A MODERN ITALIAN

A MODERN
ITALIAN GRAMMAR

FREDERIC J. JONES

M.A., B.Litt. (Oxon), D.U.P.

Professor of Italian Studies,
University College, Cardiff

HODDER AND STOUGHTON
LONDON SYDNEY AUCKLAND TORONTO

ACKNOWLEDGMENTS

GRATEFUL acknowledgment is due to the following for permission to reproduce passages from copyright works: Casa Editrice Garzanti (*Il Re Porcaro, Opere di Guido Gozzano*, Garzanti 1953); Casa Editrice Mondadori (Grazia Deledda: *Romanzi e Novelle*, 5th ed. Vol. 1, Mondadori; Massimo Bontempelli: *I Sette Savi*, Mondadori 1925; Giovanni Verga: *Mastro Don Gesualdo*, Riccardo Ricciardi 1955; Fabio Tombari: *Tutta Frusaglia*, Mondadori 1929; Alfredo Panzini: *Sei Romanzi fra due Secoli, Il Mondo è Rotondo*, Mondadori); Casa Editrice Rizzoli (Giovanni Guareschi: *Mondo Piccolo*, Rizzoli 1953); Casa Editrice Vita e Pensiero (Alfredo Obertello: *L'Oro che è Cibo*, Vita e Pensiero 1956); Gli Eredi di Curzio Malaparte (*La Pelle*, Aria d'Italia 1951); Gli Eredi di Luigi Pirandello (*L'Uomo Solo*, Mondadori 1949; *Uno, Nessuno, e Cento Mila*, Bemporad 1926); Gli Eredi di Luciano Zuccoli (*La Volpe di Sparta*, Treves 1918); Silvio Giovaninetti (*Gli Ipocriti*, Ed. di Circoli 1932).

Acknowledgements are also extended to the following in respect of illustrations: The Italian State Tourist Office (facing pages 65 (top) and 224); Miss Patricia Haynes (facing page 97 (top)); Paul Popper Ltd.(facing pages 64, 65 (foot), 96, 97 (foot), 192, 193, 225).

ISBN 0 340 15637 6

First published 1960
Second edition with revisions 1981
Second impression 1982
Third impressions 1984

Printed in Great Britain for Hodder and Stoughton Educational, a division of Hodder and Stoughton Ltd, Mill Road, Dunton Green, Sevenoaks, Kent by J. W. Arrowsmith Ltd., Bristol.

PREFACE

THIS book has been written with two purposes in mind. It aims at providing the beginner with a complete course in Italian, and at the same time it is designed to serve as a work of reference for the advanced student. It should, therefore, satisfy the needs not only of Grammar School pupils and students attending evening classes, but also of University students preparing for a degree in Italian.

The character of the book is modern and conversational rather than literary or commercial. It does, however, contain a number of passages from modern writers and examples of business letters. A serious defect of some Italian Grammars in the past has been the inclusion of much deadwood in the shape of literary archaisms which purport to help the student to grapple with the difficulties of his set books. The result has inevitably been that the student, through not knowing how to distinguish between literary and everyday idiom, has learned a quasi-archaic Italian from the beginning. This defect, it is hoped, has been obviated by the adoption of a rigorously modern idiom in the first part of this book (up to Lesson XXV), and by limiting, in general, the reading passages in the second part to selections from twentieth-century Italian writers. It seems to me that the acquisition of literary idiom and expression should follow at a later stage and be acquired where it is immediately recognised as such — in literary works themselves.

With regard to the content of the Grammar, an attempt has been made to build up a general picture of the structure of the language in the first twenty-five lessons and to leave the subjunctive mood and less important points, such as the weather, the days of the week, dates, the time, etc., to be dealt with later. Such a method, in my opinion, is more useful to the serious student than a more diversified but fragmentary scheme in which emphasis is placed principally on the learning of words and phrases in the early lessons. The basic forms of grammar should, I feel, be clearly set out from the beginning. Too much unsystematised memory work tends to confuse the mind of the student.

The vocabulary of this book is based generally on a system of word-repetition, but it may be divided into two parts: an active vocabulary, which the student is obliged to use in the translation exercises and which amounts to approximately 2,000 words, and a passive vocabulary which appears in the grammatical sections and reading exercises only. The passive vocabulary is intended to help the student in his general reading and is based on the belief that word-recognition and understanding precede a student's ability to recall and apply the vocabulary which he has acquired. It is considerably wider than the active vocabulary and amounts to some 3,200 words.

My thanks are due to Mr B. J. Morse and my other colleagues, past and present, of the Italian Section at the University College, Cardiff for reading the manuscript and giving me the benefit of their advice. I should also like to thank Mr J. Parry Lewis who, although knowing no Italian, nevertheless consented to read the manuscript from the point of view of the student and made some interesting suggestions.

F. J. J.

CONTENTS

SELECTIVE BIBLIOGRAPHY
of works of reference

Barbieri G.: *Le strutture della nostra lingua*, La Nuova Italia, Florence 1971.
Battaglia S. and Pernicone V.: *Grammatica Italiana*, Loescher-Chinatore, Torino (no date).
Camugli S.: *Précis de Grammaire Italienne*, Hachette, Paris 1942.
Lepschy A. L. and G.: *The Italian language today*, Hutchinson, London 1977.
Lipparini G.: *La Nostra Lingua*, Signorelli, Milan 1956.
Provenzal D.: *Perché si dice cosí?* Hoepli, Milan 1958.
Radford A.: *Italian Syntax, Transformational and Relational Grammar*, Cambridge University Press, 1977.
Shewring W.: *Italian Prose Usage*, Cambridge University Press, 1948.
Trabalza C. and Allodoli E.: *La Grammatica degli Italiani*, Le Monnier, Florence 1947.

Dictionaries:

Hazon M.: *Dizionario Inglese-Italiano, Italiano-Inglese*, Garzanti, Milan 1961.
Hoare A.: *An Italian Dictionary*, Cambridge University Press, 1915.
Hoare A.: *Short Italian Dictionary* (2 vols), Cambridge University Press, 1931.
Macchi V.: *Sansoni-Harrap Standard Italian-English, English-Italian Dictionary*, London/Florence (4 vols) 1972.
Panzini A.: *Dizionario Moderno*, Hoepli, Milan 1950. (Contains only modern words not be found in other dictionaries.)
Purves J.: *Dictionary of Modern Italian*, Routledge & Kegan Paul, London 1953.
Rebora P.: *Italian-English, English-Italian Dictionary*, Cassell, London 1958.
Reynolds B. (Gen. Ed.): *The Concise Cambridge Italian Dictionary*, Cambridge University Press and Penguin Books, 1975.
Tommaseo N.: *Dizionario di Sinonimi*, Vallardi, Milan 3rd ed. reprint 1957.

INTRODUCTION

English words which are given in this introduction as equivalents for Italian letters or words are only rough approximations. This book does not attempt to replace the teacher who alone can indicate the right pronunciation and accent of a language.

The Italian alphabet consists of twenty-one letters which are as follows:

LETTER	PRONUNCIATION	LETTER	PRONUNCIATION
A, a	ah	N, n	ennay
B, b	bee	O, o	fort
C, c	cheap	P, p	pea
D, d	dee	Q, q	coo
E, e	say	R, r	erray
F, f	effay	S, s	essay
G, g	jeer	T, t	tea
H, h	accah	U, u	boon
I, i	ee	V, v	voo
L, l	ellay	Z, z	dzeta
M, m	emmay		

NOTE. None of the -ay sounds given above should be pronounced as a diphthong but as a pure vowel.

The letters j, k, w, x, y (i lunga, kappa, doppio vu, ics, i greca) only appear in foreign words and do not figure in the modern Italian alphabet. The combination ph is reduced to f in Italian.

PRONUNCIATION AND SPELLING

VOWELS

There are five vowels in Italian, a, e, i, o, u, but the vowels e and o have two pronunciations, one open and one close.

The pronunciation of each vowel is as follows:

a sounds like 'a' in 'far' and varies little in quality:
> ama   darà   ma   sarai   cara   sappia.

e is either open or close. Open *e* is like 'e' in 'then':
> mensa   erba   pessimo   dieci   cappello   tieni.

Close *e* is like 'ey' in 'they':
> cena   penna   sera   pera   nero   meno.

NOTE. Any *e* not bearing the tonic stress in a word is close.

i sounds like 'i' in 'machine' and varies little in quality:
> ivi   mi   in   dica   finire   binario.

o has two sounds, one open and one close. Open *o* is like 'o' in 'off':
> collo   porco   notte   posta   costo   vostro.

Close *o* is like 'o' in 'more':
> solo   corte   bocca   amore   fiore   nome.

NOTE. Unstressed *o*, like unstressed *e*, is always close.

u sounds like 'oo' in 'soon':
> cura   burro   una   ulula   crudo   muto.

When followed by a vowel it tends to shorten to 'w':
> guerra   guado   guasto   guanto   guida.

There are no diphthongs in Italian, so that a group of vowels is read as two or three separate vowels:
> E-u-ro-pa   pa-u-ra   mi-e-i   bu-o-i   a-e-re-o   a-i-u-ta.

CONSONANTS

The consonants *b*, *d*, *f*, *l*, *m*, *n*, *q*, *t*, *v*, are pronounced approximately as in English.

c has two sounds. It is hard as in 'cat' before *a*, *o*, *u*:
> casa   cosa   bocca   con   culla   cane,

and before all consonants including *h*:
> credo   accludo   occhio   chiaro   che   chi,

but it is soft as 'ch' in 'change' before *e* or *i*:
> cera   cecità   cena   cima   difficile   cinema.

g also has two sounds, one hard as in 'gun' before *a*, *o*, *u* and all consonants including *h*:

> gatto grande ghiacciare ghiaia gota guarda,

and one soft as in 'general' before *e* or *i*:

> gente gita gelo giro getto Giorgio.

h is never pronounced in Italian but often indicates a hard pronunciation of *c* and *g*:

> ghiaia ghiaccio larghi amiche beccheggiare schedario.

r is somewhat shriller than in English and is rolled like a Scottish 'r':

> raro ridere rischio rosa rughe rapa.

s is pronounced in a number of different ways according to its position in the word:

  (i) As a single initial consonant it is pronounced like 's' in 'sad':

> servo seta seme sa sopra silenzio.

  (ii) It also has the same sound when doubled:

> passo cassa ammasso basso lasso messo.

  (iii) When intervocalic it has a sound like 's' in 'rose':

> casa mese palese morboso peso caso.

   NOTE. In Tuscany, however, there are numerous exceptions: *casa*, *così*, etc., which are pronounced like (i), i.e. as 's' in 'sad'.

  (iv) It has two sounds when initial and followed by a consonant, one similar to the 's' in 'rose' before *b*, *d*, *g*, *l*, *m*, *n*, *r*, *v*:

> sdrucciolo sleale snodare sradicare sviare svignarsela,

and one similar to the 's' in 'sad' before the other consonants:

> stivale spia sferzo spendereccio spiumato sforzo.

  (v) When preceding *ce*, *ci*, it is pronounced as a group like the 'sh' in 'shall':

> scelta scemo scena scivolare scipito scende.

NOTE. When *ce*, *ci*, *ge*, *gi* and *sce*, *sci* are followed by another vowel the *e* and *i* are not pronounced:

cielo   ciarle   già   giallo   sciame   sciagura.

(vi) *Sc* followed by *a*, *o*, *u*, or by a consonant (including *h*) is pronounced like the 'sk' in 'skip':

schiatta   schiude   sconto   scrive   scala   scuola.

z has two pronunciations, the usual one being 'ts':

pezzo   piazza   chiazza   palazzo   zio   zucchero.

The other pronunciation is 'ds', some examples of which are:

pranzo   mezzo   sozzo   dozzina   scandalizzare.

NOTE. ~~All~~ Most verbs in -*izzare* have the 'ds' pronunciation of *z*.

gn is pronounced like the similar French sound in *agneau* or as the 'ni' in 'onion':

agnello   segno   sogni   campagna   montagna   bagno.

gl is sounded like 'lli' in 'postillion':

figlio   meglio   convoglio   giglio   tagliare   miglia.

NOTE. The *i* following *gl* is hardly pronounced before another vowel.

Exceptions: *negligere* and its derivatives, and a few foreign words are pronounced with the English 'gl' sound.

DOUBLE CONSONANTS

All double consonants must be pronounced in Italian. ~~Some are separated in pronunciation~~:

ab-bat-to   car-ro   bel-lo   tet-to   san-no   strap-pa,

~~and others~~ *All* ~~are merely~~ lengthened:

faccia   regge   passo   razzo   mezzo   secco.

Great care should be taken to pronounce combinations of such consonants in the correct way, and *not* as if they were a single consonant.

ACCENT AND STRESS

1. Formerly only the grave accent (`) was used in Italian and it served to indicate tonic stresses falling on final syllables: e.g. città, università, etc., or to distinguish between words

of the same form but of different meanings: e.g. è (*is*),
e (*and*); dà (*gives*), da (*from*), etc. Nowadays, however,
the acute accent (´) is also used for a number of purposes:

(i) On final stressed vowels in the case of *i* and *ú*, e.g.
costituí, virtú, piú, etc.
(ii) On final close *é*, e.g. perché, dacché (and all compounds of *che*), né, sé, etc.

NOTE. Some good Italian writers still keep the old form of
accentuation.

2. The regular stress in Italian is placed upon the penultimate
syllable and this type of word is called a *parola piana*:

> vedere capire capit*a*no guardo dire cane.

Whenever the stress falls on the last syllable, it is indicated by an accent according to the rules given above.
This type of word is called in Italian a *parola tronca*:

> ciò città virtú università costituí bensí.

A number of words in Italian are *parole sdrucciole* and
the main stress in such words falls on the third syllable
from the end (antepenultimate). This stress, however, is
never indicated by an accent and each word bearing it
must be learned separately:

> cr*e*dere scr*i*vono c*a*none par*e*ntesi r*i*dere s*i*ndaco.

NOTE. **The stressed syllables of *sdrucciolo* words will be
italicised only on their first appearance in this book.
However, the stresses of all irregular words which do
not appear in the vocabularies to the reading exercises are given in the general vocabulary at the end
of the book.**

Finally, a few words have their main stress on the fourth
syllable from the end, and these are called *parole
bisdrucciole*:

> cap*i*tano f*a*bbricano *a*bitano d*a*ndomene s*e*minano
> and*a*ndovene.

ELISION AND APOCOPATION

Elision is the dropping of a final vowel in a word when it precedes another word beginning with a vowel. It is indicated by an apostrophe in Italian in the following circumstances:

(i) In the case of articles before nouns:
l'amico   l'*a*nitra   l'occhio   l'ora   l'anno.

(ii) With conjunctive personal pronouns before verbs:
L'ha comprato.   Egli l'apre.   Non m'importa.

(iii) With demonstrative and certain other adjectives:
Quell'alunna   un grand'uomo   Sant'Anna.

(iv) With the preposition *di*:
il libro d'un ragazzo   un'*o*pera d'arte.

Apocopation is the dropping of a final vowel or even an entire syllable before another word whether it begins with a vowel or a consonant. Students will come across such forms in their reading but are advised not to coin them themselves. Examples of normal apocopation are:

far vedere   *to show*
un buon ragazzo   *a good boy*

but, especially in poetry, we often find effective stylistic apocopation:

fatal giorno   *fatal day*
cor lasso   *weary heart*

These latter examples should not be imitated.

CAPITAL LETTERS

Capital letters are used in much the same way in Italian as in English but the following minor differences should be noted:

(i) Adjectives referring to countries do not take a capital unless they are used as nouns:

la lingua inglese   *the English language*
un libro italiano   *an Italian book*

but:

gli Inglesi (*the English*)   gli Italiani (*the Italians*).

(ii) Titles do not require a capital in Italian:
il signor conte   il professor Azegli.

(iii) The pronoun *io* (I) never takes a capital unless it is used at the beginning of a sentence.

(iv) The pronouns *Ella*, *Lei* and *Loro*, on the other hand, usually require a capital in Italian when they mean *you*.

PUNCTUATION

Punctuation marks are approximately the same in Italian and in English and have, by and large, the same uses. However, the dash (*lineetta*) is often used to denote a change of speaker in conversation and a series of dots (*punti sospensivi*) is employed in place of the English dash.

The following is a list of the principal punctuation marks in Italian:

.	punto	—	lineetta
,	virgola	...	punti sospensivi
;	punto e virgola	" "	virgolette
:	due punti	( )	parentesi
?	punto interrogativo	[ ]	parentesi quadra
!	punto esclamativo	}	grappa
-	trattino	*	asterisco

READING EXERCISES

1. Vowels *a*, *i*, *u* and single consonants:
italiano mari luna cara imparando ululava pali caricatura
prima capitano pingui calmo stivali coltivazioni virtú
radio bauli salti mulini margarina animali punti bucato
puro urna guida.

2. Vowels *e*, *o* and double consonants:
penna concetti bella cappelli terra vendetta cenni pecchi
pelle attento pessimo fetta sella venni rallenta mezzo
pezzo mezzano benedetto dialetto tenne spennato nevvero
uscirebbe dette ebbro regge.

3. Combinations of letters:
chìmica larghe figlio agnello riuscire schiavo ogni occhi negligente scemo schiatta ghiaccio giglio campagna tocchi anglicano miglio meglio ghianda scellino vecchio magnolia fichi trascinare scrive bisogno maglia gladiatore gleba globo.

4. Unpronounced letters:
cielo sciame pigliare sciocco scheggia aglio mangiare cominciamo ciancia accompagniamo cianfrusaglie ragguaglia giovare luglio camicia sciupare peggio foggia ciuco sciopero Giotto giusto leggiamo ciuffo rovescio ciglio figlia.

5. Read the following passages in Italian:
(i) A buon intenditor poche parole. A caval donato non si guarda in bocca. Acqua cheta rovina i ponti. Bisogna battere il ferro mentre è caldo. Cane che abbaia non morde. Cavar sangue da una rapa. Chi dorme non piglia pesci. Chi la dura la vince. Chi non risica non rosica. Chi non semina non raccoglie. Chi ride in gioventú, piange in vecchiaia. Chi troppo abbraccia, nulla stringe. Chi si loda s'imbroda. Dal dire al fare c'è di mezzo il mare. Chi va al mulino s'infarina. Dimmi con chi vai, e ti dirò chi sei. Esser tra l'incudine e il martello. L'abito non fa il monaco. La pratica val piú della grammatica. La volpe perde il pelo, ma non il vizio. Passata la festa, gabbato il santo. Molto fumo e poco arrosto. Oggi a te, domani a me. Patti chiari, amicizia lunga. Prendere due piccioni con una fava. Quando non c'è il gatto, i sorci ballano. Ride bene chi ride ultimo. Una rondine non fa primavera. L'uomo propone e Dio dispone.

(ii) Prima di andare in Italia decidemmo di passare una notte a Londra. Trovammo due camere presso la stazione e poi uscimmo per vedere la città. Pioveva un po' ma non ce ne accorgemmo, tant'era il fascino delle strade illuminate. Il mio amico Giovanni non parlava inglese ed io dovetti tradurre ogni cosa per lui. Alle otto entrammo in un ristorante per cenare. Io presi una bistecca con patate e carote, ma Giovanni preferí mangiare un po' di spaghetti. Ci perdemmo mentre ritornavamo all'albergo, ma un quarto d'ora piú tardi vedemmo all'angolo la porta dove eravamo entrati qualche ora prima. Entrammo nell'albergo e, poiché avevamo sonno, ci coricammo immediatamente. La mattina seguente partimmo per l'Italia. Sul treno Giovanni mi disse che si era molto divertito in Inghilterra e sperava che il mio soggiorno in Italia mi sarebbe piaciuto. Gli risposi che il mio piú grande desiderio era di andare a Roma per visitare i famosi monumenti dell'antichità.

A. THE DEFINITE ARTICLE

1. The definite article is as follows in Italian:

SINGULAR		PLURAL	
masc.	*fem.*	*masc.*	*fem.*
il	la	i	le
lo		gli	
l'	l'	{ gli	le
		gl'	

2. The article **il** is used with any masculine noun beginning with a consonant except *gn, ps, s impure* (i.e. *s* + consonant) and *z*:

   il libro   *the book*   il cane   *the dog.*

   The plural of **il** is **i**:

   i libri   *the books*   i cani   *the dogs.*

   Exception: il dio – gli dei   *Gods.*

3. **Lo** is used with all masculine nouns beginning with *s impure* and *z*, together with the few nouns beginning with *gn* and *ps*:

   lo specchio   *the mirror*   lo zio   *the uncle*
   lo gnomo   *the gnome*   lo psicologo *the psychologist.*

   The plural of **lo** is **gli**:

   gli specchi   *the mirrors*   gli zii   *the uncles*
   gli gnomi   *the gnomes*   gli psicologi *the psychologists.*

4. **Lo** is abbreviated to **l'** before masculine nouns beginning with a vowel:

   l'Americano   *the American*   l'amico   *the friend.*

   The plural of **l'** is **gli** unless the noun begins with *i*, then it is either **gli** or **gl'**:

   gli Americani   *the Americans* gli amici   *the friends,*

   but: $\begin{cases} \text{gl'Italiani} \\ \text{gli Italiani} \end{cases}$ *the Italians* $\begin{cases} \text{gl'Inglesi} \\ \text{gli Inglesi} \end{cases}$ not common *the English.*

21

5. **La** is the definite article for all feminine nouns beginning with a consonant:

la donna   *the woman*   la zia   *the aunt.*

Le is the plural of **la**:

le donne   *the women*   le zie   *the aunts.*

6. **L'** is used for all feminine nouns beginning with a vowel:

l'amica   *the friend*   l'artista (*f.*)   *the artist.*

The plural of **l'** is **le**†:

le amiche   *the friends*   le artiste   *the artists.*

(See also Lesson XVI B.)

B. NOUNS

1. All nouns are either masculine or feminine in Italian. There are three principal declensions with the following endings:

	SINGULAR	PLURAL
1.	-a	-e
2.	-o	-i
3.	-e	-i

2. Nearly all nouns of the first declension are feminine:

la figlia   *the daughter*   la sorella   *the sister*
le figlie   *the daughters*   le sorelle   *the sisters.*

Exceptions are as follows:

(a) A few nouns referring to males:

il boia   *the executioner*   il capoccia   *the foreman*
il poeta   *the poet*   il Papa   *the Pope.*

(b) A number of nouns denoting profession:

il dentista   *the dentist*   il farmacista   *the chemist*

NOTE. Nouns ending in *-ista* and *-cida* may be either masculine or feminine:

il violinista   *the violinist*   il suicida   *the suicide*
la violinista   *the violinist*   la suicida   *the suicide.*

(c) A number of nouns of Greek origin ending in *-ma*:

† *Le* is rarely shortened to *l'* before *e* in modern Italian, e.g. *le eliche* (the propellers).

il dramma	the play	il problema	the problem
il telegramma	the telegram	il tema†	the theme.

(d) Some other nouns which cannot be classified:

il boa	the boa	il gorilla	the gorilla
il sosia	the double, twin	il vaglia	the money order.

The plural of these masculines in -a is in -i, not in -e:

i poeti	the poets	i drammi	the plays

but quite a few of them are invariable:

il boa – i boa	il boia – i boia
il capoccia – i capoccia	il gorilla – i gorilla
il sosia – i sosia	il vaglia – i vaglia.

3. There are two irregular feminine plurals:

l'arma – le armi	weapon, arm
l'ala – le ali	wing.

4. Almost all nouns of the second declension are masculine:

il ragazzo	the boy	lo schiavo	the slave
i ragazzi	the boys	gli schiavi	the slaves.

An irregular plural is:

l'uomo – gli uomini   man – men.

The following nouns, although belonging to the second declension, are feminine:

l'auto – le auto	car
la dinamo – le dinamo	dynamo
la eco (l'eco) – gli echi	echo
la foto – le foto	photo
la mano – le mani	hand
la radio – le radio	radio.

It will be noted that all these nouns, except *mano* and *eco*, are invariable, and that *eco* has a masculine plural.

5. Nouns of the third declension present no difficulties with regard to number but they may be either masculine or feminine:

il padre	the father	la madre	the mother
i padri	the fathers	le madri	the mothers.

Two irregular plurals in this declension are:

il bue – i buoi	the ox	la moglie – le mogli	the wife.

(See also Lessons XVII and XLII.)

† *La tema* also exists but it means *fear*.

MODERN ITALIAN GRAMMAR

MODERN ITALIAN GRAMMAR

VOCABULARY

(Throughout the book no words which have been included in the grammatical sections are repeated in the vocabularies.)

a (al)	to, at	libro	book
accanto a	beside	molto	much, very
adesso	now	oggi	today
alunno, -a	pupil	ora (di buon'ora)	hour (early)
andare (vanno)	to go (they go)	parlare	to speak
avuto	had	penna stilografica	fountain pen
buono, -a	good	poltrona	armchair
casa	house, home	professore (m.)	teacher
classe (f.)	class	scrivere	to write
che cosa? cosa?	what?	scuola	school
con	with	sedersi (si siede)	to sit (he sits)
di (delle)	of (of the)	sempre	always
e (ed)	and	sono	are
fare	to do, make	sottolineare	to underline
fuoco	fire	stimare	to esteem
giungere	to reach /arrive	studiare	to study
intanto	meanwhile	uno, -a	a, one
leggere	to read	volenteroso, -a	willing eager
lezione (f.)	lesson		

A CASA

Giulia e Giovanni giungono adesso a casa. Che cosa fa Giovanni? Si siede[1] su una poltrona accanto al fuoco, legge un libro, e sottolinea le cose importanti con una penna stilografica. Giulia intanto parla con la madre delle lezioni avute in classe oggi. Giulia e Giovanni sono ragazzi volenterosi ed[2] intelligenti e buoni alunni. Vanno[3] sempre a scuola di buon'ora e studiano molto. Stimano molto i professori.

NOTES

[1] **Si siede :** *Sedersi* is a reflexive verb and *si* is the third person reflexive pronoun. For the conjugation of reflexive verbs see Lesson XII A.

[2] **ed** and **e :** *E* is the usual word for *and*, but sometimes, especially before an *e*, a *d* is attached to it to avoid an ugly hiatus.

[3] **Vanno :** Italian verbs do not always require pronouns as subjects, for the person is always indicated by the verb ending.

zio — tsio

EXERCISES

A. Put the definite article before the following nouns:
   dentista, zii, uomini, zie, Inglesi, professore, madri, mani,
   farmacista, dramma, case, penna, fuoco, lezioni, gnocco,
   psicologi, specchio, dei, amiche, studio, poeta, libri, ragazze,
   alunni, scuola, classe.

B. Translate into Italian:
   1. They are beside the fire.
   2. John's father is writing a book. (*Il padre di*)
   3. Julia reads a book and John speaks with his (the) mother.
   4. What is Julia doing now?
   5. John and Julia are good pupils.
   6. They esteem the teachers at school.
   7. The pupils always go to school early.
   8. Julia is speaking with her (the) father about the (*sulle*)
      lessons received today in school.
   9. The house is (*è*) beside the (*alla*) school.
   10. John underlines important things with his (the) fountain
       pen.

C. Answer the following questions in Italian:
   1. Di che cosa parla Giulia?
   2. Il padre e la madre sono con gli alunni?
   3. Che cosa fa il padre di Giovanni?
   4. Vanno gli alunni a scuola di buon'ora?
   5. Sono intelligenti i ragazzi?

A. THE INDEFINITE ARTICLE

1. The indefinite article is formed in the following way in Italian:

MASC.	FEM.
un	una
uno	un'

2. **Un** is used with all masculine nouns beginning with a consonant *or a vowel*, except *gn*, *ps*, *s impure* and *z*:

   un pranzo   *a dinner*   un uovo   *an egg.*

3. **Uno** is used only before masculine nouns beginning with *gn*, *ps*, *s impure* and *z*:

   uno gnocco†   *a dumpling*   uno psicologo *a psychologist*
   uno sforzo   *an effort*   uno zio   *an uncle.*

4. **Una** is used before all feminine nouns beginning with a consonant:

   una scrivania   *a writing-desk*   una tazza   *a cup*

5. **Un'** (always feminine) is generally used, in preference to **una**, before a feminine noun beginning with a vowel:

   un'arancia   *an orange*   un'insalata   *a salad.*

B. THE VERB

1. There are three regular conjugations in Italian, but the third must be divided into two sections:

1	2
TROVARE *to find*	VENDERE *to sell*
trovo *I find, am finding, etc.*	vendo *I sell, am selling, etc.*
trovi	vendi
trova	vende

† *Un* is tolerated these days with *gn* (un gnomo).

26

noi troviamo	vendiamo
voi trovate	vendete
essi tròvano	vèndono
esse	

3a	3b
FINIRE *to finish*	DORMIRE *to sleep*
finisco *I finish, am finishing,*	dormo *I sleep, am sleeping,*
finisci *etc.*	dormi *etc.*
finisce	dorme
finiamo ⎱ *no sc*	dormiamo
finite ⎰	dormite
finìscono	dòrmono

NOTE. (1) The tonic stress of the third person plural should be carefully studied since it always falls on the root of the word and *never* on the ending.

(2) The tonic stress of the infinitives of second conjugation verbs falls on the root. (See, however, Lesson III A.)

2. The **dormire** type of verb is rare. The main verbs conjugated in the same way are:

aprire	*to open*	partire	*to depart*
bollire	*to boil*	pentirsi†	*to repent*
consentire	*to consent*	seguire	*to follow*
cucire	*to sew*	sentire	*to hear, feel*
divertirsi†	*to amuse oneself*	servire	*to serve*
fuggire	*to fly*	soffrire	*to suffer*

3. The present tenses of **avere** and **essere** are as follows:

AVERE *to have*	ESSERE *to be*
ho *I have, am having, etc.*	sono *I am, etc.*
hai	sei
ha	è
abbiamo ⎱ *no h*	siamo
avete ⎰	siete
hanno	sono

† Reflexive verbs, see Lesson XII A.

VOCABULARY

[handwritten: tutte le mattine more common thur ogni mattina]

alcuno, -a	*some, few*	non	*not*
allo	*to the*	ogni	*every*
altro, -a	*other*	ottimo	*very good*
appunto	*note*	parola	*word*
arrivare	*to arrive*	pezzo	*piece*
banco	*school-desk*	prendere	*to take*
chi?	*who?*	puntuale	*punctual*
come	*as, how?*	quaderno	*exercise book*
compagnia	*company*	quando	*when*
difficile	*difficult*	quasi	*almost*
due	*two*	ragazzo, -a	*boy, girl*
essi	*they* *[handwritten: (sono)]*	in ritardo *[handwritten: (sin)]*	*late*
gesso	*chalk*	scambiare	*to exchange*
insieme	*together*	di solito	*usually*
lavagna	*blackboard*	soprattutto	*above all*
loro	*them*	stesso, -a	*same*
ma	*but*	sul	*on the*
matita	*pencil*	tornare *[handwritten: ritornare]*	*to return*
mattina	*morning*		

A SCUOLA

Giovanni e Carlo sono due ottimi amici. Vanno a scuola insieme ogni[1] mattina. Quando arrivano a scuola, scambiano sempre alcune parole con il professore. Si siedono insieme allo stesso banco. Carlo, di solito, scrive sul quaderno con una penna stilografica e non con una matita come fa Giovanni. Gli altri alunni sono quasi sempre in ritardo ma loro due sono sempre puntuali. Quando il professore scrive sulla lavagna con un pezzo di gesso, essi prendono appunti, soprattutto quando le lezioni sono molto[2] difficili. Tornano sempre a casa in compagnia di Barbara. Chi è Barbara e che cosa fa a scuola? Barbara è la sorella di Carlo e studia insieme con i ragazzi. È una ragazza molto intelligente.

NOTES

[1] **ogni**: This word is invariable and always takes a singular noun.

[2] **molto:** This word is invariable when it means *very* but inflects when it means *much* or *many* (molti ragazzi – *many boys*, but: una ragazza *molto* bella – *a very beautiful girl*).

EXERCISES

A. Put the indefinite article before the following nouns:

uomo, donna, casa, artista, padre, alunna, poeta, cane, opinione (*f.*), specchio, idealista, anno, figlio, scuola, classe, zia, psicologo, architetto, bacinella, sbarco, influenza, intervento, lazzo, legno, sbirro, boia, gorilla, arma, vaglia.

B. Translate into Italian:

1. John exchanges a few words with the teacher.
2. Charles's sister is a very intelligent girl.
3. What is the pupil writing in his (*sul*) exercise book?
4. I am in school now.
5. We write with a fountain pen, not with a pencil.
6. With what are you writing, Charles?
7. The other pupils are always late but John and Charles are punctual.
8. The boys go home in the company of Barbara.
9. When the pupils arrive, the teacher speaks with them.
10. Who is reading the book?

C. Answer the following questions in Italian:

1. Chi trova difficile la lezione?
2. Chi va a scuola di buon'ora?
3. Chi è Barbara?
4. Che cosa fa il professore quando gli alunni arrivano?
5. Con che cosa scrive il professore sulla lavagna?
6. Sono intelligenti gli alunni?
7. Con chi tornano a casa Giovanni e Carlo?
8. Chi è la sorella di Carlo?
9. Quando prendono appunti gli alunni?
10. Chi ha una penna stilografica?

D. Put the correct person of the verb in the following sentences:

1. Carlo (finire) la lettera.
2. A chi (scrivere) Giulia?
3. Gli alunni (arrivare) a casa.
4. Carlo ed Elena (tornare) alla stazione.
5. Giovanni (seguire) gli altri alunni.

1. - See lesson 2
2. - Present regular
3. - See irregular verbs list
4. - See below

A. IRREGULAR VERBS OF THE SECOND CONJUGATION

1. Some irregular verbs of the second conjugation have the main stress on the ending of the infinitive instead of on the root of the word like *vendere*. These verbs have many irregularities in their present tenses and some of the more important ones are conjugated below:

VEDERE *to see*	TENERE *to hold, to keep*	VOLERE *to want*
vedo	tengo	voglio
vedi	tieni	vuoi
vede	tiene	vuole
vediamo	teniamo	vogliamo
vedete	tenete	volete
vedono	tengono	vogliono

POTERE *to be able*	DOVERE *to have to, to owe*	SAPERE *to know*
posso	devo (debbo)	so
puoi	devi	sai
può	deve	sa
possiamo	dobbiamo	sappiamo
potete	dovete	sapete
possono	devono (debbono)	sanno

A complete list of these verbs follows:

1	avere†	*to have*	3 parere	*to appear*
2	cadere†	*to fall*	2 persuadere†	*to persuade*
3	dolere	*to hurt*	3 piacere	*to please*
4	dovere	*to have to, to owe*	4 potere	*to be able*
3	giacere	*to lie*	3 rimanere	*to remain*

† The derivatives of these verbs also belong to the group.

30

4 sapere	to know	4 tenere†	to hold
3 sedere†	to sit	3 valere†	to be worth
3 solere	to be accustomed	4+2 vedere†	to see
3 tacere	to be silent	4 volere	to want
2 temere	to fear		

2. The verbs **volere, potere, dovere, osare** and **sapere** (the modal verbs) are often used as auxiliaries before other verbs. In these cases, they are followed by an infinitive without a preposition:

> Devo scrivere una lettera a macchina. *I must type a letter.*
> Posso vedere la merce? *Can I see the goods?*
> Voglio rimanere qui. *I want to stay here.*
> So giocare a carte. *I can (know how to) play cards.*
> Non oso tornare a casa. *I do not dare return home.*

NOTE. One must learn to distinguish between the uses of **potere** and **sapere**, both of which translate the English *can*. The former denotes physical possibility, the latter a skill which has been learned:

> Non posso andare in città. *I cannot go to town.*

but:

> So nuotare adesso. *I can (know how to) swim now.*

For a more detailed study of the modal verbs see Lesson XXXIII B.

3. Other important irregular verbs are:

ANDARE *to go*	FARE *to do, to make*	VENIRE *to come*
vado (vo‡)	faccio (fo‡)	vengo
vai	fai	vieni
va	fa	viene
andiamo	facciamo	veniamo
andate	fate	venite
vanno	fanno	vengono

Andare and **fare** resemble **avere** in their present tense, while **venire** resembles **tenere**, apart from its second person plural form.

† The derivatives of these verbs also belong to the group
‡ Rare in modern Italian.

B. PREPOSITIONS
WITH THE DEFINITE ARTICLE

1. A number of prepositions combine with the definite article in the following manner:

	IL	LO	I	GLI	L'	GL'	LA	LE
a (*to, at*)	al	allo	ai	agli	all'	agl'	alla	alle
con (*with*)	col	collo†	coi	cogli†	coll'†	cogl'†	colla†	colle†
da (*from*)	dal	dallo	dai	dagli	dall'	dagl'	dalla	dalle
di (*of*)	del	dello	dei	degli	dell'	degl'	della	delle
in (*in*)	nel	nello	nei	negli	nell'	negl'	nella	nelle
su (*on*)	sul	sullo	sui	sugli	sull'	sugl'	sulla	sulle

Examples of the uses of these prepositions are as follows:

> Egli mi parla della vita inglese.
> *He speaks to me about English life.*

> Entro nella camera a cercare un libro.
> *I go into the bedroom to look for a book.*

> Giovanni va in chiesa col padre.
> *John goes to church with his father.*

NOTE. The abbreviated form **in** with the noun (see the last example) is very often used instead of the longer form with the article, but this is never possible when the noun is qualified by an adjective. Some set expressions also require **a**, such as: a scuola (*at school*), a casa (*at home*) etc.

2. None of the prepositions elides with the indefinite article in modern Italian except **di**:

su una tavola‡ *on a table*	in una scatola *in a box*
but: di una donna ⎱*of a woman*	di un padre ⎱*of a father*
or: d'una donna ⎰	d'un padre ⎰

NOTE. Never elide *da*:
   da una donna *from a woman*   da un segretario *from a secretary*.

---

† These forms with **con** are now rare while the preposition **per** (*for, through*) no longer combines with the article in modern Italian.

‡ One can also say: su di una tavola.

VOCABULARY

appuntamento	*appointment*	nuovo, -a	*new*
azienda	*office, works*	occupato, -a	*busy*
bene	*well*	ordine (*m.*)	*order*
caporeparto	*head of depart-*	piú	*more*
	ment	poi	*then*
che (*rel. pr.*)	*who, which*	posta	*post (office)*
chiedere	*to ask for*	posto	*place*
cominciare	*to begin*	prender nota	*to take note*
convocare	*to call together*	produzione (*f.*)	*production*
cosí	*so, thus*	pronto, -a	*ready*
dare	*to give*	proprio	*own*
dettare	*to dictate*	resoconto	*return, account*
diretto, -a	*direct*	responsabile	*man-in-charge*
disposizione (*f.*)	*disposal*	ricevere	*to receive*
distribuire	*to distribute*	richiesta	*inquiry*
diverso	*various*	rispondere	*to reply, answer*
dopo	*after*	scrivere a	*to type*
filiale (*f.*)	*branch office*	macchina	
firma	*signature*	tardi (*adv.*)	*late*
giorno, -ata	*day*	trattare	*to deal with,*
impiegato, -a	*employee*		*treat*
lavorare	*to work*	tutto, -a	*all*
magazzino	*warehouse*	ufficio	*office*
merce (*f.*)	*goods*	vendita	*sale*
notte (*f.*)	*night*	visitare	*to visit*

ALL'UFFICIO

Di solito nell'azienda Rossi gl'impiegati cominciano a lavorare di buon'ora. Le impiegate distribuiscono la posta nei vari uffici e prendono nota degli appuntamenti della giornata. Quando il principale arriva, tutto è al proprio posto. Le segretarie sono a diretta disposizione del principale. Egli detta le lettere per i vari clienti e risponde alle richieste che riceve. Le segretarie scrivono a macchina tutto il giorno[1] e tengono pronte le lettere per la firma.

Poi, il principale convoca i capireparto[2] e chiede i resoconti del giorno precedente. Dopo, egli dà[3] i nuovi ordini. Passa piú tardi a trattare con i responsabili delle vendite e prende

MIG B

nota della merce che rimane in magazzino. Quando vede che tutto va bene, parte per visitare le diverse filiali. È così occupato che non[4] finisce di lavorare che[4] a tarda notte.

NOTES

[1] **tutto il giorno**: It should be noted that *tutto* takes the definite article directly after it when used as an adjective. (Exception: when followed by a numeral: tutti e due *i* ragazzi = both boys).

[2] **capireparto**: The plural of this compound noun is formed by inflecting its first element only.

[3] **dà**: Note the accent on 3rd person singular of present tense of *dare* to distinguish it from the preposition *da*.

[4] **non . . . che**: *Non* before a verb followed by *che* means *only*.

EXERCISES

A. Put the correct person of the verb in the following sentences:
  1. Il principale (vedere) i capireparto.
  2. Le segretarie (scrivere) a macchina tutto il giorno.
  3. Giovanni (volere) parlare a Carlo.
  4. (Sapere) la lezione, *E*lena?
  5. L'impiegato (tenere) la penna in mano.
  6. La segretaria (rispondere) alle richieste che riceve.
  7. Il caporeparto (prendere) nota della merce che rimane in magazzino.
  8. Maria (andare) all'ufficio ogni mattina.
  9. Che cosa (fare) il principale adesso?
  10. Chi (venire) all'ufficio stamane?

B. Translate into Italian:
  1. They begin to work early at the Rossi office.
  2. The secretaries take note of the day's appointments.
  3. The director finishes work late at night.
  4. The head of department visits the warehouse.
  5. The secretaries keep the letters ready for signature.
  6. The director replies to the client's inquiry.
  7. The boys visit the office.
  8. The director passes on to deal with those in charge of sales.
  9. The works has many branches.
  10. The director gives new orders.

C. Answer the following questions in Italian:
  1. Da chi riceve i resoconti il principale?
  2. Che cosa scrive il principale al cliente?
  3. Che cosa fanno le segretarie tutto il giorno?
  4. Quando vede che tutto va bene, che cosa fa il principale?
  5. Chi detta le lettere ai clienti?

D. Translate into Italian:
  Charles and John go to school early. They pass in front (*davanti a*) of the Rossi office when they are near (*vicino a*) the school. They see the secretaries who are typing letters. Those in charge of sales are very busy. Two employees are carrying (*portare*) goods into the warehouse. The boys are very interested (*interessati*). They speak to their teacher about (*di*) the production. The teacher gives (*fare*) a lesson on (the) industry (*industria*).

A. SUBJECT PRONOUNS

1. Italian subject pronouns are as follows:

SINGULAR		PLURAL	
io	*I*	noi	*we*
tu	*you (thou)*	voi	*you*
lui egli esso	*he*	loro essi	*they (m.)*
lei ella essa	*she*	loro esse	*they (f.)*
Lei Ella	*you*	Loro	*you*

2. **Lei** and **Loro** (usually written with capitals) are a *third person* form of *you* and they are nowadays the normal polite form of address:

    Lei scrive.   *You write.*   Loro parlano.   *You speak.*

Ella is only used on very formal occasions when one addresses a person of very high rank:

    Che cosa ne pensa Ella, signor Presidente?
    What is your opinion, President?

3. **Tu** is only used for members of the family, for close friends, for children and for animals. To all other persons one should use the **Lei** form which is a polite singular. **Voi** is the familiar plural for **tu**, but it is often a term of respect in Southern Italy. It is also the normal form of address in business letters.

4. The pronouns **lui** and **lei** (with a small letter), although not strictly speaking nominative forms, are rapidly replacing all the other third person singular pronouns,

especially in speech. **Egli** and **ella** usually refer to persons only, while **esso, -a** can refer to both persons and things.

B. USE OF SUBJECT PRONOUNS

1. Subject pronouns are not normally required with Italian verbs. They are used mainly for emphasis, especially with **anche** (*also, too*) and in exclamations:

> Voglio andare in città anch'io.
> *I want to go to town too.*
>
> Non voglio scrivere io. Scrivi tu!
> *I don't want to write. You write!*

2. They are often used when the subject of the verb changes, especially when both subjects are pronouns:

> Egli scrive mentre noi parliamo.
> *He writes while we speak.*
>
> Tu chiudi la porta quando io apro la finestra.
> *You close the door when I open the window.*

However, the rule is not strict and one usually has a choice of insertion or omission, particularly when one of the subjects is a noun:

> Mentre egli scrive, Giovanni legge.
> *While he writes, John reads.*
>
> or: Mentre scrive, Giovanni legge.

3. The subject pronouns are also used with **stesso, -a** (*same*) to express *myself, yourself*, etc.:

io stesso -a	noi stessi -e
tu stesso -a	voi stessi -e
lui stesso (egli stesso)	
lei stessa (ella stessa)	loro stessi -e
Lei stesso -a	Loro stessi -e

The forms *esso stesso, essa stessa*, etc. are less used because of the ugly juxtaposition of similar sounds.

NOTE. A further pronoun **sé** exists which combines with **stesso** to give **se stesso** and **se stessi** (both without the accent), which mean *himself*, *herself*, and *themselves* respectively. This pronoun is used almost exclusively in the accusative case and the word **stesso** is sometimes omitted:

> Egli pensa sempre a se stesso.
> *He is always thinking of himself.*

or: Egli pensa sempre a sé.

It is *obligatory* to use *sé* in place of *lui stesso*, *lei stessa*, etc., whenever these pronouns refer back to the subject of the sentence, as in the above examples.

VOCABULARY

accadere	*to happen*	ne (*before verb*)	*of it, of them*
ascoltare	*to listen to*	negozio	*shop*
banda	*gang*	ottenere	*to obtain*
biglietto	*ticket*	parola	*word*
caffè (*m.*)	*coffee*	perché	*why? because*
caramella	*sweet*	poliziotto	*policeman*
c'è, ci sono	*there is, are*	prima di	*before (of time)*
cinema (*m.*)	*cinema*	qualcosa	*something*
comprare	*to buy*	questo, -a	*this*
decidere	*to decide*	rappresentazione (*f.*)	*performance*
direttamente	*directly*		
domani	*tomorrow*	sabato	*Saturday*
dove?	*where?*	sera	*evening*
fine (*f.*)	*end*	solo, -a	*only, single*
fortunatamente	*fortunately*	specie (*f.*)	*kind*
gruppo	*group*	stanco, -a (morto)	*tired (dead)*
guardare	*to look at*		
latte (*m.*)	*milk*	subito	*at once*
letto	*bed*	tanto (ogni tanto)	*so much (now and again)*
mangiare	*to eat*		
mentre	*while*	trattarsi di	*to treat of, to be about*

ANDIAMO AL CINEMA

Giovanni e Filippo sono grandi amici e decidono di passare la sera al cinema. Dopo la scuola, vanno direttamente in città dove, per non perdere[1] tempo, prendono solo[2] un caffè-latte in un bar. Poi, prima di ottenere[3] i biglietti, entrano in un negozio e comprano qualcosa da mangiare[4] durante la rappresentazione. Prendono caramelle perché piacciono molto a Filippo.[5] Giovanni parla ogni tanto nel cinema, ma Filippo trova il film cosí interessante che non ascolta le parole dell'amico. Si tratta di un gruppo di banditi e di poliziotti. Questa specie di film sti*m*ola l'immaginazione dei due ragazzi. Mentre guardano le varie avventure che accadono alla banda, mangiano le caramelle. Non ne rimane una sola alla fine della rappresentazione. I ragazzi tornano a casa molto contenti e vanno subito a letto stanchi morti. Fortunatamente domani è sabato e non ci sono lezioni.

NOTES

[1] **per non perdere :** *Per* before an infinitive means *in order to, so as to,* but it can only be used if the subject of the sentence is also the subject of the infinitive.

[2] **solo :** This word is either an adjective meaning *alone* or an adverb meaning *only.* As an adverb it is always invariable.

[3] **prima di ottenere :** Always use an infinitive after a preposition.

[4] **da mangiare :** *Da* is used before an infinitive when purpose is implied (i.e. something for the purpose of eating).

[5] **piacciono . . . a F. :** Study the construction with *piacere.* It is the opposite to the English (i.e. Il libro piace a Roberto, *Robert likes the book*).

EXERCISES

A. Translate into Italian:

1. While John is reading, I am writing.
2. You are going to the cinema with Philip.
3. I too am going to the cinema with Philip.
4. John is always thinking of (*a*) himself.
5. Tomorrow there are no lessons.
6. Philip likes the film very much.
7. It is about a gang of bandits and the police.
8. He is speaking for himself and not for us.
9. Charles wants something to eat before going to school.
10. Does she know how to play cards?

B. Put the personal pronoun in the blank spaces:

  1. — scrivete una lettera a un amico.
  2. Mentre — leggono, — parliamo.
  3. Quando — viene, — andate al cinema.
  4. Pensa sempre a —.

  5. Da dove viene — ?
  6. Che cosa leggono — nel libro di lettura?
  7. Non voglio leggere questo libro — !
  8. — sai giocare a carte?
  9. — prendono un caffè in un bar.
  10. — guarda le varie avventure che accadono alla banda.

C. Answer the following questions in Italian:

  1. Chi va al cinema con Giovanni?
  2. Perché prendono solo un caffelatte in un bar?
  3. Che specie di film stimola l'immaginazione dei due ragazzi?
  4. Cosa piace a Filippo?
  5. Dove entrano i due ragazzi per comprare qualcosa da mangiare?
  6. Dove decidono di passare la sera?
  7. Sono grandi amici Giovanni e Filippo?
  8. Chi parla ogni tanto durante la rappresentazione?
  9. Che cosa comprano in un negozio?
  10. Perché non ci sono lezioni domani?

D. Translate into Italian:

Philip and John are good friends. They go to school together every day. Tonight (*stasera*) they are going to the cinema. The kind of film which they see pleases the two boys; it is about bandits and policemen. When they arrive in town, they take a coffee in a bar. After the end of the film they go straight home. The film finishes very late. John and Philip go straight to bed when they return. They are dead tired.

[handwritten annotations in margins:]
always follow - nationality.
una ragazza italiana
- colour.
un vestito rosso
- denoting shape
una stanza quadrata
always after if
modified by adverb
- una casa molto nuova
molto is
invariable

LESSON V

A. ADJECTIVES

1. Italian adjectives belong to two declensions:

DECLENSION 1

SINGULAR		PLURAL	
masc.	*fem.*	*masc.*	*fem.*
nuovo (*new*)	nuova	nuovi	nuove

DECLENSION 2

masc.	*fem.*	*masc.*	*fem.*
felice (*happy*)	felice	felici	felici

It will be noticed that the first declension has four forms, while the second has only two.

2. All adjectives agree in number and gender with the nouns they qualify. If an adjective agrees with two nouns of varying genders, it is the masculine plural form which prevails:

   un cattivo ragazzo *a bad boy*   una cattiva ragazza *a bad girl*

but: un ragazzo e una ragazza cattivi *a bad boy and girl.*

3. Most adjectives follow the noun in Italian, but a small number of very common adjectives often precede it. The more important of them are as follows:

bello†	*fine, beautiful*	pessimo	*very bad*
bravo	*good*	piccolo	*little, small*
breve	*brief*	povero	*poor*
brutto	*ugly*	quello†	*that*
buono†	*good*	questo	*this*
corto	*short*	santo†	*holy*
giovane	*young*	solo	*alone*
grande†	*great, big*	sommo	*highest*
lungo	*long*	unico	*single*
nuovo	*new*	vecchio	*old*
ottimo	*very good*		

† These adjectives present irregularities (see Lesson XII B).

41

However it should be noted that even these adjectives follow the noun if they are modified by an adverb:

un povero uomo *a poor man* una bella donna *a beautiful woman*

but: un uomo molto povero   *a very poor man*

          una donna molto bella   *a very beautiful woman.*

4. Some of these adjectives also change their meaning according to their position:

un grand'uomo *a great man* un uomo grande *a tall man*

un caro ragazzo *a dear boy*   un orologio caro *an expensive watch*

          un povero ragazzo *a poor boy* (*unfortunate*)

          un ragazzo povero *a poor boy* (*penniless*).

5. Other adjectives only precede the noun occasionally when certain effects of style are sought.

(See also Lesson XVII A.)

B. POSSESSIVE ADJECTIVES

1.

SINGULAR			PLURAL		
il mio	la mia	*my*	i miei	le mie	*my*
il tuo	la tua	*thy*	i tuoi	le tue	*thy*
il suo	la sua	*his, her, its, your*	i suoi	le sue	*his, her, its, your*
il nostro	la nostra	*our*	i nostri	le nostre	*our*
il vostro	la vostra	*your*	i vostri	le vostre	*your*
il loro	la loro	*their, your*	i loro	le loro	*their, your*

It should be carefully noted that there is a third person form meaning *your* which corresponds with *Lei* and *Loro*:

SINGULAR		PLURAL	
il suo libro	*your book*	il loro libro	*your book*
i suoi libri	*your books*	i loro libri	*your books*

2. The definite article precedes the possessive adjective in Italian and must be repeated before every word:

il suo libro e la sua penna   *your book and pen.*

3. The definite article, however, is omitted with the names of the family as long as the following provisions are observed: (a) the noun must be in the singular; (b) it must not be qualified by an adjective; (c) it must not be an augmentative† or diminutive† form; (d) the possessive adjective must not be **loro**:

> mio fratello   *my brother*   mio genero   *my son-in-law*
> mia cognata   *my sister-in-law*   mio cugino   *my cousin*

but:

> i miei cognati   *my brothers-in-law* (with a plural noun)
> il mio povero nipote   *my poor nephew* (with an adjective)
> il mio fratellino   *my little brother* (with a diminutive)
> i loro suoceri   *their mother and father-in-law* (with **loro**).

NOTE. In some parts of Italy **nonno** and **nonna** (*grandfather* and *grandmother*) still take the article, while many grammarians insist on it with **babbo** (*daddy*) and **mamma** (*mummy*) which are regarded as diminutives. Most Italians, however, omit it in all cases. papà

4. In direct address the article is never used:

> Non è difficile, amico mio.   *It is not difficult, my friend.*

In such cases the possessive follows the noun.

5. Whenever there is no doubt about the identity of the possessor, the possessive can be safely omitted:

> I soldati combattono per la patria.
> *The soldiers fight for* their *country.*

6. Finally, it is omitted in certain idiomatic expressions: *article*

> è colpa mia   *it is my fault*   a casa mia   *in my house*
> a sua volta   *in his turn*   a mio parere   *in my opinion.*

(See also Lesson IX A.) secondo me

more common

VOCABULARY

abbastanza - en

amaro, -a	*bitter* barley	appena	*hardly*
anche	*also* gen. abre	arrosto	*roast*
antipasto	*hors-d'œuvre* verb	in attesa di	*while waiting to*
apparecchiare	*to lay* (table)	bere	*to drink*

† The meaning of Italian nouns is often modified by a suffix (*e.g.* ragazzo – ragazzino *boy – little boy*).

bicchiere (m.)	glass	un po' di	a little
di casa	domesticated	pomodoro	tomato
coltello	knife	presentazione (f.)	presentation
cucchiaio	spoon	prima	first
dolce	sweet	quindi	then
fetta	slice	sala (da pranzo)	(dining) room
forchetta	fork	salame (m.)	spiced sausage
frutta	fruit	sbucciare	peel
genitore (m.)	parent	sugo	sauce
ghiotto	glutton	tavola	table
mela	apple	torta	tart, pie
mettere	to put	tranne	except
noto	well-known	tre	three
ognuno	everyone	uva	grapes
la partita a dama	the game of	vino	wine
	draughts	zolletta	lump (of sugar)
patata	potato	zucchero	sugar
peperone (m.)	(red) pepper	zucchino	Italian bush
piatto	plate		marrow

A TAVOLA

Giovanni invita Carlo a pranzo. Appena questi[1] arriva, Giovanni fa le presentazioni; prima i genitori, poi la sorella Elena. Questa è una ragazza molto intelligente e di casa. Mentre la madre prepara il pranzo, Elena apparecchia la tavola nella sala da pranzo. Mette piatti, forchette, coltelli, cucchiai al loro posto. Mette anche i bicchieri per il vino perché — come è noto — gl'Italiani bevono vino a tavola.

Quando il pranzo è pronto, si siedono a tavola. Come antipasto prendono un po' di salame. Poi mangiano spaghetti al sugo di pomodoro. Come secondo[2] c'è arrosto con patate, peperoni e zucchini. Quindi, come dolce, una fetta di torta, e poi la frutta. Ci sono mele, arance, uva, e banane; Carlo — che è ghiotto di arance — prende un'arancia e la sbuccia col coltello.

Per il caffè, ognuno mette nella tazza tre zollette di zucchero tranne Giovanni che preferisce il caffè amaro.

Dopo il pranzo, i ragazzi vanno in sala a fare[3] una partita a dama in attesa di ritornare a scuola.

NOTES

¹ **questi**: This is a masculine singular despite its apparently plural ending, and it means *the latter*. See Lesson XIV B.

² **come secondo**: Italians use this abbreviated form with *piatto* understood, but other ways of saying the same thing would be *come seconda portata* or *come seconda pietanza* which would mean *as a second dish*.

³ **vanno in sala a fare**: Verbs of motion and position (i.e. *restare*, to remain) take *a* before an infinitive if purpose is not being emphasized.

EXERCISES

A. Put the various possessive adjectives before the following nouns: uomo, donna, zio, cugini, sorelle, ragazzo, suocero, genero, babbo, zii, tavola, specchi, artiste, sedia, genitori, fratello, zie, madre, donne, gnocchi, poltrona, cognate, nonna, piatti.

B. Translate into Italian:

in the small house; with the beautiful girls; on the large tables; for their dinner; by the good men; with the new pen; in the old cup; through the old street.

C. Translate into Italian:

1. Where is Helen's book?
2. Charles is a very good boy.
3. Because they have to return to school, they eat their lunch at once.
4. When the boys arrive home, Helen lays the table.
5. While they are taking their lunch, John's little sister goes into the garden (*giardino*).
6. What does she do in the garden?
7. Who is talking to John in the dining-room?
8. Helen does not like grapes.
9. The boys speak of their lessons while they eat.
10. They put three lumps of sugar in their cups.

D. Answer the following questions in Italian:

1. Chi viene a casa di Giovanni?
2. Perché mangiano presto?
3. Che cosa fanno i ragazzi dopo il pranzo?
4. Che cosa bevono gl'Italiani a tavola?
5. Come preferisce il caffè Giovanni?
6. Di chi è sorella Elena?

7. Cosa prendono per antipasto?
8. Chi fa le presentazioni?
9. Cosa fa Carlo con un'arancia?
10. Chi apparecchia la tavola?

E. Translate into Italian:
John and Charles go for dinner (*a pranzare*) to a friend's house. They arrive early. Their friend is Philip. He introduces his friends to his (the) parents. The boys take their dinner at once because they must go back to school. For hors-d'œuvres they take a little salame. Then they eat roast meat with potatoes and finish with (the) fruit. After the meal (*pasto*) the boys play at draughts before returning to school.

REVISION EXERCISES (*Lessons I–V*)

1. Put the definite article before the following nouns:
giorno, giornata, case, serata, alunni, sorelline, lavagne, poeta, muri, specchio, studi, indirizzi, zampa, zero, cucchiaino, impiegati, tappeti, lezioni, parole, sbagli, linguaggio, sale, richiesta, bagni.

2. Put the indefinite article before the following:
alunno, salotto, latte, pacco, vizio, scrivania, sedia, gnocco, psicologo, verso, poesia, madre, caffè, specie, città, disposizione, ordine, produzione, boia, filiale, sbaglio, parola,pezzo, zio.

3. Give the plurals with the article of the following:
dinamo, mano, poeta, artista, radio, bue, padre, moglie, penna, dramma, schiavo, auto, foto, alunna, matita, uomo, dio, classe.

4. Give the correct person of the present tense of the following and the meaning of the verb:
cucire, 2nd plur.; finire, 1st plur.; soffrire, 3rd plur.; potere, 3rd sing.; dovere, 3rd plur.; sapere, 1st plur.; volere, 1st plur.; vedere, 2nd sing.; dormire, 1st sing.

5. Translate into Italian:
in the class; in a box; from a boy; on industry; in the works; of the uncle; with a zero; in church; on the carpet; in the bedroom; through the street; to school; at home; from the secretary; in the books.

6. Put the correct person of the verb in the following sentences:
    1. Loro non (parlare) a Giovanni.
    2. Essa (scrivere) delle lettere.
    3. Mi (piacere) questi libri.
    4. Voi (fare) il vostro lavoro.
    5. Io (tenere) la penna in mano.

7. Translate into Italian:
    1. He is always talking about himself.
    2. While we are writing, he is speaking.
    3. I too want to speak to Charles.
    4. She is a very beautiful girl.
    5. I want something to eat.
    6. Before leaving, John exchanges a few words with his teacher.
    7. As a sweet, we have ice-cream (*gelato*).
    8. She is typing all day long.
    9. I dislike this sort of film very much.
    10. They are a happy man and woman.

8. Translate into Italian:
    In my house. It is your fault. She writes on the blackboard in her turn. It is not easy, my boy. My sister-in-law is coming to my house today. The grandparents of the little girl are dead. In my opinion, he is intelligent. What is your daddy speaking of? Where is Charles coming from?

A. THE PARTITIVE ARTICLE

1. The partitive article is formed in Italian by combining the preposition **di** and the definite article. It may be used in the singular or the plural and means *some* or *any*†:

> Ho dei fratelli.   *I have some brothers.*
> Ho delle sorelle.   *I have some sisters.*
> Ha dei fiammiferi?   *Have you any matches?*
> Ha degli amici in casa.   *He has some friends in his house.*

2. In the negative singular only, the partitive is replaced by the indefinite adjective **nessuno, -a**‡ which inflects like the indefinite article and takes **non** before the verb:

> Non ho nessun fratello.   *I have no brothers.*
> Non ho nessuna sorella.   *I have no sisters.*
> Non ha nessun amico in casa.   *He has no friends in the house.*
> Non c'è nessun'alunna qui.   *There are no girl-pupils here.*

> NOTE. Since **nessuno** means *not one*, it cannot be used with materials, such as paper, bread, etc. (See 7 below.)

3. In the negative plural the partitive is dropped completely:

> Non ha fratelli.   *He has no brothers.*
> Non vedo libri qui.   *I see no books here.*
> Non abbiamo né penne né matite.   *We have neither pens nor pencils.*

4. The partitive can be dropped even when the verb is positive under certain circumstances. They are as follows:

> (a) When a list of things is given:

>> Vende libri, penne e matite.   *He sells books, pens and pencils.*

> (b) When a contrast is made, whether it is expressed or not:

>> Vedo uomini, non donne.   *I see men, not women.*
>> Vedo uomini io!   *I see men!* (*not anybody else*).

† *Some* or *any* may, of course, be omitted in the English sentence.
‡ *Alcuno, -a* is occasionally employed instead of *nessuno, -a* in this function:

> Non gettate alcun oggetto fuori del finestrino.
> *Don't throw anything out of the window.*

However, students are advised not to use this form.

(c) When it is used in a general or an indefinite sense:

Abbiamo professori molto bravi a scuola.
We have very good teachers at school.

Leggiamo libri molto difficili quest'anno.
We are reading very difficult books this year.

NOTE. The student should study the different meanings
of the following:

Gli uomini sono buoni.   *Men are good. (general)*

Ci sono degli uomini buoni, ma anche dei cattivi.

There are good men, but also bad ones. (particular)

5. The partitive article can be replaced by a number of other
indefinite adjectives besides **nessuno**. They are **qualche**
and **alcuni, -e,** the first of which is always used in the
singular even if the meaning is plural, the second always
in the plural:

Compro qualche libro.   *I buy a few (some) books.*
Ci sono alcuni ragazzi in classe.   *There are a few boys in the class.*

NOTE. Always use **alcuni** instead of the partitive when the
partitive is in an emphatic position:

Mi piacciono alcuni generi di film, ma non tutti.
I like some kinds of film, but not all.

It would be quite wrong to use **dei** instead of **alcuni** here
because of the emphatic nature of *some* in the English
sentence.

6. In the restricted sense of *just a few* the adjective **poco, -a**
is used:

Pochi libri mi piacciono.   *I like few books.*

7. With materials, foodstuffs, and other uncountable things,
use the partitive or **un po' di** (*a little of*) in the affirmative,
never **qualche** or **alcuni**:

Compro della carta.   *I buy some paper.*
Mangio un po' di pane.   *I eat a little bread.*

In the negative, the noun stands alone:

Non mangio pane.   *I do not eat bread.*

8. **Qualunque** and **qualsiasi** translate *whatsoever* or *some or other*:

Quel ragazzo è capace di qualsiasi cosa.
That boy is capable of literally anything (of anything whatsoever).

Egli manda un libro qualunque a Giovanni.
He sends some book or other to John.

B. THE IMPERATIVE

1. The imperative of regular verbs is as follows in Italian:

SECOND SING.	FIRST PLUR.	SECOND PLUR.
trova (*find*)	troviamo (*let us find*)	trovate (*find*)
vendi (*sell*)	vendiamo (*let us sell*)	vendete (*sell*)
finisci (*finish*)	finiamo (*let us finish*)	finite (*finish*)

2. The negative plural forms are rendered by placing **non** before the positive imperative, but the negative second singular form is identical with the negative infinitive:

non trovare   non vendere   non finire

3. A few verbs present irregularities in the imperative:

andare (*to go*)	va'	andiamo	andate
avere (*to have*)	abbi	abbiamo	abbiate
dare (*to give*)	da'	diamo	date
dire (*to say*)	di'	diciamo	dite
essere (*to be*)	sii	siamo	siate
fare (*to do*)	fa'	facciamo	fate
sapere (*to know*)	sappi	sappiamo	sappiate
stare (*to stand*)	sta'	stiamo	state
volere (*to want*)	vogli	vogliamo	vogliate

4. Polite forms of the imperative also exist and they are identical with the third persons (singular and plural) of the present subjunctive (see Lesson XXIV B).

VOCABULARY

abbastanza	enough, quite	meraviglia	marvel
acquistare	to acquire	negozio (di ge-	shop (grocer's
alimentare	alimentary	neri alimentari)	shop)
asciutto, -a	dry	paio	pair
autobus (m.)	'bus	pasta (asciutta)	paste (spa-
bigliettaio	conductor		ghetti)
calzolaio	cobbler	però	however
carne (f.)	meat	proprio	just
cena	supper	pure	even, also
chilo	kilo	quanto, -a	how much
ciò	that	riprendere	to fetch
compera (far	purchase (to do	scarpa	shoe
delle compere)	shopping)	scendere	to go down
costume da	swimming	scialle (m.)	shawl
bagno	costume	spesa (con poca	expense (at
cotoletta	cutlet	spesa)	little expense)
duecento	two hundred	stagione (f.)	season
fermo, -a	standing, firm	troppo	too much
fruttivendolo,-a	fruiterer	uscire (escono)	to go out
invece di	instead of	vestito	dress, clothes
lira	lira	vetrina	shop-window
lontano	far	viaggio	journey
macelleria	butcher's shop	vitello	calf, veal

chiedere al qc.

IN CITTÀ

Elena e sua cugina Barbara vanno in città per fare delle compere. Prendono l'autobus e chiedono due biglietti da due-cento lire[1] al bigliettaio. Il centro della città è abbastanza[2] lontano. Dopo venti minuti di viaggio, arrivano nella strada principale dove ci sono molti grandi negozi. Scendono dall'autobus e vanno a vedere i vestiti in una vetrina. Vedono un costume da bagno che è una meraviglia, ma costa troppo. Invece del costume, acquistano con poca spesa uno scialle, quindi vanno dal calzolaio[3] a riprendere un paio di scarpe di Silvia. Dopo ciò, entrano in una macelleria per comprare un po' di carne per la cena. Prendono un chilo di cotolette di vitello che piacciono tanto al babbo di Elena. Le ragazze passano quindi in un negozio di generi alimentari per comprare gli spaghetti per la pasta asciutta e dalla fruttivendola per comprare frutta. Prendono un chilo di arance ed un chilo di uva. Vogliono prendere pure delle mele che in questa stagione sono molto buone. Quando escono dalla fruttivendola vedono Giovanni fermo[4] a guardare in una vetrina. 'Buon giorno, Giovanni,' dice Elena. 'Arrivi proprio in tempo per accompagnare Barbara e me a casa. Prima, però, andiamo dal dentista a prendere un appuntamento per Carlo.' Cosí i tre ragazzi tornano insieme a casa.

NOTES

[1] **da duecento lire:** Note the use of *da* in this and similar expressions where we would say *of* in English. Compare with: un francobollo da cento lire, *a stamp worth* 100 *lire.*

[2] **abbastanza:** Note that this word, even when meaning *enough*, comes before the adjective in Italian. It is invariable, as is *troppo*, when used as an adverb. *Troppo*, however, can be used as an adjective as well: i.e. troppe cose, *too many things.*

[3] **dal calzolaio:** *Da* is used to mean *at the house of* in the same way as *chez* in French. However, when used with a pronoun, it must never refer to the subject of the sentence:

Vado da lui.   I go to his house.

but not: Vado da me.   *I go alone.*

In this case, to say *I go to my house* one uses *vado a casa mia.*

[4] **fermo:** Literally *firm*, but a number of Italian adjectives have a verbal force which is rendered in English by the present or past participles. (See Lesson XLI B.)

EXERCISES

A. Fill in the blanks, whenever necessary, with the appropriate form of the partitive article or with an indefinite adjective:

1. Compro — mele dalla fruttivendola.
2. Vado in bottega a cercare — carta.
3. Egli mi mostra — specchi.
4. Vedo — uomini, non — ragazzi.
5. Mi piace leggere — libri, ma non tutti.
6. Mi dà — penne.

7. Non trovo — matite nella sala da pranzo.
8. Voglio — carne.
9. Egli dà — libri ad Arturo.
10. Non ha — amici.

B Translate into Italian:
1. Do not speak to Charles.
2. Give the book to John.
3. Take the book and read the lesson.
4. Do not write to Barbara.
5. Tell John the news (*notizia*).
6. Let us go home with Helen.
7. Be (*stare*) good (*bravo*) and study your lessons.
8. Do everything possible (*tutto il possibile*) to help John.
9. Buy some apples for Helen.
10. Go to the cobbler's when you are in town.

C. Translate into Italian:
John likes sweets very much and when he goes to school, he buys sweets at a shop in the high street. Then he calls at (*passare da*) a friend's house and they go to school together. John eats his sweets in class and the teacher is displeased (*scontento*). 'What have you in your mouth (*bocca*)?' he asks. 'A sweet, sir (*signore*).' 'You are a very naughty boy. Put the sweet in the wastepaper basket (*cestino*) at once.' John puts the sweet in the wastepaper basket and returns to his desk.

D. Answer the following questions in Italian:
1. Le ragazze come vanno in città?
2. Dove ci sono molti grandi negozi?
3. Cosa fa Giovanni in città?
4. Che cosa acquista Elena con poca spesa in un negozio?
5. Chi viene proprio in tempo per accompagnare le ragazze a casa?
6. Le ragazze da chi comprano le mele?
7. Da dove viene Giovanni?
8. Che cosa chiedono le ragazze al bigliettaio?
9. Cosa c'è in vetrina che piace alle ragazze?
10. Perchè vanno in una macelleria?

E. Write in Italian a few lines on a trip to town.

A. SOME IRREGULAR VERBS

PRESENT TENSE

BERE *to drink*	COGLIERE *to gather*	DIRE *to say*
bevo	colgo	dico
bevi	cogli	dici
beve	coglie	dice
beviamo	cogliamo	diciamo
bevete	cogliete	dite
bevono	colgono	dicono

VALERE *to be worth*	SALIRE *to go up*	USCIRE *to go out*
valgo	salgo	esco
vali	sali	esci
vale	sale	esce
valiamo	saliamo	usciamo
valete	salite	uscite
valgono	salgono	escono

Parere (*to seem*) is mostly used impersonally and is consequently rare except in the third persons which are: pare, paiono (*it seems, they seem*).

B. CONJUNCTIVE PERSONAL PRONOUNS
CARDINAL NUMBERS

1. *Direct Object*

	SINGULAR			PLURAL	
1st	mi	*me*	ci	*us*	
2nd	ti	*thee*	vi	*you*	
3rd	lo, la	*him, her, it*	li, le	*them (m. and f.)*	
	la	*you*	li, le	*you (m. and f.)*	

54

2. *Indirect Object*

	SINGULAR			PLURAL	
1st	mi	*to me*		ci	*to us*
2nd	ti	*to thee*		vi	*to you*
3rd	gli, le	*to him, to her, to it*		loro†	*to them*
	le	*to you*		Loro	*to you*

3. All the conjunctive pronouns precede a finite verb (see Lesson X) except **loro** which always follows it:

  Gli do un libro. *I give him a book.*

but: Do loro un libro. *I give them a book.*

NOTE. The third person feminine alone is used to express the indirect form *to you* (**le**) whether the person referred to is masculine or feminine; this is also the case for the singular of the direct object form (**la**), but in the plural both **li** and **le** are used according to the gender of the persons referred to:

  Le do un libro. *I give you a book* (*m. and f.*).

  La prego di partire. *I beg you to go* (*m. and f.*).

but: Li (*or* le) prego di partire. *I beg you to go* (*m. or f.*).

The past participle agrees with the feminine form **la** even when it refers to a male:

  La ho incontrata a Roma. *I met you* (*m.*) *at Rome.*

4. *Proclitic Adverbs* (used to refer to places previously mentioned):

  ci, vi *there*   ne *from there*

5. The proclitic adverbs, besides meaning *there* and *from there*, sometimes mean *in it, to it* (**ci, vi**), and *of it, of him, of her, of them* (**ne**):

  Ci vado subito. *I go there at once.*

  Ne torno proprio adesso. *I am returning from there right now.*

but: Ecco la scatola; ci metto il libro.

  Here is the box; I put the book in it.

  Ne prendo uno. *I take one* (*of them*).

It is always necessary to use **ne** in conjunction with numerals and adjectives of quantity in the last type of expression even though it may seem superfluous in English.

  There is no difference in meaning between **vi** and **ci**, although **ci** is rather more common nowadays.

      † *loro* is often replaced by *gli* in speech.

6. The first twenty cardinal numbers are as follows:

1.	uno, -a	11.	undici
2.	due	12.	dodici
3.	tre	13.	tredici
4.	quattro	14.	quattordici
5.	cinque	15.	quindici
6.	sei	16.	sedici
7.	sette	17.	diciassette
8.	otto	18.	diciotto
9.	nove	19.	diciannove
10.	dieci	20.	venti

VOCABULARY

accaduto	*happening*	gridare	*to shout*
additare	*to point out*	incamminarsi	*to make one's way*
andare a finire	*to end up*		
attraversare	*to cross*	incidente (*m.*)	*accident*
cavarsela	*to get out of*	investire	*to run over*
cenare	*to sup*	lungo (*prep.*)	*along*
di certo	*certainly*	macchina	*car*
chiamare	*to call*	paura	*fear*
di colpo	*suddenly*	persino	*even*
comunque	*however*	prima	*first*
conducente (*m.*)	*driver*	principale	*principal*
contro	*against*	proprietario, -a	*owner*
crocevia (*m.*)	*crossroads*	risposta	*answer*
dietro	*behind*	riuscire a	*to succeed in*
dimenticare	*to forget*	senza	*without*
farabutto	*rascal*	signore, -a	*Mr., Mrs.*
fare in tempo a	*to have time to*	sopraggiungere	*to come up*
fermarsi	*to stop*	spiegare	*to explain*
per filo e per segno	*the ins and outs*	spiegazione (*f.*)	*explanation*
		strada	*road, street*
fracasso	*crash*	stradale (*adj.*)	*of the street*
freno	*brake*	stridore (*m.*)	*squeal*
fuori	*out, outside*	testimonio	*witness*
furibondo	*furious*	non veder l'ora di	*to long for*
giornale (*m.*)	*newspaper*		

UN INCIDENTE STRADALE

Il signor Rossi[1] compra il giornale della sera e s'incammina lungo la strada principale della città. È stanco e non vede l'ora di arrivare a casa per cenare. Ad un crocevia dimentica persino di fare attenzione nell'attraversare[2] la strada, e per poco non[3] si fa investire[4] da un autobus. Questo si ferma di colpo con uno stridore di freni, ma la macchina che è subito dietro non fa in tempo a fermarsi e va a finire contro l'autobus con gran[5] fracasso. Il proprietario ne esce fuori e comincia a gridare contro tutti. Sopraggiunge un poliziotto ed il conducente dell'autobus gli spiega per filo e per segno l'accaduto. 'Di certo,' dice, 'è colpa sua', e addita il signor Rossi. Il poliziotto prende nota e chiede al signor Rossi una spiegazione. Naturalmente le sue risposte non piacciono ai due conducenti furibondi. Tutt'e due lo chiamano farabutto. Fortunatamente per il signor Rossi, non ci sono testimoni, ed egli se la cava con un po' di paura. Comunque ora egli non attraversa piú[6] le strade senza prima guardare.

NOTES

[1] **Il signor Rossi**: Nearly all titles take the definite article in Italian. Nouns ending in -*ore* drop the final -*e* before a proper or common noun: il professor Umberti, il signor conte, etc.

[2] **nell'attraversare**: Infinitives can be used as nouns in Italian and are always masculine in gender.

[3] **per poco non**: Study this expression which means *almost*; the verb must always be in the negative.

[4] **si fa investire**: Literally *makes oneself run over*. Many such expressions are used in Italian. (See Lesson XXXVII B.)

[5] **gran**: A shortened form of *grande* (*big*). (See Lesson XII B.)

[6] **non . . . piú**: *Non* before the verb and *piú* after it is a construction parallel to *non . . . che* and means *no more* or *no longer*.

EXERCISES

A. Translate into Italian:

1. We often (*spesso*) go there.
2. Are you coming back from there now?
3. They give the books to us.
4. We write a letter to you.
5. He sends it to them.
6. He offers us some newspapers and I take one of them.
7. We do not give him books because we do not like him.
8. We do not speak of it now.
9. There is an accident and John is a witness of it.
10. I want two and John wants one.

B. Answer the following questions in Italian:

1. Cosa dice il conducente dell'autobus al poliziotto?
2. Da dove viene il signor Rossi?
3. Chi è furibondo?
4. Perché il signor Rossi è stanco?
5. Cosa fa il proprietario della macchina dopo l'incidente?
6. A chi chiede il poliziotto una spiegazione?
7. Chi attraversa la strada senza guardare?
8. Perché è fortunato il signor Rossi?
9. Chi non fa in tempo a fermarsi?
10. Chi chiama farabutto il signor Rossi?

C. Translate into Italian:

1. We drink some wine in the shop.
2. They gather apples in the garden (*giardino*).
3. John goes up (*su*) the mountain (*montagna*).
4. We go out of (from) the room.
5. Those houses seem big.

D. Translate into Italian:

Mr. Rossi buys a paper and makes his way along the road. He sees John who is coming from school and he speaks to him for a moment. He speaks to him about his lessons. John takes the bus to go home but there is an accident along the street. A bus stops suddenly in order not to run over a gentleman and a car which is directly behind does not stop in time. It hits (*urtare contro*) the bus with a loud crash. Fortunately there are no injured (*feriti*) and John gets off with a bit of a fright.

E. Substitute *ci, vi* or *ne* for the nouns in the following sentences:

1. Egli esce dalla sala da pranzo.
2. Veniamo da Roma adesso.
3. Andate a casa subito?
4. Prende due mele.
5. Vanno a teatro stasera.
6. Entriamo in sala subito?
7. Egli è nel suo studio.
8. Desidero un po' d'inchiostro.
9. Torno da Londra proprio adesso.
10. Mandano essi due libri, Giovanni?

not translated if English verb can be replaced by relative clause eg a bird singing in the tree, - a bird who is singing in the tree.

A. THE GERUND

1. The gerund is formed by adding **-ando, -endo** and **-endo** respectively to the roots of the infinitives of the first, second and third conjugations. The Italian gerund takes over many of the functions of the English present participle and no distinction will be made here between the two parts of speech:

I	II	III
trovando *finding*	vendendo *selling*	dormendo *sleeping*
		finendo *finishing*

2. All gerunds are regular in Italian but contracted infinitives should be replaced by their original long forms when the root is to be found for gerundial formation: e.g., **fare < facere** gives **facendo**.

3. The gerund is an invariable form. It *always* (usually) refers to the subject of the sentence in modern Italian† and *never* takes a preposition before it:

> Parlando con Carlo cammino lungo la strada.
> *While speaking to Charles, I walk along the road.*
>
> Entriamo in sala fumando una sigaretta.
> *We enter the room smoking cigarettes.*
>
> Aprendo la porta vedo Giovanni.
> *On opening the door I see John.*

It will be noticed from the examples given above that the Italian gerund translates a variety of English phrases.

(See also Lesson XXII B.)

† The gerund rarely has a subject of its own in modern Italian:
Andando noi a scuola, il signor Rossi ci spiega come la sua azienda è organizzata.
While we are going to school, Mr. Rossi explains to us how his factory is organised.
but it may be used impersonally:
Lo faccio occorrendo.
I shall do it if need be.

Stare + gerund = is doing eg sto facendo - I am doing

B. THE PAST PARTICIPLE

1. The past participles of regular verbs are formed by adding **-ato, -uto, -ito** respectively to the infinitives of the first, second and third conjugations:

I	II	III
trovato *found*	venduto *sold*	dormito *slept*
		finito *finished*

2. Many past participles, however, are irregular and are listed in the table of irregular verbs at the end of the book. Some of the more common ones are as follows:

aprire – aperto *to open*	nascere – nato *to be born*
chiedere – chiesto *to ask*	offrire – offerto *to offer*
chiudere – chiuso *to close*	parere – parso *to seem, appear*
cogliere – colto *to gather*	prendere – preso *to take*
convincere – convinto *to convince*	rendere – reso *to give back*
	ridere – riso *to laugh*
correre – corso *to run*	rimanere – rimasto *to remain*
cuocere – cotto *to cook*	rispondere – risposto *to answer*
decidere – deciso *to decide*	scendere – sceso *to go down*
dire – detto *to say*	scrivere – scritto *to write*
fare – fatto *to do, make*	stare – stato *to stand, be*
giungere – giunto *to reach*	togliere – tolto *to take away*
leggere – letto *to read*	vedere – visto (veduto) *to see*
mettere – messo *to put*	venire – venuto *to come*
morire – morto *to die*	vivere – vissuto *to live*
muovere – mosso *to move*	volgere – volto *to turn*

3. The past participle is sometimes used as a simple adjective:
   l'anno passato *last year*   la settimana scorsa *last week*.

4. Sometimes it replaces a relative clause:
   Dopo le cose dette alla conferenza, la testa mi gira.
   After the things (which were) said in the lecture, my head is spinning.

5. And it is used ~~very frequently~~ in absolute constructions:
   Detto fatto. *No sooner said than done.*
   Partito lui, vado in città. *He having departed, I go to town.*
   Finita la messa, andiamo a casa.
   Mass having finished, we go home.

The rules of agreement in absolute constructions are: (a) with a transitive verb the past participle agrees with its object; (b) with an intransitive verb it agrees with its subject.

6. The past participle is also used to form the compound tenses. (See Lesson XIII A.)

VOCABULARY

tra l'altro	among other things	marciapiede (*m.*)	platform, pavement
ancora (di piú)	again (still more)	non tanto	not too much
anzi	rather, on the contrary	permesso!	excuse me!
avanti	forward	pieno, -a	full
bagno	bath	raccontare	to relate
biglietto d'ingresso	entrance or platform ticket	rispondere	to reply
binario	track, pair of rails	ritirare	to withdraw, take from
capitare	to happen	sala (d'aspetto)	(waiting) room
carrozza	carriage	sembrare	to seem
cercare	to look for	sentirsi	to feel (ill, etc.)
cosí cosí	so, so!	soffocare	to stifle
dimagrito	thin	solito	usual
all'estero	abroad	sportello	door (of carriage), ticket-office hatch
far caldo	to be hot (of weather)	stare (Come stai?)	to be, stand (How are you?)
ferrovia	railway	fare strada verso	to lead the way towards
fin dove	(up) to where	farsi strada verso	to make one's way to
fra, tra	amid, among		
francese	French	treno	train
frastuono	noise	uscita	exit
grazie (*f. plur.*)	thank you	vacanze (*f. plur.*)	holidays
incontrare	to meet	valigia	suitcase
incredibile	incredible	venire incontro a	to come up to
ingrassare	to get fat	verso	towards
lucente	gleaming	viaggiatore (*m.*)	traveller
macchinista (*m.*)	engine driver		

(handwritten annotations in margins and at bottom:)
magro – their (reason)
dimagrire – to lose weight

non *(above)* tanto
viaggiatrice (B)

fare il bagno – to take a bath
fare la doccia – to take a shower

ALLA STAZIONE

Carlo e Giovanni vanno alla stazione per incontrare un amico. Prendono l'autobus che è pieno di gente. Il bigliettaio dice loro di passare avanti. 'Permesso,' dicono, e si fanno strada fin dove si siede il conducente. Arrivati alla stazione di buon'ora, vanno allo sportello a comprare due biglietti d'ingresso. Poi entrano nella sala d'aspetto con i viaggiatori. Dopo poco, il treno arriva al marciapiede numero due e la locomotiva si ferma con un grande stridore di freni sui lucenti binari. Il macchinista è sempre molto occupato. Adesso i viaggiatori cominciano ad aprire gli sportelli e a scendere dalle carrozze. I due ragazzi non vedono l'ora di incontrare il loro amico. Ecco che[1] viene loro incontro.[2] Certo, non è dimagrito. Anzi, è ingrassato ancora di piú. 'Buon giorno, Gino,' gridano i due ragazzi tra il frastuono tumultuoso della stazione. 'Come stai, vecchio mio?' 'Cosí cosí,' risponde Gino mentre Giovanni gli prende[3] la valigia e gli fa strada[4] verso l'uscita. 'Grazie,' dice Gino. 'Prego,'[5] risponde Giovanni. 'Che caldo fa[6] oggi!' dice Gino, 'mi sento soffocare.' 'Sei stanco del viaggio?' chiede Carlo. 'Mica tanto, ma voglio fare un bel bagno.' I ragazzi sono adesso all'uscita ed il controllore ritira loro i biglietti. Carlo va a cercare un taxi e cosí vanno subito a casa. Intanto Gino racconta per filo e per segno tutte le solite avventure che possono capitare ad ogni ragazzo che va all'estero per le vacanze. Dice tra l'altro che i treni francesi vanno ad una velocità incredibile ma che egli preferisce sempre viaggiare in Italia.

NOTES

[1] **Ecco che :** This is a typical way of being emphatic in Italian.

[2] **viene loro incontro :** There are two possible constructions with prepositional verbs in Italian: *gli viene incontro* or *viene incontro a lui*. Similarly, *stiamo vicino a lui*, or *gli stiamo vicino*; but it is necessary for the preposition to be one of a group which requires *a* before a pronoun (see list in Lesson XXXVIII), since

those which require *di* such as *fuori di* (outside) do not admit of this construction.

³ **gli prende**: One takes something *to* someone in Italian, not *from* someone.

⁴ **gli fa strada**: Literally *makes the road to him*, i.e., *leads the way*. Note also *farsi strada* (to make one's way).

⁵ **Grazie ... Prego**: When an Italian says *Thank you*, the person addressed always answers *I beg you*. One might compare this with the American: *You're welcome*.

⁶ **che caldo fa**: Expressions indicating the state of the weather may take *fare* or *essere* with the adjective in Italian.

EXERCISES

A. Translate into Italian:

three books, one pen, nineteen houses, twenty boxes, five pencils, nine apples, fourteen desks, twelve tables, seventeen boys, eight men.

B. Translate into Italian:
1. We walk along the road smoking.
2. On seeing John, I go up to him.
3. Being ill (*ammalato*), I want to go home.
4. On opening the carriage door, he sees his friend.
5. Wishing to speak to Charles, I set out for his house.
6. On entering the room, I see Barbara seated (*seduto*) at a table.
7. Not wanting to reply to Helen, I go away (*andar via*).
8. Seeing John on the platform, I carry (*portare*) his suitcase to him.
9. Not knowing (the) English, Charles speaks Italian.
10. Unable to go to the cinema, Silvia reads.

C. Translate into Italian:
1. No sooner said than done.
2. Some of the words written in this book are very difficult.
3. Having finished his lessons, Charles goes home.
4. The twenty lira found by John are on the table.
5. I am giving back the book borrowed (*prendere in prestito*) by Charles.

EARLY MORNING IN VENICE

PISA

THE HARBOUR, PORTOFERRAIO, ELBA

D. Translate into Italian:

John and Charles are two great friends of Gino's. Gino is spending his holidays abroad. He is coming home today. His friends go to the station to (a) meet the traveller. The train is late and they have to go to the waiting-room. When the train arrives, the passengers get out of the carriages. Charles sees Gino coming towards him. John leads the way to the exit. They take a taxi to get home. Gino relates to them the usual adventures of a traveller abroad.

E. Answer the following questions in Italian:

1. Chi va all'estero?
2. Da chi comprano i biglietti i ragazzi?
3. Perché i ragazzi vanno alla stazione?
4. Cosa preferisce Lei, viaggiare in treno o in autobus?
5. È con un amico che Giovanni va all'estero?
6. Le piace leggere quando viaggia in treno?
7. Da dove arriva Gino?
8. Chi scende dal treno?
9. È molto grande la valigia di Gino?
10. Cosa fa Giovanni quando Gino viene loro incontro?

F. Write a few lines on a visit to the station.

A. POSSESSIVE ADJECTIVES (*cont.*)

1. The definite article may be replaced in Italian before a possessive by the following parts of speech: the indefinite article, an adjective of quantity, a numeral or a demonstrative adjective:

> un mio abito   *one of my suits*
> molti miei quadri   *many of my pictures*
> due miei amici   *two of my friends*
> questa mia sedia   *this chair of mine.*

The Italian idiom corresponding to *one of my . . . etc.* should be carefully noted, although it is also possible to translate literally: *uno dei miei abiti*, etc.

2. Italian is generally a far more impersonal language than English, so that with parts of the body and dress the possessive is omitted, provided the possessor is the subject of the sentence:

> Mette le mani in tasca.
> *He puts his hands in his pocket.*
>
> Mette la testa sul guanciale.
> *He puts his head on the pillow.*
>
> Si tolgono il cappello.
> *They take off their hats.*

NOTE. The distributive singular in example 3 should be carefully studied. It is used with parts of the body, clothes and other close possessions, when the individuals from a group possess only *one* each of the things mentioned.

3. If possession is indicated, it is done by means of an indirect conjunctive pronoun, sometimes a reflexive:

> Bruno si copre la faccia con le mani.
> *Bruno covers his face with his hands.*

Si asciugano le mani.
They wipe their hands.

Gli laviamo le mani.
We wash his *hands.*

When the subject of the sentence is not the possessor, as in example 3, it is also permissible to use the possessive:

Laviamo le sue mani.

4. If confusion should arise in the meaning of the third person possessive **suo** or **loro** which can mean *his, her, its, your,* and *their* and *your* respectively, the forms **di lui, di lei, di Lei, di loro** and **di Loro** are used in their stead:

Egli parla a un amico di lei.
He speaks to her friend.

but:

Egli parla a un suo amico.
He speaks to his (own) friend.

5. The adjectives **proprio** meaning *own* and **altrui** meaning *others* also indicate possession:

Ognuno parla dei propri affari.
Everyone is speaking of his own affairs.

Non dovete prendere la roba altrui.
You must not take other people's things.

6. Possessives are sometimes used in an idiomatic sense:

Questa è senza dubbio un'altra delle sue.
This is undoubtedly another of his tricks.

Io dico la mia e tu dici la tua.
I'll tell you my opinion and you tell me yours.

Anch'io ho avuto le mie.
I too have had my troubles.

In each of these sentences the noun which the possessive qualifies is omitted. Here, they may well be *burla* (a trick), *opinione* (*f.*) (an opinion), and *disgrazie* (misfortunes).

B. POSSESSIVE PRONOUNS

1. The possessive pronouns are identical with possessive adjectives:

SINGULAR		PLURAL		
il mio	la mia	i miei	le mie	*mine*
il tuo	la tua	i tuoi	le tue	*thine*
il suo	la sua	i suoi	le sue	*his, hers, its, yours*
il nostro	la nostra	i nostri	le nostre	*ours*
il vostro	la vostra	i vostri	le vostre	*yours*
il loro	la loro	i loro	le loro	*theirs, yours*

2. Sometimes the article is omitted and sometimes it is not. It is generally used for emphasis when one is selecting something from a group of objects and asserting possession:

> Questa valigia è la mia.
> *This case is mine* (being selected from a number of cases).

but:
> Questa valigia è mia.
> *This case is mine* (i.e. and not anyone else's).

There is no great difference in the meaning of these expressions, but the latter possessive is, strictly speaking, an adjective.

VOCABULARY

affare (*m.*)	*business*	desiderare	*to want, wish*
angolo	*corner*	discorso	*talk, conversation*
bambino, -a	*baby*		
battere (in un batter d'occhio)	*to beat (in a twinkling)*	educato, -a	*well-bred, well brought up*
ben tenuto	*well-kept*	fatto (saper il fatto suo)	*fact (to know one's job)*
bottega	*shop*		
burro	*butter*	formaggio	*cheese*
ciò che	*what*	frequentatissimo	*very frequented*
commesso	*shop-assistant*	fresco, -a	*fresh*
comportarsi	*to behave*	gente (*f.*)	*people*
conserva	*tomato purée*	impeccabile	*impeccable*
curioso, -a	*curious*	inoltre	*besides*

intromettersi	*to interfere*	pulito, -a	*clean*
mestiere (*m.*)	*trade, job*	qualità	*quality*
olio	*oil*	ragione (*f.*)	*reason*
onesto	*honest*	sbagliarsi	*to make a mistake*
padrone (*m.*)	*owner*	sí	*yes*
da parte di	*on the part of*	soddisfatto, -a	*satisfied*
piazza	*square*	trovarsi	*to be (situated)*
prosciutto	*ham*	veramente	*really*

LA BOTTEGA

È del signor Tosi la bottega all'angolo di Piazza Garibaldi? Sí, la bottega del signor Tosi si trova all'angolo della piazza ed è una bottega di generi alimentari. Potete sempre trovare merce fresca e di prima qualità dal signor Tosi — olio, formaggio, prosciutto, burro, conserve e frutta — perché conosce bene il suo mestiere. È un negozio molto ben tenuto e pulito. I clienti sono serviti sempre in un batter d'occhio e il modo di trattare la gente da parte del padrone e dei commessi è veramente impeccabile. Tutti sono soddisfatti e, per questa ragione, egli fa degli ottimi affari.

Sa veramente il fatto suo e non si sbaglia mai su ciò che desiderano i vari clienti. Inoltre, non è mai curioso, non s'intromette nei discorsi dei clienti quando parlano fra di loro[1] in attesa di essere serviti, ed è sempre pronto a fare qualche complimento ai bambini. Anche per queste ragioni il suo negozio è frequentatissimo. In città è difficile trovare[2] molti negozi di generi alimentari che fanno cosí buoni affari. Il signor Tosi si comporta sempre da persona[3] educata, onesta e prudente.

NOTES

[1] **fra di loro**: With pronouns a number of prepositions take *di* even though they stand by themselves before a noun, e.g., *Conta su di te, Giovanni.* (He is counting on you, John.) However, the double preposition is not always obligatory.

[2] **È difficile trovare**: Impersonal expressions formed from *essere* and an adjective do not take a preposition before a following infinitive.

³ **da persona:** The preposition *da* often replaces *come* (as) when the underlying meaning is *in the manner of* or *as characteristic of*. It is never used with the article in this sense.

EXERCISES

A. Translate into Italian:
1. This is one of my books.
2. John's mother is drying his hands with a towel (*asciugamano*) (*m.*).
3. He is washing his face with his hands.
4. Where are those oranges of mine?
5. The men are fighting for their lives (*vita*).
6. We take off (*togliere*) his coat (*giacca*).
7. We do not wish to speak with her friends.
8. This is my own house.
9. He is talking to a friend of his.
10. You must not take other people's belongings, John.

B. Fill in the blanks in the following sentences:
1. Ha il — cappello Lei?
2. Perché impostano le — lettere cosí tardi?
3. Le laviamo — mani.
4. Ecco Giovanna! Carlo parla con un'amica di —.
5. Ognuno ama la — casa.
6. Dov'è la — penna, Maria?
7. Prende sempre in prestito i libri —.
8. Ancora un'altra delle —, mi pare!
9. Questa valigia è — e quest'altra —.
10. Questa macchina non è —.

C. Answer the following questions in Italian:
1. Di chi è la bottega all'angolo?
2. Sono ben serviti i clienti del signor Tosi?
3. Che specie di persona è il signor Tosi?
4. Perché non s'intromette negli affari dei suoi clienti?
5. È di prima qualità la merce del signor Tosi?

D. Translate into Italian:
Where are you going, Charles? I am going to Mr. Tosi's shop in order to buy some milk. Will (*volere*) you come with me. Yes, I want to buy some ham and fruit because Philip is coming to our house for dinner. Is he a friend of yours then (*allora*)? But of course. We are in the same class at school. John and

Charles walk along the street to Mr. Tosi's shop at the corner of the square and go into it. There are many customers and the two boys have to wait (*aspettare*). When they are served they go straight home because their mothers want the things they buy to prepare dinner.

E. Write out a short conversation between a shopkeeper and a customer.

A. ORDER OF PERSONAL PRONOUNS WITH THE VERB

1. Personal pronouns, as we have seen in Lesson VII, precede *finite* verbs, except **loro** which invariably follows them:

Mi scrive una lettera.   *He writes me a letter.*
Ti parlo di quella signora.   *I am speaking to you of that lady.*

but:

Egli parla loro con autorità.   *He speaks to them with authority.*

2. All personal pronouns, however, follow and are attached to (a) an infinitive; (b) an imperative affirmative; (c) a gerund; (d) a past participle used alone; (e) **ecco** (here is):

    (a) Posso mandargli una lettera.
        I can send him a letter.
    (b) Vendimi questo libro.
        Sell me this book.
    (c) Scrivendole, domandale di venire.
        While writing to her, ask her to come.
    (d) Dettogli questo, egli va via.
        Having told him this, he goes away.
    (e) Eccoli adesso che vengono.
        Here they come now.

(a) It will be noted that the final *e* of the infinitive is dropped when the pronoun is attached. With certain auxiliaries like **potere, dovere,** *etc.* it is also possible to put the pronoun before the auxiliary and this is very frequent in Italian:

    e.g. Gli posso mandare una lettera.

(b) When an imperative is monosyllabic or stressed on the final syllable, the consonant of the pronoun attached to it is doubled except in the case of **gli**:

    Dille!   *Tell her!*   Dammi!   *Give me!*

but:

Digli di scrivere loro. *Dgli di scrivergli*
Tell him to write to them.

The negative imperative admits of two forms, ~~but the first one given is the more usual~~:

Non darmi quel quadro.
Don't give me that picture.

or: Non mi dare quel quadro. ~~(rare)~~

Non datemi quel quadro.
Don't give me that picture.

or: Non mi date quel quadro. ~~(rare)~~

Non andiamoci stasera.
Let us not go there tonight.

or: Non ci andiamo stasera. ~~(rare)~~

(c) It should be noted that **loro** never attaches itself even to these parts of the verb:

Da' loro i libri. *Give them the books.* (Dagli)
Bisogna scrivere loro. *We must write to them.* (scrivergli)

(d) The attachment of a pronoun (or even a series of pronouns) to a gerund or an infinitive does not alter their tonic stresses which fall on the gerundial or infinitive endings, except in the case of second conjugation verbs, where the infinitive stress is on the root of the verb:

dandomelo *giving it to me.*
Devo mandarglielo. *I must send it to him.*

but:

Devo scrivergli una lettera. *I must write him a letter*

(e) The stress also remains unchanged on **ecco** despite the addition of a pronoun:

Eccoli! *There they are!*

(f) Whenever a past participle is used as part of a verb form (i.e. the compound tenses), the pronoun precedes the auxiliary verb and is never attached to the past participle. (See Lesson XIII A.) *Lo ho datto le ho scritto*

3. When two pronouns are used together the indirect object precedes the direct object. **Mi, ti, si, ci, vi** become **me, te, se, ce, ve** before **lo, la, li, le, l', ne,** and **gli** and **le**

both become **glie.** In this latter case, the whole combination is written as a single word: **glielo, gliela, glieli, gliele, gliene.** Examples of the various possibilities are as follows:

Ve lo dico io!	*I tell you so!*
Ce la manda a casa.	*He sends it home for us.*
Non me lo dà.	*He does not give it to me.*
Gliela scrive.	*He writes it to her (you, him).*
Glieli mandiamo.	*We send them to him (her, you).*

Loro retains its position after the verb:

Lo vendo loro.	*I sell it to them.*

4. When two pronouns are appended to an infinitive, imperative, gerund or past participle, the whole combination becomes one word, but the same order (*i.e.* indirect before direct object) is maintained:

Posso mandargliela.	*I can send it to him.*
Dandomelo.	*Giving it to me.*
Dimmelo.	*Tell it to me.*
Dettomelo.	*Having said it to me.*

Once again the tonic stresses are unaffected by the addition of pronouns.

5. The conjunctive adverbs **ci, vi** and **ne** behave exactly like personal pronouns:

Ve li manda.	*He sends them there.*
Ne parla con loro.	*He speaks about it with them.*

Since **ci, vi** mean *us* and *you* in addition to their adverbial sense, we are sometimes led into complications. Whereas we can say:

Mandamici!	*Send me there!*

one cannot say **mandacici** to translate *send us there.* In such cases one should use other methods of saying the same thing:

Mandaci là!	*Send us there.*

6. Italians often use the reflexive pronoun **si** to mean *one* like the French *on*:

Si può vedere il mare quando si è in cima alla montagna.
One can see the sea when one is on top of the mountain.

When so used, a special order of pronouns is required in combination with it:

Lo si vede.	*One sees it.*
Se ne parla.	*One speaks of it.*
Ci si può andare.	*One can go there.*

The rule is that all pronouns (apart from *loro*) precede the indefinite **si** except **ne** which always follows it.

B. INTERROGATIVE PRONOUNS

1. Interrogative pronouns are as follows in Italian:

chi? *who?*   a chi? *to whom?*   di chi? *of whom? whose?*

che? ⎫	a che? ⎫	di che? ⎫
che cosa? ⎬ *what?*	a che cosa? ⎬ *to what?*	di che cosa? ⎬ *of what?*
cosa? ⎭	a cosa? ⎭	di cosa? ⎭

There is no difference between the three forms of *what?* and they can be interchanged at will. Students should be careful not to confuse **chi?** (who?) with the relative pronoun **che** which is also translated by *who* in English. Some examples of the use of interrogatives are given below:

Chi ti parla adesso?	*Who is speaking to you now?*
Di chi è questo libro?	*Whose book is this?*
A chi scrivi?	*To whom are you writing?*
Di che cosa si tratta?	*What is it we are dealing with?* (*What is it all about?*)
Cosa dice lui?	*What is he saying?*
A che cosa alludi?	*What are you alluding to?*

2. All the interrogatives can also be used in indirect questions:

Dimmi chi è.	*Tell me who he is.*
Dimmi che cosa vuoi.	*Tell me what you want.*
Voglio sapere di che si tratta.	*I want to know what it is all about.*

VOCABULARY

accendere	*to light*	alzarsi	*to get up*
affrettarsi	*to hurry*	amore (*m.*)	*love*
almeno	*at least*	ansia	*anxiety*

apparire	to appear	personaggio	character
attesa	expectancy	platea	pit, stalls
attore (m.), -trice (f.)	actor, actress	a poco a poco	little by little
		programma (m.)	programme
avvenimento	event	quarto	quarter
bisbiglio	whisper	rappresentare	to play
campanello	bell	ribalta	footlights
in carne ed ossa	in flesh and blood	ritardatario	latecomer
		far sfoggio	to display
in cerca di	in search of	sipario	curtain
comparire	to appear	smorzare	to die down
compleanno	birthday	spegnere	to put out
di cui	whose	sportello della biglietteria	ticket-office window
diciottesimo	eighteenth		
galleria	gallery	squillo	ringing
già	already	tanto piú che	all the more so because
infatti	(in fact,) indeed		
inizio	beginning	terzo	third
lasciare	to leave, let	vanitoso, -a	vain
luce (f.) (luci della ribalta)	light (foot-/lime lights)	non è vero?	isn't it?
		vivissimo, -a	very (acute)
mancare	to lack	voce (f.) (ad alta voce)	voice (aloud)
palcoscenico	stage	volta	turn, time

A TEATRO

Questa sera tutta la famiglia Zallio va a teatro. Ci sono il padre, la madre, i due figli, e la figlia Franca che oggi celebra il suo diciottesimo compleanno. Il signor Zallio va prima allo sportello della biglietteria ad acquistare cinque biglietti di platea. Entrano quindi in sala. Manca un quarto d'ora all'inizio dello spettacolo e già molta gente prende posto; anzi, la galleria è completa. C'è molta attesa per il nuovo spettacolo. Infatti, viene rappresentato[1] per la prima volta sul palcoscenico della città *Sei personaggi in cerca d'autore* di Pirandello. L'ansia è vivissima, tanto piú che appare il grande Vittorio Gassman. Tutto il pubblico vuole vedere in carne ed ossa questo attore cosí famoso. In sala molti commentano ad alta voce l'avvenimento; altri leggono il programma, e altri ancora osservano gli abiti nuovi di cui le signore fanno sfoggio. Infatti, molte persone vanno a teatro piú per comparire in società che per vero amore del teatro, non è vero? Cosí, almeno, pensa Franca. Ma essa non è una persona vanitosa e tutte queste superficialità la lasciano indifferente. Ecco finalmente l'ora della rappresentazione e tutti sono seduti tranne i soliti ritardatari che si affrettano ai propri posti. Si spengono[2] le luci in sala, si smorza a poco a poco il bisbiglio del pubblico, si accendono le luci della ribalta e al terzo squillo di campanello si alza il sipario.

NOTES

[1] **viene rappresentato**: *Venire* as well as *essere* is used in Italian to form the passive voice. The former is preferred with verbs of action. (See Lesson XXXVII A.)

[2] **Si spengono**: The passive voice can be avoided in Italian by using the reflexive verb.

EXERCISES

A. Translate into Italian:
  1. Give me the piece of chalk.
  2. Write it on the blackboard.
  3. Don't let's send her there now.
  4. When you are speaking to me, don't laugh!
  5. Finish it at once.
  6. I am sending it to her today.
  7. Take the 'bus, you are very late.
  8. I must talk to them about it.
  9. Here they are now.
  10. While writing to her, tell her to (*di*) come to the theatre tomorrow night.

B. Replace the nouns in the following sentences by the requisite pronouns:
  1. Giovanni dà il libro a Elena.
  2. Elena manda tre lettere ai suoi genitori.
  3. Il professore parla dell'Italia ai ragazzi.
  4. Non dare il tuo libro a Federico.
  5. È impossibile parlare a Giovanni di ciò.

6. A Giovanni non piace scrivere delle lettere a sua sorella.
7. Tuo padre parla al professore del tuo lavoro.
8. Vado a scuola di buon'ora.
9. Giovanni va in un negozio per comprare delle caramelle.
10. Vendo la mia macchina a Giovanni.

C. Translate into Italian:
1. What are you talking about?
2. To whom are you sending that box of pencils?
3. Every time that I see him, he asks me what I am doing.
4. He wants to know what it is all about.
5. Write to me to say who is coming to the cinema with us.

D. Answer the following questions in Italian:
1. Con chi va Franca a teatro?
2. Che cosa celebra questa ragazza oggi?
3. Quanto tempo manca all'inizio della rappresentazione?
4. Che dramma rappresentano stasera?
5. È una persona vanitosa Franca?
6. Chi è il famoso attore che appare sul palcoscenico stasera?
7. Di che cosa fanno sfoggio le signore?
8. Che cosa succede all'ora della rappresentazione?
9. Quando si alza il sipario?
10. Chi si affretta all'inizio della rappresentazione?

E. Translate into Italian:
Barbara and Helen are going to the theatre this evening. After school they go directly to town in order not to be late for the first performance. They have a cup of tea in a bar and then go into the theatre. At the box office they buy two tickets for the stalls and sit down to read the programme. The gallery is already full and Helen whispers (*bisbigliare*) to her friend that Ruggiero Ruggieri is taking part (*prendere parte*) in the play. Suddenly the lights go out and the play begins.

REVISION EXERCISES (*Lessons VI–X*)

1. Fill in the blanks in the following sentences:
   1. Giovanni vuole comprare — carta.
   2. Egli non ha — sorella.
   3. Dagli un libro — .
   4. — generi di film mi piacciono, ma non tutti.
   5. Ha — zii Antonio?

2. Translate into Italian:
   1. We have apples, sweets and grapes.
   2. It is boys I can see, not girls.
   3. Give him some sort of job (*posto*).
   4. I want some of the milk which is in the kitchen.
   5. Few books please him.

3. Translate into Italian:
   Write it to me. Send them to them. Don't let's open it. Put them in the box. He sends us to (*a*) sell old cars. Here he is returning from there right now. Come to my house. Go there at once. Take two of them and be content. Can I buy some too? Take six from him. We are coming to (*a*) meet (*incontrare*) him. We go up to them. We lead the way for him.

4. Replace the nouns in the following sentences by pronouns:
   1. Carlo compra due matite.
   2. Maria e Carlo vanno al cinema.
   3. Non dare quella penna a Filippo.
   4. Bisogna mandare a cercare Barbara ed Elena.
   5. Si parla di scuola adesso.
   6. Non si può andare in cucina.
   7. Metti là lo scialle.
   8. Da dove vengono quelle ragazze?
   9. Devo scrivere a mio padre stasera.
   10. Domanda a Giovanni come si fa questa cosa.

5. Translate into Italian:
   1. Having written the letter, Charles goes to the cinema.
   2. On entering the room, I hear Charles explaining to John the ins and outs of his journey abroad.
   3. The lesson having finished, we all go home.
   4. While speaking with you, I learn (*imparare*) a lot.
   5. By making mistakes, we learn many things.

6. Whose suitcase is this? It is mine.
7. That's just another of his tricks, in my opinion.
8. Both boys are dead tired.
9. It is difficult to find good wines in this town.
10. What are they talking about?

6. Put the definite and indefinite articles before the following words:
uomo, strada, luna, zia, scaffale, lampada, ghiribizzo, psicologo, gnomo, assegno, artista (*m.*), albero, mucchio, segnale, incidente, stridore, cinema, fine, latte, ordine, notte, filiale, stagione.

7. Translate into Italian:
1. We pick flowers in the garden of my aunt's house.
2. I go up (*su*) the hill (*collina*) with my cousin.
3. It seems very good to me.
4. Be careful in crossing the road.
5. This book is not worth much.
6. You tell me what you want.
7. Do you drink coffee?
8. I like reading very much.
9. Where does that woman come from?
10. I don't like him.

never ~~~~ che

(1) che = whom, who, that, which

(2) cui = whom, who, that, which after preposition.

(3) il quale etc = alternative to 1 a 2

(4) quel che, quello che
ciò che = what meaning that which

(5) il cui etc = whose.

(6) chi, colui che etc = he who.

[handwritten annotations:]
2 cui = whom, who, that which
   after prepositions
3 il quale etc = alternative to cui & che
5 il cui etc = whose.

A. RELATIVE PRONOUNS

1. The relative pronouns in Italian are as follows:

   Subject: che, il quale, la quale, *etc. who, which, that.*
   Direct Object: che, il quale, la quale, *etc. whom, which, that.*
   Genitive: di cui, del quale, della quale, *etc. of whom.*
   Indirect Object: a cui, cui, al quale, alla quale, *etc. to whom.*
   Generic: chi, colui che (*m.*), colei che (*f.*), coloro che
   (*m. and f.*), *he who, she who, they who.*

2. The pronoun **che** is invariable and is used in the following
   ways: *[handwritten: whom, who, that, which.]*

   Il professore che è in quella classe scrive sulla lavagna.
   The teacher who is in that class is writing on the board.

   Mi parla di quel professore che viene a scuola in bicicletta.
   *He is speaking to me of that teacher who comes to school on
   a bicycle.*

   Ecco la lettera che Giovanni deve dare al maestro.
   Here is the letter which John must give to the teacher.

   It will be noted that **che** can be used both as a nominative
   and a direct object pronoun.

3. When the antecedent of **che** is ambiguous, **il quale,
   la quale,** *etc.* replace it if the nouns are of varying genders:

   La madre di Giovanni, la quale è artista, è all'ospedale.
   John's mother, who is an artist, is in hospital.

4. Note also the following uses of **che** which are frequent in
   speech:

   Grazie per la sua gentilezza. — Non c'è di che!
   Thank you for your kindness. Don't mention it.

   Questo quadro ha un non so che di bello.
   This picture has something beautiful about it.

5. The genitive form is invariable, unless **il quale,** *etc.* is again used to avoid ambiguity:

> L'uomo di cui egli mi parla è mio zio.
> *The man of whom he is speaking to me is my uncle.*

6. The general indirect object form is **a cui,** rarely **cui** alone, and **il quale,** *etc.* can once again be used in cases of ambiguity:

> Il ragazzo a cui (al quale) scrivo è ammalato.
> *The boy whom I am writing to is ill.*

7. The generic forms are used in the following ways:

> Chi dice questo ha torto.
> *He who says this is wrong.*
>
> Chi rompe paga e i cocci sono suoi.
> *Who breaks things pays for them and the bits are his.*
>
> ·Colui che guadagna ha il diritto di spendere.
> *He who earns has the right to spend.*

Chi always requires a singular verb and care should be taken not to confuse it with the interrogative pronoun of the same form. It also has another use, since it sometimes means *some . . . others . . .* , or *the one . . . the next* (*the other*):

> Chi la vuol cotta, chi la vuol cruda.
> *Some want things cooked, others want them raw* (i.e., *there's no accounting for taste*).
>
> C'è nel bar chi mangia, chi beve, e chi parla.
> *There are people in the bar eating, drinking and talking.*

8. *What* when used as a relative is translated by **quel che, quello che** or **ciò che:**

> Elena mi parla di quel che fa a scuola.
> *Helen speaks to me of what she does at school.*

All that is translated by putting **tutto** before any one of these phrases:

> Elena mi parla di tutto ciò che fa a scuola.
> *Helen speaks to me of all that she does at school.*

One should note the difference between the relative and

interrogative pronouns in indirect speech, even though they can frequently be interchanged:

> Dimmi ciò che vuoi.
> *Tell me ~~anything you like~~.* what you want.
> Dimmi cosa vuoi.
> *Tell me what you want.*

The indirect question, unlike the relative clause, asks the question: *What do you want?*

B. RELATIVE, INTERROGATIVE
AND EXCLAMATORY USES OF ADJECTIVES

1. **Quale, che** and **quanto** are used in a variety of ways, but **il cui, la cui** can only be used as a relative adjective:

> È il professore la cui madre sta molto male.
> *It is the teacher* whose *mother is very ill.*

It can be replaced by **quale**:

> (È il professore, la madre del quale sta molto male.)

2. **Quale, quanto** and **che** are all used as interrogative adjectives:

> Qual è il libro che leggi, Giovanni?
> *Which book are you reading, John?*
> Che libro leggi, Giovanni?
> *What book are you reading, John?*
> Quanti libri ci sono in quell'armadio?
> *How many books are in that cupboard?*

[margin notes: quale = which; quanto = how much; quanti = how many; che = what]

The same distinction exists between **che?** and **quale?** as between *what?* and *which?* in English.

[margin note: which]

NOTE. **Quanto** has another function as a pronoun meaning *how much, as much as* or even *what*:

> Voglio sapere quanto costa.
> *I want to know how much it costs.*
> Ecco quanto posso dirti.
> *That is as much as I can tell you.*
> A quanto dicono, Pietro arriva stasera.
> *From what they say, Peter is arriving tonight.*

3. **Che, quanto** and **quale** can also be used in exclamatory sentences:

> Che bella giornata!
> *What a beautiful day!*
>
> Che meraviglia!
> *What a marvel!* how wonderful
>
> Quale sorpresa per lui!
> *What a surprise for him!*
>
> Quanta gente c'è in questo teatro!
> *What a lot of people there are in this theatre!*

NOTE. **Come** is widely used also in exclamations:

> Come è bella quella ragazza!
> *How beautiful that girl is!*
>
> Come lavora quel pazzo!
> *How that madman works!*

The order of the words (*i.e.,* How is beautiful that girl!) should be carefully studied.

VOCABULARY

banchina	*quay*	pastiglia	*pill*
beccheggio	*pitching*	personale di	*crew*
a bordo	*on board*	bordo	
cabina	*cabin*	piroscafo	*liner, ship*
capitano	*captain*	pochissimo, -a	*very little*
circa	*about*	ponte (*m.*)	*deck*
controllare	*to control* check	porto	*port*
dott. (dottore)	*doctor*	presto	*soon*
facchino	*porter*	prolungato, -a	*prolonged, long*
fischio	*whistle, siren*	ricorrere a	*to resort to*
godersi	*to enjoy*	ritenere	*to consider*
lavoro	*work*	rullio	*tossing*
lubrificare	*to oil*	segnale (*m.*)	*signal*
magnifico, -a	*wonderful*	sfortunatamente	*unfortunately*
mal di mare	*seasickness*	spettacolo	*sight*
la Manica	*the Channel*	staccarsi	*to move away*
marinaio	*sailor*	stazza	*displacement*
mille	*a thousand*	torretta	*bridge*
nave (*f.*)	*ship*	trasportare	*to transport*
oltre	*besides*	viaggiare	*to travel*
partenza	*departure*		

SUL PIROSCAFO

Appena il treno si ferma a Calais, il dott. Bertora che viaggia con la moglie chiama il facchino e fa trasportare le valigie sul piroscafo. Si tratta di un piroscafo normale, non di grande stazza, ma sufficiente a trasportare circa mille passeggeri, oltre il personale di bordo. Tutti i marinai sono al lavoro. C'è chi pulisce il ponte, chi lubrifica le macchine, chi accompagna i passeggeri nelle diverse cabine. Il capitano, dall'alto della torretta, controlla tutto. Quando tutti i passeggeri sono a bordo, dà il segnale della partenza. Si sentono tre fischi prolungati, e la nave si stacca dalla banchina.

La Manica è calma, e quasi tutti sono sul ponte a godersi il magnifico spettacolo. La nave ha pochissimo beccheggio e rullio, e il dott. Bertora, che di solito soffre il mal di mare,[1] non ritiene necessario ricorrere all'uso delle pastiglie. Pure lui è sul ponte a godersi la magnifica giornata. Sfortunatamente, il viaggio non è molto lungo, ed il piroscafo entra presto nel porto di Dover.

NOTE

[1] **soffre il mal di mare**: It should be noted that this verb is very often transitive in Italian and does not require a preposition as in English. Occasionally, however, it takes the preposition *di*.

EXERCISES

A. Translate into Italian:
1. The man who is speaking now is John's father.
2. The girl who is coming in is my sister.
3. Thank you for the book. Don't mention it.
4. Listen to those who love you (*volere bene*).
5. The door through which we are walking is very large.
6. Who is the man asking questions (*fare domande*) about John?
7. The customer to whom I am writing wants some goods which are in the warehouse.
8. Tell me what you want before going to town.
9. Tell me all you can about your visit (*visita*) to the theatre.
10. How many letters do you type every day?

B. Put the relative adjective or pronoun in the following sentences:
1. Ascolta — ti dà buoni consigli (*advice*).
2. L'uomo con — vai in Italia non è molto serio.
3. Ecco — si può ottenere da loro.
4. La strada per — scendiamo è molto bella.
5. — dorme non piglia pesci.
6. — poveri ci sono in questo mondo!
7. — sono i giorni della settimana (*week*)?
8. A — dicono, ci devo andare oggi.
9. — è grande questa sala!
10. — bella poesia! La voglio rileggere subito.

C. Translate into Italian:
1. How well he speaks English now.
2. What a lot of things he knows.
3. Which is your house?
4. Whose is this desk?
5. The man with whom you are speaking is an Italian poet.
6. How hot it is today.
7. Tell me who the person is you are speaking to.
8. The car which does not stop in time runs over the fruit-seller.
9. How wonderful it is to be on a boat crossing the Channel today.
10. What a lot of pitching and tossing this ship does!

D. Translate into Italian:
Anthony and John decide to (*di*) cross the Channel and visit England (*l'Inghilterra*) because they now speak English very well. They go on board the steamer at Calais and watch the sailors working on the deck. A porter carries their luggage on to the ship and they give him (a) hundred (*cento*) lire. Soon the boat moves off from the quay and they are on (*in*) the high sea(s). The sea is very calm so John does not suffer from sea-sickness. Unfortunately, the voyage is very short and the steamer soon enters the port of Dover.

E. Answer the following questions in Italian:
1. Chi attraversa la Manica con la moglie?
2. Che cosa fa il capitano del piroscafo?
3. Il piroscafo ha molto beccheggio e rullio?
4. Chi dà il segnale della partenza?
5. È lungo il viaggio da Dover a Calais?

6. Chi non trova necessario ricorrere all'uso delle pastiglie?
7. Soffre il mal di mare Lei?
8. Chi pulisce il ponte e chi lubrifica le macchine?
9. È sempre calma la Manica?
10. Chi trasporta le valigie sul piroscafo?

A. REFLEXIVE VERBS

1. Reflexive verbs are conjugated in the following way in the present tense in Italian:

ALZARSI *to get up*	ACCORGERSI *to notice*	PENTIRSI *to repent*
mi alzo	m'accorgo	mi pento
ti alzi	t'accorgi	ti penti
si alza	s'accorge	si pente
ci alziamo	ci accorgiamo	ci pentiamo
vi alzate	vi accorgete	vi pentite
si *alzano*	si accorgono	si pentono

These reflexive verbs are normally used in the following manner:

> Mi alzo di buon'ora per prendere il treno.
> *I get up early to catch the train.*

> Carlo si accorge di aver sbagliato.
> *Charles sees he has made a mistake.*

> Si pente d'aver agito così.
> *He repents having acted like that.*

2. Many verbs, although not natural reflexives, can become so in certain circumstances:

(a) Verbs with a reciprocal meaning:
> Si scrivono ~~(l'un l'altro)~~   scrivono l'un l'altro
> *They write to one another.*

> Si amano molto.
> *They love one another very much.*

> Si parlano ~~fra loro.~~ / parlano fra loro
> *They speak to one another.*

(b) Verbs with the reflexive pronoun referring back to the subject:

> Egli si crede una grande personalità.
> *He thinks himself an important person.*

NOTE. One must not, however, confuse this type of verb with the intensive form:

> Ho intenzione di farlo io stesso!
> *I intend doing it myself.*

(c) The indefinite form with **si** (one) is ~~actually a reflexive~~, ~~not~~ a subject pronoun, as may be seen from the following examples:

> In quella bottega si vende anche il pane.
> *In that shop they also sell bread.*

but:

> In quella bottega si vendono mele.
> *In that shop they sell apples.*

In actual fact, *pane* and *mele* are the subjects of the verb and the **si** merely turns the expression into a passive (*i.e.* Apples *are sold* in that shop). One must not, therefore, be led astray by the use of *one* in English or *on* in French. A fuller account of this form will be given in Lesson XXIII B.

(d) The reflexive can be used in a large number of cases instead of the passive voice:

> Si dice che quell'uomo è molto ricco.
> *It is said that that man is very rich.*

(e) A number of idiomatic phrases are also formed with the reflexive verb and the feminine pronoun **la** which replaces such words as *la cosa* (the thing), *le busse* (blows), *la vita* (life), etc.

> Quel ragazzo se la prende con tutti.
> *That boy quarrels with everybody.*

> Giovanni, sta zitto, se no, a momenti te le prendi.
> *John, be quiet, if not, you will catch it in a minute.*

> Ce la godiamo sempre quando andiamo al mare.
> *We always enjoy ourselves when we go to the seaside.*

(f) Some verbs are not only reflexive but take **ne** as well. They usually, though not always, have colloquial meanings:

> Sono stanco, basta cosí! Me ne vado. _andarsene_
> *I am tired, that is enough! I am leaving.*

> Tu inviti persone noiose, poi però te ne scappi.
> *You invite troublesome people, then, however, you slip away.*

> Di solito all'ufficio lavoro fino a mezzogiorno e poi me ne esco.
> *Usually, I work till midday at the office and then I go out.*

> Egli se ne sta seduto senza parlare.
> *He just sits there without speaking.*

(g) The reflexive pronoun is often used pleonastically with certain verbs:

> Non sai quel che ti dici (ti fai), figlio mio.
> *You don't know what you are saying (doing), my son.*

> Il fatto si è che voi avete torto ed io ragione.
> *The fact is that you are wrong and I am right.*

NOTE. It is omitted when the reflexive verb is dependent on **fare** (to make), **lasciare** (to let), ~~sentire (to hear)~~, ~~vedere (to see)~~:

> Lo facciamo pentire (not pentirsi).
> *We are making him repent.*

B. IRREGULAR ADJECTIVES

1. A number of common adjectives undergo modifications depending upon the noun they qualify. They are **bello, quello, buono, grande** and **santo**. Their forms are as follows:

(a) **Bello** and **quello** follow the same rules as the definite article:

un bel ragazzo	quel ragazzo
una bella ragazza	quella ragazza
_l/_ un bello specchio	quello specchio
dei bei ragazzi	quei ragazzi
delle belle ragazze	quelle ragazze
dei begli specchi	quegli specchi.

s improve after adj.

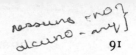

(b) **Buono** follows the rules of the indefinite article:

un buon ragazzo	una buona ragazza
un buono zio	una buona zia
dei buoni ragazzi	delle buone ragazze
dei buoni zii	delle buone zie
una buon'alunna	delle buone alunne.

(c) **Grande** and **santo** (only when it means *saint*) are contracted in certain cases:

un gran ragazzo	una grande (gran) ragazza
un grande specchio	una grande artista
un grand' uomo	delle grandi case.
dei gran quadri	
dei grandi specchi	*exists but not always used.*
San Pietro	Santa Maria
Sant'Andrea / Antonio	Sant'Anna.
Santo Stefano	

but: Il Santo Padre (*The Pope*).

Non mi piace lavorare tutto il santo giorno.
I don't like working all the blessed day.

The rules are that **gran** is used before a masculine noun unless it begins with an *s impure*, a *z* or a *vowel*, while in the feminine singular one can usually choose either form; **santo** is contracted only before a proper noun and not when it means *holy*, or *blessed* in the colloquial sense.

2. A few adjectives are invariable:

un numero pari	*an even number*
dei numeri pari	*even numbers*
un numero dispari	*an odd number*
dei numeri dispari	*odd numbers.*

A similar word **impari** is used only in the more general sense of *unequal*:

una lotta impari	*an unequal struggle*
delle lotte impari	*unequal struggles.*

The word **fu** regularly precedes the noun:

Il fu Giorgio Quinto   *The late George V*
La fu Anna   *The late Anne.*

VOCABULARY

abbisognare	to need	già che	since
acquisto	purchase	gran che	much
affollato, -a	crowded	grigio, -a	grey
allora	then	guanto	glove
altro (tutt'altro)	other (far from it)	innanzitutto	above all
		invernale (adj.)	winter
angolo	corner	logoro, -a	worn
approfittare	to profit	magari	even
benissimo	very well	magazzino	store
aver bisogno di	to need	mercato	market
blu	blue	mondo	world
boccata (d'aria)	breath (of fresh air)	no	no
		nailon	nylon
borsetta	hand-bag	necessitare	to need
calza	stocking	occasione (f.)	occasion
camicia	shirt	orecchino	ear-ring
campione (m.)	sample	paio	pair
capo di	item of clothing	parecchi, -ie	several
vestiario		da parte tua	for yourself
cappellino	hat	perla	pearl
cappotto	overcoat	pomeriggio	afternoon
fare al caso mio	to suit my purpose	portamonete (m.)	purse
		proprio	really
cercare di	to try to	prossimo, -a	next
collana	necklace	raso (bleu)	satin (blue)
commissione (f.) (far commissioni)	errand (to do shopping)	(ri)fornito	stocked
		rinnovare	to renew
		ritenere	to consider
confezionare	to make	sarto	tailor
cravatta	tie	scegliere	to choose
cuoio	leather	sin d'ora	here and now
detto	told	smagliato, -a	laddered
dunque	therefore	spiacere	to displease
estivo, -a (adj.)	summer	stoffa	material
fabbisogno	needs, requirements	tailleur (m.)	tailor-made costume
finto, -a	imitation, false		

ABITI DA UOMO E DA DONNA

— Alberto, ti spiace uscire con me, questo pomeriggio?

— Tutt'altro; non ho molto da fare oggi, e poi sento proprio[1] il bisogno di prendere una boccata d'aria. Dove devi andare?

— Devo fare diverse commissioni, innanzitutto devo andare ai Magazzini Generali per fare vari acquisti.

— Benissimo, approfitto dell'occasione per comprare un abito nuovo, perché questo è logoro, e qualcos'altro.

— Vuoi comprare una camicia nuova?

— Magari due!

— Ti spiace se passiamo un momento anche in un negozio di scarpe?

— Già che ci andiamo, voglio comprare anch'io un paio di scarpe. Va benissimo.

— Dunque, passiamo innanzitutto dai Magazzini Generali. Per me[2] è necessario un vestito di raso blu, della stoffa per un tailleur, un cappellino nuovo, un paio di calze di nailon perché le vecchie sono smagliate, e una borsetta di cuoio. Nello stesso tempo, cerchiamo di trovare una collana di finte perle come quella della cugina Laura, e un paio d'orecchini. Questo è sufficiente per il fabbisogno invernale, ma l'anno prossimo devo rinnovare parecchi capi di vestiario. Da parte tua, cosa ti abbisogna?

— Non molto. Devo comprare un abito nuovo perché, come ti ho già detto, questo è logoro. Un abito grigio, credo, fa al caso mio. Di cravatte non ne ho bisogno,[3] come non ho bisogno di cappotto. Mi necessita invece un paio di guanti e un portamonete. Se lo ritieni opportuno, prendiamo sin d'ora un campione di stoffa per un abito estivo. Lo voglio far confezionare dal sarto Marini che è un sarto famoso in tutto il mondo.

— È una buon'idea.

— Per le scarpe, in che negozio preferisci andare? Da Rossi qui all'angolo?

— Oh no! Non è un negozio molto ben rifornito. Non vi trovo gran che da scegliere. Bianchi ha un ottimo negozio. Vi trovo sempre ciò che mi abbisogna.

— Allora usciamo subito dopo pranzo; oggi è giorno di mercato ed i negozi sono affollati.

NOTES

   ¹ **proprio**: This word can be used in a variety of ways, as we have already seen. A list of its usages is as follows:

        Questa è la mia propria casa.
        This is my own house.
        Ci vado proprio adesso.
        I am going there right now.
        È proprio per questa ragione che ci vado.
        It is precisely for this reason that I am going there.
        Sento proprio il bisogno di riposarmi.
        I really feel the need for rest.

   ² **Per me**: A strong pronoun is required after a preposition, see Lesson XIV B.

   ³ **Di cravatte . . .** : Note in this phrase the pleonastic use of *ne*. The construction is a frequent one in Italian.

EXERCISES

A. Translate into Italian:
  1. He is always inviting troublesome people and then slipping off.
  2. He repents having said that.
  3. The boys make their way towards the exit.
  4. He thinks he is very intelligent.
  5. They write to each other every day.
  6. I've no intention of acting so foolishly (*scioccamente*) myself.
  7. They buy books in that shop.
  8. They don't give samples of that material.
  9. He doesn't know what he is saying.
 10. We make them get up early.

B. Put the correct form of *buono, bello, grande, santo* or *quello* before the following nouns:

occasione, specchio, cuoio, guanti, cappellino, stoffe, porta-monete, Giorgio, collana, capitano, camera, Anna, piroscafi, segnale, spettacolo, marinai, Stefano, facchino, riva, passeggeri, mercato, orecchini, Guglielmo, perle, sarto, camicie, stazza, fischi, zie, città, pane, giorno, Padre, appetito, fuoco, nave, lotta, Matteo.

C. Translate into Italian:

John and Mary set out for town very early in order to buy some clothes. They visit many shops and make many purchases, but Mary is unable to find material for a tailor-made costume. 'This is very good material,' says the tailor, but Mary does not like it. 'This is better (*migliore*),' answers John, pointing to a piece of cloth on a shelf (*scaffale* (*m.*)). 'Ah, yes!' says Mary, 'that is indeed another kettle of fish (*un altro paio di maniche*). I like it very much.' She buys four metres to have the costume made up by a friend.

D. Answer the following questions in Italian:
1. Chi vuol andare ai Magazzini Generali?
2. Che cosa desidera Alberto innanzitutto?
3. Che cosa deve rinnovare la moglie di Alberto l'anno prossimo?
4. Che specie di borsetta desidera lei?
5. Ha bisogno di un cappotto Alberto?
6. Perché vuol prendere un campione di stoffa?
7. Dove vanno per comprare delle scarpe?
8. Perché sono affollati i negozi?
9. Chi vuole trovare una collana di finte perle?
10. Chi è un sarto famoso in tutto il mondo?
11. Perché la moglie di Alberto vuole comprare un paio di calze di nailon?

E. Write ten lines on a visit to the tailor's.

A. THE PERFECT TENSE

1. The perfect tense is formed in Italian by using the present tenses of **avere** or **essere** and the past participle of the verb:

Regular Verbs

TROVARE	VENDERE	FINIRE
ho trovato *I have found*	ho venduto *I have sold*	ho finito *I have finished*
hai trovato	hai venduto	hai finito
ha trovato	ha venduto	ha finito
abbiamo trovato	abbiamo venduto	abbiamo finito
avete trovato	avete venduto	avete finito
hanno trovato	hanno venduto	hanno finito

Verbs with ESSERE as auxiliary

ANDARE	VENIRE
sono andato, -a *I have gone*	sono venuto, -a *I have come*
sei andato, -a	sei venuto, -a
è andato, -a	è venuto, -a
siamo andati, -e	siamo venuti, -e
siete andati, -e	siete venuti, -e
sono andati, -e	sono venuti, -e

Reflexive Verbs

LAVARSI	ACCORGERSI	PENTIRSI
mi sono lavato, -a *I have washed*	mi sono accorto, -a *I have noticed*	mi sono pentito, -a *I have repented*
ti sei lavato, -a	ti sei accorto, -a	ti sei pentito, -a
si è lavato, -a	si è accorto, -a	si è pentito, -a
ci siamo lavati, -e	ci siamo accorti, -e	ci siamo pentiti, -e
vi siete lavati, -e	vi siete accorti, -e	vi siete pentiti, -e
si sono lavati, -e	si sono accorti, -e	si sono pentiti, -e

DIRUPI DI LARSEC, DOLOMITES

GALLERIA, MILAN

Most intransitive verbs and all reflexives take **essere** in their perfect tenses.

2. Some of the more common verbs requiring **essere** are a follows:

andare	*to go*	restare	*to stay*
arrivare	*to arrive*	rimanere	*to remain*
correre†	*to run*	riuscire	*to succeed*
cadere	*to fall*	salire	*to go up*
essere	*to be*	scendere	*to go down*
morire	*to die*	scoppiare	*to burst*
nascere	*to be born*	tornare	*to return*
parere	*to seem*	uscire	*to go out*
partire	*to set out*	venire	*to come*
piacere	*to please*		

3. The perfect tenses of **avere** and **essere** are as follows:

AVERE		ESSERE	
ho avuto	*I have had*	sono stato, -a	*I have been*
hai avuto		sei stato, -a	
ha avuto		è stato, -a	
abbiamo avuto		siamo stati, -e	
avete avuto		siete stati, -e	
hanno avuto		sono stati, -e	

B. AGREEMENT OF PAST PARTICIPLES

1. The past participles of verbs taking **essere** (apart from reflexive verbs) always agree with the subject of the sentence:

Giovanni ed io siamo andati al cinema questo pomeriggio.
John and I went to the cinema this afternoon.

Barbara è venuta a trovarci oggi.
Barbara came to see us today.

† This verb sometimes takes *avere* when used transitively:
Egli ha corso un grave pericolo.
He has run a grave danger.

2. The agreement of the past participle with reflexive verbs is optional, either with the subject or the object:

> Si sono tolto il cappello. (subject)
> *They took off their hats.*
> Si è lavate le mani. (object)
> *He washed his hands.*

However when there is no direct object or when the direct object is the reflexive pronoun itself, then the past participle agrees with the subject:

> La ragazza s'è lavata.
> *The girl washed herself.*

Although usage varies the student is nowadays advised in all other cases to make the past participle agree with the subject, especially when that subject is an otherwise unspecified feminine person or thing:

> Si è tolta il cappello.
> *She took off her hat.*

3. It is obligatory to inflect the past participle of verbs taking **avere** only if a direct object pronoun precedes the verb. The past participle then agrees with this pronoun:

> Li abbiamo mandati in città stamattina.
> *We have sent them into town this morning.*
>
> Gliele ho date.
> *I have given them to him.*

NOTE. **Ne** also causes the past participle to inflect if it is a direct object:

> Abbiamo detto che ci piacciono le pere e ce ne ha date.
> *We said that we like pears and he gave us some.*

In all other cases agreement is optional, provided the direct object comes before the verb:

> Ecco la casa che abbiamo comprato (comprata).
> *Here is the house we have bought.*

VOCABULARY

non ... affatto	*not at all*	orgoglioso, -a	*proud*
assicurare	*to assure*	ottimamente	*very well*
augurio	*wish, greeting*	di persona	*in person*
caro, -a	*dear*	piacere (*m.*)	*pleasure*
complimentarsi	*to compliment*	preoccupare	*to worry*
contare su	*to count on*	procedere	*to procede*
cordiale	*cordial*	rimodernamento	*modernisation*
corr. (corrente)	*inst.* (*current*)	salute (*f.*)	*health*
ferie (*f.pl.*)	*bank holiday*	saluto	*greeting*
Genova	*Genoa*	scrupoloso, -a	*scrupulous*
iniziativa	*initiative*	sindaco	*mayor*
interessato, -a	*interested*	sogno	*dream*
inviare	*to send*	soprintendenza	*supervision*
lieto, -a	*happy*	sperare	*to hope*
migliore	*better*	Torino	*Turin*
minimo, -a	*slightest*	trasformazione	*transformation*
ministro	*minister*	(*f.*)	
avere modo di	*to have the chance to*	vero e proprio	*real*
		da vicino	*from close to*
municipio	*town hall*	visita	*visit*
notizia	*news item*	vivamente	*warmly*
novità	*news*		

UNA LETTERA

Caro Giovanni,

Ho ricevuto con piacere la tua lettera del 19 corr. Sono lieto di saperti in ottima salute. Anch'io sto ottimamente,[1] e ti assicuro che tutto procede bene.

La nostra casa sembra ora un sogno. Dopo che Filippo ha preso l'iniziativa di dirigere i lavori di rimodernamento c'è stata una vera e propria trasformazione. E adesso è una meraviglia.

Appena finito a casa nostra, Filippo è stato subito chiamato dal sindaco della città alla soprintendenza dei nuovi lavori in municipio. Come vedi, s'è fatto un'ottima posizione, e noi, naturalmente, ne andiamo orgogliosi. È di natura molto scrupolosa e vuol vedere e seguire da vicino ogni minimo lavoro.

L'altro giorno ha visto di persona il Ministro dei Lavori Pubblici che era in visita alla nostra città. Appena presentato al Ministro, ha avuto anche modo di illustrare il suo progetto. Il Ministro si è dimostrato molto interessato e si è vivamente complimentato con lui.[2] Certo ha da lavorare[3] molto, ma ciò non lo preoccupa affatto.

A Genova che novità ci sono? Quando vieni a trovarci a Torino? Spero di vederti prima dell'inizio delle ferie. Posso contarci? Sperando di ricevere presto tue notizie, ti invio, con i migliori auguri i piú cordiali saluti.

Tuo,
Carlo.

NOTES

[1] **Anch'io sto . . .** : When discussing conditions of health, *essere* is often replaced by *stare*: *sto bene, sto meglio*, but *egli è ammalato* (he is ill).

[2] **complimentato con . . .** : A number of verbs which take direct objects in English require *con* in Italian: *congratularsi con* (to congratulate); *rivaleggiare con* (to rival) and *complimentarsi con* (to compliment).

[3] **ha da lavorare . . .** : *Avere da* can replace *dovere* when it means *to have to*. One should not, however, use the phrase too frequently and it should be noted that a direct object is placed between the verb and the dependent infinitive:

Ho tanto lavoro da fare.   *I have so much work to do.*

EXERCISES

A. Translate into Italian:
1. He has washed his hands.
2. John and Mary came to our house this afternoon.
3. We cleaned his shoes this morning.
4. Did you find your fountain pen, Charles?
5. John ran a grave danger in crossing the street at that hour.
6. The three boys ran along the street.
7. We did not notice (+*inf.*) we had made a mistake.

8. As has been seen, Philip has made a very good position for himself.
9. Where did those books come from?
10. The boys climbed up (*su*) the mountain.

B. Put the perfect tense of the verb given in brackets in the following sentences:

1. Giorgio e Filippo (farsi) un'ottima posizione nell'amministrazione.
2. Roberto (nascere) l'anno passato.
3. Noi (partire) di buon'ora per la campagna.
4. Il ministro (complimentarsi) con noi.
5. Gli uomini (togliersi) il cappello.
6. Elena e Barbara (camminare) per due ore.
7. Scusatemi, signore, io (sbagliare).
8. Mi (dispiacere) molto aver dovuto mandarti via.
9. Giovanni mi (guardare), e non (dire) niente.
10. Non ci (rimanere) nessuna penna in bottega.

C. Translate into Italian:

1. We have written three letters to him.
2. You have not given him them.
3. How much did you sell them (for)?
4. Have you succeeded in (*a*) opening that box?
5. She took the apples and ate them all.
6. Charles and John came up to us and Charles took our case while John led the way to the exit.
7. The car did not stop after the accident.
8. The two boys played draughts before returning to school.
9. Helen has come to see us.
10. What part of Italy did you visit this year?

D. Answer the following questions in Italian:

1. A chi scrive Carlo?
2. Che cosa ha fatto Filippo a casa sua?
3. Quando Filippo ha illustrato il suo progetto al ministro, che cosa ha fatto quest'ultimo?
4. Quando spera Carlo di vedere Giovanni?
5. È bella adesso la casa di Filippo?
6. È preoccupato Filippo di avere molto da fare?
7. Chi ha chiamato Filippo alla soprintendenza dei lavori in municipio?
8. Si è mostrato interessato il ministro nel progetto di Filippo?
9. Dove abitano Giovanni e Carlo?
10. Chi s'è fatto un'ottima posizione?

E. Translate into Italian:

John and Charles are two friends but John lives in Genoa and Charles in Turin. They write to one another very often. John hopes to go to Turin before the bank holiday because the trains are crowded then. It is a journey of four hours between the two cities (*le due città*). Charles' brother has directed (p.p. *diretto*) the work of modernisation in (*di*) their house and now it is a dream. He wants to show it to John because they are both very proud of it. John tells Charles that he can count on a visit from him very soon.

Passato Prossimo. [handwritten]

A. USES OF THE PERFECT TENSE

Recent past [handwritten]

1. This tense is generally used to translate the corresponding English tense *I have found, etc.*, that is, it is used to describe an action taking place in the past but continuing up to the present: *I have done / did etc.* [handwritten]

> Quest'anno ho scritto tre libri.
> *This year I have written three books.*

2. It further describes an action taking place at an unstated time in the past:

> Ho letto quel libro.
> *I have read that book.*

3. Finally, it describes an action which has taken place in the same period of time in which it is related:

> Stamane sono andato al mercato.
> *I went this morning to the market.*
> Oggi Giorgio è venuto a trovarmi.
> *George came to see me today.*

NOTE. Northern Italians extend the use of this tense to many descriptions of past events, ~~where the past definite tense would be more appropriate (see Lesson XIX). This usage is gradually becoming more widespread.~~ *which are not recent & have no connection with present. But this does not usually occur in formal written prose.* [handwritten]

B. DEMONSTRATIVE ADJECTIVES AND PRONOUNS

1. There are three main demonstrative adjectives in Italian: **questo,** this; **quello**, that; and **codesto,** that (near you). The third adjective is rapidly dying out and can be entirely dispensed with in practice.

2. **Questo** presents no difficulties, being used to correspond to its English equivalent in the normal way:

> questo libro   *this book*
> quest'uomo   *this man.*
> questo uomo

3. **Quello,** however, offers in the first place difficulties of inflection (see Lesson XII B), since it conforms to the pattern of the definite article:

> quell'uomo   *that man*
> quegli uomini   *those men.*

It also has other idiomatic uses:

(a) As an emphatic pronoun:

> Eccolo qua quel mascalzone!
> *There he is, the rascal!*

(b) In elliptical phrases with the noun understood:

> In quel di Milano.
> *In Milanese territory.*

(c) As a pronoun to avoid repeating a noun:

> Non ho potuto trovare il mio libro, così ho portato quello di mio fratello.
>
> *I could not find my book so I brought my brother's.*

NOTE. As a pronoun **quello** is never shortened to **quel** in the singular nor is **quelli** shortened to **quei** in the plural.

4. Two *masculine singular* demonstrative pronouns exist meaning *the former* and *the latter.* *The former* is translated by **quegli** and *the latter* by **questi**. Italians, however, always put **questo** before **quegli** in a sentence, thereby referring to *the latter . . . the former,* instead of to *the former . . . the latter,* as in English:

> Churchill e Garibaldi sono due grandi uomini; questi è Italiano e quegli è Inglese.
>
> *Churchill and Garibaldi are two great men; the latter is Italian and the former English.*

5. The same rule applies in the feminine, except that the pronouns are **questa** and **quella**:

Hazel e Giovanna sono due belle ragazze; questa è Italiana, quella Inglese.

Hazel and Giovanna are two beautiful girls; the latter is Italian, the former English.

However, a ~~more modern and~~ less confusing way of saying the same thing is to use the words **primo, -a** (the first) and **secondo, -a** (the second) or **ultimo, -a** (the last):

Churchill e Garibaldi sono due grandi uomini, il primo Inglese e il secondo Italiano.

6. Two other demonstrative pronouns, **colui** (*m.*), **colei** (*f.*), **coloro** (*plur. m. and f.*) meaning *that man, that woman, those people* respectively, and **costui** (*m.*), **costei** (*f.*), **costoro** (*plur. m. and f.*) with the same meaning, are less frequently used. The latter pronouns often have a derogatory meaning:

Chi è costui? *Who is that fellow?*
Chi è costei? *Who on earth is she?*

7. **Ciò,** unlike **quello,** ~~is a neuter pronoun and~~ cannot replace a noun. ~~It is used to refer to an immediately preceding sentence or phrase:~~

Maria è andata in città e ciò non piace a sua madre.
Mary has gone into town and her mother doesn't like it.

VOCABULARY.

abbassare	*to lower*	campo d'aviazione	*airfield*
acuto, -a	*shrill*		
aereo	*aeroplane*	carrello	*undercarriage*
ampio, -a	*ample, wide*	deciso, -a	*decided*
apparecchio	*plane*	decollare	*to take off*
aspettare	*to await*	decollo	*take-off*
atterraggio	*landing*	dichiarazióne	*declaration*
atterrare	*to land*	disposto, -a	*arranged*
autorità	*authority*	dolcèmente	*softly*
avviarsi verso	*to make one's way to*	giornalista (*m.*)	*journalist*
		giro	*turn*
avvicinare	*to bring up*	impazienza	*impatience*

indietro	*backwards*	radiotelegrafista	*wireless*
inquadrare	*to sight*		*operator*
lentamente	*slowly*	a reazione	*jet*
linea (di linea)	*line (main*	recinto	*enclosure*
	line)	scaletta	*landing steps*
manovra	*handling*	schermo	*screen*
messaggio	*message*	sempre piú	*more and*
mettersi a	*to start*		*more*
mettere in moto	*to start (of*	sibilare	*to whistle, to*
	engines)		*hiss*
microfono	*microphone*	sorridente	*smiling*
mila (*plur.*)	*thousands*	sud	*south*
motore (*m.*) a	*jet motor*	torre (*f.*)	*control tower*
reazione		comando	
perfetto, -a	*perfect*	a un tratto	*suddenly*
pista di decollo	*runway*	veloce	*fast*
planare	*to glide*	volo	*flight*
puntare	*to head for*	voltarsi	*to turn*
quadrimotore	*four-engined*	volto	*face*
(*m.*)	*plane*	vorticosamente	*whirlingly,*
quota	*height*		*madly*
radarista	*radar operator*		

IL VIAGGIO AEREO DEL MINISTRO

I giornalisti e le autorità disposti in un piccolo recinto aspettano con impazienza. Ad un tratto l'aereo, che è già pronto sulla pista di decollo, mette in moto i motori. L'apparecchio è un gran quadrimotore di linea e quando girano i motori a reazione sibilano acuti. Ecco che il ministro giunge a bordo di una grande auto nera. Saluta le autorità e fa alcune dichiarazioni ai microfoni, seguito attentamente dai giornalisti. Poi si avvia verso l'aereo, sale la scaletta, e si volta indietro a salutare. L'aereo, prima lentamente, e poi sempre piú[1] velocemente si mette a correre sulla pista, decolla, prende quota, fa un giro sul campo d'aviazione e poi punta decisamente verso il sud. Alla torre comando giunge il primo messaggio inviato dal radiotelegrafista: 'Tutto bene a bordo.' I radaristi tengono l'apparecchio sotto controllo sullo schermo radar. Dopo due ore di volo a una quota di circa sei mila metri l'aereo viene annunciato alla torre di

controllo di Roma. Il ràdar lo inquadra perfettamente. Ecco
che ora appare sul campo e fa un ampio giro mentre abbassa il
carrello; poi comincia a planare dolcemente e atterra con manovra perfetta sulla pista d'atterraggio. Appena fermo, la scaletta
viene avvicinata allo sportello di uscita, questo si apre, e appare il
volto sorridente del ministro.

NOTE
[1] **sempre piú**: This is the neatest way of translating *more and
more* into Italian, although it is also possible to say *di piú in piú*.

EXERCISES

A. Translate the following sentences into Italian:
1. The radar screen has sighted it perfectly.
2. Who on earth is that fellow?
3. The handling of the 'plane has been perfect during (durante) the flight.
4. Before take-off we watched them start the engines.
5. The aeroplane gained height and headed towards the south.
6. The minister made a declaration on the radio this morning.
7. He did not like travelling in an aeroplane.
8. They have just brought up the landing steps.
9. The 'plane has been announced at the Rome control tower.
10. The 'plane has lowered its undercarriage and is landing on the runway.

B. Answer the following questions in Italian:
1. Chi è partito dal campo d'aviazione?
2. Da dove viene l'apparecchio che atterra adesso?
3. Perché l'aereo fa un ampio giro del campo prima di atterrare?
4. Dopo quante ore appare l'aereo del ministro sul campo d'aviazione di Roma?
5. Cosa si fa appena l'aereo si ferma sulla pista?
6. A che quota vola l'apparecchio durante il viaggio?
7. Che cosa dice il radiotelegrafista nel suo messaggio alla torre comando?
8. Che cosa inquadrano i radaristi sullo schermo?
9. Che specie di aereo trasporta il ministro a Roma?
10. Che specie di rumore fanno i motori a reazione?

C. Translate into Italian:
  1. These jet engines make a lot of noise (*far chiasso*).
  2. The minister has entered (*salire*) that plane on the runway.
  3. When the minister set out this morning, he made a declaration to the journalists.
  4. Why did you bring this book? Because I could not find John's.
  5. Who is that person who is always shouting?
  6. There he is, the rogue!
  7. Charles and Gino are two intelligent pupils, the former is the son of a teacher, the latter the son of a works manager.
  8. The man who wrote that is not a very likeable (*simpatico*) person.
  9. Your case has been carried (*portare*) to the plane by that porter.
  10. While the plane took off, it went faster and faster along the runway.

D. Put the correct demonstrative pronoun or adjective in the following sentences:
  1. Ho comprato (quello) specchio in città stamane.
  2. Avendo perduto i miei appunti, prendo (quello) di Carlo.
  3. Le truppe sono entrate in (quello) di Egitto.
  4. Hazel e Maria sono due belle ragazze, — è Inglese e — è Italiana.
  5. Quell'uomo è — che ho visto nel bar stamane.

E. Translate into Italian:
  The journalists await the arrival of the minister at the airfield. Here he is now in the usual big black car in which important persons of the Administration travel when they leave the country (*paese*). He says a few words into the microphone and then makes his way towards the four-engined plane on the runway. Before entering the plane, he turns around and waves. Almost immediately after the plane begins to race down the runway, takes off and gains height. It makes a wide circle around the field and then heads towards Rome.

A. THE FUTURE TENSES

1. The future tense of regular verbs is formed in Italian by attaching modified forms of the present tense of **avere** to the infinitive. However, in the first conjugation, **-are** is changed to **-er**† before one attaches the ending denoting the future:

TROVARE	VENDERE	FINIRE
troverò *I shall find*	venderò *I shall sell*	finirò *I shall finish*
troverai	venderai	finirai
troverà	venderà	finirà
troveremo	venderemo	finiremo
troverete	venderete	finirete
troveranno	venderanno	finiranno

NOTE. In the first and third singular, the stress is on the last syllable; in the third plural, it is on the ending **-anno**.

2. The verbs **essere** and **avere** have irregular futures:

ESSERE	AVERE
sarò *I shall be*	avrò *I shall have*
sarai	avrai
sarà	avrà
saremo	avremo
sarete	avrete
saranno	avranno

3. An irregular contracted future occurs with some other verbs. They are listed as follows:

andare (*to go*): andrò, andrai, *etc.*
cadere (*to fall*): cadrò, cadrai, *etc.*
dovere (*to owe, to have to*): dovrò, dovrai, *etc.*
morire (*to die*): morrò (morirò), morrai (morirai), *etc.*
parere (*to appear, seem*): parrà, parranno.

† Exceptions: *dare, darò, fare, farò, stare, starò.*

potere (*to be able*): potrò, potrai, *etc.*
rimanere (*to remain*): rimarrò, rimarrai, *etc.*
sapere (*to know*): saprò, saprai, *etc.*
tenere (*to hold*): terrò, terrai, *etc.*
valere (*to be worth*): varrò, varrai, *etc.*
vedere (*to see*): vedrò, vedrai, *etc.*
venire (*to come*): verrò, verrai, *etc.*
vivere (*to live*): vivrò, vivrai, *etc.*
volere (*to want*): vorrò, vorrai, *etc.*

NOTE. (1) All verbs with contracted infinitives (i.e., **dire** < **dicere**) form their future tense by adding the usual endings to their contracted form:

dire (*to say*): dirò, dirai, *etc.*
fare (*to do*): farò, farai, *etc.*

(2) Verbs ending in **-ciare** and **-giare** drop the **i** before the **-er** of the future tense:

cominciare (*to begin*): comincerò, comincerai, *etc.*
mangiare (*to eat*): mangerò, mangerai, *etc.*

4. The future perfect tense is formed by using the future tense of **avere** or **essere** in combination with the past participle of the verb:

ANDARE		VENDERE	
sarò andato, -a	*I shall have*	avrò venduto	*I shall have*
sarai andato, -a	*gone*	avrai venduto	*sold*
sarà andato, -a		avrà venduto	
saremo andati, -e		avremo venduto	
sarete andati, -e		avrete venduto	
saranno andati, -e		avranno venduto	

There are no exceptions to the general rule in this tense.

B. USES OF THE FUTURE TENSES

1. The future tense is used to express an English future:
Andrò in Italia l'anno prossimo.
I shall go to Italy next year.

2. To express an implied future in English after **se** (if) or after a conjunction of time when the main verb of the sentence is also in the future:

> Se lo vedrò, gliene parlerò.
> *If I see him, I shall speak to him about it.*
>
> Quando lo vedrò, gliene parlerò.
> *When I see him, I shall speak to him about it.*
>
> Quando avremo finito questo lavoro, ce ne andremo.
> *When we have finished this work, we shall go away.*

NOTE. In the case of **se** the present tense is now tolerated in this type of clause.

3. To indicate probability:

> Saranno andati in città oggi.
> *They have probably gone to town today.*
>
> Avrà perduto l'orologio.
> *He has probably lost his watch.*
>
> Saranno i miei fratelli che tornano a casa.
> *It is probably my brothers who are returning home.*

4. As in English, it occasionally replaces an imperative:

> Amerai il prossimo tuo come te stesso.
> *Thou shalt love thy neighbour as thyself.*

5. The future is sometimes replaced by the present tense in Italian:

> Ci vado io!   *I shall go there!*

VOCABULARY

acceso, -a	*inflamed, wild*	domenica	*Sunday*
arbitrale (*adj.*)	*of the referee*	dovuto, -a	*due*
arbitro	*referee*	eccitazione (*f.*)	*excitement*
attendere	*to await*	essenzialmente	*essentially*
avvenire	*to take place*	europeo, -a	*European*
calcio	*football*	folla	*crowd*
capro espiatorio	*scapegoat*	giocatore (*m.*)	*player*
contegno	*behaviour*	gioco	*game*
corretto, -a	*correct*	giudizio	*decision*
dimenticare	*to forget*	improperi	*reproaches*
discutibile	*doubtful*	(*m. pl.*)	
disparato, -a	*varied*	incontro	*match*
diventare	*to become*		

all'indirizzo di	in the direction of, at	rendersi conto di	to realise
ingiurioso	insulting	rendimento	efficiency
invasione (f.)	invasion	sconfitta	defeat
lanciare	to hurl	seguente	following
limitarsi	to confine one-self	in seguito a	as a result of
		sovente	often
di gran lunga	by far	spesso	often
nazione (f.)	nation	squadra	team
nomignolo	name, nick-name	sudamericano, -a	South-American
oppure	or else	tifo	enthusiasm
partita	match	tifoso	supporter
popolarissimo, -a	very popular	trepidazione (f.)	trepidation
		vincere	to win
popolo	people	a volte	at times
presso	with, near		

UN INCONTRO DI CALCIO

Presso i popoli[1] europei e sudamericani il gioco del calcio è diventato popolarissimo. In alcune nazioni esso è diventato lo sport[2] di gran lunga preferito, e al sabato e alla domenica intere folle di spettatori affollano i campi da gioco.[3] Il tifo delle folle è a volte eccessivo e spesso avvengono vere e proprie invasioni di campo in seguito a qualche discutibile giudizio arbitrale, oppure al contegno poco corretto di qualche giocatore. In alcuni casi, invece, i tifosi si limitano a lanciare all'indirizzo dell'arbitro gl'improperi piú ingiuriosi e i nomignoli piú disparati. Sanno bene che la propria squadra deve vincere e, in caso di sconfitta, l'arbitro diventa sovente il capro espiatorio. Ma appena l'eccitazione è passata, anche i piú accesi tifosi si rendono conto che la sconfitta è essenzialmente dovuta al cattivo rendimento della propria squadra. Per questa ragione arbitro e incontro sono presto dimenticati e si attende con trepidazione la partita seguente.

NOTES
[1] **i popoli . . .** : Care must be taken not to confuse the word *popolo* with *gente* since both are translated by 'people' in English.

Popolo refers to national population, while *gente* is used in a more general sense:

> Il popolo inglese   *The English people.*
> C'è troppa gente.   *There are too many people.*

² **lo sport** : The Italians have taken the English word for *sport* but it is invariable in Italian. One says, for example, *tutti gli sport.*

³ **i campi da gioco** : To express the use or purpose of an object in Italian is the function of the preposition *da* in nearly all cases: *un cane da caccia* (a hunting dog); *una nave da guerra* (a man-o'-war); *degli occhiali da sole* (sun-glasses); *una barca da pesca* (a fishing boat), *etc.*

EXERCISES

A. Translate into Italian:
1. I shall need a table and two chairs.
2. Will John be able to come with us?
3. We shall send an employee to his house to see if he is there.
4. If we sell the factory, what shall we do with the money (*danaro*)?
5. He will probably have arrived this evening.
6. When John has gone home, we shall stop working.
7. I can't find my exercise book. — You have probably lost it in (*per*) the street.
8. It will rain (*piovere*) tomorrow in my opinion.
9. If we play draughts, he will want to play as well.
10. If our team has lost, Charles will be very pleased.

B. Translate the following:
I shall give; he will remain; we shall have done; she won't have replied; you will go; they will die; we shall have been able; they will pick; I shall come; he will say; they will have spoken; you will hold; I shall stay; he will throw; we shall realise it; it will appear; you will be worth; they will await; we shall become; they will have forgotten; you will play; he will be able to win; they will confine themselves to hurling reproaches at the referee.

C. Answer the following questions in Italian:
1. Dove è diventato popolare il gioco del calcio?
2. Chi diventa il capro espiatorio quando una squadra perde una partita?
3. In che nazioni affollano i campi da gioco gli spettatori?
4. Perché il tifo della folla diventa a volte eccessivo?

5. A che cosa è dovuta una sconfitta?
6. Come si attende la partita seguente?
7. Il contegno dei giocatori è sempre corretto?
8. Chi sa bene che la propria squadra deve vincere?
9. Qual è lo sport di gran lunga preferito in Italia?
10. Quando si gioca al calcio di solito?

D. Insert the future of the verbs given in brackets in the following sentences:
1. Sono sicuro che (piovere) stasera.
2. Quando Giovanni (partire) andremo al cinema.
3. Egli (vivere) a Roma l'anno prossimo.
4. Quando (venire) a visitarci, Giovanni?
5. Che cosa (scrivere) a Giovanni per chiedere scusa?

E. Translate into Italian:
Mr. Rossi has accompanied his brother-in-law to a football match. This game is now very popular in Italy. The field is very crowded and Mr. Rossi is unable to see the players. Suddenly there is a great deal of excitement and the crowd hurls the most insulting reproaches at the referee. Mr. Rossi's brother-in-law's team wins, so he is very happy. They return home contented after a very pleasant (*piacevole*) afternoon.

REVISION EXERCISES (*Lessons XI–XV*)

1. Translate into Italian:
1. The ship on which we travelled has now returned to London.
2. The steamer which has just moved away from the quay is not big.
3. I have heard (*sentire*) all you are telling me before.
4. Anyone who breaks a glass must pay (for) it.
5. Some talk in the dining-room, others in the drawing-room (*salotto*).
6. What cabin have you taken, Bruno?
7. What a lot of people are in this room.
8. From what the porter has said, it is difficult to find a seat (*posto*) on the train.
9. How beautiful the Channel is today!
10. I know he is ill, but that is all I can tell you.

2. Insert the correct person of the present and the perfect tenses of the verbs given in the infinitive in the following sentences:
    1. Giovanni e Maria (alzarsi) di buon'ora stamane.
    2. Guido (accorgersi) di non averne approfittato.
    3. Essi (cavarsela) con un po' di paura.
    4. In quel negozio (vendere) orecchini e collane.
    5. Loro (credersi) persone importantissime.

3. Translate into Italian:
    1. They are both ready to (a) give up (*rinunciare a*) that unequal struggle.
    2. The late Mr. Tacchi has been buried (*seppellire*) today.
    3. It is precisely because the sea was (*era*) calm that I did not suffer from seasickness.
    4. John has given some of them to you.
    5. Where are the newspapers you have bought?
    6. John took off his spectacles and cleaned them.
    7. I lost my way (*perdersi*) as soon as I arrived in Rome.
    8. Shakespeare and Dante are two famous men, the former is English and the latter Italian.
    9. The plane has just landed on the runway now.
    10. This work has become more and more difficult lately (*recentemente*).

4. Give the required forms of the verbs given in the infinitive: essere (future 1st plur.); tenere (perfect 2nd sing.); volere (future 2nd plur.); valere (present 1st sing.); dire (future 3rd sing.); rimanere (perfect 3rd plur.); parere (present 3rd plur.); sapere (imperative 2nd sing.).

5. Translate into Italian:
    1. John has probably already come, for I heard someone going up (*salire per*) the stairs (*le scale*).
    2. You will talk to him after I have seen him.
    3. I hope to (*di*) go to Turin this year, but I shall pass through Paris (*Parigi*).
    4. I shall live in Italy during (*durante*) my holidays next year.
    5. I shall speak to him about it when he comes home.
    6. I congratulated him warmly.
    7. Few people can rival him in that game.
    8. I almost fell from the train.
    9. I shall have to write to John at once.
    10. What will you do with all these reports?

A. DISJUNCTIVE PERSONAL PRONOUNS

1. The disjunctive personal pronouns are as follows in Italian:

SINGULAR		PLURAL	
me	*me*	noi	*us*
te	*you*	voi	*you*
lui, esso	*him*, *it* (*m.*)	loro, essi	*them* (*m.*)
lei, essa	*her*, *it* (*f.*)	loro, esse	*them* (*f.*)
sé	*himself, herself, itself*	sé	*themselves*
Lei	*you*	Loro	*you*

2. The disjunctive pronouns are used in the following cases:

(a) After prepositions:

Andiamo al cinema con loro.
Let us go to the cinema with them.

Carlo mi ha parlato di Lei.
Charles has spoken to me of you.

Il ragazzo ha fatto l'esercizio da sé.
The boy has done the exercise by himself.

NOTE (1) One sometimes finds the expressions **meco, teco,** and **seco** replacing **con me, con te** and **con sé** but they are dying out in Modern Italian.

(2) Some prepositions always require **di** before a disjunctive personal pronoun: **contro** (against); **dietro** (behind); while with others it is optional: **senza** (without); **dopo** (after); **verso** (towards). (See Lesson XXXVIII A.)

(b) When a verb has two pronouns as direct or indirect objects:

Egli chiama lui e te.
He is calling him and you.

Maria ha scritto a te e a Giovanni.
Mary has written to you and to John.

(c) When one wishes to be emphatic:

> Biasimo te non lui, perché è stata veramente colpa tua.
> *I blame you not him because it was really your fault.*

(d) In exclamations:

> Beato lui! *Happy he!*   Povero me! *Poor me!*

3. It should be noted that those disjunctive pronouns which are not identical with the subject pronouns cannot be used in the nominative case:

> Non sei piú tu! (*not* te)
> *You are no longer yourself.*
>
> Ci vado io. (*not* me)
> *I shall go there.*

Exception: Ci andremo io e te.
> *Both you and I shall go there.*

Te must be used instead of **tu** when linked with another subject pronoun.

B. IDIOMATIC USES
OF THE DEFINITE ARTICLE

1. The definite article is necessary in the following cases:

(a) Before abstract nouns unless they are being used to replace an adjective:

> La vita non è un sogno.
> *Life is not a dream.*
>
> La virtú è il piú grande dono di Dio.
> *Virtue is the greatest gift of God.*

but: I bambini hanno bisogno di lunghi periodi di felicità.
> *Children need long periods of happiness* (i.e., *happy periods*).

(b) Whenever nouns are used in a general or all-inclusive sense:

> Gl'Italiani amano la musica.
> *Italians like music.*
>
> Le penne si usano per scrivere.
> *Pens are used to write with.*

One should compare the first of these sentences with:

Ci sono degli Italiani che amano la musica.
There are Italians who love music.

In the second case, the noun is taken in a partitive, not in a general sense, thereby distinguishing a particular category from the whole.

(c) With the names of titles:

Il conte Bertazzi. *Count Bertazzi.*
Il signor Rossi. *Mr. Rossi.*

(d) With well-known surnames, especially in literature and in history:

Il Tasso   Il Parini   l'Ariosto   Il Manzoni
but: Garibaldi   Mazzini.

One must not use an article before a Christian name if it is masculine:

Dante   Michelangelo

NOTE. *Il Dante* exists but it means Dante's works.

However, in colloquial or familiar speech **la** is sometimes found with the Christian names of women:

Ho cercato la Luigia dappertutto.
I have looked for Louise everywhere.

(e) Rivers and mountains usually require the article:

Il Po *The Po*   Il Tamigi *The Thames*
L'Etna *Mount Etna* Le Alpi *The Alps*

(f) For the article with the names of countries, see Lesson XXXV A.

(g) Parts of the body and clothes require the article instead of the possessive (see Lesson IX A):

Egli alza la mano.
He lifts up his hand.
Si sono tolti il cappello.
They took off their hats.

(h) The article generally precedes the possessive adjective (see Lesson V B).

(i) The verb **giocare a** (to play at) sometimes requires the article with the names of games, but at other times it is optional or never used:

  (i) With the article:

    Giochiamo alla palla, al pallone.
    Let us play ball, football.

    Giocano alla roulette.
    They are playing roulette.

  (ii) With the article optional:

    Giochiamo a (alle) carte.
    Let us play cards.

    Giocano a (agli) scacchi.
    They are playing chess.

  (iii) With omission of the article:

    Giochiamo a palla canestro, a palla nuoto.
    Let us play basket ball, water polo.

    Giocano a domino, a tennis, a mosca cieca, a golf.
    They are playing dominoes, tennis, blind man's buff, golf.

2. The definite article is omitted:

(a) Before titles used in direct address:

    Che desidera, signorina?
    What do you want, Miss?

    Buona sera, signor conte.
    Good evening, Count.

(b) In proverbs:

    Amore e tosse non si celano.
    Love and a cough cannot be hidden.

(c) With **di** followed by a noun used in a purely adjectival sense:

    una giacca di lana.   *a woollen jacket.*
    l'ambasciatore d'Italia.   *the Italian ambassador.*
    un bicchier d'acqua.   *a glass of water.*

(d) Usually with nouns in apposition, even when modified by a possessive, but not when they are the antecedents of a relative clause:

    Roma, capitale d'Italia.
    Rome, capital of Italy.

L'Italia, sua patria.
Italy, his country.

but: Firenze, la città che si trova sull'Arno, è molto bella.
Florence, the town which stands on the Arno, is very beautiful.

(e) In many set phrases:
Andiamo in città. *Let us go to town.*
Che fame ho! *How hungry I am!*
Abbiamo sete. *We are thirsty.*

(f) The names of towns usually do not take the article unless qualified by an adjective or descriptive phrase:
Veniamo da Napoli. *We are coming from Naples.*
Vanno a Firenze. *They are going to Florence.*

but: La Firenze del Rinascimento. *Florence of the Renascence.*
La Roma classica. *Classical Rome.*

NOTE. Sometimes the article is part of the name of the town itself and in this case it must always be used:

La Spezia   il Cairo   L'Aia (*The Hague*)   la Mecca

Siamo venuti dalla Spezia.
We have come from La Spezia.

(g) With **parlare** when speaking of a language:
Io parlo italiano. *I speak Italian.*
but: Io insegno l'italiano. *I teach Italian.*

VOCABULARY

agilmente	*agilely*	davanti a	*in front of, before*
animale (*m.*)	*animal*		
arrampicarsi	*to climb*	descrivere	*to describe*
avventura	*adventure*	entrata	*entrance*
bestia	*animal*	esilarante	*exhilarating*
buffo, -a	*funny*	estasiato, -a	*delighted*
chiamare	*to call*	gabbia	*cage*
coccodrillo	*crocodile*	gettare	*to throw*
condurre	*to take*	godimento	*enjoyment*
dappertutto	*everywhere*	impadronirsi	*to take possession of*
dare origine a	*to give rise to*		

indescrivibile	*indescribable*	saltare	*to jump*
infine	*finally*	scena	*scene*
ippopotamo	*hippopotamus*	scimmia	*monkey*
lanciare un	*to give a roar*	selvaggio, -a	*wild*
ruggito		serpente (*m.*)	*snake*
leggero, -a	*light*	soffermarsi	*to linger*
leone (*m.*)	*lion*	soglia	*threshold*
marzo	*March*	sole (*m.*)	*sun*
nipotino, -a	*grandson,*	spaventare	*to frighten*
	daughter	tale	*such*
nocciolina	*nut*	di tanto in tanto	*from time to*
occhio	*eye*		*time*
pantera	*panther*	tigre (*f.*)	*tiger*
pregustare	*to look forward*	varcare	*to cross*
primaverile	*spring-like*	vento	*wind*
rincorrersi	*to chase*	a vicenda	*in turn*
ruggito	*roar*	vista	*sight*

UNA VISITA AL GIARDINO ZOOLOGICO

In una bella giornata di marzo con un sole caldo ed un leggero vento primaverile, Nonno Battista decide di condurre Angela e Giuseppe, i suoi nipotini, al giardino zoologico. Cosí, nel primo pomeriggio, tutti e tre prendono l'autobus che li conduce[1] proprio davanti all'entrata principale. Dopo aver acquistato[2] i biglietti, essi varcano la soglia di quel gran giardino. Che spettacolo si offre subito alla vista dei bambini! Gli animali piú selvaggi stanno davanti ai loro occhi, in carne ed ossa. Estasiati, i bambini si soffermano davanti ad ogni recinto. Vedono prima i coccodrilli e gli ippopotami, poi i leoni, uno dei quali lancia un gran ruggito tale da spaventare tutti i presenti. Poi vedono le tigri, le pantere e infine i serpenti che non lasciano un'impressione troppo bella. Ma dove i bambini si divertono immensamente, è nel recinto delle scimmie. Quale godimento alla vista di cosí piacevoli bestie! Esse saltano da una parte all'altra della gabbia, si rincorrono a vicenda, s'arrampicano agilmente dappertutto e molto spesso si fermano ed osservano in modo buffo gli spettatori. Questi, di tanto in tanto, gettano qualche nocciolina, al che³ le bestie, per impadronirsene, danno origine alle piú esilaranti scene. La felicità dei bambini è indescrivibile e già pregustano l'ora del ritorno per poter descrivere al babbo e alla mamma ciò che essi chiamano la loro piú bella avventura.

NOTES

¹ **conduce**: *Condurre*, like many verbs with contracted infinitives, is conjugated in the normal way in the present tense, just as if the contraction had not taken place: *conduco, conduci, conduce, conduciamo, conducete, conducono.*

² **Dopo aver acquistato**: The past infinitive is used after *dopo* but one can also use an expression similar to the English preposition and participle:

Dopo mangiato, è partito.   *After eating, he departed.*

³ **al che**: When the antecedent of *che* is a whole clause, the article is used with it.

EXERCISES

A. Translate into Italian:
1. I have given him the book, not you.
2. How on earth (*come mai*) did you discuss (p.p. *discusso*) it with him?
3. Poor him, I don't know what to do to help (*aiutare*) him.
4. Don't let's blame ourselves, it is not our fault.
5. John and you will have to go home now.
6. He intends to go there by himself.
7. We like playing golf.
8. Buy some sweets for me and a pencil for him.
9. My friend will take his nephews to the zoo tomorrow.
10. Having crossed the threshold, the children see many wild animals.

B. Put the definite or partitive articles in the spaces left blank in the following sentences:
1. Giovanni ha visto — serpenti nel giardino zoologico.
2. — uomo perde tutto alla fine della vita.
3. Non mi piacciono — mele.
4. Essi parlano sempre di — virtú ma sono viziosissimi.
5. Carlo ama molto — vino.

6. Abbiamo detto che ci piacciono — pere ma ci ha dato — mele.
7. — libri di matematica sono sempre difficili.
8. — ippopotami sono — bestie enormi.
9. Leggo — giornali ogni mattina.
10. Non ci sono — scimmie in quella gabbia.

C. Translate into Italian:
  1. Tasso and Garibaldi are two great Italians.
  2. I have just seen a picture of Michelangelo's.
  3. Mount Etna is in Italy.
  4. We took off our hats when we entered the room.
  5. What would you like, Mr. Rossi?
  6. Here is an iron (*ferro*) box.
  7. Let's go to Paris for our holidays.
  8. The lion gave a great roar and frightened all the onlookers.
  9. Monkeys are funny animals.
  10. Grandfather Battista took us to the zoo today.

D. Translate into Italian:
  Guido and Giovanna are the grandchildren of Mr. Rossi and they live in a big house outside the town. One day Mr. Rossi decides to take them to the zoo and they set out in the early afternoon in order to be back before evening. The bus takes them right to the door and, as soon as they cross the threshold, they see all the wild animals. It is the monkeys which interest the children most (*di più*) and they throw nuts to them and watch them while they chase one another in turn in their cage. At the end of their visit, they want to hurry home (*tornare in fretta*) in order to tell their mother and father about all they have seen.

E. Answer the following questions in Italian:
  1. Chi è andato al giardino zoologico questo pomeriggio?
  2. Quanti nipotini ha Nonno Battista?
  3. Che cosa fanno prima di varcare la soglia del giardino zoologico?
  4. Quanto costa per entrarci?
  5. Che cosa fa un leone?
  6. Quali animali divertono di più i bambini?
  7. Chi getta di tanto in tanto delle noccioline nella gabbia delle scimmie?
  8. Sono felici i bambini dopo la visita?
  9. Quale impressione lasciano i serpenti?
  10. Perché vogliono tornare a casa i bambini?

A. FURTHER DECLENSIONS, IRREGULAR PLURALS OF NOUNS AND ADJECTIVES

1. All monosyllables, and nouns ending in a consonant, an accented vowel or unaccented -i are invariable:

il re – i re	*king*
il lapis – i lapis	*pencil*
il revolver – i revolver	*revolver*
la città – le città	*city*
la virtú – le virtú	*virtue*
la crisi – le crisi	*crisis*

Nearly all nouns ending in -à, -ú and -i (exc.: *il brindisi* (the toast)) are feminine.

Two other common words which are invariable are **la specie – le specie** (kind) and **la serie – le serie** (series).

2. Feminine nouns and adjectives ending in -ca and -ga form their plurals in -che and -ghe:

la barca – le barche	*boat*
la bottega – le botteghe	*shop*
sporca – sporche	*dirty*
larga – larghe	*wide, broad*

3. Nouns and adjectives ending in unaccented -cia and -gia form their plurals in -cie and -gie if the preceding consonant is single, in -ce and -ge if it is double or in combination with another consonant:

l'audacia – le audacie	*bravery*
la roccia – le rocce	*rock*
la cupidigia – le cupidigie	*lust*
la spiaggia – le spiagge	*beach*
sudicia – sudicie	*dirty*
liscia – lisce	*smooth*
malvagia – malvagie	*wicked*
greggia – gregge	*raw* (of materials)

This rule, however, is sometimes broken; we find **provincie** alongside **province, valigie** alongside **valige,** *etc.*

4. Masculine nouns and adjectives ending in **-co** form their plurals in **-chi** if the penultimate syllable is stressed:

il fico – i fichi — *fig*
ricco – ricchi — *rich*

NOTE. The same rule applies to masculine nouns in **-ca**:

il monarca – i monarchi *monarch*

However, if the main stress is on the antepenultimate syllable, the plural is in **-ci**:

il medico – i medici — *doctor*
autentico – autentici — *authentic*

Exceptions:

(a) When the stress is on the penultimate syllable:

l'amico – gli amici — *friend*
il nemico – i nemici — *enemy*
il porco – i porci — *pig*
il Greco – i Greci — *Greek*

(b) When the stress is on the antepenultimate:

lo stomaco – gli stomachi *stomach*
carico – carichi — *loaded*
etc. etc.

5. Masculine nouns ending in **-go** and **-ga** and adjectives in **-go** form their plurals in **-ghi**:

l'albergo – gli alberghi — *inn*
il collega – i colleghi — *colleague*
largo – larghi — *wide*

Exceptions: a few nouns ending in **-ago** and **-ogo** whose stress falls on the antepenultimate:

l'asparago – gli asparagi *asparagus*
l'astrologo – gli astrologi *astrologer*
but: il catalogo – i cataloghi *catalogue*
il dialogo – i dialoghi *dialogue*

6. Masculine nouns and adjectives ending in unaccented **-io** form their plurals by dropping the **-o**:

lo specchio – gli specchi *mirror*

lo studio – gli studi   *study*
grigio – grigi   *grey*

7. All nouns ending in stressed **-io** and **-ia** form their plurals in **-ii** or **-ie**:

il mormor*io* – i mormor*ii*   *murmur*
la nostalg*ia* – le nostalg*ie*   *nostalgia*

8. Some masculine nouns ending in **-o** have feminine plurals in **-a**:

centinaio – centinaia   *hundreds*
il lenzuolo – le lenzuola   *sheet*
il miglio – le miglia   *mile*
il paio – le paia   *pair*
il riso – le risa   *laugh*
l'uovo – le uova   *egg*

9. Others have two singulars or two plurals, one masculine and one feminine:

il braccio – le braccia, i bracci   *arm*
il cervello – le cervella, i cervelli   *brain*
il ciglio – le ciglia, i cigli   *eyelid*
il corno – le corna, i corni   *horn*
il dito – le dita, i diti   *finger*
il frutto, la frutta – i frutti   *fruit*
il fuso – le fusa, i fusi   *spindle*
il ginocchio – le ginocchia, i ginocchi   *knee*
il grido – le grida, i gridi   *shout*
il labbro – le labbra, i labbri   *lip*
il legno, la legna – i legni   *wood*
il membro – le membra, i membri   *limb*
il muro – le mura, i muri   *wall*
l'orecchio – le orecchie, gli orecchi   *ear*
l'osso – le ossa, gli ossi   *bone*

There is little difference between the two plurals of **ginocchio** and **grido**, but in some other cases the feminine plural is used for the everyday object and the masculine form is reserved for a figurative or wider sense:

Le braccia del corpo.   *The arms of the body.*
I bracci di mare.   *The arms of the sea.*
Le ciglia della ragazza.   *The girl's eyelids.*
I cigli della strada.   *The sides of the road.*

Le corna del cervo.	*The stag's horns.*
I corni del dilemma.	*The horns of the dilemma.*
Le dita della mano.	*The fingers of the hand.*
Questi due diti mi fanno male.	*These two fingers hurt.*
Le labbra del bimbo.	*The baby's lips.*
I labbri della ferita.	*The lips of the wound.*
Le membra del corpo.	*The limbs of the body.*
I membri della commissione.	*The members of the commission.*
Le mura della città.	*The city walls.*
I muri della casa.	*The walls of the house.*
Le ossa del corpo.	*The bones of the body.*
Gli ossi trovati per la strada.	*Bones found in the street.*

NOTE. (1) **Fusi** and **fusa** have entirely different meanings:

I fusi per filare.	*Spindles for spinning.*
Il gatto fa le fusa.	*The cat purrs.*

(2) **La frutta** is only used for fruit on the table, while **frutto** and **frutti** are used for fruit on the tree or in the figurative sense:

> Alla fine del pranzo abbiamo mangiato frutta.
> *At the end of the dinner we ate fruit.*

> Quell'albero porta una grande quantità di frutti.
> *That tree bears a great quantity of fruit.*

> Questi sono i frutti dei miei studi.
> *These are the fruits of my studies.*

(3) **Il legno** is the usual word for the substance *wood* but **la legna** is *firewood*.

B. FORMATION OF ADVERBS

1. Adverbs are commonly formed by adding **-mente** to the feminine form of the adjective:

sincera – sinceramente	*sincere*
piena – pienamente	*fully*
lenta – lentamente	*slowly*

2. If the feminine of the adjective ends in **-le** or in **-re**, the **-e** is dropped before **-mente**:

facile – facilmente	*easily*
particolare – particolarmente	*particularly*

The **-e** remains, however, if it is preceded by *two* consonants:

acre – acremente	*bitterly*
folle – follemente	*madly*

3. Certain adverbs end in **-oni**:

bocconi	*flat on one's face*	a cavalcioni	*astride*
carponi	*on all fours*	penzoloni	*hanging down*

4. Some adverbs have special forms:

al di là	*beyond*	laggiú	*over there, down there*
altrimenti	*otherwise*	lassú	*up there*
bene	*well*	lungi	*(far) from*
là, lí	*there*	qua, qui	*here*
		volentieri	*willingly*

There is no difference in meaning between **qua** and **qui** but **là** means *yonder*, while **lí** refers to a spot in reasonable proximity to the speaker. Other forms are:

costà, costí	*there (where you are)*	quaggiú	*down here*
colà	*yonder*	quassú	*up here, in heaven*

The student should always use **lí** and **là** instead of **costí** and **costà**.

5. Certain adjectives are used as adverbs in their masculine singular form. A number of these are listed below:

alto	*highly, loudly*	poco	*little*
chiaro	*clearly*	sicuro	*surely*
fermo	*firmly*	sodo	*hard*
forte	*strongly*	solo	*only*
giusto	*rightly, clearly*	vicino	*nearby*
piano	*slowly, softly*		

Essi hanno gridato alto.	*They shouted loudly.*
Egli ha visto giusto.	*He has seen clearly.*
Abitiamo vicino.	*We live nearby.*

It will be noted that these adverbs never inflect.

6. One can often avoid an adverb in Italian by using the following type of construction:

Il cielo è d'un azzurro magnifico oggi.
The sky is magnificently blue today.

VOCABULARY

abituale	*usual*	inclinarsi	*to yield, bow*
accettare	*to accept*	indicibile	*ineffable*
accrescere	*to increase*	intento, -a	*intent*
aria	*air*	lato	*side*
arrivo	*arrival*	libertà	*liberty*
assordante	*deafening*	lontano, -a	*far*
attorno	*around*	maggiormente	*greatly*
benvenuto	*welcome*	paesino	*village*
biondeggiante	*yellowing, ripening*	parete (f.)	*wall*
		passaggio	*passage, passing*
calesse (m.)	*trap, horse-carriage*		
		pensiero	*thought*
caloroso, -a	*warm*	prato	*meadow*
campagna	*countryside*	provare	*to experience*
campo	*field*	puro, -a	*pure*
canto	*song*	respirare	*to breathe*
cavallo	*horse*	ridente	*smiling*
contadino, -a	*countryman, -woman*	ringraziamenti	*thanks*
		rumore (m.)	*noise, sound*
costretto a	*forced to*	senso	*sense*
esprimere	*to express*	settimana	*week*
fisico	*bodily health*	stazione (f.)	*station*
frizzante	*sparkling, sharp*	tenuta	*estate*
		trascorrere	*to pass*
gioia	*joy*	trotterellare	*to trot*
giulivo, -a	*joyful*	verde	*green*
grano	*grain, wheat*	volerci	*to lack, need*
impegno	*duty, work*		

UN VIAGGIO IN CAMPAGNA

Il signor Enzo Bocca viene invitato dall'amico Luigi Visconti a trascorrere alcuni giorni nella sua tenuta di campagna. Con quale gioia accetta l'invito! Costretto a vivere per tutta la settimana in città, tra le pareti del suo studio, alcuni giorni all'aria aperta sono proprio quel che ci vuole[1] per il suo fisico. Cosí, lasciata di buon'ora la città, si avvia con il treno verso un paesino distante dieci miglia.[2] Alla stazione d'arrivo trova l'amico che l'attende su di un calesse e si avvia con lui alla tenuta. Quale piacere per il signor Bocca respirare l'aria pura e frizzante dei campi! La campagna attorno, bella e ridente, pare dargli un caloroso benvenuto. Da un lato della strada i biondeggianti grani paiono inclinarsi al suo passaggio, dall'altro, verdi prati gli fanno provare un senso di indicibile piacere. E mentre il cavallo trotterella giulivo verso la tenuta, gli giungono i canti lontani dei contadini intenti ai lavori dei campi. Questo non è certo uno spettacolo abituale per il signor Bocca. Il pensiero di vivere alcuni giorni in piena libertà, lontano dai rumori assordanti della città e dagli impegni d'ufficio, accresce maggiormente la sua gioia. Per questo esprime all'amico i più sinceri e calorosi ringraziamenti.

NOTES

¹ **ci vuole :** *Volerci* means *to need* and is used in a large number of idiomatic expressions:

Ci vuole ben altro! *Something far better is required!*

Ci vogliono due uomini per aiutarci. *We need two men to help us.*

(See Lesson XXXIII B.)

² **distante dieci miglia:** One can also say: *a dieci miglia di distanza* . . . , but this expression is neater.

EXERCISES

A. Form the plurals of the following nouns:

crisi, lapis, autobus, becco, nemico, raggio, virtú, astrologo, contumacia, frangia, caccia, fiducia, socia, baco, drago, ferocia, mormorio, bugia, farmacia, ciglio, ginocchio, fico, fuoco, studio, brulichio, zio, sindaco, monaco, rigo, porco, palco, ciliegia, denuncia, stomaco, dialogo, specchio, nostalgia, monologo, obbligo, calpestio, bacio, ozio, valico, collega, fuso, dito.

B. Give the masculine and feminine plurals of the following adjectives:

bigio, elettrico, eroico, sporco, ricco, largo, ligio, greco, grigio, greggio, fradicio, teorico, autentico, lungo, presago, poco, vigliacco, cattolico, proprio, vario, savio.

C. Translate into Italian:

1. The cat purrs in the kitchen.
2. The members of the committee (*comitato*) spoke of the dangers of war (*guerra*).
3. The dog brought bones into the dining-room.
4. What sort of fruit shall we eat after supper?
5. The baby has very red (*rosso*) lips.
6. These are the fruits of my labour.
7. John went slowly along the road.
8. This problem (*problema (m.)*) is not particularly difficult.
9. You must go to the cinema now, otherwise it will be too late.
10. Charles fell flat on his face when he opened the door.

D. Translate into Italian:

Mr. Rossi has been invited by his friend Mr. Lamberti to pass the weekend on his estate in the country. Mr. Rossi is very happy to accept the invitation because he does not like spending all his time in town. He catches a train to a little village five miles away, near which Mr. Lamberti has his country house. On arriving at the station he sees Mr. Lamberti waiting for him with a trap. As the horse trots snappily down the road Mr. Rossi hears the songs of the peasants in the distance (*in lontananza*). He passes a very pleasant few days with his friend before returning home on Sunday (*la domenica*) in order to be ready to start work in the office the next day.

E. Answer the following questions in Italian:

1. Quanto tempo passa il signor Bocca in campagna?
2. Chi l'attende alla stazione del paese?
3. Che cosa gli giunge alle orecchie mentre va alla tenuta dell'amico?
4. Che cosa fa il signor Bocca durante la settimana?
5. Come gli pare la campagna quando arriva?
6. Perché è costretto a vivere in città?
7. Come si chiama il suo amico?
8. Perché la campagna non è uno spettacolo abituale per il signor Bocca?
9. Di che colore sono i campi?
10. Perché ringrazia l'amico?

A. THE IMPERFECT AND PLUPERFECT TENSES

1. The imperfect tense is formed in Italian as follows:

Imperfect

TROVARE	VENDERE	FINIRE
trovavo	vendevo	finivo
I was finding,	*I was selling,*	*I was finishing,*
I used to find	*I used to sell*	*I used to finish*
trovavi	vendevi	finivi
trovava	vendeva	finiva
trovavamo	vendevamo	finivamo
trovavate	vendevate	finivate
trovavano	vendevano	finivano

NOTE. The stress of the third person plural of this tense should be carefully noted.

The only irregular verb in the imperfect tense is **essere**:

ESSERE

ero	*I was, etc.*	eravamo
eri		eravate
era		erano

2. The pluperfect is formed by using the imperfect tenses of **avere** or **essere** and the past participle of the verb:

Pluperfect

TROVARE	VENDERE	FINIRE
avevo trovato	avevo venduto	avevo finito
I had found	*I had sold*	*I had finished*
avevi trovato	avevi venduto	avevi finito
aveva trovato	aveva venduto	aveva finito
avevamo trovato	avevamo venduto	avevamo finito
avevate trovato	avevate venduto	avevate finito
avevano trovato	avevano venduto	avevano finito

VENIRE	LAVARSI
ero venuto, -a *I had come*	m'ero lavato, -a *I had washed*
eri venuto, -a	t'eri lavato, -a
era venuto, -a	s'era lavato, -a
eravamo venuti, -e	c'eravamo lavati, -e
eravate venuti, -e	v'eravate lavati, -e
erano venuti, -e	s'erano lavati, -e

B. USES OF THE IMPERFECT AND PLUPERFECT TENSES

1. The imperfect tense is used for the following cases:

   (a) Descriptions in the past:

   > La montagna era coperta di neve.
   > *The mountain was covered with snow.*
   > Il tempo era cattivo.
   > *The weather was bad.*

   (b) To express incomplete actions in the past:

   > Mentre Maria scriveva, i ragazzi parlavano.
   > *While Mary was writing, the boys were speaking.*

   (c) To express continuous or repeated actions and continuous states in the past:

   > Le due ragazze chiacchieravano nel salotto.
   > *The two girls were chatting in the drawing-room.*
   > Carlo era solito andare da Filippo ogni sera l'anno scorso.
   > *Charles used to go to Philip's house every evening last year.*
   > A destra c'era il nemico, a sinistra il mare.
   > *To the right was the enemy, to the left the sea.*

   The tense should never be confused with the Perfect and the Past Definite (see Lesson XIX), both of which express single, completed actions in the past.

2. The pluperfect tense is used to translate the equivalent English tense except in the rare cases when the past anterior tense (see Lesson XIX) is used:

Carlo mi ha dato il libro su cui Giovanni aveva scritto alcuni appunti.
Charles has given me the book on which John had written a few notes.

VOCABULARY

accattivarsi	*to capture, attract*	grandezza	*size, bigness*
affarista	*business-seeking*	infrangibilità	*unbreakableness*
balenare	*to flash*	ininterrotto, -a	*unbroken*
bambino, -a	*baby, child*	massaia	*housewife*
buttare	*to throw, hurl*	mondo	*world, lot*
calcolatore, -trice	*calculating*	orazione (*f.*)	*oration*
commerciante	*merchant*	ovunque	*everywhere*
convinto, -a	*convinced*	posto di ritrovo	*rendez-vous*
costo	*cost*	prodotto	*product*
credulone	*credulous person*	risparmiatore, -trice	*economical*
dimostrare	*to demonstrate*	rivivere	*to relive*
esporre	*to display*	roteare	*to wave, roll*
espressione (*f.*)	*expression*	scongiurare	*to swear*
farmaco	*drug*	semplice	*simple*
fegato	*liver*	sostenere	*to maintain*
fertilizzante (*m.*)	*fertilizer*	stupefatto, -a	*astonished*
fiducia	*faith, trust*	sveglio, -a	*wide awake*
fine (*m.*)	*aim*	terra	*ground*
formula	*formula*	terreno	*land*
fare a gara	*to vie, compete*	tipo	*type*
		venditore, -trice	*seller*

IL MERCATO

Il mercato, si sa bene, è uno dei posti piú interessanti di una città. Ogni mercato può variare da un altro per grandezza o per le diverse merci che vengono esposte e vendute, ma l'atmosfera è ovunque la stessa. Esso è il posto di ritrovo di ogni tipo di persona: dalla massaia risparmiatrice e calcolatrice al contadino credulone, dal commerciante sveglio ed affarista al semplice spettatore. Ogni venditore fa a gara per

accattivarsi prima l'interesse e poi la fiducia dei presenti al
fine di¹ poter vendere il proprio prodotto.

Ancor oggi torno sovente col pensiero a rivivere i momenti
in cui già da bambino mi soffermavo con interesse ad
ascoltare le ininterrotte e lunghe 'orazioni' dei diversi
venditori. C'era chi buttava per terra piatti al fine di
dimostrare la loro infrangibilità, chi aveva farmachi speciali
contro il mal di fegato, chi sosteneva di possedere formule
speciali per speciali fertilizzanti di terreno, e c'era persino
chi scongiurava di vendere sotto costo. Ed io mi divertivo
un mondo ad osservare le diverse espressioni dei venditori,
seguivo il roteare delle loro braccia, il rapido balenare dei
loro occhi. Alla fine riuscivano quasi sempre a vendere il
loro prodotto agli stupefatti spettatori, i quali tornavano a
casa convinti di aver fatto un ottimo affare.

NOTE
    ¹ **al fine di**: One should not confuse *il fine* (the aim) with
la fine (the end). This expression is a useful variation for *per*
with the infinitive.

EXERCISES

A. Translate into Italian:
  1. The merchant was throwing plates on to the ground in
     order to demonstrate their unbreakableness.
  2. We watched the seller's eyes flashing as he sold his goods.
  3. John told me that he had not gone to the cinema last night.
  4. The weather was very warm when we were going to the
     country.
  5. We often used to go to John's house last year.
  6. When Mary was typewriting I used to read the paper.
  7. My head was spinning when I came out of the lecture.
  8. I saw Guido every week in the summer holidays.
  9. He didn't know what his friend was doing.
  10. To the left and to the right the fields looked very green.

B. Give the required form of the following verbs:
     lavarsi (3rd plur. pluperfect); essere (2nd plur. imperfect);
     dormire (2nd sing. imperfect); avere (3rd plur. pluperfect);

venire (1st plur. imperfect); mangiare (3rd sing. pluperfect);
accorgersi (3rd plur. pluperfect); dare (1st plur. imperfect).

C. Answer the following questions in Italian:
1. Che cosa fanno i venditori in un mercato?
2. Da dove vengono i prodotti dei fruttivendoli sul mercato?
3. Con chi parlano i commercianti?
4. Perché si buttano piatti per terra?
5. Chi torna a casa convinto di aver fatto un ottimo affare?
6. Quale specie di persona si trova spesso al mercato?
7. In che modo si esprimono i commercianti?
8. I mercati sono sempre della stessa grandezza?
9. Che specie di merci si vende al mercato?
10. I venditori riescono sempre a vendere il loro prodotto?

D. Translate into Italian:
John and Helen went to the market this morning to buy some
fruit. The market was not very crowded so the merchants
were waving their arms and making their eyes flash as they
spoke of their products to their astonished clients. At one
spot (*luogo*) a man was hurling plates on the ground, in
another one merchant swore he was selling under cost price.
John and Helen bought apples, pears, grapes and oranges at
the fruitseller's and then came straight back home.

E. Give a short description in Italian of the market in your town.

A. THE PAST DEFINITE AND PAST ANTERIOR TENSES

1. The past definite tense of regular verbs is formed in Italian as follows:

TROVARE	VENDERE	FINIRE
trovai *I found*	vendei (-etti)† *I sold*	finii *I finished*
trovasti	vendesti	finisti
trovò	vendé (-ette)	finí
trovammo	vendemmo	finimmo
trovaste	vendeste	finiste
trovarono	venderono (-ettero)	finirono

NOTE. The stress of the third person plural should once more be noted for this tense.

2. The past definite of **avere** and **essere** are irregular:

AVERE	ESSERE
ebbi *I had*	fui *I was*
avesti	fosti
ebbe	fu
avemmo	fummo
aveste	foste
ebbero	furono

3. The past anterior tense is formed with the past definite tense of **avere** or **essere** and the past participle of the verb:

TROVARE	VENDERE	FINIRE
ebbi trovato	ebbi venduto	ebbi finito
I had found	*I had sold*	*I had finished*
avesti trovato	avesti venduto	avesti finito
ebbe trovato	ebbe venduto	ebbe finito

† Do not use this form with verbs whose root ends in *t: potei*, not *potetti*.

avemmo trovato	avemmo venduto	avemmo finito
aveste trovato	aveste venduto	aveste finito
ebbero trovato	ebbero venduto	ebbero finito

VENIRE	LAVARSI
fui venuto, -a *I had come*	mi fui lavato, -a *I had washed*
fosti venuto, -a	ti fosti lavato, -a
etc.	*etc.*

B. USES OF THE PAST DEFINITE AND PAST ANTERIOR TENSES

1. The past definite tense is used exclusively to describe single actions in the past:

> Giovanni ci piantò in asso.
> *John left us in the lurch.*
> Tornando a casa, incontrai Luigi.
> *While returning home, I met Lewis.*

It is always used in the narration of historical events:

> Napoleone morí nel 1821.   *Napoleon died in 1821.*

2. It may be distinguished from the perfect tense by its tendency to refer to more specific times in the past and is especially used in clauses where we find such expressions as *l'anno scorso* (last year), *mesi fa* (months ago), *ieri* (yesterday), etc.

> Comprai un cappotto due mesi fa.
> *I bought an overcoat two months ago.*

but: Ho comprato un cappotto oggi.
> *I bought an overcoat today.*

3. The past anterior is used only in subordinate clauses introduced by a conjunction of time, when the verb of the main clause is in the past definite tense:

> Quando ebbi finito il mio lavoro, me ne andai.
> *When I had finished my work, I went away.*
> Appena ebbe proferite quelle parole, si morse la lingua.
> *Hardly had he uttered those words, when he bit his tongue.*
> (*Manzoni*)

The past anterior is not used in speech in which it is generally replaced by the past definite:

Quando finii il mio lavoro, me ne andai.
When I finished my work, I went away.

4. The verb **nascere** presents a special difficulty. **È nato** (was born) is used for someone still living; **era nato** is used with the same meaning for someone who has recently died; **nacque** is used historically for someone long dead:

Il bambino è nato stamani.
The baby was born this morning.

Il morto era nato quasi un secolo fa.
The dead man was born almost a century ago.

Quel poeta nacque due secoli fa.
That poet was born two centuries ago.

VOCABULARY

le Alpi (*f.*)	*the Alps*	freddo, -a	*cold*
arte (*f.*)	*art*	frontiera	*frontier*
artistico, -a	*artistic*	galleria (d'arte)	*tunnel (art gallery)*
battistero	*baptistry*		
campanile (*m.*)	*belfry*	giú	*down*
canale (*m.*)	*canal*	golfo	*bay*
canzone (*f.*)	*song*	gondola	*gondola*
capitale (*f.*)	*capital*	incantare	*to entrance*
celebre	*famous*	incantevole	*charming*
cioè	*that is*	indimenticabile	*unforgettable*
cittadina	*town*	iniziare	*to begin*
confine (*m.*)	*border, frontier*	laborioso, -a	*hard-working*
		lago	*lake*
doganale	*of the customs*	laguna	*lagoon*
duomo	*cathedral*	legare	*to link, tie*
per eccellenza	*par excellence*	mancare (venire a mancare)	*to lack (be short)*
fabbrica	*factory*		
filare	*to go fast, to speed along*	marinaro, -a	*maritime*
		meraviglioso, -a	*wonderful*
Firenze	*Florence*	monumento	*monument*
fontana	*fountain*	museo	*museum*

napoletano, -a	*Neapolitan*	ricordo	*memory*
operoso, -a	*hard-working,*	riviera di	*Italian Eastern*
	industrious	Levante	*riviera*
paese (*m.*)	*country*	romantico, -a	*romantic*
palazzo	*large building,*	scenario	*scenery*
	palace	soggiorno	*stay*
parco	*park*	storia	*history*
Parigi	*Paris*	Svizzera	*Switzerland*
pendente	*leaning, hang-*	tenace	*tenacious*
	ing	torre (*f.*)	*tower*
perciò	*therefore*	tradizione (*f.*)	*tradition*
Piemonte (*m.*)	*Piedmont*	turista (*m.*)	*tourist*
piovigginoso, -a	*drizzly*	vetta	*peak*
piuttosto	*rather*		

UN VIAGGIO IN ITALIA

L'anno scorso il signor Rossi e sua moglie decisero di visitare l'Italia. Il treno lasciò Parigi in una sera piovigginosa e piuttosto fredda diretto alla frontiera italiana. Nelle prime ore della mattina, passata la stazione doganale di Modane e la galleria sotto le Alpi, arrivarono a Bardonecchia, il posto di confine italiano. Bella e ridente sullo scenario magnifico delle Alpi le cui vette erano ancora coperte di neve, la prima cittadina italiana diede[1] il benvenuto ai nostri viaggiatori già stanchi del lungo viaggio.

La prima città che visitarono fu Torino, la grande ed operosa capitale del Piemonte, famosa per le sue fabbriche di automobili Fiat e Lancia; poi andarono a Genova, la tenace, laboriosa e famosa città marinara, ricca di storia e di tradizione. Da Genova il treno filò lungo la bella riviera di Levante e i nostri viaggiatori arrivarono presto a Pisa dove passarono la prima notte del soggiorno in Italia. Andarono a vedere[2] la torre pendente, il Duomo e il Battistero e poi partirono per Roma. Arte e storia sono legate a Roma come in nessun'altra città del mondo; perciò visitarono musei, monumenti, gallerie d'arte, palazzi, giardini, fontane, cioè tutti i posti famosi che incantano i turisti d'ogni paese. Poi

giú verso Napoli, la città del Vesuvio col suo golfo incantevole, Posilippo, Mergellina, dalle celebri canzoni napoletane.
Da Napoli iniziarono il viaggio di ritorno, attraversarono gli
Abruzzi con il famoso parco nazionale diretti verso la verde
Umbria. Si fermarono a Orvieto per vedere il duomo e poi
andarono ad Assisi che lasciò in tutti e due un ricordo
indimenticabile. Infine passarono alcuni giorni a Firenze e
a Venezia. A Firenze andarono a vedere le gallerie d'arte
perché questa è la città artistica per eccellenza, poi il Duomo,
il campanile di Giotto, la chiesa di Santa Croce e tanti altri
posti interessanti. Restarono tre giorni a Venezia, famosa per
la sua laguna, piazza San Marco, i suoi canali e le romantiche
gondole. Ma poi venne a mancare il tempo e dovettero
ritornare in Inghilterra. Partirono di mattina[3] per la Svizzera
e arrivarono a Londra la sera del giorno seguente.

NOTES

[1] **diede** : Past definite of *dare* (to give); the complete conjugation of the verb in this tense is given in Lesson XXII A.

[2] **Andarono a vedere** : Verbs of motion mostly take *a* before
an infinitive. They take *per* instead only when the motivation of
the action expressed is uppermost in the speaker's mind and not
the thought of proceeding to a place.

[3] **di mattina** : This expression can be extended to all periods
of the day, to the seasons and to the months of the year: *di
pomeriggio* (in the afternoon); *di notte* (in the night); *di sera* (in
the evening); *d'inverno* (in the winter); *di settembre* (in September),
etc.

EXERCISES

A. Translate into Italian:
1. He said (*disse*) they had gone to Italy last week, but were
   now on the way back.
2. Anthony carried the suitcase into the compartment (*scom-
   partimento*).
3. We didn't have time to (*di*) see John and his friends when
   we were in Naples.
4. I bought some apples this morning before I went to the
   factory.

5. When I had given (*fare*) my lesson, I slipped off.
6. The train sped along the rails towards Florence.
7. At the frontier post, the train stopped for two hours.
8. We saw monuments, museums, art galleries, and very large buildings in Rome.
9. We crossed Switzerland on our way home.
10. Hardly had he opened the door, (when) John entered the room in a fury (*furibondo*).
11. Dante died many years ago, but his Divine Comedy (*Divina Commedia*) is famous throughout the world.
12. We went to Orvieto this summer, but many tourists were there.

B. Insert the past definite of the verb in brackets in the following sentences:

1. Cessata la pioggia, (riprendere) il nostro cammino.
2. Nel pensare alla patria lontana i miei occhi (bagnarsi) di lacrime.
3. Ieri (andare) a trovare Carlo e Giulio.
4. Quando andammo in campagna, (cominciare) a piovere.
5. Emilio (contentarsi) di poco.
6. Assisi (lasciare) in loro un ricordo indimenticabile.
7. Barbara (seguire) suo fratello lungo la strada.
8. Noi (uscire) dopo cena per andare a vedere un film.
9. Scritta la lettera, io non ci (pensare) piú.
10. Voi (comprare) una penna stilografica in quel negozio.

C. Give the required form of the following verbs:

andare (1st sing. pres.); lavarsi (2nd plur. past ant.); venire (3rd plur. imperf.); chiedere (2nd sing. past def.); variare (2nd plur. past def.); mangiare (3rd plur. fut.); filare (1st sing. past def.); sedersi (1st plur. pluperf.); pensare (1st plur. fut.); chiamare (2nd plur. imperf.); proferire (1st sing. past def.); potere (3rd sing. past def.); finire (3rd sing. past def.); applaudire (1st plur. past def.); seguire (1st plur. past ant.); vendere (3rd plur, pas ant.).

D. Translate into Italian:

Last month John and I went to Italy for our holidays. We took the train at London and crossed the Channel from Dover to Calais. From Calais we went to Paris where we passed a few days. Then we continued our journey to Italy. We reached the Italian frontier in the early hours of the morning. Bardonecchia was the first Italian town we saw. The Alps were all around (*tutt'intorno*) and their peaks were still covered in snow. From Bardonecchia we sped towards Turin where we visited the huge Fiat works. Then we set out for Rome, which is called the eternal (*eterno*) city. In Rome art and history are linked together as in no other city of the world. We visited all sorts of monuments and museums when we were there. Now, however, time was getting short and we had to return to England. We crossed Switzerland when returning and arrived in London in the evening of the following day.

E. Translate into Italian:
1. We went out to see the city after supper.
2. We know John will come to help us.
3. Let's go to see a play at the theatre tonight.
4. She went there to give him the tickets.
5. We climbed up the mountain to see the countryside.

A. THE CONDITIONAL TENSES

1. The present conditional tense is formed by adding the appropriate tense endings to the infinitive of the verb, with the **-are** ending of the infinitive of the first conjugation once more being changed to **-er** before the tense is formed, as in the future tense:

TROVARE	VENDERE	FINIRE
troverei	venderei	finirei
I should find	*I should sell*	*I should finish*
troveresti	venderesti	finiresti
troverebbe	venderebbe	finirebbe
troveremmo	venderemmo	finiremmo
trovereste	vendereste	finireste
troverebbero	venderebbero	finirebbero

NOTE. Those verbs which are irregular in their future tense (see Lesson XV) are also irregular in their conditional tense.

2. The present conditional of **avere** and **essere** is as follows:

AVERE	ESSERE
avrei *I should have*	sarei *I should be*
avresti	saresti
avrebbe	sarebbe
avremmo	saremmo
avreste	sareste
avrebbero	sarebbero

3. The conditional perfect tense is formed by using the conditional tenses of **avere** or **essere** and the past participle of the verb:

TROVARE	VENDERE	FINIRE
avrei trovato	avrei venduto	avrei finito
I should have found	*I should have sold*	*I should have finished*
avresti trovato, *etc.*	avresti venduto, *etc.*	avresti finito, *etc.*

There are no irregularities in this tense.

B. USES OF THE CONDITIONAL TENSES

1. The conditional tenses are used as follows:

(a) To express an English conditional tense:

> Dice che dovrei andare a scuola.
> *He says I should go to school.*
>
> Lasciò detto che sarebbe venuto domani.
> *He left word that he* would be coming *tomorrow.*

It is very important to note the sequence of tenses in the second example. Whenever the main verb is in the past tense in Italian, the conditional tense used must also be in the past.

(b) To express a wish or a question more politely, or to make an assertion more modest:

> Mi accompagneresti alla stazione?
> *Will you accompany me to the station?*
>
> Potrei avere un po' di frutta, per favore?
> *Can I have a little fruit, please?*
>
> Vorrebbe accompagnarci al teatro.
> *He wants to accompany us to the theatre.*
>
> Direi che domani pioverà.
> *I should say it will rain tomorrow.*

(c) When a statement is reported as hearsay, on the authority of another person:

> Secondo il ministro, la produzione sarebbe cresciuta del doppio durante gli ultimi cinque anni.
> *According to the minister, production* has increased *twofold during the last five years.*
>
> A quanto dicono i giornali, il re sarebbe morto.
> *From what the papers say, the king* has died.

VOCABULARY

abbonamento	radio licence, subscription	irradiare	to transmit
		Iugoslavia	Jugoslavia
abbonato	subscriber	per mezzo di	by means of
ampiezza	size	montano, -a	mountainous
angolo	angle, corner	nascosto, -a	hidden, remote
annuo, -a	annual	nero, -a	black
antenna	mast, aerial	nonostante	notwithstand-
apparecchio	set		ing, despite
attraverso	through, across	numeroso, -a	numerous
bianco	white	paese (m.)	country
bruciare	to burn (out)	periodo	period
cambiare	to change	pezzo	piece, part
carattere (m.)	character, kind	pollice (m.)	thumb, inch
catena	chain	potenziamento	development
cavo coassiale	co-axial cable	prezzo	price
cifra	figure	privato	private (person)
collegare	to link	quotidiano, -a	daily
completo	complete	radioaudizione	sound broad-
comprendere	to include	(f.)	casting
compreso, -a	included	rapidamente	quickly
comune	common	regionale	regional
concorrenza	competition	rete (f.)	net, network
condensatore(m.)	condenser	ripetitore, -trice	repeater
coprire	to cover	satellite (m.)	satellite
decina	ten(s), half-score	serale (adj.)	evening
diminuire	to diminish	settecento-	seven hundred
distinguersi	to distinguish	cinquanta	and fifty
dividere	to divide, separate	sorgere (sorto)	to rise (risen)
		sostanzialmente	substantially
entro	in, within	stazionario, -a	stationary
Francia	France	studio	studio
fronteggiare	to meet, resist	essere allo	to be under study
garantire	to guarantee	studio	
gratuitamente	free, without payment	sviluppo	development
		Svizzera	Switzerland
immagine (f.)	image, picture	tavolino	table
impervio	impassable, impervious	teleschermo	television screen
		televisivo, -a	
iniziare	to begin	(adj.)	television
internazionale	international	territorio	territory

terzo, -a	third	tredici	thirteen
trasformatore		uso	use
(m.)	transformer	valvola	valve
trasmittente	transmitting	venti	twenty
trasmettere	to transmit	video	screen

RAI – RADIOTELEVISIONE ITALIANA

Il programma di sviluppo della televisione in Italia è ora completo e copre il territorio nazionale con tre reti televisive. Per gli sviluppi futuri dobbiamo aspettare il potenziamento dell'uso di satelliti che già sono allo studio da alcuni anni. A parte le reti nazionali, si possono ricevere in Italia anche programmi delle nazioni vicine, Francia, Monaco, Svizzera, Iugoslavia. Le varie stazioni trasmittenti sono collegate fra di loro per mezzo di cavi coassiali e antenne ripetitrici che, nonostante le impervie catene montane che dividono l'Italia, portano l'immagine negli angoli piú nascosti. Dagli studi di Roma e di Milano, e da altri di minore importanza, vengono irradiati numerosi programmi quotidiani; alcuni sono al pomeriggio come la T.V. per i ragazzi, ma i piú importanti sono quelli serali. Recentemente la legislazione è cambiata e i privati possono installare stazioni trasmittenti e trasmettere programmi. Sono sorte cosí centinaia di stazioni di radio e decine di stazioni televisive, e ogni grande città ha almeno una televisione privata. Mentre le prime due reti della RAI non si distinguono sostanzialmente l'una dall'altra, la terza rete è stata iniziata per fronteggiare la concorrenza delle trasmittenti private, e ha carattere piú locale e regionale.

Alcuni anni fa iniziarono le trasmissioni a colori, e ora gli apparecchi in bianco e nero stanno diminuendo rapidamente. Le varie ampiezze del video o teleschermo sono quelli internazionali, i piú comuni televisori sono da ventun[1], ventidue e ventisei pollici. Il prezzo di un televisore da ventisei pollici è di circa settecentocinquanta mila lire[2] compreso il tavolino e l'antenna. Poiché tutti gli apparecchi sono garantiti per un anno, se entro tale periodo si brucia qualche valvola o qualche condensatore, o anche lo schermo, questi pezzi vengono cambiati gratuitamente.

Gli abbonati alla televisione sono attualmente oltre tredici milioni, e questo significa che praticamente ogni famiglia possiede un apparecchio. L'abbonamento è cinquanta mila lire annue, ma questa cifra comprende anche l'abbonamento alle radioaudizioni.

NOTES

[1] **Da ventun:** *Da* is used as a complement of measure or value in Italian (see Lesson XXXIX A.) The numbers *ventuno, trentuno,* etc. are shortened to *ventun, trentun,* etc. before a noun and are invariable in modern Italian (see Lesson XXVIIA).

[2] **È di circa settecentocinquanta mila:** With estimates of any kind (i.e., distance, value, etc.) the preposition *di* is necessary after the verb *essere.*

EXERCISES

A. Translate into Italian:
1. I would like to watch the television tonight.
2. From what they have been saying on the radio, Italy has beaten England in the international football match.
3. He left word that he could not come to see you today.
4. The price of a television set would be about 750,000 lira in Italy.
5. When we changed the valve the transformer burned out.
6. The whole of Italian territory has been covered by a television network in a period of twenty years.
7. Would you like to see the television at my house this afternoon?
8. It has been said that we could not continue our industrial expansion (*espansione* (*f.*)) without an atomic (*atomico*) programme.
9. How much would a television licence cost in England?
10. A number of repeating aerials would help to (*a*) transmit our programmes to the public.

B. Answer the following questions in Italian:
1. Chi ha ora il permesso di installare stazioni trasmittenti?
2. Qual è la differenza tra il terzo programma e i due altri della R.A.I.?
3. Da dove vengono irradiati i programmi televisivi in Italia?

4. Quanto è l'abbonamento alla televisione in Italia?
5. Quali sono le ampiezze comuni del teleschermo?
6. In che modo portano gli Italiani l'immagine negli angoli piú nascosti?
7. C'è un programma per ragazzi in Italia?
8. Quali parti di un apparecchio televisivo vengono cambiate gratuitamente quando è sotto garanzia?
9. Quanto è il prezzo di un apparecchio televisivo in Italia?
10. Che cosa è allo studio adesso?

C. Translate into Italian:

Now that the television network in Italy is complete, future developments will come from the use of satellites. Three different networks have been developed by R.A.I., but many other private programmes have arisen from a recent change in legislation and these are transmitted by private stations. There are two hours of programmes for children in the afternoon and at least six others in the evening. Many Italians used to go to a café to see the television but now there is a television set in almost all families. Many people say that the development of satellites should go ahead (*andare avanti*) quickly because we could then have a network which would cover the whole of Europe (*L'Europa*). Probably these developments will be complete in about ten years.

D. Give 1st person singular of the present and perfect conditionals of the following verbs:

vivere; avere; scrivere; cadere; amare; andare; mangiare; accorgersi; stare; vedere; essere; venire.

E. Write a few lines on television in England.

REVISION EXERCISES (*Lessons XVI–XX*)

1. Translate into Italian:
   1. He was speaking of you, not of me.
   2. They frightened him and her.
   3. We did not show it to him, only to them.
   4. I sent them to him and to you.
   5. I have no faith (*fede* (*f.*)) in them.

2. Fill in the blanks (if necessary) in the following sentences:
   1. L'ambasciatore — Francia ritornò a Parigi.
   2. Voglio — volontari per aiutarmi a portare questo sacco in cantina.
   3. Parla sempre di — onestà, ma è un farabutto.

4. Gli asciugo — mani.
5. Ho cercato dappertutto — Giovanna.
6. Come sta oggi, — signorina Azegli?
7. Il leone ha lanciato — ruggiti quando eravamo nel giardino zoologico.
8. Ci siamo andati — pomeriggio.
9. Il professore ci ha parlato di — Dante stamane.
10. Abbiamo dovuto camminare per due ore senza fermarci, — che non fu molto divertente.

3. Give the plurals of the following nouns with the definite article:
giacca, roccia, stomaco, astrologo, albergo, studio, nostalgia, amico, monarca, fico, greco, specchio, dito, osso, labbro, orecchio, ciglio, miglio, uovo, autobus, specie, revolver, barca, cupidigia, raggio, ciliegia, metà, valigia, spiaggia, brindisi, dialogo, lega, spago.

4. Give the masculine and feminine plurals of the following adjectives:
autentico, fradicio, malvagio, greggio, largo, liscio, ricco, bigio, carico, sporco, opaco, bellico, sudicio.

5. Translate into Italian:
The two arms of the lake. The dog carried the bone into the house. These fingers are hurting me. The walls of the city are very old. The cat began to purr. We are on the horns of a dilemma. We had fruit after dinner. We walked for more than two miles. He put the sheets on the bed. There are ten members of this commission.

6. Put in the correct tenses of the verbs given in the infinitive:
1. Quando (finire) di lavorare, uscii con due miei amici.
2. Stamani (andare) in biblioteca per riportare un libro che (prendere) in prestito.
3. Napoleone (nascere) in Corsica.
4. Mi dicono che il primo ministro (partire) per l'America.
5. Mentre Giovanni (leggere), Filippo (continuare) a parlare.
6. I due fratelli (venire) ogni anno a Milano per vedere il loro vecchio zio ma questi morí due anni fa.
7. La casa (bruciare) quando arrivai.
8. Mi disse che me ne (parlare) piú tardi.
9. (Volere) sapere il tuo nome, ragazzino.
10. Partirò quando (fare) questo lavoro.

A. NEGATIVE EXPRESSIONS

1. If an expression of negation follows a verb, it requires **non** before the verb itself:

> Non ho nessun giornale.
> *I have no newspaper.*
>
> Egli non scrive a nessuno.
> *He doesn't write to anybody.*
>
> Non sono mica andato a Milano, sai!
> *I really didn't go to Milan, you know!*
>
> Non voglio niente (*or* nulla).
> *I don't want anything.*
>
> Non gli parlano mai.
> *They never speak to him.*
>
> Non ho visto né Giovanni né Lorenzo.
> *I saw neither John nor Lorenzo.*
>
> Mio padre non lavora piú.
> *My father no longer works.*
>
> Non ho che una sola sigaretta.
> *I have only one cigarette.*
>
> Stasera non ci vado nemmeno per lui.
> *I shall not go there tonight, not even for him.*
>
> Non potevo dirtelo perché non lo sapevo neppure.
> *I could not tell you because I didn't even know.*
>
> Non ho affatto fame.
> *I am not at all hungry.*

It will be noted in example three that **mica** is merely an intensification of **non** and is thus not translatable into English except by some adverb such as *really*, etc.

2. If the expression of negation precedes the verb, **non** is never used:

> Nessuno partirà.
> *No one will leave.*
>
> Nulla è impossibile per chi lavora sodo.
> *Nothing is impossible for him who works hard.*

Non lo so e neanche lo voglio sapere.
I don't know and don't even want to know it.

Né Giovanni né Filippo sanno scrivere.
Neither John nor Philip can write.

NOTE. Some of these expressions never appear before the verb (i.e., **non . . . che** or **non . . . piú**) so that the rule does not apply to them.

3. **Niente** is often used as an adjective meaning *no* in absolute expressions:

Niente pane, grazie.
No bread, thank you.

and is commonly used to mean *not at all* in the following type of sentence:

Grazie per avermi prestato aiuto ieri sera. – Di niente.
Thank you for having helped me yesterday. – Not at all.

B. SUFFIXES IN ITALIAN

1. Suffixes are added to Italian words to modify their meanings, and many of them refer to size or to quality. Those which tend to enlarge an object we call augmentatives, those that tend to diminish it we call diminutives.

2. The important augmentative suffixes are **-one, -otto, -ozzo, -occio.**

(a) **-one** emphasizes sheer physical size and, except in a few cases, changes a feminine noun into a masculine one:

un libro (*a book*)   un librone (*a huge book*)
una donna (*a woman*)   un donnone (*a huge woman*)

With adjectives and nouns which have both masculine and feminine forms, a form **-ona** is used to prevent confusion:

una ragazza (*a girl*)   una ragazzona (*a big girl*)
una vecchia (*an old woman*) una vecchiona (*a huge old woman*)

The words **ragazzone** (*m.*) and **vecchione** (*m.*) can thus be kept exclusively for males.

The **-one** ending is also added to adjectives and adverbs occasionally and it strengthens the quality represented by such words:

> Come sta oggi? – Benone!
> *How are you today? – Very well indeed!*

(b) **-otto** often means *sturdy* or *strong*:

un giovane (*a youth*)   un giovanotto (*a strapping fellow*)

but it also denotes the young of some animals:

una lepre (*a hare*)   un leprotto (*a young hare*)
una tigre (*a tiger*)   un tigrotto (*a tiger cub*).

(c) **-ozzo** is rare and implies unpleasantness:

una predica (*a sermon*)   un predicozzo (*a scolding*).

(d) **-occio** is used with adjectives to mean *rather*:

> È un uomo grassoccio.
> *He is a fattish man.*

3. Diminutives are far more numerous and can be subdivided into pure diminutives and endearments, although distinctions cannot always be clearly drawn.

(a) Simple diminutives:

il gatto – il gattino	*cat – kitten*
il naso – il nasetto	*nose – small nose*
il giovane–il giovanetto	*youth – lad*
il vento – il venticello	*wind – breeze*
il fiume – il fiumicino	*river – stream*
il figlio – il figliuolo	*son – child*
la pastora – la pastorella	*shepherdess– young shepherdess*
la mano – la manina	*hand – small hand*
la casa – la casetta	*house – cottage*
la campana–il campanello	*bell – door-bell*.

It will be noticed from the last example that some feminine nouns have masculine diminutives. However, no rule can be laid down for such cases and each one must be memorized.

(b) Endearing diminutives:

la casa – la casina	*the house – the pretty little house*

Maria – Mariuccia   *Mary – dear little Mary*
la vecchia – la vecchierella   *old woman – dear old woman*

But **-uccia** is often derogatory with a common noun:

la casa – la casuccia   *the house – the poor house*

It should also be remembered that some diminutives combine the ideas of smallness and endearment, so that **la manina,** for example, often means a pretty, as well as a tiny, hand.

(c) Diminutives are sometimes attached to adjectives or adverbs and give a variety of meanings:

povero – poveretto   *poor – poor* (expressing sympathy)
facile – facilino   *easy – very easy*
bene – benino   *good – quite good*

4. A number of derogatory endings exist in addition to **-uccia** with a common noun which we have already mentioned:

(a) **-accio, -a** means *wicked*:

ragazzo – ragazzaccio   *boy – wicked boy*
tempo – tempaccio   *weather – foul weather*
donna – donnaccia   *woman – wicked woman*
parola – parolaccia   *word – swear word*
roba – robaccia   *stuff – rubbish.*

(b) **-astro** often means *a quack* or *a fake*:

medico – medicastro   *doctor – quack*
poeta – poetastro   *poet – poetaster*

but it also indicates relationship:

fratello – fratellastro   *brother – half-brother*
sorella – sorellastra   *sister – half-sister.*

(c) **-aglia** means *the dregs of*:

gente – gentaglia   *people – rabble*
plebe – plebaglia   *plebs – scum*

but also something widespread or large:

bosco – boscaglia   *wood – woody district*
muro – muraglia   *wall – long high wall.*

5. Sometimes two or more endings are added to a noun to express certain shades of meaning:

| casa – casettina | *house – delightful little house* |
| pesce – pesciolino | *fish – pretty little fish.* |

6. **-ame, -ime** and **-ume** denote quantities of material or stuff:

rottame	*wreckage*
ferrame	*scrap iron*
mangime	*chicken feed*
becchime	*birdseed*
biancume	*white stuff*
nerume	*black stuff*
sudiciume	*filth.*

All nouns formed with these endings are masculine.

7. **-ata** usually means *a blow with* or *a something full of*; but it also has other meanings:

un piede – una pedata	*foot – kick*
un gomito – una gomitata	*elbow – dig of the elbow*
bocca – boccata	*mouth – mouthful*
mano – manata	*hand – handful*
cucchiaio – cucchiaiata	*spoon – spoonful*
telefono – telefonata	*telephone – telephone call*
riso – risata	*laugh – burst of laughter*
giorno – giornata	*day – length of a day*
mattina – mattinata	*morning – matinée* (or *morning*)
sera – serata	*evening – evening's entertainment* (or *evening*).

8. Typical adjectival suffixes are:

verde – verdognolo	*green – greenish*
giallo – giallognolo	*yellow – yellowish*
rosso – rossiccio	*red – reddish*
bianco – biancastro	*white – whitish.*

9. Some verbs also take diminutives:

cantare – canterellare	*to sing – to hum*
rubare – rubacchiare	*to steal – to pilfer*
saltare – salterellare	*to jump – to hop*
trottare – trotterellare	*to trot – to mince*
piangere – piagnucolare	*to weep – to snivel*
parlare – parlottare	*to talk – to chatter.*

NOTE. It is not possible to attach suffixes to nouns, adjectives or verbs indiscriminately in Italian. The student is advised never to use a suffix with any word unless he has come across it before.

VOCABULARY

albicocca	*apricot*	melone (*m.*)	*melon*
allietare	*to gladden*	mensa	*table*
autunno	*autumn*	minestra	*thick stew*
ben di Dio	*God's abundance*	minestrone (*m.*)	*vegetable stew*
bollito	*boiled food*	muscolo	*mussel*
bolognese	*Bolognese*	sott'olio	*in oil*
budino	*pudding*	ostrica	*oyster*
cacciagione (*f.*)	*game*	pagina	*page*
carciofo	*artichoke*	pesca	*peach*
castello	*castle*	piccante	*piquant*
categoria	*category*	piemontese	*Piedmontese*
cetriolo	*cucumber*	pollo	*chicken, poultry*
ciambella	*small cake*		
ciliegia	*cherry*	prugna	*plum*
cipollina	*small onion, shallot*	quanto a	*as for*
		raggruppare	*to group, divide*
compiuto, -a	*complete*		
concernere	*to concern*	ragú	*ragoût*
contenere	*to contain*	riccio	*sea-urchin*
contorno	*garnishing*	richiedere	*to require*
crema	*custard*	salume (*m.*)	*salted pork-meat*
estate (*f.*)	*summer*		
fritto, -a	*fried*	a seconda di	*according to*
frutto di mare	*shell-fish*	sí che	*so that*
fungo	*mushroom*	sottaceti	*pickles*
gambero	*crayfish*	stufato	*stew*
gamma	*gamut, range*	svariato, -a	*varied*
giardiniera	*mixed pickles*	tagliatelle (*f. plur.*)	*tagliatelle*
infinito, -a	*infinite*		
inverno	*winter*	toscano, -a	*Tuscan*
lista	*list*	vasto, -a	*vast*
luogo	*place*	verdura	*greens, vegetables*
maionese (*f.*)	*mayonnaise*		
manzo	*beef*		

LA CUCINA ITALIANA

È molto difficile parlare compiutamente della cucina italiana poiché le sue specialità sono cosí immense e cosí varie a seconda dei luoghi, che una semplice lista richiede parecchie pagine.

Gli antipasti variano dal prosciutto cotto a quello crudo serviti con melone, ai frutti di mare, quali[1] ostriche, ricci, muscoli, oppure gamberi in maionese, ai salumi di ogni tipo, ai carciofi e funghi sott'olio, ai vari sottaceti, come cipolline e cetrioli o a quell'insalata di sottaceti chiamata giardiniera.

Le minestre si dividono in tre grandi categorie, le minestre in brodo, i minestroni e le pastasciutte. Le minestre in brodo hanno il brodo di carne di bue o di pollo e contengono svariatissimi tipi di pasta. I minestroni sono fatti di verdura e possono contenere o no pasta, mentre le pastasciutte sono cosí dette perché la minestra è al sugo o al ragú. I tipi piú noti sono gli spaghetti napoletani al sugo di pomodoro e le tagliatelle bolognesi al ragú di carne.

I secondi piatti sono infiniti. Ma i vari tipi si possono raggruppare in bolliti, stufati, arrosti e fritti molto spesso accompagnati da un contorno d'insalata. Oltre a secondi di carne di bue, manzo[2] o vitello, si possono avere vari secondi di pesce o cacciagione. L'Italia produce una vasta gamma di formaggi, da quelli dolci a quelli piccanti. Quanto alla frutta quasi ogni tipo di frutto cresce in Italia, sí che essa allieta la mensa tutto l'anno, dalle ciliege in aprile alle albicocche, alle pesche, alle prugne in estate, all'uva e ai fichi in autunno, alle mele e alle pere in inverno.

Per ciò che concerne i dolci si può dire che ogni famiglia ha la sua specialità, dalle creme ai budini, alle ciambelle. E per tanto ben di Dio ci sono moltissimi vini, dal Barbera alla Freisa e al Grignolino, piemontesi, al Chianti toscano, al vino dei Castelli Romani, al Marsala della Sicilia. Per queste ragioni ed altre, la cucina italiana è famosa in tutto il mondo.

NOTES
¹ **quali** : *Quale* is used without the article to mean *such as* and often replaces *come* in this sense.

² **manzo** is actually a calf after it has shed its milk teeth and its meat would be regarded as beef in England. In Italy, however, a distinction is maintained between *manzo* and *carne di bue*.

EXERCISES

A. Translate into Italian:
1. I have no cherries.
2. Neither John nor Charles will come to town with us this afternoon.
3. I've really not decided to leave for Italy, you know.
4. He can no longer continue to (*a*) help us.
5. We shall never speak to him about it.
6. I have only one (*un solo*) match left.
7. No ham, thank you.
8. I have had nothing to eat today.
9. No one shall go to the cinema tonight.
10. Thank you for having written to him for me. — Not at all.
11. I have never thought of (*a*) this.
12. Nothing is difficult if one works hard.
13. He hasn't even written to me.

B. Translate the following expressions into Italian by using suffixes:
A big old man; a good scolding; six enormous books; a pile of white stuff; a sturdy youth; a pretty little house; a breeze; two small kittens; a pretty little hand; a fattish woman; quite good; a wicked girl; a swear word; a half-brother; a pretty little fish; poor fellow; bird-seed; yellowish books; a spoonful of sugar; a peal of laughter; scrap iron; rabble; a woody district; those two have been chattering for a long time.

C. Answer the following questions in Italian:
1. Perché è difficile parlare compiutamente della cucina italiana?
2. Che cos'è l'antipasto?
3. In quante categorie si dividono le minestre?
4. Contengono sempre pasta i minestroni?
5. Quali specie di formaggio produce l'Italia?
6. Quali tipi di pastasciutta sono ben noti?

7. Che frutta mangiano gli Italiani in inverno?
8. Quali sono le regioni famose per il vino?
9. Con che cosa si mangia un piatto fritto?
10. Quando vengono le pesche e le albicocche in Italia?

D. Translate into Italian:

Charles and Anthony decide to go on a gastronomic tour (*fare un giro gastronomico*) of Italy. They first visit Bologna since this town is famous for its kitchen and they go into a restaurant and order (*ordinare*) a large meal. As an hors-d'œuvre they take tagliatelle since the waiter (*cameriere*) tells them that they are very good and they also buy some Chianti. As a second dish they decide to take roast veal and, while Charles orders a garnishing of marrows, Anthony takes a lettuce (*lattuga*) salad. They both like Gorgonzola cheese and order two slices, then, as a sweet, they have peaches because they are not dear in Italy. The bill (*il conto*) for their meal is three thousand lire.

E. Give a description of a meal in an English restaurant.

A. THE PAST DEFINITE OF IRREGULAR VERBS

1. Irregular past definites have three irregular forms only: the 1st person singular, the 3rd person singular and the 3rd person plural. The three other forms are regular and they are formed by attaching the past definite endings to the stem of the infinitive of the verb.

2. Italian irregular verbs can be generally divided into groups:
   (a) Those that change their radical vowel (1) without a consonant doubling, (2) with a consonant doubling:

   (1) *Without consonant doubling*

FARE *to do*	VEDERE *to see*
feci	vidi
facesti	vedesti
fece	vide
facemmo	vedemmo
faceste	vedeste
fecero	videro

   (2) *With consonant doubling*

SAPERE *to know*	ROMPERE *to break*
seppi	ruppi
sapesti	rompesti
seppe	ruppe
sapemmo	rompemmo
sapeste	rompeste
seppero	ruppero

Verbs conjugated in a similar way to the first examples are: **fondere** (to melt) – **fusi, fondesti, fuse,** *etc.*; **mettere** (to put) – **misi, mettesti, mise,** *etc.*; **redimere** (to redeem) – **redensi, redimesti, redense,** *etc.* Verbs similar to the second examples are:

condurre (to lead) – **condussi, conducesti, con-
dusse,** *etc.*; **dirigere** (to direct) – **diressi, dirigesti,
diresse,** *etc.*; **redigere** (to draw up) – **redassi,
redigesti, redasse,** *etc.*

The verbs **stare** and **dare** are both exceptions in
that they keep their modified radical throughout the
conjugation of the tense:

DARE *to give*	STARE *to be, stand*
diedi (detti)	stetti
desti	stesti
diede (dette)	stette
demmo	stemmo
deste	steste
diedero (dettero)	stettero

(b) Many irregular verbs double a consonant without
changing their radical vowel:

VOLERE *to want*	CONOSCERE *to know*	CADERE *to fall*
volli	conobbi	caddi
volesti	conoscesti	cadesti
volle	conobbe	cadde
etc.	*etc.*	*etc.*

Verbs conforming to this pattern are: **crescere** (to
grow, increase) – **crebbi, crescesti, crebbe,** *etc.*;
piovere (to rain) – **piovve**; **tenere** (to hold) – **tenni,
tenesti, tenne,** *etc.*; **venire** (to come) – **venni,
venisti, venne,** *etc.*

(c) Change of consonant to **-si** without a change of
radical:

CHIUDERE *to shut*	CORRERE *to run*	RISPONDERE *to reply*
chiusi	corsi	risposi
chiudesti	corresti	rispondesti
chiuse	corse	rispose
etc.	*etc.*	*etc.*

There are many verbs conforming to this pattern: **accendere** (to light) – **accesi, accendesti, accese,** *etc.*; **cogliere** (to gather) – **colsi, cogliesti, colse,** *etc.*; **porre** (to place, put) – **posi, ponesti, pose,** *etc.*; **scendere** (to go down) – **scesi, scendesti, scese,** *etc.*; **spegnere** (to extinguish) – **spensi, spegnesti, spense,** *etc.*; **spendere** (to spend) – **spesi, spendesti, spese,** *etc.*; **valere** (to be worth) – **valsi, valesti, valse,** *etc.*; **vincere** (to win) – **vinsi, vincesti, vinse,** *etc.*; **volgere** (to turn) – **volsi, volgesti, volse,** *etc.,* *etc.*

(d) Change of consonant to **-ssi**:

DIRE *to say*	SCRIVERE *to write*	MUOVERE *to move*
dissi	scrissi	mossi
dicesti	scrivesti	movesti
disse	scrisse	mosse
etc.	*etc.*	*etc.*

Verbs conforming to this pattern are: **concedere** (to concede) – **concessi, concedesti, concesse,** *etc.*; **cuocere** (to cook) – **cossi, cuocesti, cosse,** *etc.*; **percuotere** (to strike) – **percossi, percuotesti, percosse,** *etc.*; **reggere** (to rule, support) – **ressi, reggesti, resse,** *etc., etc.*

(e) Verbs adding the suffix **-qui**:

PIACERE *to please*	NASCERE *to be born*
piacqui	nacqui
piacesti	nascesti
piacque	nacque
etc.	*etc.*

An important verb belonging to this group is **tacere** (to be silent).

3. Some verbs have both strong and weak past definites:

      aprire (*to open*) – aprii (apersi)
      bere (*to drink*) – bevei (bevvi)

soffrire (*to suffer*) – soffrii (soffersi).

The tendency is for the irregular forms to die out in the modern language.

4. The past definites of the more important irregular verbs are included in the list at the back of the book.

B. THE PAST GERUND

1. The past gerund is formed by combining the present gerunds of **avere** or **essere** with the past participle of the verb:

TROVARE	VENDERE	FINIRE
avendo trovato	avendo venduto	avendo finito
(*having found*)	(*having sold*)	(*having finished*)

ANDARE	ESSERE	LAVARSI
essendo andato, -a	essendo stato, -a	essendosi lavato, -a
(*having gone*)	(*having been*)	(*having washed*)

2. The past gerund is used to translate the English perfect participle (i.e., having found, sold, *etc.*). It is distinguishable from the present gerund in that it expresses an action which is in the past with relation to the main clause:

Avendo comprato l'orologio, uscí dal negozio.
Having bought the watch, he left the shop.

Essendo partiti i miei amici, cominciai a studiare.
My friends having left, I began to study.

Avendo capito che non venivano, andai a dormire.
Having understood that they were not coming, I went to bed.

NOTE. Unlike the present gerund, the past gerund often has a subject of its own (see the second example) and does not then refer to the subject of the main clause.

3. The absolute construction with the past participle very often replaces the past gerund both in speech and in writing:

Comprato l'orologio, uscí dal negozio.
Partiti gli amici, cominciai a studiare.

The past particle in these cases agrees with the accompanying noun or nouns.

VOCABULARY

aggirarsi su	to average about	mese (m.)	month
apprestarsi a	to prepare for	metodo	method
coltivabile	cultivable	mietitura	reaping, harvesting
concime (m.)	manure, fertilizer	milione (m.)	million
		ondeggiare	to wave
condurre a termine	to bring to an end	ottanta	eighty
		passato	past
duplicare	to double	proporzionato, -a	proportional
durare	to last		
fatica	effort, fatigue	quantità	quantity
faticoso, -a	tiring, wearying	quintale (m.)	100 kilos
		raccolto	crop
frumento	wheat	regione (f.)	region
gettito	yield	risparmiare	to spare, save
giugno	June	scala	scale
grazie a	thanks to	sino a	up to
impiego	use, employment	solere	to be accustomed
maggiore	greater	svolgere	to carry out
media	average	triplicare	to triple

LA MIETITURA

La maggior parte del terreno coltivabile in Italia è riservata al frumento. Il Piemonte, la Lombardia e l'Emilia sono le regioni italiane che danno il maggior gettito di grano e quando giugno arriva, quando i campi ondeggiano biondeggianti, i contadini si apprestano alla mietitura. Nel passato tutto il lavoro della mietitura era svolto a mano. I contadini solevano iniziare il lavoro nelle primissime ore del giorno, e, tolto qualche breve intervallo nelle ore più calde, procedevano sino a tarda notte. Era un lavoro faticosissimo — come si può facilmente immaginare — e durava almeno un mese. Inoltre, la quantità del raccolto non era mai proporzionata alle fatiche spese. Oggi invece, grazie all'impiego delle macchine, il lavoro è condotto a termine in un periodo di tempo abbastanza breve, ed al contadino vengono risparmiate le piú gravi fatiche. L'uso dei concimi su larga scala fatto con metodi razionali, ha inoltre contribuito a duplicare, ed a volte triplicare, la quantità del raccolto. La media annuale di frumento si aggira per l'Italia sugli ottanta milioni di[1] quintali.

NOTE

[1] **sugli ottanta milioni di**: *Su* is often used with figures to express an approximation. It should also be noted that *milione*, being a noun, requires *di* before the noun denoting the quantity measured.

EXERCISES

A. Insert in the following sentences the past definite of the verbs given in brackets:
1. Il contadino (vedere) due cavalli nel campo.
2. Egli non (sapere) che fare.
3. Io non (volere) andare in città con lui.
4. Giovanni e Carlo (correre) giú per la strada.
5. Mi (rispondere) di sí, ma (dire) di non poter venire questa settimana.
6. Non gli (piacere) venire con noi.
7. Quando (arrivare) i poliziotti, ci (essere) un fuggi fuggi generale.
8. I due grandi uomini (nascere) in Italia.
9. Giovanni me ne (scrivere) l'anno scorso.
10. Mi (dire) che non solevano lavorare di mattina.

B. Translate into Italian:
1. The harvest having been finished, we left for the town.
2. Having congratulated him, we asked him what he was hoping to do next year.
3. Having used machines on a large scale, we sold our wheat cheaply (*a buon mercato*).
4. Having tripled the yield of corn, we were very happy.
5. The yield, having averaged about 80 million quintals for three years, suddenly fell to sixty (*sessanta*) million quintals.

C. Answer the following questions in Italian:

    1. Perché è piú facile lavorare in campagna adesso?

    2. Su quale cifra s'aggira la media annuale di frumento in Italia?

    3. Nel passato quanto tempo ci voleva per fare la mietitura?

    4. A che ora cominciava la mietitura nel passato?

    5. Fin quando lavoravano?

    6. Che cosa ha fatto triplicare il raccolto recentemente?

    7. Che cosa s'apprestano a fare i contadini in giugno?

    8. Quali sono le regioni italiane che danno il maggior gettito di frumento?

    9. Come era svolta la mietitura nel passato?

    10. Cosa fanno i contadini nelle ore piú calde?

D. Translate into Italian:

Mr. Tozzi took the family to the country during the harvesting. The peasants were singing very happily in the fields and the sun was shining (*brillare*). The children wanted to help the workers but the work had been almost completely finished before their arrival. Towards evening the wind began to blow (*tirare vento*) and Mrs. Tozzi decided it was time to go home. As they went along the road in the car they could see the ripe corn swaying in the wind. When they reached home, they all agreed (*essere d'accordo*) that the trip (*la gita*) had done them all good.

E. Translate into Italian:

    1. John got out of the carriage.

    2. Charles went down (*per*) the road.

    3. Barbara went up (*per*) the stairs.

    4. Philip came down (from) the mountain.

    5. Giovanna set out along the road.

A. THE PRESENT AND PERFECT SUBJUNCTIVE

1. The present subjunctive of regular verbs is as follows:

TROVARE	VENDERE	FINIRE
trovi	venda	finisca
trovi	venda	finisca
trovi	venda	finisca
troviamo	vendiamo	finiamo
troviate	vendiate	finiate
trovino	vendano	finiscano

The **dormire** type verbs of the third conjugation are conjugated in the present subjunctive without the inchoative -isc- of the **finire** type verbs.

2. The present subjunctive of **avere** and **essere** is as follows:

AVERE	ESSERE
abbia	sia
abbia	sia
abbia	sia
abbiamo	siamo
abbiate	siate
abbiano	siano

3. A large number of verbs have irregular present subjunctives and some of the more important ones are as follows:

andare: vada, vada, vada, andiamo, andiate, vadano.
dare: dia, dia, dia, diamo, diate, diano.
dovere: debba, debba, debba, dobbiamo, dobbiate, debbano.
morire: muoia, muoia, muoia, moriamo, moriate, muoiano.
parere: paia, paiano.
potere: possa, possa, possa, possiamo, possiate, possano.
rimanere: rimanga, rimanga, rimanga, rimaniamo, rimaniate, rimangano.

sapere: sappia, sappia, sappia, sappiamo, sappiate, sappiano.
stare: stia, stia, stia, stiamo, stiate, stíano.
tenere: tenga, tenga, tenga, teniamo, teniate, tengano.
venire: venga, venga, venga, veniamo, veniate, vengano.
volere: voglia, voglia, voglia, vogliamo, vogliate, vogliano.

Most irregular present subjunctives are formed from the stem of the first person singular, present indicative. The present subjunctives of other irregular verbs may be found in the list of irregular verbs given on pp. 330-42.

4. The perfect subjunctive is formed by using the present subjunctive of **avere** or **essere** with the past participle of the verb. There are no exceptions to this rule.

TROVARE	ACCORGERSI	VENIRE

abbia trovato, *etc.* mi sia accorto, -a, *etc.* sia venuto, -a, *etc.*

B. *SI* AS AN INDEFINITE PRONOUN

1. As has already been pointed out (see Lesson XII A), **si** is really a reflexive and not an indefinite pronoun. Consequently, it requires a plural verb when the direct object is plural in English, because this direct object becomes a subject in Italian:

> Si vede ch'egli ha ragione.
> *One can see he is right.*

but: Si vendono mele in questo negozio.
> *Apples are sold in this shop.*
> (*One sells apples in this shop.*)

2. In the past tense it requires the auxiliary **essere**:

> S'è detto che Roberto è molto intelligente.
> *It is said that Robert is very intelligent.*

> Giovanni, come s'è visto, è campione di tennis.
> *John, as has been seen, is tennis champion.*

3. With reflexive verbs, **si** is not repeated but is replaced by **ci**:

> Quando ci si avvicina al mare, l'aria diventa più fresca.
> *When one approaches the sea, the air becomes fresher.*

4. As already pointed out (Lesson X A), all other pronoun except **ne** and **loro** come before **si** in this indefinite sense

> Lo si dice in paese.
> *They are saying it in the village.*

but:
> Se ne parla in tutta la città.
> *It is spoken of in the whole town.*

NOTE. A Tuscan expression combines **si** with **noi** to express *we*, but it should be used sparingly both in writing and in speech:

> Noi si dice che egli ha torto.
> *We say that he is wrong.*

5. **Si** requires a plural adjective after verbs conjugated with **essere** in their compound tenses and also after **essere** itself:

> Si è partiti di buon'ora.
> *We set out early.*

> Bisogna viaggiare quando si è giovani.
> *One must travel when one is young.*

This is also the case with an infinitive:

> È difficile stare allegri quando si ha mal di denti.
> *It is difficult to be cheerful when one has toothache.*

But it is *not* the case with verbs which, when not used with **si**, take **avere** as their auxiliary:

> Si è dormito bene stanotte, non è vero?
> *We slept well last night, didn't we?*

VOCABULARY

albero	tree	migliore	best
carota	carrot	minuto	minute
cavolfiore (*m.*)	cauliflower	nocciola	hazel-nut
cavolo	cabbage	noce (*f.*)	walnut
cipolla	onion	orto	garden
curare	to look after	paradiso	paradise
dedicare	to dedicate	passatempo	pastime
energia	energy	passeggiare	to walk
immaginabile	imaginable	passione (*f.*)	passion
insomma	in short	pensionato, -a	pensioner
mandorla	almond	prezzemolo	parsley
in meno di	in less than	qua e là	here and there

quasi (*conj.*)	*as if*	sicuro, -a	*sure*
sedano	*celery*	sparso, -a	*scattered*
sentiero	*path*	susina	*plum*

NELL'ORTO

L'orto del signor Antonio Gallinotti non è molto distante dal paese; ci si arriva in meno di quindici minuti. Fu cosí che un pomeriggio Giuseppe ed io andammo[1] a farvi una visita. Eravamo sicuri che il signor Gallinotti sarebbe stato molto felice ed orgoglioso di mostrarci quello che riteneva 'il piú bell'orto del paese'.

In verità l'orto era molto ben tenuto. Si sarebbe detto che non mancava un solo prodotto: dall'insalata alle carote, dai peperoni ai sedani, dalle cipolle alle patate, dai pomodori ai cavolfiori, dai cavoli al prezzemolo; insomma, tutta la verdura immaginabile. Ed era uno spettacolo notare con quanta attenzione il signor Gallinotti curava il suo orto. Vi dedicava tutte le sue migliori energie. Quello doveva essere il passatempo che — come spesso egli sosteneva — ogni buon pensionato avrebbe dovuto scegliere.

Ma non solo all'orto andavano le sue preferenze; egli aveva infatti una gran passione anche per gli alberi da frutta. E qua e là sparsi per l'orto, si potevano osservare le piú diverse qualità di alberi: di mele, di pere, di susine, di albicocche, di fichi,[2] di ciliegie, di noci, di nocciole. Si sarebbe detto un vero paradiso terrestre.

Il lavoro certo non mancava al signor Gallinotti, ma egli non pareva sentire la fatica; anzi, alla sera, dopo una frugale cena, soleva ritornare e passeggiare per il sentiero del suo orto quasi per voler[3] godere della buona giornata di lavoro che vi aveva dedicato.

NOTES
[1] **Giuseppe ed io:** If there are two or more subjects to a verb and one of these subjects is a first or second person pronoun, the verb must be put into the person corresponding to that pronoun.

² **di fichi . . . :** In general the names of fruits are feminine in Italian while the names of fruit-trees are masculine: *il melo –
la mela, il pero – la pera, il susino – la susina,* etc., but both the fig and the fig-tree are masculine. The same word is used to signify the two things.

³ **quasi per voler :** Provided that the person of the verb does not change, one should use infinitives instead of subordinate clauses to express quite complicated ideas in Italian. Here the translation would be: . . . *as if he wished to enjoy* . . . ; similarly one could translate the sentence: *He believed he could do all the work himself,* as follows: *Credeva di poter fare tutto il lavoro da sé.*

EXERCISES

A. Translate into Italian:
1. One would have said (it was) the loveliest garden in (*di*) the land.
2. One gets up early in summer to enjoy the sunlight.
3. Houses are not built in a day.
4. It is easy to seem pleased when things are going right.
5. At first (*dapprima*) one does not notice that one has made a mistake.
6. One hurries to catch the train in the morning.
7. We always say he is wrong.
8. It has been written about in (*su*) the papers.
9. Robert, as we have seen, is a good football player.
10. As one approached, the sea appeared to change colour.

B. Insert the right form of the present or perfect subjunctive of the verbs given in brackets in the following sentences:
1. Non vuole ch'io (alzarsi) di buon'ora.
2. Non so dove (andare) il signor Gallinotti.
3. Il professore ordina che i ragazzi (smettere) di fare gli sciocchi.
4. Cerco un ragazzo che (sapere) suonare il violino.
5. Temo che lui (essere) scontento di me.
6. Non è vero che lei (avere) sempre ragione.
7. Non crederanno che (venire) a casa mia un uomo importante come lui.
8. Qualunque cosa (dire), non ho intenzione di ascoltarlo.
9. Non credo che essi (potere) andare avanti da soli.
10. Non diciamo che egli l'(avere) perduto.

C. Translate into Italian:

John is a very good gardener (*giardiniere*). He likes to spend his time in the kitchen garden and grows (*far crescere*) all sorts of vegetables there. He says that every schoolboy ought to have a hobby and gardening (*giardinaggio*) is the one which he prefers. In the past he has grown many fruit-trees and he has some of all kinds, from the apple-tree to the cherry-tree, from the pear-tree to the walnut-tree. These trees bear many fruits and he hopes to plant (*piantare*) vines (*vite* (*f.*)) next year. He and I are so fond of grapes. After supper, he often strolls along the garden path as if he wants to enjoy the good day's work he has put into it.

D. Answer the following questions in Italian:

1. Il signor Gallinotti abita in città?
2. Che cosa si dice del suo orto?
3. Quali specie di verdura ci sono nell'orto del signor Gallinotti?
4. Che cosa soleva fare dopo cena?
5. Quale passatempo dovrebbe avere ogni pensionato, secondo il signor Gallinotti?
6. Manca il lavoro al signor Gallinotti?
7. Perché non pareva sentire la fatica?
8. Che cosa pare un vero paradiso terrestre?
9. Chi è andato a fargli una visita?
10. Che cosa è sparso per l'orto?

E. Describe your own garden in Italian.

A. THE IMPERFECT AND PLUPERFECT SUBJUNCTIVE

1. The imperfect subjunctive is formed by adding the imperfect subjunctive endings to the stem of the infinitive:

TROVARE	VENDERE	FINIRE
trovassi	vendessi	finissi
trovassi	vendessi	finissi
trovasse	vendesse	finisse
trovassimo	vendessimo	finissimo
trovaste	vendeste	finiste
trovassero	vendessero	finissero

2. The imperfect subjunctives of **avere** and **essere** are as follows:

AVERE	ESSERE
avessi	fossi
avessi	fossi
avesse	fosse
avessimo	fossimo
aveste	foste
avessero	fossero

It will be noted that the imperfect subjunctive of **essere** is irregular. Other irregular imperfect subjunctives are: **dare** (to give) — **dessi, dessi, desse, dessimo, deste, dessero**; and **stare** (to be, stand) — **stessi, stessi, stesse, stessimo, steste, stessero.**

NOTE: All verbs with contracted infinitives revert to their original long forms before the imperfect subjunctive endings are added: e.g. **fare** (to do, make) – **facessi,** *etc.*

3. The pluperfect subjunctive is formed with the imperfect subjunctive of **avere** or **essere** and the past participle of the verb:

TROVARE	ACCORGERSI	VENIRE
avessi trovato, *etc.*	mi fossi accorto, -a, *etc.*	fossi venuto, -a, *etc.*

There are no exceptions in this tense.

B. SOME USES OF THE SUBJUNCTIVE

1. As a polite imperative:

> Mi dia quel libro, per favore.
> *Give me that book, please.*

> Mi mostri il quadro che ha comprato.
> *Show me the picture you have bought.*

Since this type of imperative is in fact a finite verb, the pronouns (with the exception of **loro**) precede it in the normal way.

2. In subordinate clauses following commands:

> Digli che venga a casa mia.
> *Tell him to come to my house.*

> Ha ordinato ch'io ti accompagni alla stazione.
> *He has ordered me to accompany you to the station.*

3. In subordinate clauses after verbs expressing desire or emotion:

> Volle che si desse da mangiare ai polli.
> *He wanted the chickens to be fed.*

> Mi dispiace che egli non venga.
> *I am sorry that he is not coming.*

> Sono contento che tu sia venuto ad incontrarmi.
> *I am pleased you have come to meet me.*

> È un peccato che tu debba tornare a casa ora.
> *It is a pity you have to return home now.*

4. With verbs expressing preference, possibility or opinion:

È meglio che tu rimanga qui da noi.
It is better for you to stay here with us.

È mai possibile che Giovanni sia partito senza salutarmi?
Is it possible that John has left without saying goodbye to me?

Penso che tu abbia ragione.
I think you are right.

Credo che non ci si possa andare d'inverno.
I think one cannot go there in winter.

NOTE. Sometimes, however, if one is absolutely sure of one's facts, the future indicative is used with verbs expressing opinion:

Io credo che Giovanni verrà domani.
I believe John will come tomorrow.

5. After verbs of doubt, ignorance and denial:

Dubito che egli mi abbia spedito quella lettera ieri.
I doubt whether he sent me that letter yesterday.

Non so se abbia ragione Lei o mio fratello.
I don't know whether you are right or my brother.

Nego che mio figlio abbia fatto ciò.
I deny that my son did that.

6. After verbs of appearing,† permission, fearing and preventing:

Sembrava che avesse messo tutto a soqquadro.
It seemed he had turned everything upside down.

Non permetto che egli vada in Italia quest'anno.
I won't allow him to go to Italy this year.

Ho paura (*or* Temo) che essi si siano smarriti.
I am afraid they have got lost.

Impedí che andassero in chiesa.
He prevented them from going to church.

7. After many impersonal verbs:

Pare che egli dorma.
It seems he is asleep.

† *Che* is often omitted after these verbs:
Sembrava avesse messo tutto a soqquadro.

Bisogna che io vada subito a casa.
I must (it is necessary for me to) go home at once.

NOTE. One should avoid using a subordinate clause if the subject of the sentence does not change:

Crede di poter andare in Italia l'anno prossimo.
He believes he will be able to go to Italy next year.

Strada facendo, mi disse subito di voler tornare a casa.
On the way, he suddenly said to me that he wanted to go back home.

8. The subjunctive is very often used in indirect questions but it is not always obligatory:

Chiede dove vadano (vanno) i due ragazzi.
He asks where the two boys are going.

Mi domandò come avessi risolto il problema.
He asked me how I had solved the problem.

9. In indirect statements only doubtful observations require the subjunctive. Doubt may be expressed in the following ways:

(a) By a negative:

Non dico che non sia un buon ragazzo.
I am not saying he is not a good boy.

(b) By an interrogative:

Chi ha chiesto se tuo fratello potesse accompagnarci?
Who asked whether your brother could come with us?

(c) By an indefinite pronoun:

Si dice che sia un uomo geniale.
They say he is a brilliant man.

NOTE. When, however, no doubt exists, the indicative is obligatory:

Sono sicuro che Giovanni ci accompagnerà a teatro domani.

I am sure John will accompany us to the theatre to-morrow.

10. The subjunctive is also used in certain exclamatory expressions:

Fossi pazzo! *If I were mad!*
Volesse il cielo! *Would to heaven!*
Che lavori quel fannullone! *Let that good-for-nothing work!*

VOCABULARY

affrontare	*to face*	medicamento	*medicine*
asserire	*to assert*	nervo	*nerve*
atroce	*atrocious*	polmonite (*f.*)	*pneumonia*
avventurarsi	*to venture*	prescrivere	*to prescribe*
brancolare	*to grope*	in punto di	*at death's*
buio	*dark*	morte	*door*
cancro	*cancer*	rabbrividire	*to shudder*
circa	*about*	raffreddore (*m.*)	*cold*
contrarre	*to contract*	rassegnazione	*resignation*
cuore (*m.*)	*heart*	(*f.*)	
dolore (*m.*)	*pain*	rimanere in	*to be in doubt*
dominare	*to dominate*	forse	
effetto	*effect*	schiena	*back*
filo di voce	*ghost of a*	scienza	*science*
	voice	sconfiggere	*to overcome*
finché + *subj.*	*until*	sintomo	*symptom*
indigestione (*f.*)	*indigestion*	sollievo	*relief*
infettato, -a	*infected*	somma	*sum*
influenza	*influenza*	talvolta	*sometimes*
laconico, -a	*laconic*	tentare di	*to try to*
malattia	*illness*	tubercolosi (*f.*)	*tuberculosis*
male (*m.*)	*illness*	visitare	*to examine*

UNA VISITA DEL MEDICO

La settimana scorsa il signor Lamberti cadde ammalato e, ai primi sintomi della malattia, sua moglie decise di mandare a chiamare il medico, dicendo come un semplice raffreddore trascurato possa avere talvolta effetti molto gravi per tutta una famiglia. Naturalmente, il signor Lamberti cominciò allora a pensare a tutte le malattie che avesse potuto contrarre,[1] dalla tubercolosi alla polmonite, dall'influenza al cancro. Al solo pensiero di quest'ultimo rabbrividí perché sapeva che la scienza sembra ancora brancolare nel buio e, per quanto[2] siano spese enormi somme di danaro e lunghi e pazienti studi vi siano dedicati, nulla s'è finora trovato che possa sconfiggere questo terribile male.

Mentre aspettava la visita del medico, la sua mente saltava

da una malattia all'altra ed egli finí con lo sperare di essere infettato dalla tubercolosi per paura che fosse qualcosa di peggiore.³ Rimase cosí in forse per circa una mezz'ora prima di sentire il medico che saliva in camera sua. Poi, dominando i suoi nervi, lo affrontò con rassegnazione. Disse di avere dolori dappertutto, specialmente intorno al cuore e nella schiena. Asserí che la testa gli girava ogni volta che tentava di mettersi in piedi, e che il fegato gli faceva soffrire dei dolori atroci. Infatti, soffriva di tutto e si credeva proprio in punto di morte.

Dopo averlo visitato, il medico gli prescrisse dei medicamenti e gli disse di restare a letto finché si sentisse meglio. Con un filo di voce il signor Lamberti rispose di sí e poi s'avventurò a domandare di che cosa soffriva. Con suo gran sollievo⁴ il dottore disse laconicamente: 'D'un po' d'indigestione.'

NOTES
¹ **contrarre**: The present indicative of this verb is as follows: *contraggo, contrai, contrae, contraiamo, contraete, contraggono.*
² **per quanto**: *Per* used before an adjective and followed by a subjunctive means *however.*
³ **qualcosa di peggiore**: *Qualcosa, che, niente* and *nulla* require *di* before an adjective: *Che c'è di nuovo?* (What news is there?) See Lesson XXXIX A.
⁴ **sollievo**: With expressions of emotion and surprise, the English preposition *to* is translated by *con* and the article with the possessive is omitted.

EXERCISES

A. Translate into Italian:
1. They asked me where the two boys had gone.
2. Feed (*polite form*) the chickens, please!
3. What a pity I was unable to meet you.
4. Perhaps it would be better for me to see you in town?
5. I asked him not to turn everything upside down when looking for his book.

6. I didn't say he wasn't a good man (*uomo per bene*).
7. I need to go to see the doctor tonight.
8. He had denied that we had said anything so stupid.
9. Who said he could not follow his father's trade?
10. It is not true that George is spending his holidays with us.

B. Insert the indicative or the subjunctive of the verb given in the infinitive in the following sentences:
   1. Pare che egli (avere) molto danaro.
   2. Non so da dove (venire).
   3. Credete che essi (andarsene)?
   4. Mi disse che (partire) domani mattina di buon'ora.
   5. Ordinò che i bambini non (andare) a scuola.
   6. Voleva sapere quanto io (pagare) la mia nuova macchina.
   7. Secondo lui, la nostra squadra (vincere) la coppa.
   8. Bisogna che tu gli (parlare) di ciò.
   9. Dopo che (vedere) Carlo, incontrai sua sorella.
   10. Non c'è dubbio che egli (lavorare) per me nel passato.

C. Translate into Italian:
   One day last week Mr. Lamberti felt so ill that he decided that he must call in the doctor. His wife made a telephone call (*telefonata*) to him, and he arrived a half an hour later. Meanwhile, Mr. Lamberti began to think of all those diseases from which he could be suffering and he hoped he had pneumonia for fear that he had something worse. He heard with trepidation (*trepidazione* (*f.*)) the doctor coming up to his room and he greeted him with resignation. He swore he had pains around the heart, in the back and in his stomach and was convinced he was at death's door. When he had examined him, the doctor prescribed some medicines. In a ghost of a voice, Mr. Lamberti said: 'What is the matter with me? (*Che cosa ho?*)' and the doctor replied laconically: 'A touch of indigestion.'

D. Translate into Italian:
   1. He thought he would not have been able to go to meet Charles at the station.
   2. He finished up by hoping that he would not have to take the television-set back to the shop.
   3. He did not deny having said it to him.
   4. He wrote to say he would not be here tonight.
   5. He insisted he could not swim.

E. Describe a visit to the doctor's in Italian.

A. THE COMPARISON OF ADJECTIVES

1. Comparisons of equality are expressed by means of the forms **tanto ... quanto** or **cosí ... come.** In both cases, the first element can be included or omitted at will:

> Questa ragazza non è (tanto) intelligente quanto mia sorella.
> *This girl is not as intelligent as my sister.*
> Mio fratello non è (cosí) alto come me.
> *My brother is not as tall as I am.*

When **tanto** inflects with a noun, **quanto** also inflects by attraction:

> Non ho tante penne quante Lei.
> *I haven't as many pens as you.*

NOTE. Cosí is used alone, with a gesture, to indicate size:
> Una scatola grande cosí!
> *A box as big as this!*
> Un ragazzo alto cosí!
> *A boy as tall as this!*

2. Comparisons of inequality are expressed by **piú** (more) or **meno** (less):

> La sala è piú grande che bella.
> *The room is more spacious than beautiful.*

> La sala è meno lunga che io non credessi.
> *The room is shorter than I thought.*

3. *Than* is translated by **di** before a noun, pronoun or numeral:

> Mio padre è piú alto di mio fratello.
> *My father is taller than my brother.*

> Elena è piú pigra di lei.
> *Helen is more lazy than she.*

> C'erano piú di mille persone nel cinema.
> *There were more than a thousand people in the cinema.*

However, if the noun or pronoun is governed by a preposition, or if the noun is used in a general sense (without the article) and is compared with another noun used in the same way, then **che** is required to translate *than*:

Scrivo a Giovanni piú spesso che a lui.
I write to John more often than to him.

C'è piú acqua che vino in quella bottiglia.
There is more water than wine in that bottle.

4. *Than* is always translated by **che** before an adjective, adverb, infinitive or participle:

Questa tavola è piú solida che bella.
This table is more solid than beautiful.

È meglio lavorare sodo che sprecare tempo.
It is better to work hard than waste time.

Si guadagna piú lavorando che giocando a carte.
One earns more by working than playing cards.

5. With finite verbs the following constructions are possible:

È piú vecchio di quel che credi.
È piú vecchio che tu non creda.
È piú vecchio di quanto tu possa credere.
He is older than you think.

The first example requires the indicative, while the two others require the subjunctive. The expletive **non** after a comparative should be carefully noted in the second sentence.

6. The comparative and superlative forms of adjectives are formed by placing **piú** and **il piú** respectively before the adjective itself:

felice (*happy*)   piú felice (*happier*)   il piú felice (*happiest*).

However, when a superlative adjective follows a noun, it drops the definite article:

Questo è l'edificio piú alto del mondo.
This is the highest building in the world.

The superlative is thus often identical with the comparative in Italian but the context always makes it clear which form is being used. It should be noted that the word *in* after a superlative is always translated by **di** in Italian.

7. An absolute superlative is also used in Italian and it translates the word *very* before an adjective. It is formed by adding **-issimo, -a** to the adjective after dropping its final vowel†:

Questo grattacielo è bellissimo.
This skyscraper is very beautiful.
La signora è elegantissima.
The lady is very elegant.

NOTE. Adjectives ending in -*efico* and -*ifico* are irregular:
munìfico (*munificent*) – munificentìssimo.

The adjectives **acre** (sour), **celebre** (famous), **ìntegro** (honest, upright), and **salubre** (healthy), with a few other lesser known ones, form their absolute superlatives by adding **-errimo, -a**:

Questo pianista è celeberrimo.
This pianist is very famous.

8. Some adjectives, in addition to their regular forms, have irregular comparatives and superlatives:

buono	*good*	migliore	il migliore	ottimo
cattivo	*bad*	peggiore	il peggiore	pessimo
alto	*high*	superiore	il superiore	sommo
basso	*low*	inferiore	l'inferiore	infimo
grande	*big*	maggiore	il maggiore	massimo
piccolo	*small*	minore	il minore	minimo

The irregular forms of **buono** and **cattivo** are more common than the regular forms of the comparative and superlative, but they are very often interchangeable. On the other hand, **più grande** and **più piccolo** are used in the physical sense of *larger* and *smaller*, while **maggiore** and **minore** mean *greater* and *minor* in the figurative sense. Likewise, **più alto** and **più basso** mean *higher* and

† Adjectives ending in -*co* and -*go* retain the hard sound of the consonant: ricco – ricchissimo, *etc.*

LESSON XXV   183

lower while **superiore** and **inferiore**, except with some place names, have a figurative meaning.

NOTE. **Buono** and **cattivo** also have irregular adverbs:

| bene | *well* | meglio | il meglio | benissimo |
| male | *badly* | peggio | il peggio | pessimamente |

9. **Molto** and **poco** have only irregular comparatives and relative superlatives:

| molto | *much* | piú | *more* | il piú | *most* | moltissimo *very much* |
| poco | *little* | meno | *less* | il meno | *least* | pochissimo *very little* |

B. THE PROGRESSIVE TENSES IN ITALIAN

1. Progressive tenses exist in Italian to correspond to our English progressive, *I am finding*, etc., but they are far more emphatic and therefore less used than their English equivalents. They are formed by using **stare** or **andare** with the gerund and are found only in the present and imperfect tenses:

> Sono andato in bottega a vedere ciò che egli stava facendo.
> *I went into the shop to see what he was up to.*
> Che cosa stai facendo in salotto?
> *What are you doing in the lounge?*
> Quel ragazzo va crescendo a vista d'occhio.
> *That boy is growing under your very nose.*
> Sono convinto che sta tirando le cose per le lunghe apposta.
> *I am convinced he is dragging things out on purpose.*

It should be noted from the third example that **andare** is often used when the idea of growth is conveyed.

VOCABULARY

arricchire	*to enrich*	echeggiare	*to echo*
aspettativa	*expectancy*	festa	*festivity*
botte (*f.*)	*barrel*	festoso, -a	*joyful, merry*
carro	*cart*	filare (*m.*)	*row*
cascina	*farm*	grappolo	*cluster*
collina	*hill*	illuminarsi	*to light up*

invadere	to invade	sorriso	smile
mosto	must	stridulo, -a	shrill
pigiatura	pressing	tipico, -a	typical
raccogliere	to collect	tradire	to betray
raccolta	harvest	vendemmia	grape harvest
riempire	to fill	vigna	vineyard
sopra	upon		

LA VENDEMMIA

La vendemmia è una festa molto cara al cuore degli Italiani. Quando l'autunno arriva e le colline si arricchiscono di grappoli d'uva neri e bianchi, il volto dei contadini pare illuminarsi di un bel sorriso che tradisce la gioia dell'aspettativa. E quando il giorno della raccolta viene, uomini, donne e bambini, tutti invadono le vigne. Canti festosi echeggiano per l'aria mentre gli uomini trasportano l'uva dai filari sino al carro che si trova al margine delle vigne. Nello stesso tempo le donne procedono alla raccolta dei grappoli. Certo, questo è il gran giorno tanto atteso dai bambini! Essi riempiono l'aria con le loro voci stridule e si rincorrono a vicenda lungo i filari. Naturalmente, quando vedono un bel grappolo d'uva, vi si gettano immediatamente sopra con la trepidazione che è tipica dei bambini in queste occasioni.

Poi l'uva viene trasportata nelle cascine e qui si procede alla pigiatura. Il mosto viene raccolto in grandi botti e, dopo qualche mese, il nuovo vino, fresco e frizzante, è pronto per la tavola.

EXERCISES

A. Translate into Italian:
1. He is not as big as I am.
2. The room is very wide.
3. There is more water than milk in this bottle.
4. Our house is higher than yours.
5. Summer is warmer than autumn.

6. He is the nicest person in the world.
7. We write to Philip more often than to John.
8. This problem is not as easy as I thought.
9. It is better to sell now than to lose money later.
10. He is a very famous violinist.
11. The city is lower than the countryside around it.
12. That was the best book of the year.

B. Insert the word required in the following blank spaces:
 1. Egli è meno ricco — noi.
 2. Carlo è l'uomo piú felice — mondo.
 3. Preferisco parlare a te — a lui.
 4. Ci sono piú — duecento persone in questa sala.
 5. Egli è meno uomo d'affari — affarista.
 6. Questo dramma è piú interessante di — credessi.
 7. Quel ragazzo è piú industrioso — intelligente.
 8. Carlo è piú coraggioso — te.
 9. Mi piace piú parlare — ascoltare.
 10. Giovanna non è bella — te.

C. Translate into Italian:
 1. He kept on asking me what I was doing.
 2. That baby is growing under our very noses.
 3. They stood talking for a half hour.
 4. He was writing when we entered the room.
 5. He stays there all day long (a) reading.

D. Translate into Italian:
 The wine harvest takes place (avere luogo) in the very early days of September. As it approaches, the faces of the peasants seem to light up with the joy of expectancy. Men, women and children, all go into the fields during the summer, but they prefer to climb the hills and gather the black and white grapes from the rows in the vineyards. The grapes are brought back to the farms on carts and the wine pressing follows immediately The must is collected into large barrels and, a few months later, is ready (per) to be drunk.

E. Give the comparative and superlative forms (relative and absolute) of the following adjectives:
 buono, calmo, gentile, largo, cattivo, piccolo, santo, operoso, occupato, alto, lungo, grande, molto, sudicio, basso, bello, limpido, lontano, lento, felice, rapido, costoso, piacevole, vecchio, celebre, dolce, brutto, grave.

REVISION EXERCISES (*Lesson XXI–XXV*)

1. Translate into Italian:
    1. The clerk did not send the letters either to the client or to the director.
    2. Mr. Rossi said that he had gone to the branch office only to see what they had in the warehouse.
    3. I have never understood why he dislikes me.
    4. I was told at the factory that John didn't work there any more.
    5. I really didn't go to the cinema last night, you know.
    6. Nothing is too difficult for him.
    7. The director never replied to the client's inquiry.
    8. Thank you for letting me know (*fare sapere*). – Not at all.
    9. His ideas have only given rise to difficulties in the past.
    10. Nobody has come into the office this afternoon.

2. Translate into Italian:
    a huge book; rubbish; a strapping fellow; a fattish boy; a breeze; a doorbell; a wretched little house; a dear old woman; poor fellow; foul weather; a step-sister; scrap iron; black stuff; a party; whitish; yellowish; he is snivelling; a dig with the elbow.

3. Give the past definite of the following verbs:
    sapere, stare, piovere, fondere, soffrire, cuocere, aprire, scendere, valere, bere, tacere, dare, volere, crescere, rispondere, percuotere.

4. Translate into Italian:
    1. Having broken the window, the boys fled.
    2. My friends having gone I started to write a letter.
    3. By selling on a large scale, Mr. Tosi made a great deal of money.
    4. Having chosen a sample of material I ordered the tailor to make me a suit.
    5. Having decided to visit my uncle, we caught the train for Rome.

5. Give the present and imperfect subjunctives of the following verbs:
    andare, venire, dovere, dare, comprare, dormire, tenere, stare, volere, morire, trovare, credere, spendere, amare, parere.

6. Translate into Italian:
    1. Write me a letter when you get to Naples.
    2. Tell him to whom he must write.
    3. I shall never permit you to go to Italy alone.
    4. The countryside seemed to be greener than ever.
    5. It is probable that he will never return.
    6. What a pity you will not be able to meet us at the station on our return.
    7. I don't know whether I shall be able to come or not.
    8. Who would have thought that he could say such things.
    9. I am sorry he could (*perf.*) not stay to dinner tonight.
    10. They tell me that John is very ill.

7. Translate into Italian:
    1. That skyscraper is much higher than I thought.
    2. It is much better to be silent than to say something dis agreeable (*spiacevole*) to an old friend.
    3. This book is smaller than that one.
    4. I ordered him to stop.
    5. We suspect that he stole (*rubare*) the money.
    6. He is more kindly than intelligent.
    7. He wants me to open a bigger shop in the main street.
    8. I need more books than you seem ready to give me.
    9. We hoped he would have been able to come to see us this evening.
    10. I am very happy that Mary has passed (*essere promosso a*) her examinations.

A. SEQUENCE OF TENSES IN THE INDICATIVE

1. No hard and fast rules can be given for tense sequences in Italian, but the following will serve as a guide to the student:

(a) The present and future in the main clause may be followed by the present, future or perfect tenses in subordinate clauses according to the sense:

> Gli do ciò che desidera.
> *I give him what he wants.*
> Dice che partirà domani.
> *He says he will leave tomorrow.*
> Gli darò ciò che ha chiesto.
> *I shall give him what he has asked for.*

(b) The perfect tense in the main clause can be followed by almost any other tense in the subordinate clause according to the sense:

> Ha detto che viene domani.
> *He said he is coming tomorrow.*
> Ha detto che verrà domani.
> *He said he will come tomorrow.*
> Ha detto che è venuto stamani.
> *He said he came this morning.*

(c) The other past tenses in main clauses require past tenses in subordinate clauses, once more according to the sense:

> Gli diedi ciò che voleva.
> *I gave him what he wanted.*
> Gli diedi ciò che aveva chiesto.
> *I gave him what he had asked for.*

(d) If the main verb is in any past tense and the verb in the subordinate clause is a conditional, then, contrary to English usage, the conditional perfect tense should be used in Italian:

> Disse che sarebbe partito domani.
> *He said that he would be leaving tomorrow.*

(e) A present perfect in English may well be a concealed future perfect in reported speech after a conjunction of time:

> Dice che partirà quando avrà finito il lavoro.
> *He says he will leave when he has finished the work.*

but if a similar type of sentence contains a concealed conditional, the subjunctive should be used:

> Disse che sarebbe partito quando avesse finito il lavoro.
> *He said he would leave after he had finished the work.*

B. SEQUENCE OF TENSES IN THE SUBJUNCTIVE

1. The present, imperative, or future tenses in the main clause are followed by the present or perfect subjunctive in the subordinate clause, according to the sense:

> Voglio che tu porti questa lettera alla posta.
> *I want you to take this letter to the post.*
> Digli che venga subito.
> *Tell him to come at once.*
> Non sospetterà che tu sia andato in città.
> *He will not suspect that you have gone to town.*

2. A principal verb in any past tense requires a past subjunctive in the subordinate clause, according to the sense:

> Insistette che io andassi a casa sua per cena.
> *He insisted on my going to his house for supper.*
> Per un po' di tempo ha temuto che io l'abbandonassi.
> *For a short while he thought I would abandon him.*
> Vorrei che tu mi accompagnassi alla stazione.
> *I should like you to accompany me to the station.*

NOTE. The perfect tense in the main clause may on occasion take a present instead of a past subjunctive in the subordinate clause:

Ho sempre creduto che tu sia un buon ragazzo.
I have always thought you to be a good boy.

In this example the subordinate verb actually indicates a present or future time, so that it is quite logical for it to be in the present subjunctive.

3. It should be noted that Italian is far more strict about its tenses than English:

Mi domandò se fossi stato a casa sua ieri.
He asked me if I had been (was) at his house yesterday.

There is always the danger, as can be seen from this example, of a simple past tense in English disguising a pluperfect. In Italian the pluperfect tense is the only possible tense to use in the above case.

VOCABULARY

The student will by now have acquired a sufficiently wide vocabulary to enable him to read Italian passages without the aid of detailed lists of words. Any new words appearing in the reading exercises which follow may be found in the vocabulary at the end of the book.

IL NASO STORTO

Subito mi figurai che tutti, avendone fatta mia moglie la scoperta, dovessero accorgersi di quei miei difetti corporali e altro non notare in me.

— Mi guardi il naso? — domandai tutt'a un tratto quel giorno stesso[1] a un amico che mi s'era accostato per parlarmi di non so che affare che forse gli stava a cuore.

— No, perché? — mi disse quello.

E io, sorridendo nervosamente:

— Mi pende verso destra, non vedi?

E gli imposi una ferma e attenta osservazione, come se quel difetto del mio naso fosse un irreparabile guasto sopravvenuto al congegno dell'universo.

L'amico mi guardò in prima un po' stordito; poi, certo

sospettando che avessi cosí all'improvviso e fuor di luogo cacciato fuori il discorso del mio naso perché non stimavo degno né d'attenzione né di risposta l'affare di cui mi parlava, diede una spallata e si mosse[2] per lasciarmi in asso. Lo acchiappai per un braccio, e:

— No, sai, — gli dissi — sono disposto a trattare con te quest'affare. Ma in questo momento tu devi scusarmi.

— Pensi al tuo naso?

— Non m'ero mai accorto che mi pendesse verso destra. Me n'ha fatto accorgere, questa mattina, mia moglie.

— Ah, davvero? — mi domandò allora l'amico; e gli occhi gli risero d'una incredulità ch'era anche derisione.

(LUIGI PIRANDELLO, *Uno, nessuno e cento mila*)

NOTES

[1] **stesso:** This word changes its meaning according to its position. When it precedes a noun it means *same*, when it follows a noun it means *very*. See Lesson XXXIV A.

[2] **si mosse:** Since **muovere** is a transitive verb, it must be used reflexively when it lacks a direct object.

EXERCISES

A. Translate into Italian:

   1. He said he would be leaving the country tomorrow.
   2. I shall write to John when I have finished my homework (*compito*).
   3. I did not give him what he asked for, so he left very displeased.
   4. I would have liked him to help me with my business this evening.
   5. He told me he was at my house this morning.
   6. I have heard it said that he is a man of genius.
   7. 'Write to me when you have time,' said Mr. Rossi to his friend.
   8. I had not suspected that he had visited you while I was out.
   9. I asked him how much it cost.
   10. He insisted on my accompanying him to the station after he had made his speech.

B. Insert the appropriate form of the verb given in the infinitive in the following sentences:

1. Giovanna voleva che io (rimanere) a casa stasera.
2. Mio padre impedí che mio fratello (diventare) marinaio.
3. Ho ordinato che Carlo lo (fare) da sé.
4. Loro credono che io (cadere) in mano ai banditi.
5. Temo che Barbara non (venire).
6. Peccato che tu non (essere) da noi ieri sera.
7. Non sapevo che voi (dovere) accompagnarmi a Londra.
8. Credo che ci si (avvicinare) adesso.
9. Mi dispiace che lui non (potere) venire.
10. Mi chiese dove (andare) il suo amico.

C. Translate into Italian:

One day when I was looking in the mirror, I saw that my nose hung towards the right. I was very surprised (*sorpreso*) but my wife told me that it had always been like that (*così*). The next day I had to visit a friend who intended to talk business with me. He could see that I was very worried (*preoccupato*) and asked me what it was that was worrying me. At that moment he had come near to speak to me of some business which he considered important for himself. When I told him that my nose hung towards the right he was amazed. Then, suspecting that I had brought out this observation because I did not consider the business of which he was speaking to me worthy of attention, he shrugged his shoulders and left me on the spot.

D. Translate into Italian:

1. He prevented us from going to the zoo.
2. Who would have thought that he was an Italian?
3. We ordered them to go away.
4. I am afraid you are wrong.
5. He is much older than I thought.
6. They asked me where I was going.
7. Tell him he cannot do that.
8. We asked them how they had succeeded in (*a*) solving the problem.
9. We prevented the enemy from approaching.
10. It was a pity that he was not able to come.

E. Write a few lines in Italian on some amusing incident.

PORTOFINO

WINTER IN OVINDOLI, APENNINES

A. NUMERALS

1. The cardinal and ordinal numbers are as follows in Italian:

CARDINAL

1	uno, -a	41	quarantuno
2	due	48	quarantotto
3	tre	50	cinquanta
4	quattro	51	cinquantuno
5	cinque	58	cinquantotto
6	sei	60	sessanta
7	sette	61	sessantuno
8	otto	68	sessantotto
9	nove	70	settanta
10	dieci	71	settantuno
11	undici	78	settantotto
12	dodici	80	ottanta
13	tredici	81	ottantuno
14	quattordici	88	ottantotto
15	quindici	90	novanta
16	sedici	91	novantuno
17	diciassette	98	novantotto
18	diciotto	100	cento
19	diciannove	101	centouno
20	venti		(centuno)
21	ventuno	102	centodue
22	ventidue	108	centotto
23	ventitré	120	centoventi
24	ventiquattro	180	centottanta
25	venticinque	200	duecento
26	ventisei	300	trecento
27	ventisette	800	ottocento
28	ventotto	1000	mille
29	ventinove	1001	mille (e) uno
30	trenta	1002	milledue
31	trentuno	2000	duemila
38	trentotto	1,000,000	un milione
40	quaranta	1,000,000,000	un miliardo

193

ORDINAL

1st	primo	16th	sedicesimo
2nd	secondo		decimo sesto
3rd	terzo	17th	diciassettesimo
4th	quarto		decimo settimo
5th	quinto	18th	diciottesimo
6th	sesto		decimo ottavo
7th	settimo	19th	diciannovesimo
8th	ottavo		decimo nono
9th	nono	20th	ventesimo (vigesimo)
10th	decimo	21st	ventunesimo
11th	undicesimo	22nd	ventiduesimo
	undecimo	23rd	ventitreesimo
	decimo primo	30th	trentesimo
12th	dodicesimo	40th	quarantesimo
	decimo secondo	100th	centesimo
13th	tredicesimo	101st	centunesimo
	decimo terzo		centesimo primo
14th	quattordicesimo	102nd	centoduesimo
	decimo quarto	1000th	millesimo
15th	quindicesimo		
	decimo quinto		

2. General remarks on cardinal numbers:

(a) **Uno** is the only numerical adjective to agree in number and gender with the noun it qualifies. When used as a pronoun, the long form **uno** is always necessary for the masculine singular.

(b) **Mille** has a plural **mila** and does not quite follow the usual pattern, for 1001 usually takes **e** before **uno**.

(c) **Venti, trenta,** *etc.* drop their final vowel before **uno** and **otto**. **Tre** acquires an accent in combination with any of them since the main stress then falls on the last syllable.

(d) When **milione** and **miliardo** are used as nouns they are joined to a following noun by the preposition **di** like nouns denoting quantity. If, however, other numbers follow them, **di** is omitted:

due milioni di abitanti. *two million inhabitants.*

but: due milioni (e) cinquecento mila lire.
two million, five hundred thousand lire.

(e) When numerals are used as nouns they are always masculine.

(f) Numbers are written usually as one word, except when the conjunction **e** (e.g. *mille e uno*) is used:

duemiladuecentoquattro. *two thousand two hundred and four.*

3. **Uno** is invariable and is generally used in its shortened form **un** after **venti, trenta,** *etc.* followed by a noun:

ventun professori	*twenty-one teachers*
ventun donne	*twenty-one women.*

Although the following forms also exist, they are never used nowadays:

donne ventuna	ventuna donna.

4. **Tutto** combines with a numeral as follows:

tutti e due i ragazzi	*both boys*
tutte e tre le figlie	*all three daughters.*

5. The following construction is very important:

Eravamo in dieci al ballo.
There were ten of us at the ball.

Eravamo in quattro al ristorante.
There were four of us at the restaurant.

6. General remarks on ordinal numbers:

(a) All ordinals are adjectives and inflect with the noun.

(b) All ordinals, except for the first ten, can be formed by adding the ending **-esimo** to the cardinal number.

(c) Note the doubling of the **e** in **ventitreesimo, trentatreesimo,** *etc.*

(d) **Decimo primo, decimo secondo,** *etc.* are used mainly for the centuries, for volumes of books, *etc.*

7. Ordinals are used as in English, but the article is omitted
   before the number denoting succession with rulers:

   Enrico quarto   *Henry the Fourth*
   il terzo capitolo   *the third chapter.*

8. They are also necessary for the second part of a fraction:

   tre quarti   *three-quarters*
   undici dodicesimi   *eleven-twelfths.*

   NOTE. Never use any other form than the one in **-esimo** for
   the formation of fractions above tenths.

9. The adjective **mezzo, -a** (half) inflects before a noun but
   need not when it comes after it:

   una mezz'ora   *a half hour*
   una mezza mela   *half an apple*

   but: un'ora e mezzo (*or* mezza) *an hour and a half.*

   The noun for *half* is **la metà** but it is used sometimes as
   an adjective:

   Egli prese la metà del danaro.
   He took half the money.

   but: Eravamo a metà strada.
          We were halfway there.

10. The commonest collectives in Italian are:

    la coppia – le coppie   *the couple*
    il paio – le paia   *the pair*
    la decina – le decine   *the half score*
    la dozzina – le dozzine   *the dozen*
    la ventina – le ventine   *the score*
    il centinaio – le centinaia *the hundreds*
    il migliaio – le migliaia   *the thousands.*

    NOTE. The ending **-ina** can be added to every tenth number,
    trentina, quarantina, *etc.* up to a hundred, and they
    usually mean *about thirty, about forty, etc.*:

    C'era una trentina di persone nel gruppo.
    There were about thirty people in the group.

    The collective numbers are used in the following way:

    Le uova costano duemila lire *la* dozzina.
    The eggs cost two thousand lire a dozen.

Ci sono migliaia di foglie nella strada.
There are thousands of leaves in the street.

B. THE TIME IN ITALIAN

1. The time is told in the following manner in Italian:

È l'una.	*It is one o'clock.*
Sono le due.	*It is two o'clock.*
Sono le sei.	*It is six o'clock.*
È mezzogiorno.	*It is midday.*
È mezzanotte.	*It is midnight.*
Sono le undici e mezzo (*or* mezza).	*It is half past eleven.*
Sono le quattro meno un quarto.	*It is a quarter to four.*
Sono le otto e un quarto.	*It is a quarter past eight.*
Sono le nove e venti.	*It is twenty past nine.*
Sono le dodici meno dieci.	*It is ten to twelve.*
Che ora è? Che ore sono?	*What time is it?*

It will be noted that the verb is always in the singular for *one o'clock*, *midday* and *midnight*, but always in the plural for all the other hours. *The definite article is never omitted.*

2. When the part of the day is required, it is expressed as follows:

Le due della mattina.	*Two in the morning.*
Le tre del pomeriggio.	*Three in the afternoon.*
Le sette della sera.	*Seven in the evening.*

NOTE. The Italians often count the time in periods of twenty-four hours, hence one may also say:

Sono le quattordici.	*It is two in the afternoon.*

3. The following expressions are also useful:

Il mio orologio va avanti.	*My watch is fast.*
Il mio orologio va indietro.	*My watch is slow.*
Il mio orologio è giusto.	*My watch is right.*
Suonano le due.	*It is striking two.*

LA GUARIGIONE DI BEATUS

Il primo giorno che Beatus uscí di casa, sentí giú per le scale un odore di acido fenico. Proveniva dalla porta stemmata del marchese al primo piano.

— Perché questo fetore? — si domandò Beatus. Ma la risposta fu data dal marchese stesso che usciva in quel momento.

Il signor marchese si scontrò a naso a naso con Beatus, in quanto ambedue erano della stessa statura, e della stessa età; e non essendo deciso chi sia superiore, se un marchese o un cavaliere e uomo universitario, si salutarono contemporaneamente.

— Ma Lei sta bene, — disse il marchese non senza stupore. — La portinaia . . .

— Precorre la storia — continuò Beatus; — e avrà annunciato la mia morte.

— Questo precisamente no, — rispose il marchese, — ma la marchesa mia moglie fu impressionatissima. Volevamo andare nel nostro feudo, ma anche laggiú la malattia fa strage. Guarda, dicevamo, questa casa è la sola che sia rimasta immune . . .

— E mi sono ammalato io. Creda che ne sono mortificato.

— Già![1] E allora la mia signora sparge per le scale l'acido fenico.

Il signor marchese parlava con dignità, in modo da far cadere e far sentire tutte le sue parole.

Beatus, dunque, non era agli occhi della signora marchesa che un agente di infezione: un uomo porta-bacilli, che spaventava una dama. Che cosa sarebbe stato se la avesse spaventata con la sua bara giú per le scale? —

— Io la prego, — disse Beatus, — di presentare le mie scuse alla signora marchesa.

(ALFREDO PANZINI: *Il Mondo è Rotondo*)

NOTE

¹ **Già** : *Già* is often used instead of *sì* to mean *yes* when expressing agreement with a statement made by another person: Che tempaccio! — Già. *What dreadful weather! — Yes.*

EXERCISES

A. Express the following numbers in Italian:

19, 58, 29, 444, 987, 2,546, 1, 345, 670, 5,884,325, $\frac{3}{4}$, $\frac{1}{2}$, 2,345,678, 28th, 999, 11,111, 3,765, 101st, 967th, $\frac{1}{4}$, 2,563,872, 18, 233, 976, 78, 443, 10,001, 300, 648, 14, 13th, 11 dozen, 2,287,950, 20th, $\frac{5}{8}$, $\frac{11}{50}$, 1957, 1128, 45, 777, 31st, 666th, 739,065, 5,432, 9,876, 6,789, 234, 88,732, 12th, $\frac{5}{16}$, 3,256,785, 115,432nd, 22,345.

B. Translate into Italian:
1. There were twelve of us in the restaurant.
2. He gave his little brother three-quarters of the orange.
3. All three men left the room.
4. Italy has 48 million inhabitants.
5. We went for a walk to the next village, but halfway there we caught a bus.
6. The eggs cost three hundred and fifty lire a score.
7. There were hundreds of people in the big store.
8. We counted thirty-one people in the queue (*coda*).
9. After we had beaten the champions, 15 thousand people applauded (*applaudire*) us.
10. I opened the book at the twelfth chapter.

C. Express the following times in Italian:
12.20; 5.40; 5 o'clock; 7.45; 9.30; 1 o'clock; 10.5; 6.15; 4.27; 5.43; 2.5; 11.30; 8.15; 10.45; 11.25; 1.30; 3 o'clock; 12.45; 6.35; 7.56; 2.50; 3.55; 7.15; 12.55.

D. Answer the following questions in Italian:
1. Chi era stato ammalato?
2. Quale specie di odore proveniva dalla porta del marchese?
3. Perché era sorpreso il marchese?
4. Chi avrà annunciato la morte di Beatus?
5. Che cosa avrebbe spaventato la signora marchesa?
6. Dove avrebbe voluto andare il marchese?
7. Che cosa era Beatus per la signora marchesa?
8. Dove faceva strage la malattia?
9. In che modo parlava il marchese?
10. Dove incontrò Beatus il marchese?

E. Translate into Italian:

Mr. Lamberti had been very ill but one day he felt (*sentirsi*) well enough to (*per*) go and see his garden. While he was descending the stairs, he met the marquis who lived on the second floor. 'Good day, marquis,' he said, but the latter did not reply. He was so surprised to see Mr. Lamberti out. 'I thought . . .' 'Yes, yes, the doorkeeper's wife will no doubt have told you that I was at death's door.' 'Not precisely that,' replied the marquis, 'but she said enough to frighten my wife. The disease from which you were suffering was rife around our estate, so we decided to stay here.' 'I am very sorry, in that case, that I became ill. Please convey my apologies to the marchioness,' said Mr. Lamberti with a smile and he hurried off to see his cabbages.

LESSON XXVIII

A. DATES IN ITALIAN

1. The days of the week are as follows in Italian:

lunedí	*Monday*
martedí	*Tuesday*
mercoledí	*Wednesday*
giovedí	*Thursday*
venerdí	*Friday*
sabato	*Saturday*
domenica	*Sunday*

All the days of the week are masculine, except **domenica,** and they are written in small letters, not with a capital, unless at the beginning of a sentence.

2. The months of the year are:

gennaio	*January*	luglio	*July*
febbraio	*February*	agosto	*August*
marzo	*March*	settembre	*September*
aprile	*April*	ottobre	*October*
maggio	*May*	novembre	*November*
giugno	*June*	dicembre	*December*

The months of the year are all masculine and are also written in small letters, unless at the beginning of a sentence.

3. Dates are written by means of the cardinal numbers and the definite article, except in the case of the first day of the month when the ordinal **primo** is used:

il due giugno 1957   *2nd June 1957*
il venticinque maggio 1651   *25th May 1651*
but: il primo settembre 1944   *1st September 1944.*

If the day of the week is expressed with the date, the definite article before the numeral is omitted:
domenica sette luglio 1957   *Sunday 7th July 1957.*

4. To express repetitive actions which take place on certain days of the week, the definite article is placed before the day:

> Andiamo sempre in chiesa la domenica.
> *We always go to church on Sundays.*

5. When a year is referred to alone, it always takes the definite article, since the word **anno** is always understood:

> Nel 1957   *In 1957*   Nel 1832   *In 1832.*

6. When both the year and the month, but not the precise date, are referred to, they are written:

> Nel gennaio del 1956   *In January 1956.*

7. When one refers to the month alone, one writes:

> Eravamo di luglio.   *It was (in) July.*
> or: Eravamo in luglio.   *We were in July.*

The following expressions should be noted:

Fra otto giorni.	*In a week's time.*
Oggi a otto.	*A week today.*
Fra quindici giorni.	*In a fortnight.*
Due anni or sono	*Two years ago.*
L'altro ieri.	*The day before yesterday.*
Domani.	*Tomorrow.*
Dopodomani.	*The day after tomorrow.*
Ieri sera.	*Last night.*
Stamane, stasera, stanotte.	*This morning, this evening, tonight, (last night).*
Quanti ne abbiamo del mese?	*What date is it?*
Ne abbiamo tre. or: Siamo al tre.	*It is the third.*

8. The seasons are as follows in Italian:

La stagione	*The season*
La primavera	*Spring*
L'estate (*f.*)	*Summer*
L'autunno	*Autumn*
L'inverno	*Winter.*

In or **di** may be used with the seasons as with the months:

In primavera	*In Spring*
D'estate	*In Summer.*

9. The centuries are often written with the ordinal numbers:

Il secolo decimo quinto.   *The fifteenth century.*
Il secolo decimo ottavo.   *The eighteenth century.*

One can also say **il quindicesimo secolo** (*the fifteenth century*).

From the thirteenth century onwards, one can also write:

Il duecento (dugento)	*The thirteenth century*
Il trecento	*The fourteenth century*
Il quattrocento	*The fifteenth century*
Il cinquecento	*The sixteenth century*
Il seicento (secento)	*The seventeenth century*
Il settecento	*The eighteenth century*
L'ottocento	*The nineteenth century*
Il novecento	*The twentieth century.*

It will be noted that in this alternative, and very popular, way of indicating the centuries, the number is always one behind the century denoted.

10. Age is expressed in Italian by using the verb **avere**:

Quanti anni ha Giovanni? Ha venticinque anni.
How old is John? He is twenty-five.

Che età ha Lei? Ho ventidue anni.
How old are you? I am twenty-two.

Note also the following expressions:

Un ragazzo diciottenne.
A boy of eighteen.

Un uomo sui quaranta.
A man around forty.

Egli è un nonagenario.
He is a nonagenarian.

B. MEASURE AND THE WEATHER IN ITALIAN

1. Italians use the metric system and a working knowledge of this system will be assumed in what follows.

2. Length and breadth can be expressed in two ways:

Questa stanza è lunga sei metri e larga quattro metri e mezzo.
This room is six metres long and four and a half metres wide.

or:

Questa stanza ha una lunghezza di sei metri e una larghezza di quattro metri e mezzo.

3. Other useful expressions of distance are:

La strada misura duecento metri.
The street is two hundred metres long.

Il paese dista tre chilometri da qui.
The village is three kilometres from here.

Il fiume si estende dieci chilometri.
The river extends for ten kilometres (i.e. is ten kilometres long).

4. Cost per metre or per kilo is expressed as follows:

Ho pagato questa stoffa tremila lire al metro.
I paid three thousand lire a metre for this material.

Ho pagato le pere millecento lire al chilo.
I paid one thousand one hundred lire a kilo for the pears.

Note also:

Le mele sono duecentocinquanta lire l'una.
The apples are two hundred and fifty lire each.

5. **Fare** is often used to indicate the weather in Italian:

Che tempo fa?	*What is the weather like?*
Fa bel tempo.	
or: Fa bello.	*It is fine.*
Fa brutto.	*It is bad weather.*
Fa caldo.	*It is hot.*
Fa freddo.	*It is cold.*

NOTE. One can also say, however:

Il tempo è bellissimo oggi.
The weather is very fine today.

Other useful expressions are:

Tira vento.	*The wind is blowing.*
Piove.	*It is raining.*
Pioviggina.	*It is drizzling.*
Grandina.	*It is hailing.*
Nevica.	*It is snowing.*
Lampeggia.	*There is lightning.*

Tuona.	*It is thundering.*
Che afa!	*How close it is!*
Un temporale.	*A storm.*
Una tempesta.	*A tempest.*
Il tempo si guasta.	*The weather is getting bad.*
Gela; sgela.	*It is freezing; it is thawing.*
La nebbia.	*Fog.*
Tutto bagnato.	*Soaking wet.*

6. When one refers to one's own bodily reactions to the weather, one should use *avere*, not *fare*:

Ho freddo.	*I am cold.*
Ho caldo.	*I am hot.*

IL RE PORCARO

Un re aveva tre figliuole belle come il sole e ch'egli amava piú degli occhi suoi.

Avvenne che il Re, rimasto vedovo, riprese moglie e cominciò per le tre fanciulle una triste esistenza. La matrigna era gelosa dell'affetto immenso che il Re portava alle figlie, e le odiava in segreto. Con mille arti aveva cercato di farle cadere in disgrazia del padre, ma, visto che le calunnie non servivano che a farle amare di piú, deliberò di consigliarsi con una fattucchiera.

— Si può farle morire — rispose costei.

— Impossibile: il Re m'ammazzerebbe.

— Si può affatturarle in qualche modo...

— Vorrei una fatatura che le facesse odiare dal padre, per sempre.

La strega meditò a lungo, poi disse:

— L'avrete. Ma occorre che mi portiate un capello di ciascuna strappato con le vostre mani, e tre setole porcine, strappate con le vostre mani...

La matrigna ritornò al palazzo e la mattina seguente entrò sorridendo nelle stanze delle tre principesse, mentre le cameriste ne pettinavano le chiome fluenti.

— Figliuole mie — disse con voce affettuosa, — voglio insegnarvi un'acconciatura di mia invenzione.

E prese il pettine dalle mani delle donne, pettinò Doralice.
— Ah! mamma, che mi strappi i capelli!...
Pettinò Lionella.
— Ah! mamma, che mi strappi i capelli!...
Pettinò Chiaretta.
Ah! mamma, che mi strappi i capelli!...
Salutò le figliastre e uscí con i tre capelli attorti nel dito
*i*ndice... Attraversò i giardini, i cortili, giunse alle fattorie,
entrò nel porcile e con le sue dita inanellate, strappò tre
setole da tre scrofe. Poi ritornò dalla strega.

Alla mensa regale sedevano il Re, la Regina, le tre principesse, cinquecento dame e cinquecento cavalieri. La Regina
versò furtivamente nel calice del Re il filtro fatato e attese,
ansiosa, di vederne l'effetto. Aveva appena bevuto che il Re
stralunò gli occhi, come preso da sdegno e da meraviglia, e
si alzò accennando le figlie:
— Che beffa è questa? Chi ha messo tre scrofe al posto
delle mie figliuole?

(GUIDO GOZZANO: *Il Re Porcaro*)

EXERCISES

A. Translate the following dates into Italian:
    February 25th 1924; 11th June 1932; 14th May 1879; in
    July 1723; Sunday, 12th October 1546; Tuesday, 30th Novem-
    ber 1472; 5th August 1923; Wednesday, 6th December
    1932; 14th century; in January 1955; 1st March 1852;
    20th century; in 1884; in 1915; 16th century; in May
    1588; 14th September 1944.

B. Translate into Italian:
    1. How old are you? – I am twenty-six.
    2. What day is it today? – It is the 5th July.
    3. Dante was born in 1265.
    4. Shakespeare died in 1616.
    5. We were in September.
    6. We intend going home in a week's time.
    7. We shall set out the day after tomorrow.

8. We are very fond of 15th century art.
9. We often go to the country on Saturdays if it does not rain.
10. The room was three metres long by two and a half wide.
11. The courtyard measures 100 metres.
12. We paid a thousand lire a metre for that silk.

C. Answer the following questions in Italian:
1. Chi aveva tre figliuole belle come il sole?
2. Perché la matrigna odiava le figliuole in segreto?
3. Con chi è andata a consigliarsi?
4. Che cosa suggerisce la fattucchiera?
5. Che cosa deve ottenere la Regina?
6. Perché pettina le chiome delle sue figliastre?
7. Dove va per ottenere tre setole porcine?
8. Che cosa mette la Regina nel calice del Re?
9. Perché il re stralunò gli occhi?
10. Perché crede che qualcuno abbia messo tre scrofe al posto delle sue figliuole?

D. Translate into Italian:
1. I wonder (*domandarsi*) what the weather is like today?
2. Please close the door, I am very cold.
3. The weather was wonderful when we were in Italy.
4. We had a terrible storm last night, I went out to see a friend and got soaking wet.
5. It snows very much here in winter.

E. Translate into Italian:

There was once (*una volta*) a king who had three beautiful daughters whom he loved very much. His queen had died so he decided to take a second wife. Unfortunately, the step-mother was very jealous of the love which the king bore his daughters and she hated all of them. When she found that she was unable to bring them into disgrace she decided to consult a witch. The witch told her that she could kill them but the queen said that that was impossible. It would be better for her to bewitch them some way. The witch gave the queen a potion to put into the king's glass. When she had done this at dinner the next night, she waited anxiously to see the effect. The king, as soon as he had drunk his wine, opened his eyes wide, and, pointing to his daughters, said, 'What kind of joke is this? Who has put three sows in the place of my daughters?'

A. FURTHER USES OF THE SUBJUNCTIVE

1. The subjunctive is used after comparatives unless the expression **di quel che** is used, with which it is rare:

   Egli ha piú danaro che tu non creda.
   He has more money than you think.

   Egli ha piú danaro di quanto tu non creda.
   He has more money than you think.

2. After a superlative or the adjectives **solo** and **unico** when used as antecedents to the subordinate clause:

   Questa è la migliore casa che io abbia mai visto.
   This is the best house I have ever seen.

   Questo è il solo paio di scarpe che io abbia portato con me.
   This is the only pair of shoes I have brought with me.

   Tu sei l'unica persona di cui io possa fidarmi.
   You are the only person I can trust.

3. In a relative clause after an indefinite antecedent:

   Non trova chi lo voglia aiutare.
   He can't find anyone to help him.

   Cerco un ragazzo che sappia suonare il pianoforte.
   I am looking for a boy who can play the piano.

   Non c'è nessuno che sappia suonare il pianoforte.
   There isn't anyone who knows how to play the piano.

   But if the antecedent is definite, then the indicative must be used:

   Cerco il ragazzo che sa suonare il pianoforte.
   I am looking for the boy who plays the piano.

4. After the indefinites **chiunque** (whoever), **qualunque** and **qualunque cosa** (whatever), and the rarer forms **chicchessia** and **checché** which correspond to them respectively:

   Chiunque sia, lo faccia aspettare.
   Whoever he is, make him wait.

Qualunque siano i vostri diritti, non permetto che entriate in casa mia.
Whatever your rights are, I won't permit you to enter my house.

Qualunque cosa io faccia, trovo sempre opposizione.
Whatever I do, I always find opposition.

B. THE SUBJUNCTIVE IN ADVERBIAL CLAUSES

1. The subjunctive is used after the following conjunctions which introduce an adverbial clause:

Purpose:	perché, affinché	*so that, in order that*
Time:	prima che	*before*
	finché (*see note*)	*until*
Condition:	nel caso che	*in case*
	a meno che . . . non	*unless*
	se,† quando, qualora	*if*
	a condizione che	*on condition that*
	come (se), quasi	*as if*
	purché	*provided that*
	supposto che	*supposing that*
Concession:	benché, sebbene, quantunque	*although*
	nonostante che	*notwithstanding*
	per quanto	*however much*
	caso mai	*in case*
	quand'anche	*even if*

2. **Perché** takes the subjunctive when it implies purpose, not when it gives a reason:

Gli detti cento lire perché andasse al cinema.
I gave him one hundred lire so that he could go to the cinema.

† *Se* often takes the indicative in the present and future tenses, and when it means *whether*. (See also Lesson XXX A.)

but:

Vado a letto perché sono stanco.
I am going to bed because I am tired.

3. **Prima che** requires the subjunctive under all circumstances:

Me ne vado prima che Giovanni arrivi.
I am going before John arrives.

4. **Finché** is capable of several different constructions, only one of which requires the subjunctive:

Finché vivrò, non gli mancherà il pane.
As long as I live, he will not go in want.

L'ho aspettato finché ho potuto ma non è venuto.
I waited for him as long as I could but he didn't come.

Non si deve salire sull'autobus finché non si ferma.
One should not get into a bus until it stops.

Aspetterò finché egli torni a casa.
I shall wait until he returns home.

The subjunctive is used with **finché** (as in the fourth example) only when it means *until* and when it expresses *an intention for the future*.

5. All conjunctions expressing conditions require the subjunctive, and **a meno che** also requires an expletive **non**:

A meno che tu non voglia che io t'aiuti, farò una passeggiata.
Unless you want me to help you, I shall go for a walk.

Mi ha parlato come se niente fosse.
He spoke to me as if nothing was the matter.

Qualora il tempo si metta al bello, potremo fare una passeggiata.
If the weather improves, we shall be able to go for a walk.

It will be noted, however, that **quando** has two meanings:

Quando eri a scuola, non lavoravi.
When you were at school, you did not work.

Quando tu fossi a scuola, non lavoreresti.
If you were at school, you would not work.

6. The conjunctions expressing concession also require the subjunctive:

Mi è venuto incontro quasi (come se) volesse parlarmi.
He came up to me as if he wanted to speak to me.

Caso mai tu partissi, ricordati di avvisarmi.
In case you go away, remember to let me know.

Quand'anche te ne andassi, non me ne importerebbe niente.
Even if you were to go away, it would not matter to me.

Per quanto sia difficile il problema, tenterò di risolverlo.
However difficult the problem is, I shall try to solve it.

7. **Senza che** also takes the subjunctive, but is used only if the person changes in the subordinate clause:

Voglio partire senza che essa mi veda.
I want to leave without her seeing me.

NOTE. With these conjunctions it is sometimes possible to avoid the subjunctive:

Benché (fosse) giovane, non gli piacevano gli sport.
Although (he was) young, he didn't like sport.

Voglio partire senza essere visto da lei.
I want to leave without being seen by her.

Prima di agire, pensaci!
Before acting, think!

LA VENDITA ALL'ASTA

— Don Gesualdo . . . sentite qua!

Volse in giro un'occhiata da cospiratore e abbassò la voce:

— Una proposta seria! — e fece un'altra pausa significativa. — Prima di tutto, i danari della cauzione . . . una bella somma! . . . La disgrazia volle cosí . . . ma voi non ci avete colpa, don Gesualdo . . . e neppure, voi, mastro Nunzio . . . È giusto che non li perdiate! . . . Accomoderemo la cosa! . . . Voi signor barone Zacco, vi rincresce di lasciare le terre che sono da quarant'anni nella vostra famiglia? . . . E va bene! . . . La baronessa Rubiera adesso vuole la sua parte anche lei? . . . Ha piú di tre mila capi di bestiame sulle spalle . . . E va bene anche questo! Don Gesualdo, qui, ha danari da spendere lui pure[1]; vuol fare le

sue speculazioni sugli affitti . . . Benissimo! Dividete le
terre, fra voi tre . . . senza lite, senza puntigli, senza farvi la
guerra a vantaggio altrui . . . A vantaggio di chi, poi? . . . del
comune! Vuol dire di nessuno! Mandiamo a monte l'asta. —
Il pretesto lo trovo io! . . . Fra otto giorni si riapre sul prezzo
di prima; si fa un'offerta sola . . . Io no . . . e nemmeno loro!
. . . Il canonico Lupi! in nome vostro, don Gesualdo . . .
Ci fidiamo . . . Siamo galantuomini! Un'offerta sola sul
prezzo di prima; e vi rimangono aggiudicate le terre senza
un baiocco d'aumento. Solamente una piccola senseria per
me e il canonico . . . E il rimanente lo dividete fra voi tre,
alla buona[2] . . . d'amore e d'accordo. Vi piace? Siamo
intesi?

— Nossignore, — rispose don Gesualdo — le terre le piglio
tutte io.

Mentre gli altri erano contenti e approvarono coi cenni
del capo l'occhiata trionfante che il notaio tornava a[3] volgere
intorno, quella risposta cadde come una secchia d'acqua. Il
notaio per primo rimase sbalordito; poi fece una giravolta e
s'allontanò canterellando. Don Niní scappò via senza dir
nulla. Il barone stavolta finse di calcarsi il cappello in capo
per davvero. Lo stesso canonico saltò su inviperito:

— Allora vi pianto anch'io! . . . Se volete rompervi le
corna, il balcone è là, bell'e aperto . . . Vi offrono dei buoni
patti! . . . vi stendono le mani! . . . Io vi lascio solo, com'è
vero Dio!

Ma don Gesualdo si ostinava, col suo risolino sciocco, il
solo che non perdesse la testa in quella baraonda.

(GIOVANNI VERGA: *Mastro don Gesualdo*)

NOTES
[1] **pure :** This word has a variety of other meanings as well as
also :

(a) as an emphatic adverb:

| Venga pure! | Sia pure! | Dica pure! |
| *Do come!* | *So be it!* | *Do speak!* |

(b) as an emphatic element attached to other words:

> Possiamo andare a teatro, oppure al cinema, stasera.
> *We can go to the theatre or else to the cinema tonight.*

> Mi disse di aspettarlo alle cinque, eppure non venne.
> *He told me to expect him at five o'clock, and yet he did not come.*

(c) Before *troppo* it means *unfortunately*:

> Purtroppo, non sapevo che tu c'eri.
> *Unfortunately, I did not know you were there.*

(d) *Pur di* means *provided* or *if only*:

> Pur di andare a Torino, farebbe qualsiasi sacrificio.
> *Provided he could go to Turin, he would make any kind of sacrifice.*

² **alla buona:** A noun such as *maniera* is understood in expressions of this kind which are very frequent in Italian:

> Alla francese.   All'inglese.
> *In the French way.   In the English style.*

³ **tornare a:** This expression is used to describe a repeated action and the phrase may be translated as *cast around again* in this case. The expression never means *to turn around to*.

EXERCISES

A. Translate into Italian:

1. In case you change your mind (*idea*), let me know (it) at once.
2. Whatever the book is you read, it did not give you much information.
3. Is there no one who can write a letter to John for me?
4. That was the only time I ever met him.
5. That picture was much more beautiful than I thought.
6. I can't find anyone to play the piano in the concert (*concerto*) tonight.
7. This skyscraper is the highest building we have ever seen.
8. Whoever wrote that poem (*poesia*) was a bad poet.
9. I am looking for the boy whom I spoke to yesterday.
10. Whatever you may think, it is better to be silent.

B. Insert the right tense of the verbs given in the infinitive in the following sentences:

1. Finché (essere) il padrone, si farà ciò che dico io.
2. Prima che egli (potere) parlare, Carlo l'accusò di furto.
3. Ti ha dato quella grammatica perché (studiare) l'italiano.
4. Volle scriverle senza che suo padre lo (sapere).
5. Benché non (pentirsi) di avermi offeso, lo salutai.
6. Quando tu (andare) in Italia, saresti troppo pigro per imparare la lingua.
7. Qualora tu ne (sentire) parlare, fammelo sapere.
8. Mi domandai perché non (venire) direttamente a casa dopo scuola.
9. Ho pregato i miei amici che mi (aiutare).
10. Ci parlò quasi (perdere) la partita.

C. Translate into Italian:

1. Wait till (*che*) he leaves and I will tell you everything.
2. May no one come to disturb me!
3. Although you don't deserve (*meritare*) it, I shall help you.
4. I don't know how you can approve (of) him.
5. I shall accompany you unless you don't wish me (to).
6. Before writing to your uncle, think well of (*a*) what you intend to say.
7. I shall stay here until John comes.
8. We spoke to him as if nothing was the matter but we were in fact very worried.
9. However much you try to persuade him he is wrong, he will not listen to you.
10. I told him that he could come provided that he could make his own arrangements (*prendere gli accordi*).

D. Answer the following questions in Italian:

1. Che cosa vende all'asta il comune?
2. Perché vuole la sua parte la baronessa Rubiera?
3. Chi ha danari da spendere?
4. Perché rincresce al barone Zacco di lasciare le terre?
5. Che cosa vuole fare don Gesualdo?
6. Come cadde la risposta di don Gesualdo al notaio?
7. Cosa vuol fare il notaio per accomodare le cose?
8. Chi finisce col diventare furioso?
9. Chi è il solo a non perdere la testa?
10. Su che cosa vuol fare le sue speculazioni don Gesualdo?

E. Translate into Italian:

The mayor of the village decided to auction some land and a number of people made offers. However, he did not think these offers high enough and did not accept them. Then a rich countryman made a very high offer which the local aristocracy (*aristocrazia*) did not like, so they asked him to share the land with them. The lawyer said he would be able to find a pretext to annul the auction and that the next week he would be able to buy the land at the former price. When the countryman replied that he would not do it, the baron and the canon became furious and said that he was a very foolish man. But the countryman persisted and he was in fact the only one who did not lose his head in the tumult.

LESSON XXX

A. CONDITIONAL SENTENCES

1. When both verbs of a conditional sentence are in the present tense the indicative mood is always used:

Se vai in città, comprami un tubetto di pasta dentifricia.
If you are going to town, buy me a tube of tooth paste.

2. If the main verb is in the future tense, it is usual for the verb in the conditional clause to be put into the future tense as well:

Se verrà, gliene parlerò.
If he comes, I shall speak to him of it.

3. When the main verb is in the present conditional or perfect conditional tense the verb of the conditional clause must be in the imperfect or the pluperfect subjunctive, according to the sense:

Se venisse a casa mia, gliene direi di tutti i colori.
If he came to my house, I should tell him off soundly.

Se mi avesse scritto, sarei venuto subito.
If he had (Had he) written to me, I would have come at once.

NOTE. **Se** can *never* be followed by the conditional tense.

4. In spoken Italian the imperfect indicative often replaces both the subjunctive and the conditional tenses in such sentences:

Se mi scriveva, venivo subito.
If he had written, I would have come at once.

One can even find occasionally a combination of the imperfect indicative and the conditional:

Se mi scriveva, sarei venuto subito.
Had you written to me, I would have come at once.

The student is advised to use the form given in section 3 rather than these more colloquial ones.

B. ORTHOGRAPHIC CHANGES WITH CERTAIN VERBS

1. Verbs ending in **-care** and **-gare** insert an **h** after the **c** and the **g** when these letters are followed by **e** or **i**:

    leccare (*to lick*): lecchi, lecchiamo, leccherò, *etc.*
    pregare (*to pray*): preghi, preghiamo, pregherò, *etc.*

2. Verbs ending in **-ciare** or **-giare** drop the **i** before another **i** or before an **e**:

    lasciare (*to let*): lasci, lascerò, *etc.*
    mangiare (*to eat*): mangi, mangerò, *etc.*

3. All other verbs in **-iare** drop the **i** before another **i**:

    pigliare (*to take*): pigli, pigliamo, *etc.*
    fischiare (*to whistle*): fischi, fischiamo, *etc.*

4. Verbs ending in **-scere** insert **i** before the **u** of the past participle only:

    mescere (*to pour*): mesciuto; *but,* mescono (*they pour*).
    pascere (*to pasture*): pasciuto; *but,* pascono (*they pasture*).

5. Some verbs diphthongize† in their present tenses:

SEDERSI *to sit*	MUOVERSI *to move*	NUOCERE *to harm*
mi siedo	mi muovo	noccio (nuoccio)
ti siedi	ti muovi	nuoci
si siede	si muove	nuoce
ci sediamo	ci moviamo	nociamo
vi sedete	vi movete	nocete
si siedono	si muovono	nocciono (nuocciono)

We have already seen other verbs conjugated in this manner such as **tenere** and **venire**. The rule for diphthongization is that the open **e** or **o** of the root should bear the main stress of the word and should not be followed by more than one consonant. Hence **si siedono** (with a single consonant following the **e**)

† Strictly speaking these sounds are not diphthongs, but the term is used as a convenient one to describe this general process in Italian.

diphthongizes, while **nocciono** (with a double consonant following the **o**) usually does not.

LA FUGA SUL LAGO

Non tirava un *a*lito di vento; il lago giaceva liscio e piano, e sarebbe parso immobile, se non fosse stato il tremolare, e l'ondeggiar leggiero della luna, che vi si specchiava da mezzo il cielo. S'udiva soltanto il fiotto morto e lento frangersi sulle ghiaie del lido, il gorgoglio piú lontano dell'acqua rotta tra le pile del ponte, e il tonfo misurato di quei due remi che tagliavano la superficie azzurra del lago, uscivano ad un colpo grondanti, e si rituffavano. L'onda segata dalla barca, riunendosi dietro la poppa, segnava una striscia increspata che si andava allontanando dal lido. I passeggieri silenziosi, colla faccia rivolta indietro, guardavano le montagne e il paese rischiarato dalla luna e svariato qua e là di grandi ombre. Si discernevano i villaggi, le case, le capanne: il palazzotto di don Rodrigo, colla sua torre piatta, elevato sopra le casucce ammucchiate alla falda del promontorio, pareva un feroce che ritto nelle tenebre sopra una compagnia di giacenti addormentati, vegliasse meditando un delitto. Lucia lo vide, e rabbrividí; discese coll'occhio a traverso la china, fino al suo paesello, guardò fisso alla estremità, scorse la sua casetta, scorse la chioma folta del fico che sopravanzava sulla cinta del cortile, scorse la finestra della sua stanza; e seduta com'era sul fondo della barca, appoggiò il gomito sulla sponda, chinò su quello la fronte, come per dormire, e pianse segretamente.

(MANZONI: *I Promessi Sposi*)

EXERCISES

A. Translate into Italian:
   1. If one looked up to the top of the hill, one could see don Rodrigo's fortress.

2. Had the weather been better, we would have been able to cross the lake.

3. If the lawyer had looked at don Gesualdo's face, he would not have cast around an exultant look again.

4. Had he spoken more slowly, I would have understood him.

5. If you should go to the grocer's, order me some fruit and vegetables.

6. If he wishes to study Italian, you must send him to (*in*) Italy.

7. I would not have written to you today, had I known you would be coming to see me this evening.

8. If you do that, then I too will abandon you.

9. I would have liked to have discussed his work with him, but he was in a hurry (*aver fretta*).

10. If the boat had crossed the lake, I would have known immediately.

B. Give the correct form of the present or future tenses of the verb in brackets:

1. Giulia e Carlo (sedersi) per mangiare il loro pranzo.

2. Il troppo mangiare (nuocere) alla salute.

3. Secondo Newton, gli oggetti (muoversi) sempre in linea diretta.

4. Quando ci andrò, sono sicuro che mi (pregare) di passarci la notte.

5. Tu non (mangiare) mai il pesce? Perché no?

C. Translate into Italian:

1. I don't want this pear, you eat it.

2. You (*tu*) leave the book at John's house and I will call in (*passare da*) on him this evening.

3. Although the dog licks her hand every time she goes there, she is still terribly afraid of it.

4. I would go to Italy in the summer if I had the money.

5. If you should see her, will you explain to her what I want?

6. Had he come home earlier, we could have finished the work this evening.

7. I would have told him off at once if he had not slipped off.

8. Let me open the door.

9. The cattle are pasturing in the field.

10. He said he would go to the cinema if I would go too.

D. Answer the following questions in Italian:
   1. Come era il lago quando Lucia l'attraversò?
   2. Che cosa guardava quando la barca si staccò dal lido?
   3. Con che cosa si tagliava la superficie del lago?
   4. Dov'era il palazzotto di don Rodrigo?
   5. Che cosa si specchiava nel lago?
   6. Che cosa si sentiva intorno al ponte prima di partire?
   7. Che cosa fece Lucia quando vide il palazzotto di don Rodrigo?
   8. Dove si ammucchiavano le casucce del paese?
   9. Dov'era la casetta di Lucia?
   10. Che cosa c'era dietro la poppa durante la traversata?

E. Translate into Italian:
   The surface of the lake was smooth and motionless when the travellers set out. All that could be heard was the slow breaking of the water against the piles of the bridge. The measured plunging of the oars cut the blue surface of the lake and the moon was mirrored in the undulating of the waves. The boat left behind it a rippling strip which stretched away towards the shore. The passengers were silent and looked at the little houses crowded together at the foot of the promontory. Lucy was still able to distinguish her own home in the distance (*in lontananza*) but she soon lost sight of it (*perdere di vista*) and decided to try to sleep.

REVISION EXERCISES (*Lessons XXVI–XXX*)

1. Translate the following sentences into Italian:
    1. He said he would come to see us when he arrived in this country.
    2. We did not give him the money he had asked for.
    3. He wanted me to write to his mother to tell her the good news.
    4. It would be better for you to pay him a visit (*fare una visita*) yourself.
    5. John asked me if I saw the football match yesterday.
    6. He denied that he had said I was a scoundrel.
    7. We never believed him to be guilty (*colpevole*).
    8. They asked me how I had managed to do the work myself.
    9. He wanted to know who it was that had betrayed him.
    10. He asked me if they had worked all the morning.

2. Give the following numbers in Italian:
    1001, 5001, 1932, 88, 71st, 654th, 23, about 60, 19, 101, 345, 17th, 21 boys, 18th century, 56, 1111, 2,443,502, 3 million people, Charles the Second, 5326, 998, $\frac{3}{4}$, $\frac{3}{8}$, $\frac{4}{5}$, $\frac{29}{30}$.

3. Give the following times in Italian:
    5.36; 4.45; 2.30; 1 o'clock; 5.25; 6 o'clock; 9.20; 10.55; 7.40; 12.10; 5.45; 9.15; 4 o'clock.

4. Translate into Italian:
    1. We were in the middle of July.
    2. The January winds are always cold.
    3. Saturday March 25th is the day of the international football match.
    4. We went to France in 1956.
    5. It was in September that war broke out (*scoppiare*).
    6. I hope to (*di*) see you today week.
    7. Charles came to see us the day before yesterday.
    8. What day is it today? – It is the tenth.
    9. The room was six metres long and five wide.
    10. The town is five kilometres away from here.

5. Insert the correct form of the verb given in brackets in the following sentences:
    1. Cerco un arbitro che (potere) spiegarmi le regole del calcio.
    2. Tu sei l'unica persona a cui (osare) parlarne.
    3. Mi domandò se (finire) il mio lavoro.
    4. Gli ho scritto perché (sapere) le condizioni in cui vivo.
    5. Te lo dirò quando (venire).

6. Prima che ci (andare) vorrei sapere chi ci sarà.
7. Finché (vivere) non vi mancherà da mangiare.
8. Dopo che egli (scrivere) la lettera, uscí di casa.
9. Mi ha chiesto come si (fare) per farlo.
10. Disse che Giovanni (uscire) un quarto d'ora fa.

6. Translate into Italian:
1. Had I gone to the zoo with him, he would have insisted on my spending the whole day with him.
2. We beg you to (*di*) stay to dinner with us.
3. He told us he would give us a cup of coffee if we could wait five minutes.
4. We told him to wait at the station until John arrived.
5. Whatever he says, I am still sure that I am right.
6. We said we would have liked to help him but he replied that he could do everything himself.
7. Provided you give the boy a tip (*una mancia*), it should not be difficult to find a place.
8. We tried to prevent him leaving the country.
9. However much I try, I never succeed in (*a*) doing it.
10. Even if you were to go to his house, you would not find him in.

A. PREPOSITIONS BEFORE INFINITIVES

1. Many verbs do not require a preposition before a dependent infinitive and the most important among these are the following:

bastare†	to suffice	piacere	to please
bisognare	to need	potere	to be able
convenire	to suit	preferire	to prefer
desiderare†	to desire	sapere	to know
dovere	to have to	sentire	to feel, hear
fare	to do, make	solere	to be accustomed to
giovare	to be useful	toccare	to be one's turn to
importare	to be important	udire	to hear
lasciare†	to let, allow	usare	to be used to
occorrere	to be necessary	vedere	to see
osare	to dare	volere	to want, wish

Many, but not all, of these verbs fall under the following headings:

(a) The modal verbs (**dovere, osare, potere, sapere, solere, usare, volere,** etc.):

> Carlo voleva andarci ma non osava uscire.
> *Charles wanted to go there but dared not go out.*

(b) Impersonal verbs:

> Non mi conviene farlo. *It does not suit me to do it.*
> Giova notare. *It is useful to note.*
> Mi piacerebbe andarci. *I would like to go there.*
> Occorre scrivergli. *One must write to him.*

NOTE. Some impersonal verbs, however, require a preposition:

> Mi rincresce di vederlo. *I am sorry to see him.*
> Mi pare di‡ averlo visto altrove. *I seem to have seen him elsewhere.*

† These verbs also permit of other constructions (see Lesson XXXII A).
‡ *Di* is often omitted with *parere* and *sembrare*.

(c) Verbs indicating the various senses:

L'ho visto arrivare.	*I saw him arriving.*
L'ho sentito cantare.	*I have heard him sing.*

2. Impersonal expressions with **essere** do not require a preposition before a dependent infinitive:

È un piacere farlo.	*It is a pleasure to do it.*
È un peccato dire bugie.	*It is a sin to tell lies.*
È inutile insistere.	*It is useless to insist.*
È difficile farlo.	*It is difficult to do it.*

but:

Questi problemi sono difficili a risolvere.
These problems are difficult to solve.

In the last example the subject of **essere** is no longer impersonal so that the adjective is followed by the preposition which it usually requires.

3. After **chi, che, dove** and **onde** (*whence*) in certain indirect questions no preposition is required before the infinitive:

Non so a chi rivolgermi.
I don't know who to apply to.

Non sapevo che rispondere.
I didn't know what to answer.

Gli ho spiegato dove andare per ottenere quella merce.
I explained to him where to go to get that merchandise.

4. Verbs which require **a** before a dependent infinitive are fairly numerous and some of the most important are the following:

abituarsi	*to be accustomed to*	continuare	*to continue*
		costringere	*to compel*
affrettarsi	*to hurry*	esitare	*to hesitate*
aiutare	*to help*	forzare	*to force*
andare	*to go*	imparare	*to learn*
apprestarsi	*to prepare*	incoraggiare	*to encourage*
arrivare	*to arrive*	insegnare	*to teach*
cominciare	*to begin*	invitare	*to invite*
consentire	*to consent*	mandare	*to send*

PONTE VECCHIO, FLORENCE

ISOLA DEI PESCATORI, LAKE MAGGIORE

mettersi	*to set about*	riuscire†	*to succeed*
obbligare†	*to oblige*	stare	*to be, stand*
ostinarsi	*to persist*	stimolare	*to stimulate*
persuadere	*to persuade*	tardare†	*to delay*
prepararsi	*to prepare*	tornare	*to do again*
rinunciare	*to give up*	uscire	*to go out*

These verbs can often be recognized since many of them
fall into the following categories:

(a)   Verbs of motion:

Tocca a Lei andare a vederlo adesso.
It is up to you to go and see him now.

Venne ad incontrarlo alla stazione.
He came to meet him at the station.

(b)   Verbs of beginning, continuing or preparing:

Cominciavo a divertirmi quando egli venne a trovarmi.
I was beginning to enjoy myself when he came to find me.

Continuò a parlarmi sottovoce.
He continued to speak to me in a whisper.

Mi apprestai a partire.
I prepared to leave.

(c)   Verbs of learning and teaching:

Imparo a parlare italiano.
I am learning to speak Italian.

(d)   Verbs indicating compulsion:

Mi costrinse ad accompagnarlo.
He forced me to accompany him.

(e)   After *far bene* (to do right), *far male* (to do wrong)
and *far meglio* (to do better):

Ho fatto bene a dirglielo.
I did right to tell him.

Ha fatto male a disprezzare il mio aiuto.
He did wrong to despise my help.

Farebbe meglio a rimanere.
He would do better to stay.
(It would be better for him to stay.)

† These verbs also permit of other constructions in certain cases (see
Lesson XXXII A).

Note. Study the personal and impersonal uses of **riuscire** (to succeed):

>Non riesco a farlo.
>*I can't succeed in doing it.*

but: Non mi riesce (di) farlo.
>*I can't succeed in doing it.*

5. **A** is also used before an infinitive of narration:

>E tutti a ridere.
>*And everybody laughed.*
>
>E il nemico a fuggire da ogni parte.
>*And the enemy fled in all directions.*

Note. This use of the infinitive is found only in particularly graphic or literary expressions.

6. **Essere** followed by a numeral, **solo** or **ultimo,** also takes *a* when preceding an infinitive:

>Fu il primo a farlo.
>*He was the first to do it.*
>
>Fu il solo ad aiutarmi.
>*He was the only one to help me.*

B. QUESTIONS IN ITALIAN

1. Questions may be asked in a number of ways in Italian, many of which have already appeared in the reading exercises. The following are the usual methods of interrogation:

(a) By inversion, as in English:

>Dove va Giovanni?
>*Where is John going?*

or: Giovanni dove va?
>*Where is John going?*
>
>Cosa sta facendo Lei?
>*What are you doing?*

(b) By inflection of the voice:

>Carlo è andato al cine stasera?
>*Did Charles go to the cinema tonight?*

(c) By the use of **non è vero? vero?** or **nevvero?**:

> Carlo è andato al cinema stasera, vero?
> *Charles has gone to the cinema tonight, hasn't he?*

(d) By placing **è vero che** . . . or some similar expression at the beginning of the sentence:

> È vero che Carlo è andato al cinema stasera?
> *Is it true that Charles has gone to the cinema tonight?*

> È possibile che Carlo sia andato al cinema stasera?
> *Is it possible that Charles has gone to the cinema tonight?*

NOTE. The inversion method should not be abused, for instance:

> Hai trovato il libro?
> *Have you found the book?*

is much better than:

> Hai tu trovato il libro?

UNA PARTITA A CARTE

La signora Alice riceve il prevosto diritta accanto la grande tavola rotonda su cui fumiga un grosso lume a petrolio portabile, munito di un paralume a frange molticolori. S'inchina al sacerdote, gli porge la mano, dice: 'Buona sera, reverendo.' Comanda: 'Una sedia, Gionemín.' La sedia c'è, eccola, Gionemín fa solo il gesto di porgerla. E sono tutti e tre seduti, ultima Gionemín, con ritegno e sempre visibile memoria e atto che lei è serva ammessa per bisogno e non per complimento e parità.

La partita è subito iniziata, incominciando da dove fu lasciata la sera prima. La signora Alice chiama: 'Chiara.' Chiara, una giovane esile, biondiccia, di puro incarnato, esce dal salotto accanto. 'Eccomi,' dice. E 'Buona sera, reverendo,' aggiunge con un inchino. Il suo posto è vuoto, siede. Ha già le sue carte dal prevosto che, leccandosi di quando in quando il dito con un soffio della lingua come se spegnesse una candela, è tutto occupato a distribuire senza far sotterfugi sotto lo sguardo fermo della signora Alice.

La partita in quattro è seria e muta. Il mantice che

solleva il cupo silenzio è quel grosso petto del prete. La continua novità è quel suo leccarsi un dito o due o quattro addirittura[1] per poi buttare, dopo molti pensieri e pentimenti e occhi stravolti al cielo con enormi soffiate della bocca, una carta che invariabilmente è sbagliata. La signora Alice non può soffrire né quella lingua *u*mida che bagna continuamente i polpastrelli e le carte . . . che schifo! . . . né quelle lunghe soste sopra pensiero. Ma le piace lo sbaglio. Gionemín le manda in quelle occasioni occhiate dolci di soll*u*chero servizievole. Sa che la padrona gode.

(ALFREDO OBERTELLO: *L'Oro che è Cibo*)

NOTE
[1] **addirittura**: This word may be used in a number of ways, depending on the tone of one's voice:

(a) to express surprise:

Indovina un po' dove siamo arrivati. A Milano. — Addirittura!
Just guess where we have arrived. At Milan. — Really?

(b) or incredulity:

Indovina un po' dove siamo arrivati. A Milano. — Addirittura!
Just guess where we have arrived. At Milan. — Don't be silly!

(c) or for emphasis, as in the example in the passage above:

Siamo andati addirittura a Milano.
We went right to Milan.

EXERCISES

A. Translate into Italian:
1. He didn't dare say anything.
2. We were the first to arrive.
3. They need something to drink.
4. I heard him say he was going home at once.
5. You are not accustomed to doing this kind of work.
6. It is a pity to stop before the job is completed.
7. It is necessary to go there at once.
8. We did not hesitate to accept his offer.
9. It did not suit me to go there so late.

10. We say he was forced to accept our conditions (*condizione*
    (*f.*)).
11. It would be better to do our shopping before dinner.
12. We prepared to receive him in the study.

B. Put a preposition (if required) into the following blank spaces:
1. E i ragazzi — fuggire in disordine.
2. Siamo andati alla stazione — incontrarla.
3. Mi basta — sapere che non è stato ferito.
4. Vuol aiutarci — portare i bagagli in casa?
5. Quel ragazzo non imparerà mai — scrivere il proprio nome.
6. Preferisco — andare in macchina che in bicicletta.
7. Sarà un piacere — farvi quel servizio.
8. Non mi conviene — andare a trovarlo adesso.
9. Bisogna che tu ti affretti — finirlo.
10. Non ha consentito — vendercelo.
11. S'è messo — lavorare subito.
12. Non mi piace — fare ciò.

C. Translate into Italian:
1. What is he doing now?
2. Why is the priest continuing to lick his fingers?
3. Has John really gone to visit the old castle?
4. She started to give her mistress sugary glances.
5. He is right, isn't he?
6. Let's go to the theatre tonight, shall we?
7. Did you find the cards in that old box?
8. Is it true that Charles has got a new job?
9. You know we would like to help you, don't you?
10. Has the game begun yet?

D. Answer the following questions in Italian:
1. Quante persone giocano a carte in casa della signora Alice?
2. Che cosa fa il prete mentre dà le carte?
3. Perché esita il prevosto prima di giocare una carta?
4. Che specie di luce c'è nella sala?
5. Dove riceve la signora il prevosto?
6. Chi è Gionemín?
7. Che cosa fa quando il prete mette giú una carta sbagliata?
8. Come si chiama la quarta persona della partita?
9. Quale rumore solleva il cupo silenzio?
10. Perché Gionemín si siede per ultima?

E. Translate into Italian:

The provost often comes in the evening to play cards with Alice, her niece and the servant. They do not have electric light (*luce elettrica*) in Alice's house, so the room is lit by an old oil lamp with a lampshade of many colours. As soon as the priest arrives, the game is started, beginning where it was left off the night before. The provost disgusts (*far schifo*) Alice by licking the balls of his fingers as he gives out the cards. The game itself is played in silence and with many pauses (*pausa*) since the priest often sighs loudly (*forte*) and casts his eyes heavenwards before playing a card. And then, it is generally the wrong one. This delights Alice and her servant sends her soft, sugary glances since she knows how well her mistress enjoys the priest's mistakes.

A. PREPOSITIONS BEFORE INFINITIVES (*cont.*)

1. The majority of Italian verbs take *di* before a dependent infinitive and some of the most important are the following:

accettare	to *accept*	ingegnarsi	to *strive to*
accorgersi	to *notice*	mancare	to *fail, lack*
ardire	to *dare*	meravigliarsi	to *be amazed*
assicurare	to *assure*	offrire	to *offer*
badare†	to *take care (to)*	parere†	to *seem*
		pensare	to *think*
capitare	to *happen*	pentirsi	to *repent*
cercare	to *strive to* (not when meaning *to seek*)	permettere	to *permit*
		pregare	to *pray, ask*
		preoccuparsi	to *worry*
cessare	to *cease, to stop*	pretendere	to *claim*
		promettere	to *promise*
consigliare	to *advise*	ricordarsi	to *remember*
contentarsi	to *content oneself*	rifiutare	to *refuse*
		rincrescere	to *be sorry*
credere	to *believe*	rispondere	to *reply*
dichiarare	to *declare*	scrivere	to *write*
dimenticare	to *forget*	scusare	to *excuse*
dire	to *say*	sembrare†	to *seem*
dispiacere†	to *displease*	sforzarsi	to *strive to*
evitare	to *avoid*	smettere	to *stop, leave off*
far conto	to *imagine, intend*		
		sospettare	to *suspect*
figurarsi	to *imagine*	sperare	to *hope*
fingere	to *pretend*	temere	to *fear*
finire	to *finish*	tentare	to *try*
godere	to *enjoy*	vantarsi	to *boast*
impedire	to *prevent*	vietare	to *forbid*

These verbs may be classified as follows:

(a) Verbs denoting belief, opinion, hope, expectancy, knowing, suggestion:

Credo di poter farlo.   *I believe I can do it.*

† These verbs also permit of another construction (see Lesson XXXI A).

Spero di vederlo.	*I hope to see him.*
So d'aver errato.	*I know I have erred.*
Non vedo l'ora di andare a casa.	*I am longing to go home.*
Gli ho suggerito di diventare avvocato.	*I suggested he should become a lawyer.*

(b) Verbs denoting commands, permission and prohibition:

Gli ordinò di non andarci.	*He ordered him not to go there.*
Gli ho permesso di farlo.	*I have permitted him to do it.*
Ti proibisco di parlare.	*I forbid you to speak.*

(c) Verbs of saying, affirming, requesting, asking and denying:

Ti ho detto di lasciarmi.	*I told you to leave me alone.*
Ti prego di accompagnarmi.	*I beg you to accompany me.*
Gli ho chiesto di scriverti.	*I have asked him to write to you.*
Nego di averlo fatto.	*I deny having done it.*

(d) Verbs denoting completion and omission:

| Ho finito di scrivere. | *I have finished writing.* |
| Tralasciò di informarcene. | *He omitted to inform us of it.* |

(e) Verbs expressing doubt or uncertainty:

| Dubita di poter venire oggi. | *He doubts whether he can come today.* |
| Sospettavo di essere stato imbrogliato. | *I suspected I had been cheated.* |

(f) Verbs expressing astonishment, emotion and fear:

Mi meravigliai di vederti in casa di Giovanni.
I was amazed to see you in John's house.

Temo di aver perduto il tuo danaro.
I am afraid I have lost your money.

(g) Verbs of trying, striving and endeavouring†:

Si sforzarono di riuscire.
They struggled to succeed.

† Exceptions are: *provare a* (to try) and *stentare a* (to do with difficulty).

Tentò di capire ma senza riuscirci.
He tried to understand but without succeeding.

2. Many nouns and adjectives require **di** before an infinitive:

Non ho voglia di aiutarlo   *I am unwilling to help him.*

Non vale la pena (di) partire   *It is not worthwhile going*
domani.   *away tomorrow.*

Ho bisogno di parlare con te.   *I need to speak to you.*

Sono felice di vedervi.   *I am happy to see you.*

3. Many prepositions also require **di** before an infinitive:

A forza di lavorare, si stancò molto.
As a result of working, he tired himself greatly.

Prima di partire, me ne parlò.
Before leaving, he spoke to me about it.

4. Some constructions with verbs requiring **di** are worth noting:

(a) **Capitare** used impersonally:

Se vi capita di andarci, salutatemi gli amici.
If you happen to go there, remember me to my friends.

(b) **Smettere** meaning *to stop* in the sense of *to cease*:

Smetti di litigare.   *Stop quarrelling.*

But when motion is implied, **fermarsi** must be used:

Il treno si fermò subito.   *The train suddenly stopped.*

(c) **Cercare** has two constructions:

Cerco di riparare il mio orologio.
I am trying to repair my watch.

È andato a cercare un medico.
He has gone to look for a doctor.

(d) **Rincrescere** and **dispiacere** are both used impersonally:

Mi rincresce (dispiace) di non essere venuto.
I am sorry I didn't come.

(e) **Badare** permits of several constructions:

Bada di non cadere giú dalle scale.
Mind you do not fall downstairs.

Si badi a distinguere fra queste due forme.
Be careful to distinguish between these two forms.

Bada ai fatti tuoi.
Mind your own business.

The difference between **badare di** and **badare a** is slight, but the former usually takes a negative infinitive. Note that the verb requires **a** before a complement.

(f) **Dimenticare** is replaced by **dimenticarsi** in absolute constructions:

Hai dimenticato di dirglielo? Sí, mi sono dimenticato.
Did you forget to tell him? Yes, I forgot.

5. Some verbs admit of a number of constructions with dependent infinitives and they fall into two groups, (a) those with a single meaning but with alternative constructions; (b) those whose meanings vary with the construction used:

(a) **Bastare** and **desiderare** admit of alternative constructions with no change in meaning:

Basta dirglielo.   *It is sufficient to tell him.*
Queste parole bastarono a calmarlo.
These words were sufficient to calm him.
Desidero (di) andarci.
I want to go there.

NOTE. **Bastare** takes no preposition when used impersonally; in all other cases it requires **a**.

(b) **Lasciare, obligare** and **pensare** permit of two constructions with different meanings for each:

Mi lasci parlare.
Let me speak.
Non lascia mai di annoiarmi.
He never ceases annoying me.
Mi ha obbligato a servirlo.
He has forced me to serve him.
Mi obbligo di fare ciò che egli ha rifiutato di fare.
I undertake to do what he has refused to do.
Non pensa che a divertirsi.
He only thinks of amusing himself.

Non ho mai pensato di farlo.
I have never thought of doing it.

In the case of **pensare** the distinction between the two meanings, although slight, is very real. The first example implies purposeful thinking towards a single end, the second a resolution to do or not to do something.

6. **Da** is used before an infinitive in a number of ways:

(a) With the verbs **astenersi** and **contenersi**:

Mi sono astenuto dal bere.
I have abstained from drinking.

Non potevo contenermi dal piangere.
I could not restrain myself from weeping.

(b) To translate *the wherewithal to* :

Mi dia da mangiare, per piacere.
Give me something to eat, please.

Ci diede da pensare.
He gave us something to think about.

(c) To imply purpose or aim:

casa da vendere.	*house for sale.*
macchina da scrivere.	*typewriter.*

(d) To translate *so . . . as to* in combination with **tanto**:

La casa era tanto bella da entusiasmarci.
The house was so beautiful as to delight us.

(e) To express futurity, usually with a passive force:

Cosa c'è da fare?
What is to be done?

Questi sbagli sono da evitare.
These mistakes are to be avoided.

NOTE. The infinitive is sometimes made reflexive in writing but less often in speech to emphasize the passive force of the verb:

Questi sbagli sono da evitarsi.

B. ADJECTIVES FOLLOWED BY PREPOSITIONS

1. Certain adjectives govern the preposition **a** and the most important of these are the following:

adatto	*suitable for*	inutile	*useless for*
avvezzo	*accustomed to*	lento	*slow to*
buono	*good for*	pericoloso	*dangerous to*
disposto	*disposed to*	pronto	*ready to*
facile	*easy to*	simile	*similar to*
fedele	*faithful to*	utile	*useful to*

Non sono disposto a fare ciò.
I am not disposed to do that.

Carlo è lento a decidersi.
Charles is slow in making up his mind.

Giovanni è fedele ai suoi amici.
John is faithful to his friends.

2. Others require **da**:

alieno	*foreign to*	immune	*immune to*
assente	*absent from*	indipendente	*independent of*
bandito	*banished from*	lontano	*far from*
cieco	*blind in*	monco	*maimed in (an arm)*
differente	*different from*		
diverso	*different from*	zoppo	*lame in*

Egli è cieco da un occhio.
He is blind in one eye.

Questa spiegazione è del tutto diversa dalla mia.
This explanation is quite different from mine.

NOTE. **Lontano** usually takes **di** before **qui** or **là**:

Quel paese è lontano di qui.
That village is far from here.

The adverb **lungi** also requires **da**:

Lungi da farmi amico con lui, non voglio piú vederlo.
Far from becoming his friend, I do not want to see him again.

3. A large number of adjectives govern **di**, of which the following are a short selection:

abbondante	*abundant*	impaziente	*impatient*
avido	*greedy, avid*	invidioso	*jealous, envious*
bramoso	*desirous, eager*	lieto	*happy*
certo	*certain*	ricco	*rich*
contento	*content*	sicuro	*sure*
degno	*worthy*	stanco	*tired*
desideroso	*desirous*	vestito	*dressed*
geloso	*jealous*		

Quest'opera non è molto ricca di pensieri.
This work is not very rich in thought.

Erano stanchi del viaggio.
They were tired of the journey.

Era vestita di nero.
She was dressed in black.

NOTE. **Libero** (free) usually takes **da** with a noun and **di** with an infinitive:

Libero da ogni cura.
Free from all worry.

Si sentiva libero di scegliere ciò che gli conveniva.
He felt free to choose what suited him.

UN PAESAGGIO SARDO

Dopo il tramonto del giorno seguente giunsero verso il littorale, sotto le falde di un monte desolato, nero sul cielo rosso come un cumulo di carboni spenti. Un paesetto con le casupole grigie affondate in certe buche scure simili a cave di pietra abbandonate, con le strade coperte di polvere gialla, accresceva la desolazione del paesaggio. Piú in là tutto cominciò a brillare nel crepuscolo: in fondo alla landa selvaggia del littorale, fra il giallo dorato delle dune e l'azzurro del mare, lunghe chiazze di acqua paludosa vibravano argentee e rosse al riflesso del cielo come enormi pesci guizzanti sulla sabbia.

Erano arrivati ad una regione strana, melanconica; il mare

era scomparso all'orizzonte e oltre la brughiera, a sinistra verso l'interno dell'isola, sorgeva una catena di colline nerastre dentellate come scogli, ma fra un dente e l'altro s'affacciavano cime azzurre di monti lontani che lasciavano indovinare dietro la muraglia scura un paese più vago e fresco.

(GRAZIA DELEDDA: *Marianna Sirca*)

EXERCISES

A. Translate into Italian:
 1. Take great care not to frighten her.
 2. He persuaded me to help him.
 3. We imagined we were the winners (*vincitore*).
 4. Mind you don't miss (*perdere*) the train.
 5. He offered to go to London in my place.
 6. We advised him to accept that job.
 7. We enjoy going to the sea.
 8. He refused to sign it.
 9. I was sorry to see him go.
 10. He told me to stop working.

B. Put in the correct preposition in the spaces provided:
 1. Questo problema è facile — risolvere.
 2. Questo paesaggio è molto simile — quelli che si trovano in alta montagna da noi.
 3. Non sono avvezzo — fare il giardiniere.
 4. Volle essere indipendente — sua famiglia.
 5. Lungi — andarci stasera, non ho neppure intenzione di andarci domani.
 6. Roma è molto ricca — musei e — gallerie d'arte.
 7. Egli non è disposto — aiutarci.
 8. Essi sono molto stanchi — viaggio.
 9. Vuole essere libero — ogni specie d'obbligo.
 10. Giovanni è lento — muoversi.

C. Translate into Italian:
 1. We hoped he would be able to come.
 2. He boasted of having won the race (*corsa*).
 3. We were very worried in case he had lost his way (*perdersi*).
 4. Don't fail to come and see us when you return.
 5. He appeared not to know where he was going.

6. He did not stop writing till two in (of) the morning.
7. We didn't finish working till ten past twelve.
8. He finished up by hoping to see him sometime (*nel corso di*) next week.
9. It is useless writing to him today.
10. You will find this book useful in explaining difficult problems.

D. Translate into Italian:

Towards evening they reached the coast, at the foot of a chain of mountains which stood out (*risaltare*) like a pile of burnt coals against the reddish sky. The village on the sea-shore was buried in a large dark hole which seemed as if it was an abandoned stone quarry. Then, further on, along the coast stretched the dunes with long pools of water here and there which flashed like silver in the reflexion of the sky. Beyond the heath towards the south, there rose another chain of blackish hills, but their blue summits, as jagged as rocks, seemed to suggest the existence of a more beautiful countryside behind its dark wall.

E. Describe a typical English scene in Italian.

A. OMISSION OF THE INDEFINITE ARTICLE

1. The indefinite article is omitted in the following cases:

(a) Before a noun in apposition:

La Lombardia, regione d'Italia . . .
Lombardy, an Italian province . . .

(b) After **che !** or **quale !** used in exclamations:

Che bella giornata oggi!
What a lovely day it is today!

(c) Before an *unqualified* predicate indicating a profession:

Giovanni è dentista.
John is a dentist.

but:

Filippo è un buon ingegnere.
Philip is a good engineer.

(d) After **da** used to mean *like a* or *as characteristic of*:

Agí da uomo coraggioso.
He acted like a brave man.

(e) With numerals:

Ho comprato una scatola di cento spilli.
I have bought a box of a hundred pins.

(f) After the following verbs: **chiamare** (to call); **eleggere** (to elect); **nominare** (to appoint, name); **proclamare** (to proclaim):

Fu eletto Presidente.	*He was elected President.*
Mi chiamò farabutto.	*He called me a rascal.*
Fu proclamato re.	*He was proclaimed king.*
Fu nominato professore.	*He was appointed as a teacher.*

(g) Before titles of books:

Vita di Dante.	*A Life of Dante.*
Storia d'Italia.	*A History of Italy.*

B. IDIOMATIC USES OF CERTAIN VERBS

1. The various tenses of **dovere** have the following meanings:

devo	*I must, I am to, I have to, I should*
dovrò	*I shall have to*
dovevo	*I was to, I had to*
dovei (dovetti)	*I had to*
dovrei	*I ought to, I should*
ho dovuto	*I have had to, I had to*
avrò dovuto	*I shall have had to*
avrei dovuto	*I ought to have, I should have had to*
avevo dovuto	*I had had to*

Devono essere le tre.
It must be three.

Il treno deve arrivare alle tre.
The train should arrive at three.

Dovrei comprare quel libro.
I should buy that book.

Avrei dovuto parlarne con lui.
I should have spoken about it to him.

Ho dovuto ripetere quell'esame.
I have had to sit that examination again.

Avrà dovuto passare da sua zia.
He has probably had to call on his aunt.

2. The modal verbs **dovere, potere** and **volere** very often take the auxiliary of the infinitive which depends on them:

Giovanni è dovuto andare all'ufficio questo pomeriggio.
John has had to go to the office this afternoon.

Carlo non è potuto venire.
Charles could not come.

Non ci sono voluto andare.
I did not want to go there.

However, the auxiliary **avere** is also tolerated, especially in speech, in modern Italian:

Giovanni ha dovuto andare all'ufficio questo pomeriggio.
Carlo non ha potuto venire.
Non ho voluto andarci.

With reflexive verbs one of two constructions must be used:

(a) *either* the pronoun is attached to the infinitive and **avere** is used as an auxiliary:

> Non ha potuto salvarsi. *He could not save himself.*

(b) *or* the pronoun is placed before the main verb and **essere** is used as an auxiliary:

> Non si è potuto salvare. *He could not save himself.*

NOTE. In addition to the three verbs mentioned above, **sapere** conforms to the rules which govern the auxiliary to be used in conjunction with reflexive verbs:

> Non ha saputo ritirarsi in tempo. *He couldn't draw back in time.*

or:

> Non si è saputo ritirare in tempo. *He couldn't draw back in time.*

In no circumstances, however, does **sapere** behave like the other modal verbs when the infinitive is not reflexive. In such cases, the only possible construction is with **avere**:

> Non ha saputo uscirne. *He could not get out.*

3. **Sapere** is also used in the following ways:

(a) Instead of **potere** when *to be able* means *to know how to*:

> Egli sa nuotare ma non va alla piscina molto spesso.
> *He can (knows how to) swim but does not often go to the baths.*

(b) With **di** to mean *to smack of*:

> Quell'azione sa di tradimento.
> *That action smacks of treason.*

(c) **Non voler saperne di** means *not to have to do with* or *not to hear of*:

> Il signor Rossi non ne voleva sapere di quell'affare.
> *Mr. Rossi did not want anything to do with that business.*

(d) Note the polite form:

> Giovanni è a casa? — Non saprei.
> *Is John in? — I'm afraid I don't know.*

(e) The difference between **sapere** and **conoscere** is that the former means to know a fact while the latter means to know a person or a place:

> Non sa dove ha messo il libro.
> *He doesn't know where he has put the book.*
>
> Non conosco la sorella di Giovanni.
> *I don't know John's sister.*
>
> Conosco bene la Toscana.
> *I know Tuscany well.*
>
> but: Conosco (so) un po' l'italiano.
> *I know Italian a little.*

4. **Volere** can be used as follows:

(a) To express the English *it needs* when in combination with **ci**:

> Ci vuole un'ora per andare da Dino.
> *It takes (it needs) an hour to get to Dino's.*
>
> Ci vogliono dieci volontari.
> *Ten volunteers are wanted.*

NOTE. The verb in this construction agrees in number with the noun that follows it.

(b) In the following idioms:

> Sembra voglia piovere.
> *It seems it is trying to rain.*
>
> I suoi genitori gli vogliono bene.
> *His parents love him very much.*
>
> Vorrei andare in Italia.
> *I would like to go to Italy.*
>
> Non capisco ciò che Lei vuole dire.
> *I do not understand what you mean.*

5. **Potere** also has a number of idiomatic uses:

> Potrebbe essere mezzanotte.   *It may be midnight.*
> Non ne posso piú.   *I am completely exhausted.*
> Il primo ministro poté molto sul Presidente.
> *The prime minister had much influence over the President.*

It should also be carefully noted that *could* may be an imperfect, a conditional or a past definite in English:

Mi disse che non poteva venire.
He said he could not come.

Chi potrebbe crederlo?
Who could believe it?

Il ministro volle scrivere al re ma non poté farlo.
The minister wanted to write to the king but could not do it.

RIUNIONE DELLA GIUNTA A FRUSAGLIA

— La seduta è incominciata — disse il sindaco. E l'usciere tornò dentro con l'orcio del muscatello.

— Aggiungi — disse il sor Gigi — che è cominciata, ed è cominciata bene. Il segretario, da parte, sotto il lume, scriveva a rotta di collo.

— Che accidente scrivi?

— La cabala.

In quel momento entrarono anche le signore.

— Silenzio laggiú!

— Mettetevi qui — disse l'usciere alle signore — starete calde. E attente a non parlare, se no vi mando via.

La signora farmacista faceva la smorfiosa. — No, prego, prima lei, signora, prima lei. —

Cornelio nipote, sempre galante, acciò che stessero zitte, mise loro davanti una saccocciata di fave abbrustolite. Intanto a poco a poco entrava anche il pubblico. Sulla balconata, Sarcofago si divertiva a tirare i lupini sulla testa pelata del segretario.

— Io direi — cominciò il sindaco — che la ferrovia dovrebbe essere conterranea.[1]

Fu un applauso solo, un urlo di gioia. — Bene! Bravo!

Il sindaco si guardò d'attorno con soddisfazione: pareva quello che atterrò il toro con un pugno.

Ma il prevosto non si associò a quegli applausi.

— Non voglio — gridava — che il treno mi passi sotto casa. Se passa il treno, crolla il campanile.

In quel momento dal tavolo del segretario volò un calamaio contro il pubblico.

— Non cominciamo con gli scherzi — esclamò il brigadiere.

Sarcofago nell'ombra rideva come un matto.

— Niente ferrovia *conterranea* — disse il notaio con voce
ferma — si segua la retta via.

Non l'avesse mai detto.[2] Ninetta, se non lo tenevano,
faceva una strage notarile, e il garzone del mugnaio aveva
già saltata la balconata.

— Dio mio — gridavano le signore — Dio mio!

(FABIO TOMBARI: *Tutta Frusaglia*)

NOTES

[1] **conterraneo**: The word means *belonging to the village* but
it is misunderstood by the provost and the lawyer. The first
imagines it means *underground* (*sotterraneo*) and the latter thinks
it means *following the contours of the land*.

[2] **Non l'avesse mai detto**: *Would he had never said it.* (See
Lesson XXIV, B 10.)

EXERCISES

A. Translate into Italian:
   1. He has always acted as a just man.
   2. Piedmont, a region of Italy, is well known for its industry.
   3. We elected him president.
   4. There are a hundred and sixty people in that room.
   5. John is a dentist and Charles a very good chemist.
   6. What a lovely afternoon!
   7. They called him the greatest pianist in Europe.
   8. They treated us as brothers.
   9. Alessandria, a small town in Italy, is well known in history
      (*storia*).
   10. John has just been appointed head of the department.

B. Translate into Italian:
   1. It seems it is going to snow.
   2. I ought to have gone to see him but I was too busy last
      week.
   3. John told me that Philip was to catch a train at three
      o'clock.
   4. Do you know French and German?
   5. John told us that Dino had not been able to come tonight.

6. He told us he could not drive (*guidare*).
7. 'I shall have nothing to do with that business,' said Charles.
8. We said he would have to shave (*farsi la barba*) before going out.
9. He should have arrived yesterday.
10. Barbara will have to write directly to the minister.

C. Answer the following questions in Italian:
1. Dove ha luogo questa scena?
2. Perché il segretario getta il calamaio contro il pubblico?
3. Qual è il progetto del sindaco?
4. Che cosa fa Sarcofago?
5. Perché il prevosto non si associa agli applausi?
6. Che cosa vuole il notaio?
7. Chi vuol far una strage notarile?
8. Che cosa dà Cornelio alle signore?
9. Come scrive il segretario?
10. Perché l'usciere dice alle signore di non parlare?

D. Translate into Italian:
1. He wrote to tell me of all the difficulties he had met (with).
2. They did not want to speak to him about it.
3. Who wrote that book? – I couldn't say.
4. Would you like to go there by yourself?
5. I can't prevent (to) him going there.
6. Let's stop here for a moment, I am completely exhausted.
7. It took ten men to lift (*sollevare*) the machine.
8. If I understood what he meant, I would do what he wants.
9. I know England very well.
10. Did you know that John had set out for America?

E. Translate into Italian:
The town council met (*riunirsi*) last night to discuss whether we should have a railway station near the town or not. The public was allowed in but they were warned (*avvertire*) by the usher not to speak or else they would be sent out. Some nasty boy fired lupin seeds at the secretary's head, which angered (*fare arrabbiare*) him. He ended up by throwing an inkwell at the public gallery. The mayor wanted the railway to be 'belonging to the village' but the provost thought he wanted it to go underground and was afraid that the belfry would collapse. The various difficulties were, however, resolved (p.p. *risolto*) finally, and it was decided to have the station in the centre of the town.

A. INDEFINITE ADJECTIVES AND PRONOUNS

1. **Alcuno** is used in the singular only as a negative; in the plural it expresses positive quantities. It may be used both as an adjective or as a pronoun:

> Non ho comprato alcuna cosa.
> *I haven't bought anything.*
> Ho alcuni libri nella mia cartella.
> *I have a few books in my satchel.*
> Ne ho comprati alcuni.
> *I have bought a few.*

2. **Altro** is used in a variety of ways:

   (a) As an adjective and as a pronoun:

   > Ho tante altre cose da fare.
   > *I have so many other things to do.*
   > Ti può bastare quel libro? — Ci vuole ben altro.
   > *Will that book be suitable? — I need something far better.*
   > Gli uni dicono così, gli altri cosà.
   > *Some say one thing, the others another.*
   > Altro è dire, altro è fare.
   > *There is a difference between words and deeds.*

   (b) With a reciprocal meaning in conjunction with reflexive verbs:

   > Si parlano l'un l'altro.†
   > *They speak to one another.*

   but:

   > Parlano l'uno *all*'altro.
   > *They speak to one another.*

NOTE. **L'un l'altro** is an absolute phrase which never requires a preposition when used with *reflexive verbs*; on the other hand, it always requires the preposition which accompanies a given verb when there is *no reflexive*.

† *Si parlano* is usually sufficient to express the reciprocal meaning.

(c) In conjunction with other adjectives or pronouns:

> Non voglio nessun'altra cosa.
> *I want no other things.*
>
> Non voglio nient'altro oggi.
> *I want nothing else today.*

(d) **Altri** is used as a masculine singular pronoun:

> Né tu né altri ci può aiutare.
> *Neither you nor others can help us.*

(e) The following idiomatic uses of **altro** are to be noted:

> Se non altro mi ha ringraziato.
> *He thanked me if nothing else.*
>
> Mi farai questo piacere? — Senz'altro.
> *Will you do me this service? — Certainly.*
>
> Ti ha ringraziato? — Tutt'altro.
> *Did he thank you? — Far from it.*
>
> Sono tutt'altro che annoiato.
> *I am far from bored.*
>
> Non fa altro che giocare.
> *He does nothing but play.*
>
> Ho da studiare, altro che andare al cinema.
> *Far from going to the cinema, I have to study.*
>
> Noi altri Inglesi.   *We English.*
> Noi altri Italiani.   *We Italians.*

(f) **Altro che !** is also an interjection:

> Sei andato al convegno di Milano? Altro che!
> *Did you go to the congress at Milan? Rather!*
>
> Conosci Giovanni? Se lo conosco! Altro che!
> *Do you know John? Do I know him! I'll say I do!*
>
> Conosci quell'uomo? Altro che conoscerlo! È mio fratello.
> *Do you know this man? I'll say I do! He is my brother.*

(g) **Altrettanto** means *as much* and is used as follows:

> Mi diede due scellini e altrettanti a mio fratello.
> *He gave me two shillings and the same (as much) to my brother.*

> Arrivederci! Tante cose alla famiglia! Altrettanto a
> Lei, signore.
> *Goodbye! Best wishes to the family! The same to you,*
> *sir.*

In the second sentence **altrettanto** is used as a
pronoun and, therefore, does not agree with **cose**.

3. **Ciascuno** is inflected like **uno** and means *each*:

> Ciascun giudice si ritiene giusto.
> *Each judge considers himself just.*
>
> Ciascuno per sé.
> *Each for himself.*

Ciascuno is often replaced by **ogni** as an adjective and
sometimes by **ognuno** (*everyone*) as a pronoun.

4. **Nessuno** is used only as a negative pronoun or adjective
and almost always requires **non** when following the verb:

> Non vedo nessuno qui.
> *I don't see anyone here.*
>
> Non ho nessun libro.
> *I have no books.*

It may, however, be used without the negative in questions
of the following type:

> È venuto nessuno?
> *Has no one come?*

5. **Parecchi, -ie,** means *several* and is used as follows:

> Ho parecchi libri nella mia cartella.
> *I have several books in my satchel.*
>
> Ho messo parecchie matite sulla scrivania.
> *I have put several pencils on the desk.*

Parecchio in the singular is an adverb meaning *very*
much:

> Ti sei divertito durante le vacanze? — Parecchio!
> *Did you enjoy yourself during your holidays? — Very much!*

6. **Il piú** means *most* and is used in the singular in most
expressions:

> Il piú delle volte essi vanno al cinema il giovedí.
> *Mostly they go to the cinema on a Thursday.*

Note. **Per lo piú** (mostly); **per lo meno** (at least):
Per lo piú, i suoi drammi fanno furore.
His plays are mostly big hits.

7. **Poco** is used in a restrictive sense as an adjective:
> C'erano poche persone nella sala.
> *There were few people in the room.*

while **un po' di** refers to small quantities:
> Voglio un po' di carta.
> *I want a little paper.*

Note: The following idiomatic use of **un po'** is important:
> Senta un po'!   *Just listen!*
> Dimmi un po'!   *I say!*

8. **Qualche** can *only be used as an adjective* and takes a singular noun, but it combines with other words to form indefinite pronouns:
> C'è qualche fiore in quel campo.
> *There are a few flowers in that field.*
> C'è qualcuno che chiede di Lei.
> *There's someone asking for you.*
> Hai portato qualcosa per me?
> *Have you brought something for me?*

but:
> Ti devo dire una cosa.
> *I have to tell you something.*

9. **Stesso** means *same* before the noun, *very* or *himself, herself,* etc. after it:
> Quell'auto è dello stesso modello di quella di mio padre.
> *That car is the same model as my father's.*
> Carlo è arrivato il giorno stesso in cui partivo.
> *Charles arrived on the very day I was leaving.*
> Vidi venirmi incontro mio padre stesso.
> *I saw my father himself coming towards me.*

Note. **Medesimo** is used occasionally instead of **stesso**:
> Ci sono andato io medesimo.
> *I went there myself.*

10. **Tale** means *such* or *certain* and is often preceded by the article or some other supporting word:

> Non ho mai visto un tale spettacolo.
> *I have never seen such a spectacle.*

> Quel tale signore è venuto.
> *That certain gentleman has arrived.*

> La sua sciocchezza è tale da far ridere qualsiasi persona.
> *His foolishness is such as to make anyone laugh.*

> La pioggia era tale che sono stato completamente bagnato.
> *The rain was such that I was completely soaked.*

> Un tale, una tale, un Tal dei Tali.
> *Mr. So-and-So, Mrs. So-and-So, Lord So-and-So of So-and-So.*

Tale quale means *just as, like*:

> Giovanni è tale quale suo fratello.
> *John is just like his brother.*

Taluno means *some* like **alcuno** but is not so frequent:

> Ci sono taluni errori assai gravi.
> *There are some very grave errors.*

11. **Tanto** means *so much*:

> Ci sono tante matite in questa scatola!
> *There are so many pencils in this box!*

However, it has also the following idiomatic uses:

> Gli ho scritto una lettera molto franca, tanto piú che è un mio caro amico.
> *I wrote him a very frank letter, all the more so because he is a dear friend of mine.*

> Non adirarti, tanto ormai l'hai rotto.
> *Don't get angry, you have broken it and that's that.*

> A un tanto la settimana.
> *At so much a week.*

> Me ne dai ancora un tantino?
> *Will you give me a little more?*

12. **Tutto** is used in the following ways:

> Ho letto tutto il libro.
> *I have read the whole book.*

> Mi ha fatto perdere tutta una giornata.
> *He has made me waste a whole day.*

Ci parleremo in tutta libertà qui.
We shall speak to one another in complete liberty here.

Ci siamo andati tutti e due.
We both went there.

Tutto quanto means *absolutely all*:

Ci siamo andati tutti quanti.
Absolutely all of us went there.

Ho percorso tutte quante le strade.
I went through absolutely all the streets.

B. TENSES WITH **DA** MEANING *SINCE* USE OF **FRA, TRA** AND **IN** WITH EXPRESSIONS OF TIME

1. **Da** meaning *since* or *for* is used in conjunction with the present or imperfect tenses if an action or state begun in the past is still continuing in the present:

Abito a Londra da dieci anni.
I have lived in London for ten years (i.e., I still live there).

Non lavoravo da dieci anni quando mi offrí quel posto.
I had not worked for ten years when he offered me that post.
(i.e., I was still not working when offered the post.)

But, if the action or state has been interrupted, the past tense must be used, with or without the preposition **per**:

Abitai a Londra per dieci anni.
I lived in London for ten years.
or:
Abitai dieci anni a Londra.

NOTE. When *since* means *after that time* the past tense is always required, even though the state or action may be continuing up to the present. When in doubt the student is advised to substitute *after* for *since* and use the past tense if the sentence still makes sense:

Da quel tempo non l'ho visto piú.
Since (after) that time I have seen him no more.

2. **Da che** or **dacché** means *since* and usually takes the same tense as the main clause:

Da che sono qui, mi sento molto meglio.
Since I have been here, I feel much better.

or:

Da che sono stato qui, mi sono sentito molto meglio.
Since I have been here, I have been feeling much better.

3. In phrases dealing with time, **tra** and **fra** mean *after* or *at the end of* and **in** means *within*:

Arriverà fra due settimane.
He will arrive in a fortnight's time.

La casa è stata costruita in dieci settimane.
The house was built in ten weeks.

UN DIALOGO

Venditore: Almanacchi, almanacchi nuovi; lunari nuovi, lunari nuovi. Le occorrono almanacchi, signore?

Passante: Almanacchi per l'anno nuovo?

Venditore: Sí, signore.

Passante: Credete che quest'anno nuovo sarà un anno felice?

Venditore: Sí, certo, caro signore!

Passante: Come quest'anno passato?

Venditore: Assai di piú.

Passante: Come l'altro ancora?

Venditore: Di piú, di piú, caro signore.

Passante: Ma come che anno? Non vi piacerebbe che l'anno fosse come uno di questi ultimi?

Venditore: No, signore, non mi piacerebbe.

Passante: Quanti anni nuovi sono passati da che vendete almanacchi?

Venditore: Saranno vent'anni, signore.

Passante: A quale di questi vent'anni vorreste che somigliasse l'anno venturo?

Venditore: Non saprei.

Passante: Non vi ricordate di nessun anno in particolare che vi sia parso felice?

Venditore: Sinceramente no, caro signore.

Passante: Eppure la vita è una cosa bella, non è vero?

Venditore: È una cosa che si sa.

Passante: Non tornereste a vivere questi vent'anni e anche tutto il passato cominciando da quando siete nato?

Venditore: Volesse il cielo che si potesse, caro signore.

Passante: Ma se dovreste rifare tutta la vita che avete fatta, compresi tutti i dispiaceri e i dolori che avete passati?

Venditore: Questo no.

Passante: Anch'io sono dello stesso parere se dovessi rivivere e cosí tutti. Ma questo è segno che il Caso per tutto quest'anno ha trattato tutti male. La vita bella non è la vita che si conosce ma quella che non si conosce. Non la vita passata ma la futura. Con l'anno nuovo la Sorte comincerà a trattar bene voi e me e tutti gli altri e incomincerà la vita felice, non è vero?

Venditore: Speriamo.

Passante: Quindi, mi faccia vedere l'almanacco piú bello che ha, per piacere.

Venditore: Ecco signore, questo costa trecento lire.

Passante: Ecco trecento lire.

Venditore: Grazie, signore, Arrivederla. Almanacchi, almanacchi nuovi, lunari nuovi . . .

    (Adattato da GIACOMO LEOPARDI: *Operette Morali*)

EXERCISES

A. Translate into Italian:
1. We sold a few last year.
2. How much did that other book cost?
3. I don't think I need anything else today, thank you.
4. Will you do me a great favour? – But of course.
5. I have not seen him for five years.

6. I believe he is far from happy.
7. Did you enjoy the film last night? – I'll say I did.
8. There are several good films in town this week, but the best is in the cinema near the station.
9. I have been working in Paris for two years.
10. Each man was given a small bag of roasted beans.
11. On the whole, it is not too difficult to learn Italian.

B. Put the correct preposition in the blank spaces:
1. Mi riparò la macchina — due orette.
2. Speriamo di rivederla — poco.
3. Non ci vediamo — piú di due anni.
4. Abitai a Milano — cinque anni.
5. Vado in Italia — una quindicina di giorni.

C. Translate into Italian:
1. This is the very book I was looking for.
2. He was doing the same kind of work as I am.
3. I shall be with you in a few moments.
4. There are certain things which should not be said.
5. Barbara is just like her little sister.
6. We threw them all out (*mettere alla porta*).
7. His speech was so bad that it bored us all.
8. Since he has bought that huge house near the village, he thinks he is an important man.
9. Was there someone asking for (*di*) me?
10. I will give you 5,000 lire and Dino will give you the same.

D. Translate into Italian:
Buyer: What have you got there?
Seller: Calendars for the new year, sir.
B.: How much are they this year?
S.: Three hundred and fifty lire.
B.: They are much dearer than they were last year. Do all you sellers think we shall have a happy year if you all raise (*innalzare*) your prices?
S.: It is the cost of production which is getting higher and higher, sir.
B.: Where will it all end up? Everybody is getting poorer every day.
S.: I know that only too well, sir. People have so little money these days that they are unable to buy calendars. They have to spend all their money on the necessities (*necessità*) of life.

  B.: Then it must be very difficult for you to earn your
    living (*campare la vita*) now?
  S.: Yes sir, I earn very little nowadays (*oggidì*).
  B.: In that case, I will buy one of your best calendars.
    Show me one. – Ah! that one is very beautiful, how
    much does it cost?
  S.: Five hundred lire.
  B.: Here they are.
  S.: Thanks, sir. Good-day, sir, you are too kind.

E. Write an imaginary dialogue between yourself and a shopkeeper.

A. GEOGRAPHICAL LOCATIONS IN ITALIAN

1. The names of countries in Italian require the article in all
cases with the exception of certain constructions involving
di and **in**:

> La Grecia è un piccolo paese.
> *Greece is a small country.*
>
> L'Inghilterra è un'isola.
> *England is an island.*
>
> Gli Stati Uniti sono grandi.
> *The United States is large.*

2. The rules regarding **di** and **in** are as follows:

(a) Feminine names of countries require the article in
combination with **di** unless they are used in a purely
adjectival sense:

> L'Italia è piú grande dell'Inghilterra.
> *Italy is bigger than England.*
>
> I laghi della Svizzera.
> *The lakes of Switzerland.*
>
> La forza industriale della Russia.
> *The industrial strength of Russia.*

but:

> L'ambasciatore d'Italia.
> *The Italian Ambassador.*

(b) With masculine names of countries the article is
always used in combination with **di**:

> La seta del Giappone.   *Japanese silk.*

(c) Feminine names of countries drop the article after **in**
unless they are qualified by an adjective:

> Siamo in Italia.   *We are in Italy.*
> Andiamo in Isvizzera.†   *We are going to Switzerland.*

† A prothetic *i* is often placed before an initial *s impure* when it is
preceded by a consonant: *in Ispagna* (in Spain), *in iscuola* (in school), *etc.*

but: Siamo nella bella Francia. *We are in beautiful France.*
Siamo nella ricca Ger- *We are in rich Germany.*
    mania.

(d) The masculine names of countries can be used with **in**, with or without the article:

> Andiamo nel Brasile (*or* in Brasile).
> *We are going to Brazil.*
> Viviamo nel Giappone (in Giappone).
> *We live in Japan.*

When, however, the name of the country is a plural, the use of the article is obligatory:

> Siamo negli Stati Uniti.
> *We are in the United States.*

3. Continents, regions (when feminine) and large islands follow the same rules as the feminine names of countries:

Vanno in Africa.	*They are going to Africa.*
Siamo in Toscana.	*We are in Tuscany.*
Abitano in Sicilia.	*They live in Sicily.*

If masculine, the names of regions follow the same rules as masculine names of countries:

> Siamo nel Lazio (*or* in Lazio).
> *We are in Latium.*

> Viviamo nel Piemonte (*or* in Piemonte).
> We live in Piedmont.

4. The names of small islands and towns never require the article and are preceded by **a** instead of **in** when *motion towards* or *position in* is to be expressed:

> Vanno a Capri, ad *I*schia, a Cipro, etc.
> *They are going to Capri, to Ischia, to Cyprus, etc.*
> Vanno a Roma.   *They are going to Rome.*

NOTE. The preposition *in* is sometimes possible with the names of towns if position *within the town walls* is thought of:

> Quel palazzo è in Milano. *That building is in Milan.*

5. The genders of geographical locations may be classified as follows:

(a) The names of lakes are masculine:

> il Garda *Lake Garda* il Trasimeno *Lake Trasimenus*

(b) The names of mountains are masculine with few
   exceptions:
        Gli Appennini   *the Apennines*   il Giura   *the Jura*
but:
        Le Alpi   *the Alps*   le Ande   *the Andes*

(c) The names of rivers not ending in **-a** are masculine,
   those ending in **-a** (with few exceptions) are feminine:
        il Danubio   *the Danube*   il Tevere   *the Tiber*
        la Loira   *the Loire*   la Senna   *the Seine*
but:
        il Niagara   *the Niagara*   il Volga   *the Volga*

(d) The names of countries ending in **-a** are feminine,
   apart from a few exceptions:
        la Francia   *France*   L'Italia   *Italy*
but:
        il Canadà   *Canada*   il Bengala   *Bengal*

   The more common masculine names of countries are:
   il Brasile (Brazil), **il Bengala** (Bengal), **il Canadà**
   (Canada), **l'Egitto** (Egypt), **il Giappone** (Japan), **il
   Messico** (Mexico), **il Portogallo** (Portugal), **gli
   Stati Uniti** (the United States).

(e) The names of all towns are feminine except **il Cairo**
   (Cairo). In this latter case the article is always used
   with the name of the town (see Lesson XVI B).

B. THE INFINITIVE

1. The infinitive may be used as a noun in Italian and is
   always of masculine gender:
        L'arte dello scrivere.   *The art of writing.*
        Il troppo mangiare è nocivo.   *Overeating is harmful.*
        C'era un correre e uno strillare di donne.
        There was a sound of running and of women screaming.
        Aveva un bel dire, nessuno badava a lui.
        He spoke in vain, no one paid attention to him.

NOTE. Infinitives used as nouns may have direct or indirect objects:

Nel fare ciò, si mostrò colpevole.
In doing that, he showed himself to be guilty.

Finí col mandarci una lettera raccomandata.
He finished up by sending us a registered letter.

Care must be taken not to translate the word *of* in such phrases as:

Lo sprecar tempo non è lecito in questa fabbrica.
The wasting of time is not allowed in this factory.

However, one must translate it with **di** in two cases: (a) when the Italian verb always requires **di** before a complement; (b) when the infinitive used as a noun is intransitive:

Il parlare dei suoi difetti morali è poco cortese.
To speak of his moral defects is impolite.

All'apparire di Pietro, tutti tacquero.
At Peter's appearance, all were silent.

2. The infinitive may be used as an imperative when a general exhortation is to be expressed:

Per le informazioni necessarie rivolgersi all'agenzia Cook.
For the necessary information, apply to Cook's.

Rallentare all'angolo.   *Slow down at the corner.*

Non sporgersi dalla finestra. *Don't lean out of the window.*

3. Note the different meanings of the following:

Sul partire   *just before departure*
Al partire   *at the moment of departure*
Nel partire   *in process of departing*
Col partire   *after (resulting upon) departure*

Sul partire mi disse che s'era molto divertito.
On his departure he told me he had enjoyed himself.

Al partire del treno, mi strinse la mano.
As the train left, he shook my hand.

Il treno, nel partire, mandò un lungo fischio.
The train, as it started, whistled loudly.

Col partire di Giovanni, tutta la squadra si sentí giú di morale.
On John's departure, the whole team felt low-spirited.

4. The perfect infinitive is formed by using the present infinitives of **avere** or **essere** and the past participle of the verb:

TROVARE *to find*   ANDARE *to go*   LAVARSI *to wash*
avere trovato *to*   essere andato   essersi lavato *to have*
have found   *to have gone*   washed

5. The perfect infinitive is used:

(a) To translate its counterpart in English:
Mi sembra di averlo visto prima.
I seem to have seen him before.

(b) After certain prepositions:
Dopo aver cenato, andai a dormire.
After having supper, I went to bed.

(c) After certain verbs:
Si scusò di non essere potuto venire.
He apologized for not having been able to come.

GEOGRAFIA DELL'ITALIA

L'Italia è divisa in una ventina di regioni, ma queste regioni sono in gran parte soltanto espressioni geografiche, in quanto, sebbene la costituzione italiana preveda la formazione di regioni come enti territoriali usufruenti di alcune autonomie politiche e amministrative, al giorno d'oggi solo quattro regioni sono state formate con questi poteri: la Sardegna, la Sicilia, la Val d'Aosta, e il Trentino. Di uno statuto speciale gode anche Trieste ma, prescindendo da queste eccezioni, la divisione più comune che si fa dell'Italia è: Italia Settentrionale, Centrale, Meridionale, e Insulare.

Nell'Italia Settentrionale sono concentrate le maggiori industrie: il triangolo più industrializzato è quello che ha i suoi vertici a Torino, Milano e Genova, capoluoghi rispettivamente del Piemonte, della Lombardia e della Liguria. Importante centro agricolo e ferroviario dell'Italia Settentrionale è Bologna, capoluogo dell'Emilia; mentre Venezia è importante centro turistico. Nell'Italia Centrale, che comprende la Toscana, le Marche, l'Umbria, il Lazio e gli Abruzzi, le città piú importanti sono Roma, capitale d'Italia, e Firenze, importante centro artistico e culturale. L'Italia meridionale comprende la Campania, le Puglie, la Lucania e la Calabria. Napoli è certamente la piú nota città di queste regioni ma da un punto di vista commerciale ha notevole interesse anche Bari. L'Italia ha molte isole, ma le due maggiori sono la Sicilia e la Sardegna, ricche di usi e costumi tradizionali.

Quanto ai confini, l'Italia si protende nel mar Mediterraneo, il quale prende vari nomi a seconda delle coste che bagna: Mar Ligure, Mar Tirreno, Mar Ionio, Mare Adriatico. Al Nord è cinta dalle Alpi mentre per tutta la sua lunghezza è percorsa dagli Appennini.

Si dice che l'Italia abbia un buon clima, e quest'è vero, ma d'inverno, e specialmente nella pianura padana, esso è rigido forse piú che un inverno inglese.

EXERCISES

A. Translate into Italian:
   1. We went to Egypt for our holidays this year.
   2. I have never been to the United States.
   3. What does John want to go to Corsica for?
   4. The blue skies of Italy are a wonderful sight for one who rarely sees the sun.
   5. We get our timber from Canada.
   6. Brazil is one of the biggest countries in the world.
   7. The President of France spoke on the wireless last night.
   8. How long is it since you were in Sicily?
   9. That building is in Rome, not in Florence.
   10. The train passed through Tuscany on the way to the capital of Italy.

B. Answer the following questions in Italian:
   1. Quante regioni ci sono in Italia?
   2. Che cosa prevede la costituzione italiana?
   3. Quante regioni godono dell'autonomia locale?
   4. Che parte d'Italia è piú industrializzata?

    5. Che specie d'importanza ha la città di Bologna?
    6. Qual è la divisione piú comune che si fa dell'Italia?
    7. Che cosa percorre tutta la lunghezza dell'Italia?
    8. In che parte dell'Italia l'inverno è molto rigido?
    9. Quali sono le città piú importanti dell'Italia meridionale?
  10. Come si chiamano le isole maggiori italiane?

C. Translate into Italian:
    1. Writing books is difficult.
    2. Having taken supper, we went to bed.
    3. Whoever does not do his duty is not worthy of being respected.
    4. The setting (*tramontare*) of the sun is a wonderful sight.
    5. While going (infin.) to school, I met two of my friends.
    6. He spoke in vain, no one was listening.
    7. To want to know everything is madness (*pazzia*).
    8. Promising and giving are two very different things.
    9. I couldn't help (*contenersi da*) laughing.
  10. On (*a*) first entering the room, he felt very nervous (*nervoso*).
  11. We shall begin by reading the first chapter of the book.
  12. There was a shout, a sound of running and of weeping.

D. Put the correct preposition in the blank spaces:
    1. I vini — Portogallo sono ben conosciuti.
    2. Siamo — fertile Toscana.
    3. Il re — Inghilterra è partito per la Scozia.
    4. La parte piú industriale — Italia è la Lombardia.
    5. Non sono mai andato — Ischia.

E. Translate into Italian:
Italy is generally divided into four parts, Northern, Central,
Southern and Insular Italy. The North is rich in industry
while the South is very poor with few large towns and little
trade. Central Italy is an agricultural region but it also
contains Rome, the capital of Italy, and Florence which is
well known for its artistic traditions. The Italian climate is
said to be very good, but in winter it is often very cold, even
colder perhaps, than in an English winter.

REVISION EXERCISES (*Lessons XXXI–XXXV*)

1. Translate into Italian:
    1. It is enough for me to know you are working hard.
    2. He had wanted to repent.
    3. I am hoping to see that film.
    4. It is a pity you cannot come with us.
    5. I explained to him who to discuss the matter with when he arrived.
    6. He made John write the letter to his friend.
    7. It's a real pleasure to be able to help.
    8. I think I would do better by staying at home than by going there.
    9. Whose turn is it to play?
    10. You certainly did right to remind him of it.
    11. We were the last to get on the bus.
    12. What has happened to John since I saw him last?
    13. What is he up to in the garage (*autorimessa*)?
    14. Where has Charles gone?
    15. He declared he had never been there.
    16. Stop doing that.
    17. They are always boasting of the money they earn.
    18. He tried to prevent us from speaking to you.
    19. It is not possible to ask him to help us.
    20. It would have seemed as if he had forgotten what he promised to do if he had not returned at once.
    21. He denies he said such a thing.
    22. I'm afraid I shall not be able to join (*associarsi con*) you in your new business.
    23. It is not worth while disturbing (*disturbare*) them for so little.
    24. He claimed he had solved the problem in a few minutes.
    25. I am sorry to hear what has happened.

2. Fill in the blank spaces with the appropriate preposition if required:
    1. Sono molto felice — incontrarla.
    2. Non mi è piaciuto — andarci.
    3. Mi ha mandato — cercare.
    4. Si è sforzato — finire il lavoro.
    5. Non esitiamo — negarlo.
    6. Ho fatto bene — rimanere qui.

264

7. Ero il solo — ottenere un premio.
8. Mi costrinsero — seguirli.
9. E poi uscimmo — riveder le stelle.
10. Mi hanno vietato — andare a casa.

3. Translate into Italian:
1. Take care lest you spill (*rovesciare*) the milk.
2. Has he forgotten the book? Yes, he has.
3. That gave them something to think about.
4. We never thought of doing such a thing.
5. This machine is not suitable for that work.
6. We all like to think ourselves free from prejudice (*pregiudizio*).
7. He was ready to depart at that very moment.
8. That poor man is one-armed.
9. I should like to know what is to be done.

4. Give the correct tense of the verb in brackets:
1. Mi hanno domandato se (essere) in Italia.
2. Disse che essi (dovere) alzarsi subito.
3. Giovanni, come si (vedere), ha vinto il premio.
4. Io (volere) sapere dove era andato a finire.
5. Se avessi trovato la tua penna, te la (consegnare).

5. Translate into Italian:
1. I ought to have known that what he said was the truth (*verità*).
2. It must be at least eleven o'clock.
3. It seems as if it is going to rain tonight.
4. Do you know what the capital of Italy is?
5. I was to go to see the doctor yesterday but I couldn't leave the office.
6. We don't quite understand what you mean.
7. We wanted to continue our walk (*passeggiata*) but he said he was completely exhausted.
8. I know the North of Italy very well.
9. Charles wouldn't have anything to do with our plan (*piano*).
10. We shall need at least an hour to do this work.
11. Just listen, our cousins will be coming today and we have not yet begun to prepare to receive them.
12. Do you know Philip? — Do I know him? He is my best friend.
13. If nothing else, we have succeeded in making him decide what he intends to do.

14. A certain man came to see you this morning while you were out.
15. I would have thought that the rain was so heavy as to prevent you from going out.
16. Would you like a little more meat? Yes, just a little, please.
17. There were many pupils in the class, some reading, some writing.
18. I've been in Florence for ten years.
19. They went to Rome ten years ago.
20. We intend going to Italy for a fortnight's holiday.
21. He did the work in half an hour.
22. We do not care for Japanese pictures.
23. When did you say you would be going to Switzerland?
24. The Volga is the longest river in Europe.
25. Just as we were leaving, he shook hands with us.

6. Put in the correct preposition in the blank spaces:
1. Vorrei andare — Messico l'anno venturo.
2. Se andassimo — Spagna, vorrei passare qualche giorno — Siviglia.
3. Il clima — Italia è molto buono.
4. Vanno — Egitto per le loro vacanze.
5. Abbiamo passato due settimane — bella Sicilia.
6. Mi piace molto il caffè — Brasile.
7. La potenza industriale — Inghilterra è molto grande.
8. L'Italia è piú grande — Grecia.
9. Impossibile andare — Cipro quest'anno.
10. Le foreste — Canadà sono immense.

A. VERBS TAKING BOTH **AVERE** AND **ESSERE** IN THEIR COMPOUND TENSES

1. Some verbs take **avere** or **essere** in their compound tenses according to whether they are transitive or intransitive:

Ho corso un grave pericolo.
I have run a grave danger.

Sono corso giú per la strada.
I have run down the road.

La sua salute è migliorata.
His health has improved.

Abbiamo migliorato la nostra situazione finanziaria.
We have improved our financial position.

È vissuto per due anni in America.
He has lived in America for two years.

Ha vissuto una vita da eroe.
He has lived a hero's life.

Ho salito i gradini.
I climbed the steps.

Siamo saliti in macchina.
We got into the car.

Hai cessato d'importunarmi?
Have you finished worrying me?

La guerra è cessata.
The war has finished.

Abbiamo convenuto il prezzo.
We have agreed about the price.

Siamo convenuti qui per onorare un grande uomo.
We have assembled here to honour a great man.

2. Impersonal verbs dealing with the weather take **avere** or **essere** almost indifferently:

Ha piovuto. ⎫
È piovuto. ⎬ *It has rained.*

Ha nevicato.
È nevicato. } *It has snowed.*

NOTE. All other impersonal verbs require **essere** in their compound tenses:

Mi è dispiaciuto che tu non abbia potuto assistere alla ceremonia.
I was sorry you were unable to attend the ceremony.

Mi è parso strano che egli non potesse venire a casa mia.
It seemed strange to me that he could not come to my house.

B. IDIOMS WITH CERTAIN COMMON VERBS

1. **Stare** often takes over the duties of **essere,** especially with adverbs:

Egli sta un po' meglio oggi.
He is a little better today.

Sta bene cosí.
It's all right like that.

Non sta bene comportarsi cosí.
It is not right to behave like that.

2. **Stare a** conveys the idea of a lengthy duration of time:

Che i due stessero ad aspettare qualcuno era cosa troppo evidente. (Manzoni)
That the two were standing there waiting for somebody was only too evident.

but it is also used in the following type of expression:

Stia a sentire!   *Just listen!*

3. **Stare per** means *to be about to*:

Stavo per partire quando mi richiamò.
I was about to leave when he recalled me.

NOTE. One can also say:

Stavo lí lí per cadere quando mi afferrò la mano.
I was about to fall when he grasped my hand.

This expression means *to be on the very verge of* and is generally used to describe narrow escapes from disaster, etc.

4. The following idioms are worth remembering:

stare in piedi	*to be standing*
stare tranquillo	*to be quiet, calm*
Come sta?	*How are you?*
Quel vestito ti sta male.	*That dress is a bad fit.*
stare seduto	*to remain seated*
Fatto sta che tu ci sei andato.	*The fact remains that you went there.*
stare tra il sí e il no	*to hesitate*
stare in forse	*to be in doubt*
lasciare stare	*to leave alone*
Lascia stare, farò io.	*Leave it alone, I'll do it my-self.*
Bene mi sta!	*It serves me right!*

5. **Essere per** means the same as **stare per** but it is rarer:

Ero per partire quando mi richiamò.
I was about to leave when he called me back.

6. **Essere** usually requires a complement, and if one does not exist in English, a neutral **lo** is placed before the verb in Italian:

Siete voi Giovanni Lanfredi? — Lo sono.
Are you John Lanfredi? — I am.
È professore cosí come lo sono io.
He is a teacher as I am myself.

7. Note the following expressions:

Chi è là? — Sono io.	*Who is there? — It is I.*
Che n'è stato del signor Tosi?	*What has become of Mr. Tosi?*
Mi domando se tu c'eri.	*I wonder if you were there.*
Chi è in bottega? — Ci sono loro.	*Who is in the shop? They are.*
Cosa c'è?	*What is the matter?*

But where people are concerned, one must use **avere**:

Cos'hai oggi?	*What's the matter with you today?*

In Italian **sono io, sei tu,** *etc.* replace *it is I, it is you, etc.* in response to a question.

8. The following idioms with **dare** are important:

dare su	*to overlook, to look on to*
La finestra dà sul giardino.	*The window overlooks the garden.*
darla a bere (a)	*to take someone in*
dare ai nervi	*to get on one's nerves*
dare del tu, del Lei, del voi	*to address with tu, Lei, voi*
Dagli al ladro!	*Stop thief! (After the thief!)*
darsela a gambe	*to take to one's heels*
Può darsi + subj.	*It is possible that . . .*
dare nell'occhio	*to attract attention*
Quel vestito ti dà nell'occhio.	*That dress hits you in the eye.*
darsi a	*to devote oneself to*
Si è del tutto dato allo studio.	*He is completely devoted to study.*
darsi per	*to admit*
Mi son dato per vinto.	*I admitted defeat.*
dare inizio	*to initiate*
dare alla testa	*to go to one's head*
I soldi gli han sempre dato alla testa.	*Money has always gone to his head.*
dare il benvenuto a	*to welcome*
dare addosso ad uno	*to attack*
Appena mi vide, mi diede addosso.	*Hardly had he seen me when he attacked me.*

9. **Andare** means *to fit* or *to suit* in some phrases:

Queste scarpe non mi vanno bene.	*These shoes do not fit me well.*

10. **Andare** is also used with some adjectives instead of **essere**:

andare orgoglioso	*to be proud (of)*
andare pazzo	*to be mad (over)*
andare fiero	*to be proud (of)*
andare matto	*to be mad (over)*

Giovanni ha vinto il premio e ne andiamo orgogliosi.
John has won a prize and we are proud of him.

11. The following idioms are important:

andare a piedi	*to go on foot*
andare a cavallo	*to go on horseback*

andare a monte	*to go wrong, awry*
andare a male	*to go bad (food)*
a lungo andare	*in the long run*
andare a meraviglia	*to go swimmingly*
andare a genio	*to please, suit*
lasciare andare	*not to take notice of*
Lascia andare, tutti sanno che è un ignorante.	*Pay no attention, everyone knows he is an ignoramus.*
andare in collera, in bestia, etc.	*to get angry*

12. **Fare** sometimes means *to practise a profession*:

Carlo fa l'avvocato.	*Charles is a lawyer.*
Giovanni fa il soldato.	*John is a soldier.*

13. **Farsi** means *to become*:

Mio fratello si è fatto prete.	*My brother has become a priest.*

14. **Far sí che** is used in the following ways:

Feci sí che partisse subito.
I arranged for him to leave at once.
Il dottore fece sí che tutto andasse bene.
The doctor saw to it that all went well.
Fece sí che alla fine mi arrabbiai.
He carried on in such a way that I finally became angry.

The last example does not require the subjunctive since **sí che** in that case expresses a result, not a purpose.

15. The following idioms are also important:

bell'e fatto	*well and truly done*
strada facendo	*on the way*
fare per uno	*to suit*
Questo non fa per me.	*This does not suit me.*
farla ad uno	*to play a trick on*
Non la fa a me.	*He won't play that one on me.*
Come si fa a . . .	*How does one . . .*
Come si fa ad andare avanti di questo passo?	*How can one keep on at this pace?*
niente a che fare (vedere) con	*to have nothing to do with*
Questo problema non ha niente a che fare con la matematica.	*This problem has nothing to do with mathematics.*

UNA VISITA AD UNA PARENTE

La signora Delfina e il signor Piero Dobelli rimasero sbalorditi apprendendo da una conoscente chiacchierina che la contessa Filippeschi era da otto giorni a Milano. Dopo quattro mesi di assenza, da otto giorni a Milano e non aveva avvertito la famiglia del suo arrivo, né era andata a trovarla ...

— Che cosa si fa? — chiese Delfina.

— Si fa finta di non saper nulla, e si passa da casa sua, — rispose Piero.

Uscirono: per abitudine, Delfina andava innanzi; veniva poi Piero; e da ultimo Dick, il quale essendo vecchio e grasso camminava piano, indifferente al viavai delle strade popolose come alla vista di altri cani, che gli davano una fiutata e tiravan via. Per riguardo a Dick, camminava piano anche Piero e camminava piano anche Delfina; i tre componevano il corteo della vita pacifica.

— Di questo passo — osservò Piero, — arriveremo da Gioconda verso l'alba.

Si consultarono, diedero un'occhiata a Dick, il quale aveva bisogno di una boccata d'aria, e decisero di noleggiare una carrozza. Dick si acconciò di malavoglia tra Delfina e Piero, perché odiava le novità; e le passeggiate in carrozza erano in casa Dobelli tal novità, che Dick non ne rammentava due nella sua quattordicenne esistenza. La contessa Filippeschi era in casa. Si fecero annunziare, mentre la cameriera apriva loro l'uscio del salotto. Attesero venti minuti. Finalmente Gioconda comparve, con la sigaretta tra l'indice e il medio della sinistra.

(Luciano Zuccoli: *La Volpe di Sparta*)

EXERCISES

A. Translate into Italian:
1. It has just hailed.
2. It has pleased me to hear that you are well.
3. How do you feel today? — I feel a little better, thank you.

4. Our financial position has improved.
5. Just fancy! he warned (*avvertire*) me this would happen last month. It serves me right.
6. That dress does not suit you at all.
7. I was about to go out when John came to see me.
8. What has happened to Charles and Philip?
9. Who is there? — It is I.
10. The room looked out on to the beach.
11. That multicoloured suit of his attracts your attention at once.
12. His methods of working were laughable.
13. We are very proud of what he has done.
14. I am sure he would not play that one on me.
15. In my opinion, this has nothing to do with the problem.

B. Answer the following questions in Italian:
1. Perché rimasero sbalorditi la signora e il signor Dobelli?
2. Chi ha detto loro che la contessa era da otto giorni a Milano?
3. Che cosa consiglia di fare Piero?
4. Perché andavano piano lungo la strada?
5. A che cosa somigliavano?
6. Che cosa osservò alla fine Piero?
7. Quando arrivarono alla casa della contessa, chi aprí la porta?
8. C'era la contessa?
9. Quanto tempo hanno dovuto aspettare?
10. Fumava la contessa quando comparve?

C. Fill in the blank spaces with the appropriate tense of *avere* or *essere*:
1. Non — nevicato quest'anno.
2. Loro — vissuti a Roma per dieci anni.
3. Io — vissuto una vita da cane quando ero prigioniero di guerra.
4. Il rumore — cessato.
5. Mi — occorso andare a casa.
6. Essi — migliorato il disegno delle loro macchine.
7. Voi — corso un gran rischio nel fare ciò.
8. Mi — sembrato meraviglioso che i Russi avessero lanciato un satellite.
9. Quanto — costato quel libro?
10. Ci — rotto l'orologio.

D. Translate into Italian:

The Dobelli family decided to go out and pay a visit to a relation who had recently returned from abroad. They took their old dog, Dick, with them but he walked so slowly that they had to take a carriage. When they arrived at the countess Filippeschi's house, the door was opened by the maid who showed (*far entrare*) them into the drawing-room. The countess was very busy and made them wait a half hour before she appeared. Then she came into the room smoking a cigarette and did not excuse herself for being late.

E. Describe in Italian a visit to an old aunt in the country.

A. THE PASSIVE VOICE

1. The passive voice is generally formed in Italian by the use of the various tenses of the verb **essere** and the past participle of the verb. The past participle in this construction always agrees with the subject of the sentence:

Il pranzo è servito.   *Dinner is served.*
Un uomo è stato ucciso.   *A man has been killed.*
La ragazza è stata promossa agli esami.
The girl has passed the examination.

2. With verbs of action **venire** very frequently replaces **essere** as an auxiliary, but this is only possible in the simple, not in the compound, tenses:

La finestra era chiusa. (*state*)   *The window was closed.*
La finestra venne chiusa. *The window was (had just (action) been) closed.*

3. **Andare** with the past participle is rarely a true passive† but often indicates obligation:

Costruirò una casa come va costruita.
I shall build a house as it should be built.

Quel libro non va messo sul secondo scaffale.
That book should not be (is not to be) put on the second shelf.

4. Note the use of **rimanere** with verbs expressing emotion:

Quando gli dissi che le sue proposte non mi facevano né caldo né freddo, rimase stupefatto.
When I told him I was indifferent to his proposals, he was amazed.

5. The passive voice can also be translated as follows:

(a) By a reflexive verb:

Come si pronunciano queste parole?
How are these words pronounced?

† It is, however, a true passive with verbs of losing, wasting, destroying, etc.:
Una buon'azione non va mai persa.
A good action is never wasted.

instead of:

Come sono pronunciate queste parole?

(b) By the indefinite **si**:

Si dice che sia scoppiata la guerra.
It is said that war has broken out.

instead of:

È detto che sia scoppiata la guerra.

(c) By using a third person plural:

Dicono che sia scoppiata la guerra.
It is said that war has broken out.

B. FARE, LASCIARE, SENTIRE AND VEDERE WITH A DEPENDENT INFINITIVE

1. **Fare** with a dependent infinitive means *to have something done by someone else* and **lasciare** (to let) follows the same rules as **fare** in almost all constructions. These rules are:

(a) If there is one object only, it precedes **fare** or **lasciare** when a pronoun and follows the dependent infinitive when a noun:

Lo feci partire.   *I made him leave.*
Lo lasciai partire.   *I let him leave.*

but:

Feci correre Giovanni.   *I made John run.*

(b) If both verbs have an object, then the object of **fare** or **lasciare** becomes indirect:

Gli feci mandare la lettera. *I made him send the letter.*
Gli lasciai mandare la lettera. *I let him send the letter.*

(c) If the use of the indirect form causes ambiguity, one uses **da**:

Feci scrivere la lettera da Giovanni.
I made John write the letter.

The normal form of construction could have a different meaning in this case:

Feci scrivere la lettera a Giovanni.
I had the letter written to John.

Such ambiguity is frequent with verbs taking an indirect object of the person.

NOTE. (1) The following form of **fare** should be noted:

Fu fatto entrare.
He was caused to enter. (i.e., He was shown in.)

(2) **Lasciare** does not require the pronoun *it* in the following type of phrase:

Lascia stare.	*Leave it alone.*
Lascia fare a me.	*Leave it to me (Let me see to it).*

(3) Instead of:

Lascia fare a lei.	*Let her do it.*

one can also use the subjunctive and a subordinate clause:

Lascia che lo faccia lei.

(4) Reflexive verbs drop the reflexive pronoun after **fare** or **lasciare**:

Lo facemmo pentire.	*We made him repent.*

2. **Vedere** and **sentire** behave like **fare** when their objects are pronouns:

La vedo venire.	*I see her coming.*
La sento cantare.	*I hear her singing.*
Gliela sentii cantare.	*I heard her sing it.*
Gliene vidi portare via.	*I saw him carrying some away.*

But when the object (or objects) are nouns, then the following constructions are used:

Sentii abbaiare il cane.	*I heard the dog bark.*

Vidi Giovanni portare via delle pere.
I saw John carrying some pears away.

Sentii Maria cantare un'aria di Monteverdi.
I heard Mary singing an air by Monteverdi.

The rule is that if there is only one object, it usually follows the infinitive; if more than one, the infinitive is separated from the finite verb by the direct object of the person.

IL GRANDE ANARCHICO

Libero Vasti era figlio del solo repubblicano che fosse mai stato in paese, di Ercole Vasti capomastro. Libero non aveva tradito gl'ideali paterni consacrati in quel nome augurale; anzi li aveva spinti alle loro conseguenze estreme, diventando prima socialista, poi anarchico, o meglio libertario, come preferiva chiamarsi dopo certa avventura occorsagli in città. A diciotto anni il padre lo aveva mandato nella vicina città a lavorare. Ma Libero era un lavoratore un po' distratto e il padrone lo teneva soltanto per l'ottima sua indole e perché lo divertivano i discorsi focosamente ribelli di quel giovanotto roseo.

Una volta vi fu in città una dimostrazione operaia, un po' di tumulto. Libero vi si cacciò in mezzo, e gridava con gli altri. Scorse due sbirri che guardavano attorno, un po' perplessi, come[1] non sapessero bene che fare. Libero andò loro incontro, proclamando: — Sono un anarchico. Allora i due sbirri lo misero in mezzo e lo portarono al posto di sicurezza. La mattina dopo, essendosi divertiti un po' alle sue spalle e avendone riconosciuto la perfetta innocuità, lo rilasciarono, segnandolo sui loro registri come 'anarchico pericoloso'. Come tale lo troveran ricordato gli storici avvenire[2] quando ricercheranno negli archivi delle questure i documenti di quest'era di rivoluzione che noi stiamo, senz'accorgercene, attraversando, come molti asseriscono.

(MASSIMO BONTEMPELLI: *Il Ribelle in Riga*)

NOTES

[1] **come**: *Come* is used here in place of *come se* (as if).

[2] **avvenire**: This curious construction of an infinitive used as an adjective should be noted. It is also used as a noun meaning *the future*.

EXERCISES

A. Translate into Italian:
1. A man has just been killed in a road accident.
2. The windows are open but the door is closed.
3. When the letters had been written, the young man took them to the post.
4. When I heard the news, I was amazed.
5. I will show you how the work should be done.
6. Those plates should not be put there.
7. I have been told that John has passed his examination.
8. The visitor was shown in by the servant.
9. We were all perplexed when he accused us of stealing.
10. He wanted to know how many Italian words were pronounced.

B. Answer the following questions in Italian:
1. Chi era Libero Vasti?
2. Che specie di avventura gli è occorsa in città?
3. Perché si è fatto segnare come 'anarchico pericoloso' nei registri della polizia?
4. Come Libero s'è attirato l'attenzione dei due sbirri?
5. Perché i poliziotti si sono un po' divertiti alle sue spalle?
6. Libero era un buon lavoratore?
7. Perché lo teneva il padrone?
8. In quale specie di periodo viviamo secondo alcuni?
9. Dove cercheranno gli storici i documenti di quest'era di rivoluzione?
10. Che cosa fece Libero durante la dimostrazione operaia?

C. Translate into Italian:
1. 'Leave it alone!' said the boy's father.
2. They made him return home on foot.
3. I could hear John singing an Italian song.
4. They made Charles send a letter (even) though he did not wish to do it.
5. Let me see to it, I shall do it more quickly than you.
6. Mr. Tosi has rung up for an appointment, when shall I have him come?
7. He would not allow me to leave before six.
8. I had my mother buy a book for my friend.
9. Mr. Rossi made his son wash his hands before coming to the table.
10. I had him make me a new suit.

D. Put the correct pronouns into the blank spaces:
  1. Perché (*him*) — avete fatto venire per niente?
  2. Suo padre (*him*) — fece mettere i suoi libri in ordine.
  3. Quando (*him*) — vidi venire, me ne andai subito.
  4. Noi (*him*) — facemmo firmare la dichiarazione.
  5. Essi (*her*) — sentirono cantare.

E. Translate into Italian:

Libero was the son of a republican and he certainly did not betray his father's ideals; on the contrary, he carried them to their extreme consequences and became an anarchist. His first encounter (*incontro*) with the police took place (*aver luogo*) in the city when he was eighteen years old. He saw two policemen standing at the street corner during a demonstration and he went up to them at once, proclaiming: 'I am an anarchist.' Happy to find a victim (*vittima*), they put him between them and took him to the police station. They soon discovered, however, his perfect harmlessness and, having amused themselves a little at his expense, they let him go. They then marked him down in their books as a dangerous anarchist and it is as such that he will be remembered by those historians of the future who will search among the documents of the prefectures for the proofs (*prove*) of this age of revolution.

A. PREPOSITIONS IN ITALIAN

1. Prepositions in Italian may be classified as follows:

(a) Those which *never* require a second element such as
a or **di**:

a	*to, at*	in	*in*
attraverso	*across*	lungo	*along*
circa	*about, nearly*	mediante	*by means of*
con	*with*	per	*for, through*
da	*from*	rasente†	*skimming*
di	*of*	salvo	*except, save for*
durante	*during*	secondo	*according to*
eccetto	*except*	tranne	*except*
fuorché	*except*		

Ci siamo andati tutti fuorché Giovanni.
We all went there except John.
Glielo comunicai mediante un telegramma.
I let him know by means of a telegram.

(b) Those that may or may not take **a** before a noun and
di before a personal pronoun:

	NOUN	PRONOUN	
contro	–	di	*against*
dentro	a*	di	*in, inside*
dietro	a*	di	*behind*
dopo	–	di*	*after*
oltre	a*	di	*beyond*
presso	a*	di*	*near, at, almost*
senza	–	di*	*without*
sopra	–	di	*on, upon*

† Sometimes takes *a* with a noun.
* Denotes an option of insertion or omission of the second element.

sotto	a* (rare)	di*	*under*
su	–	di	*on*
tra (fra)	–	di*	*between, among*
verso	–	di*	*towards*

NOTE (1) **Presso** changes its meaning on occasion when used with **di**:

> Abito presso (alla) la stazione.
> *I live near the station.*

but:

> Abita presso di noi.
> *He lives at our house.*

When used in the sense of *almost* it always requires **a**:

> Ci sono presso a poco duemila sterline.
> *There are almost two thousand pounds.*

(2) **Dopo** requires **di** before a relative:

> Dopo di che, andammo a letto.
> *After which, we went to bed.*

(c) Other prepositions always require **a**:

accanto a	*beside*	innanzi† a	*in front of,*
davanti a	*in front of, before*		*before*
		intorno	*around*
dinanzi a	*in front of, before*	(attorno) a	
		quanto a	⎫
dirimpetto a	*opposite*	riguardo a	⎬ *as for*
fino a	*up till, as far as*	rispetto a	⎭
		sino a	*up till*
incontro a	*against*	vicino a	*near*

NOTE. **Dirimpetto** permits of two constructions:

> La tua casa è dirimpetto a quel gran palazzo.
> *Your house is opposite that large building.*

but also:

> Di chi è quella casa dirimpetto?
> *Whose house is the one opposite?*

† *Innanzi* is sometimes used without *a*:
  Arrivai innanzi tempo.   *I arrived before time.*

(d) There are many prepositional phrases requiring **a**:

in capo a	*at the end of (time)*
in cima a	*on the top of*
in faccia a	*to the face of*
in fondo a	*at the bottom of*
di fronte a	*face to face with, confronted by*
in mezzo a	*in the middle of*
in riva a	*on the bank of*

Arrivammo alle quattro in cima alla montagna.
We arrived at four o'clock on the top of the mountain.

Ci trovammo inaspettatamente di fronte al nemico.
We found ourselves unexpectedly face to face with the enemy.

La barca era in mezzo al fiume.
The boat was in the middle of the river.

(e) Prepositions with **di**:

fuori di	*outside*
invece di	*instead of*
per causa di	
a causa di	*because of*
per via di	
nel mezzo di	*in the middle of*
per mezzo di	*by means of*
prima di	*before (time or sequence)*
in punto di	*at the point of*

Sono andati fuori della casa.
They have gone out of the house.

Non ha voluto rimanere a causa di te.
He did not want to stay because of you.

(f) Prepositions with **da**:

fin da	*right from (time)*
giú da	*down from*
lungi da	*far from*
sin da	*right from (time)*

Sin da allora, non è piú venuto qui.
From that time, he has not been here.

(g) Prepositions with **per**:

su per   *up along*
giú per   *down along*
su su per   *right up*
giú giú per   *right down*

È corso giú per la strada.
He ran down the road.

Andò su su per le rocce verso la cima del monte.
He went right up through the rocks towards the top of the mountain.

2. Prepositions must be repeated unless a list is given:

I ragazzi camminarono nel fango e nelle pozzanghere.
The boys walked in the mud and the puddles.
but:
Non si può scrivere senza penna, inchiostro e carta.
One cannot write without a pen, ink and paper.

B. THE REPETITION OF WORDS IN ITALIAN

1. The repetition of words is used in Italian for a large number of effects. It is quite frequent with adjectives, verbs, adverbs and adverbial expressions:

(a) With adjectives:

Il tempo era cattivo cattivo.
The weather was very bad.
Il mare era calmo calmo.
The sea was very calm.

As can be seen from these examples, the repetition of the adjective has the same effect as the absolute superlative.

(b) With verbs:

Batti oggi, batti domani, un bel giorno riuscirà.
By hammering away day and night, he will succeed one day.
Gira e rigira, è sempre lo stesso problema.
Whichever way you look at it, it is always the same problem.

Ci fece delle grandi promesse ma, stringi stringi, non
   ricevemmo nulla.
*He made us great promises, but, in conclusion, we re-
   ceived nothing.*

Voglia o non voglia, lo dovrò fare.
I must do it, whether I like it or not.

It will be noted that all the verbs are in the second
person singular of the imperative in these phrases,
except the last example. No matter what the subject of the main phrase may be, these forms never
change.

(c) With adverbs and adverbial expressions:

Giovanni andò pian piano verso i suoi avversari.
John went very softly towards his opponents.

Avendo avuto una bella lavata di capo dal direttore,
   l'impiegato se ne andò mogio mogio.
*Having had a good row from the director, the employee
   went away with his tail between his legs.*

Man mano che la merce era portata dentro, Carlo la
   disponeva lungo il muro.
*As the goods were being brought in, Charles arranged
   them along the wall.*

IL MARITO FA UNA SCENATA

Adriana: M'hai chiamata?

Giacomo: Adriana, so tutto: tu hai un amante. È uno
studente. L'hai visto ieri, ier l'altro, e ti sei trovata con
lui in una pensione poco raccomandabile. È vero o non
è vero?

Adriana (*con uno scatto di gioia*): Ah finalmente! Ho capito,
Giacomo! Perché non dirlo subito? (*ride*) Uno studente
sí . . . un giovane che mi ama molto.

Giacomo (*stupito guarda Giorgio*): Ride? Confessa e ride?

Adriana: Ma sí. Povero ragazzo. È scappato di collegio
perché era innamorato. Gli ho trovato un appartamentino
modesto: gli ho anche regalato mille lire.

Giacomo: Eh?

Adriana: È mio fratello! È Augusto! (*ride*) Che sciocco! Povero figliuolo! Una predica gliel'ho già fatta io, poi un po' alla volta, gliela farai tu . . . Per il momento l'ho aiutato a nascondersi. Ecco tutto. E tu . . . chi è che t'ha informato? Scommetto che è stato lui. (*addita Giorgio*)

Giorgio: Io? Io no, glielo assicuro.

Adriana: E allora chi? Mi fai seguire forse?

Giacomo: Oh guarda, guarda! (*seccato*) Dunque non è vero. Bene, bene, ne sono lieto.

Giorgio (*gli stringe la mano*): Congratulazioni!

Giacomo (*con ira*): Ma Augusto aggiusterà i conti con me. Che cosa crede? Scappare dal collegio? A diciotto anni?

Adriana: Ha fatto benissimo. Doveva[1] scappare a diciassette. I collegi sono insopportabili.

Giacomo: Naturalmente! Questa è la tua morale. Questo è il tuo modo di vedere la vita. Nessun rispetto per niente; nessun rispetto per le convenienze. (*il telefono squilla, Giacomo prende il ricevitore*) Pronto[2]: va bene, vengo subito (*continuando*). Nessun rispetto . . .

Adriana (*affettuosa*): Ma Giacomo . . . non sei contento che io sia innocente? Non senti bisogno di chiedermi scusa?

Giacomo (*turbato*): Ah già! Perdonami . . . sono un po' avventato, lo riconosco. Non lo farò piú. (*le sfiora la fronte con le labbra*) Ti assicuro che d'ora innanzi non ti darò piú noia. (*a Giorgio*) Hanno bisogno di noi in istudio.

Giorgio: Va pure. Ti raggiungo subito.

(S. GIOVANINETTI: Gli Ipocriti)

NOTES

[1] **Doveva**: Just as we have seen in conditional clauses, the imperfect may on occasion be used instead of the conditional perfect. The meaning of the verb in this sentence is obviously *ought to have*.

[2] **Pronto**: This word is the Italian equivalent to *Hello!* when answering the telephone as well as meaning *ready*.

EXERCISES

A. Translate into Italian:
1. I have nothing against John.
2. It is nearer five pounds than three.
3. We cannot go there without him.
4. According to them, a war is about to break out.
5. Charles stood in front of the shop.
6. What is that building opposite used for (*A che serve . . .*)?
7. He put his chair beside mine.
8. We sat in the middle of the room.
9. He could not see any water at the bottom of the well.
10. We could not get out of the building because of the crowd.
11. She asked Charles to come instead of John.
12. They went right down into the valley (*la valle*) without seeing a soul (*anima viva*).

B. Put the correct preposition (if required) into the following spaces:
1. Camminavano — la strada.
2. La mia casa sta — tre chilometri di qui.
3. Udimmo strani rumori — la notte.
4. Si parlavano fra — loro.
5. Fino — quando dobbiamo rimanere qui?
6. Abitiamo presso — lui al momento.
7. Quanto — Carlo, è un bravo ragazzo.
8. Siamo andati fino — Milano.
9. Non si può contare su — lui.
10. Mise il libro sotto — la sua sedia.

C. Translate into Italian:
1. Whether we like it or not, we have to do what he tells us.
2. As they were walking across the heath, the moon was rising above the hills.
3. Whatever way you look at it, the problem is very difficult.
4. We walked slowly down the road talking.
5. After I had told him off, he went away with his tail between his legs.

D. Answer the following questions in Italian:
1. Perché il marito fa una scenata?
2. Per chi Adriana ha trovato un appartamentino?
3. Di che cosa Adriana accusa suo marito?
4. Perché Augusto è scappato dal collegio?
5. Con chi deve aggiustare i conti?

6. Chi, secondo Giacomo, non ha rispetto per le convenienze?
7. È contento Giacomo che Adriana sia innocente?
8. Che cosa egli si riconosce di essere?
9. Di chi si chiede al telefono?
10. Dove va Giacomo dopo la telefonata?

E. Translate into Italian:

Adriana's husband accuses her of betraying him but she laughs and asks whether he is having her followed. The fact is that her young brother had run away from college and she thought it her duty to find him a small apartment in town. Giacomo, her husband, hardly seems pleased when he hears the news, and, instead of asking his wife's pardon, becomes angry because Augusto has left school. Adriana replies that he ought to have left much earlier, but then her husband completely loses his temper (*uscire dai gangheri*) and accuses her of not having any respect for the proprieties. At that moment the telephone rings and he finds that he is wanted in the office. He leaves at once slamming (*sbattere*) the door behind him.

A. PREPOSITIONS (*cont.*)

1. The preposition **a** is also used:

(a) To indicate means, manner or instrument:

chiudere a chiave	*to lock*
cucire a macchina	*to sew with a sewing-machine*
imparare a memoria	*to learn by heart*
scrivere a penna	*to write with a pen*
andare a piedi	*to go on foot*
Si salvò a forza di cure.	*He saved himself by way of treatment.*
Lo minacciarono a parole e a gesti.	*They threatened him with words and deeds.*
Una diga a protezione della città.	*A dyke for the protection of the town.*
Lo riconobbi all'accento.	*I recognized him by his accent.*

(b) To mean *in the way of* (see Lesson XXIX, Notes):

all'italiana	*in the Italian fashion*
alla buona	*simply, informally*
alla rinfusa	*in confusion, in disorder*

(c) To express structure, form or make-up of something:

una barca a vela	*a sailing-boat*
una macchina a vapore	*a steam-engine*
una pittura a olio	*an oil-painting*
un mulino a vento	*a windmill*

(d) After numerals (see Lesson XXXI A 6):

il primo a venire	*the first to come*
il secondo a parlare	*the second to speak*
l'ultimo a partire	*the last to leave*

(e) In a large number of adverbial expressions closely allied to those given in (a):

andare a cavallo	*to go on horseback*
a bocca aperta	*open-mouthed*
comprare a contanti	*to buy for cash*
a destra, a sinistra	*on the right, on the left*

giocare a carte	*to play cards*
gridare a squarciagola	*to shout at the top of one's voice*
morire a migliaia	*to die in thousands*
stilla a stilla	*drop by drop*
a stento	*with difficulty*
ad uno ad uno, a due a due, etc.	*one by one, two by two, etc.*
a volo	*in flight*
ad alta voce	*aloud*

(f) Sometimes to express value:

Vendiamo le biciclette a diecimila lire l'una.
We sell the bicycles at ten thousand lire each.

(g) In idiomatic phrases with infinitives:

Giovanni, a conoscerlo bene, è un bravo ragazzo.
John, when you know him well, is a fine fellow.

Neanche a picchiarlo non parlava.
He wouldn't speak even when you beat him.

2. Further uses of the preposition **da** are:

(a) To indicate an approximate number:

C'erano da trenta a quaranta persone in quella sala.
There were from thirty to forty people in that room.

(b) In descriptions:

L'uomo dal cappello rosso.	*The man with the red hat.*
La donna dagli orecchini d'oro.	*The woman with the golden earrings.*

NOTE. **Con** may also be used in this sense.

(c) To express *in the manner of, as characteristic of* (see Lesson IX, Notes):

Ha agito da pazzo.	*He has acted like a madman.*

(d) To express value or measurement:

un francobollo da venti lire	*a twenty lire stamp*
un teleschermo da 17 pollici	*a 17-inch television screen*
un biglietto da 200 lire	*a 200 lire ticket*
un appartamento dall'affitto proibitivo	*an appartment with a prohibitive rent*

(e) To denote the use of an object:

una tazza da tè	*a teacup*
una bottiglia da vino	*a wine bottle*
una sala da pranzo	*a dining-room*
un uomo dabbene	*a good-natured man*
una vita da cane	*a dog's life*

NOTE. Compare these phrases with **una tazza di tè** (a cup of tea); **una bottiglia di vino** (a bottle of wine), *etc.*

(f) To express various ideas before an infinitive:

a passive:

casa da vendere	*house for sale*
È da sperarsi.	*It is to be hoped.*

obligation:

Ho da lavorare.	*I have to work.*
Diritti da difendere.	*Rights to defend.*

result:

un caldo da scoppiare	*hot enough to burst*
un freddo da morire	*cold enough to die*
un viso da far morire in bocca una preghiera. (Manzoni)	*a face ugly enough to stifle a prayer on the lips.*
Siamo tanto felici da non capire piú nulla.	*We are so happy, we understand nothing any more.*
nulla da dire	*nothing to say*
un po' da fare	*a little to do*
È cosí bravo da riuscire.	*He is clever enough to succeed.*

(g) To denote the origin of a person:

Guido da Siena	*Guido from Siena*
Cino da Pistoia	*Cino from Pistoia*

(h) In many adverbial expressions:

daccapo (da capo)	*from the beginning*
Ricominciamo da capo.	*Let us begin again from the beginning.*
da lontano	*from afar*
Lo vidi da lontano.	*I saw him from afar.*
da vicino	*from nearby, close to*
Non l'ho mai visto da vicino.	*I have never seen him close to.*

| davvero | *really* |
| È davvero possibile? | *Is it really possible?* |

3. Further uses of the preposition **di** are as follows:

   (a) After certain indefinite expressions:

qualche cosa di buono	*something good*
Che c'è di nuovo?	*What news is there?*
niente d'importante	*nothing important*
un non so che di misterioso	*a touch of mystery*

but:

| nient'altro | *nothing else* |
| qualcos'altro | *something else* |

NOTE. (1) The adjective is always masculine in such phrases.
(2) **Altro** never takes **di**.

   (b) To indicate the composition of an object:

un orologio d'oro	*a gold watch*
una casseruola di rame	*a copper saucepan*
una padella di acciaio	*a steel frying-pan*

NOTE. If the material is uppermost in the mind rather than the object to which one is referring, it is possible to use **in**:

| una poltrona in pelle | *a hide armchair* |

   (c) To indicate contents:

| una tazza di tè | *a cup of tea* |
| un bicchier d'acqua | *a glass of water* |

   (d) To specify certain times:

di mattina	*in the morning*
di sera	*in the evening*
di notte	*in the night*
di giorno	*in the day*
di primavera	*in Spring*
di quaresima	*in Lent*

   (e) In many other expressions and with many verbs:

Di scrittore si fece operaio.	*From a writer he became a workman.*
di paese in paese	*from country to country*
di male in peggio	*from bad to worse*
Che ceffo d'uomo!	*What an ugly-looking man!*
Quell'ignorante d'Enrico!	*That ignoramus Henry!*
multato di mille lire	*fined 1,000 lire*

circondare di filo spinato *to surround with barbed wire*
costruire di mattoni *to build with bricks*

(f) In the formation of adverbs:

di certo *certainly*
di nascosto *secretly*
di nuovo *again*
di solito *usually*

4. Further uses of the preposition **con** are:

(a) With verbs of *beginning* and *ending* when followed by an infinitive:

Cominciò col domandarmi il mio nome.
He began by asking me my name.
Finii col dargli cento lire.
I finished up by giving him a hundred lire.

(b) With verbs of congratulation:

Mi congratulai con lui per il suo successo.
I congratulated him on his success.

5. **Per** is used in the following idiomatic ways:

(a) To express motion *towards* or *through*:

Partimmo per Roma. *We set out for Rome.*
Passammo per Firenze. *We passed through Florence.*

(b) To express *by means of*:

comunicare per telefono *to communicate by telephone*

(c) To express distribution:

disporsi per tre *to arrange oneself in threes*
allinearsi per due *to line up in twos*

(d) To express multiplication:

tre per tre fa nove *three times three make nine*

(e) **Per** with an adjective and followed by a relative clause with the subjunctive means *however . . .*:

Per ricco che sia, non ha delle belle maniere.
However rich he is, he hasn't good manners.

6. **In** is used in the following idioms:

(a) To express motion *towards* or *into* without the article, provided that the noun is unqualified:

andare in sala	*to go into the room*

but:

andare nella casa grande	*to go into the big house*

(b) To specify capacity or incapacity after adjectives:

bravo in italiano	*good in Italian*
deboluccio in matematica	*weak in mathematics*
perfetto nello stile	*perfect in style*
mediocre in tutto	*mediocre in everything*

(c) In combination with **di** in phrases indicating periodicity:

di quando in quando	
di tanto in tanto	*from time to time*
di volta in volta	

(d) To indicate profession:

dottore in legge	*doctor of law*
professore in belle lettere	*professor of literature*
commerciante in frutta	*fruit merchant*

7. **Su** may be used in the following idiomatic phrases:

(a) With expressions of weight or time to indicate approximations:

Pesa sulle dieci tonnellate.	*It weighs about ten tons.*
È un uomo sui cinquanta.	*He is a man around fifty.*
Partimmo sul far del giorno.	*We left about dawn.*

(b) In adverbial expressions:

su due piedi	*instantly*
Ci lasciò su due piedi.	*He left us instantly.*
sul serio	*seriously*
Parli sul serio?	*Are you speaking seriously?*
sul tardi	*late (rather late)*
È arrivato sul tardi.	*He came rather late.*
sulla parola	*at one's word*
Lo presi sulla parola.	*I took him at his word.*

(c) In selections:

> Ne togliemmo uno su dieci.   *We took away one out of every ten.*

B. PREPOSITIONAL VERBS

1. Prepositional verbs are very often used in speech in Italy. Some of the more important are the following:

andare su	*to go up*	tagliare fuori	*to cut off*
andare giú	*to go down*	tirare su	*to pull up*
andare via	*to go away*	tirare via	*to carry on, to go ahead*
metter su	*to set up* (*house, shop, etc.*)		
portare su	*to carry up*	venire su	*to come up*
portare giú	*to carry down*	venire giú	*to come down*
portare via	*to carry away*	venire via	*to come away*

Andammo su per le scale.	*We went up the stairs.*
Venimmo giú per le scale.	*We came down the stairs.*
Abbiamo messo su casa.	*We have set up house.*
Ha portato su i bagagli?	*Has he taken the luggage up?*
Eravamo tagliati fuori dalla marea.	*We were cut off by the tide.*
Tiro su la valigia.	*I am pulling up the case.*
Mi disse di tirare via e di non parlarne.	*He told me to go ahead and not to talk about it.*

UNA VISITA AL PAESELLO DOPO LUNGHI ANNI DI ASSENZA

Il mio piú *i*ntimo amico, a detta di tutti, era un certo dottor Palumba, mai sentito nominare, il quale, poveretto, sarebbe venuto certamente ad accogliermi alla stazione, se da tre giorni appena non avesse perduto la moglie. Pur[1] sprofondato nel cordoglio della sciagura recentissima, però, il dottor Palumba agli amici, andàti a fargli le condoglianze, aveva chiesto con ansia di me, se ero arrivato, se stavo bene, dov'ero alloggiato, per quanto tempo intendevo di trattenermi in paese.

Tutti con commovente unanimità, mi informarono che non passava giorno, che quel dottor Palumba non parlasse di me a lungo, raccontando con particolari inesauribili, non solo i giuochi della mia infanzia, le birichinate di scolaretto, e poi le prime, ingenue avventure giovanili; ma anche tutto ciò che avevo fatto da che m'ero allontanato dal paese, avendo egli sempre chiesto notizie di me a quanti fossero in caso di dargliene. E mi dissero che tanto affetto, una così ardente simpatia dimostrava per me in tutti quei racconti, che io, pur[1] provando per qualcuno di essi che mi fu riferito un certo imbarazzo e anche un certo sdegno e avvilimento, perché, o non riuscivo a riconoscermi in esso o mi vedevo rappresentato in una maniera che più sciocca e ridicola non si sarebbe potuta immaginare, non ebbi il coraggio d'insorgere e di protestare:

— Ma dove mai? ma quando mai? Chi è questo Palumba? Io non l'ho sentito mai nominare!

(LUIGI PIRANDELLO: *I Nostri Ricordi*)

NOTE
[1] **Pur :** *Pur* with the gerund often means *although*.

EXERCISES

A. Translate into Italian:
1. Italy set herself up (*costituirsi*) as a republic.
2. Do they still use steam trains in England?
3. I shouted to him at the top of my voice but I could not make him hear.
4. We went into the cinema in twos.
5. John, to tell the truth, is not a great football player.
6. He is considered as a very worthy (*rispettabile*) man.
7. They were so stupid that they did not know what was going on.
8. There were teacups, wine glasses and fruit plates on the table.

9. I have never looked closely into his methods, but they seem very good.
10. Do you want to buy grapes or something else?
11. I think the financial position in his firm is going from bad to worse.
12. I want steel shelves not wooden ones.
13. I forgot to congratulate him on his success in the examinations.
14. The soldiers (*soldato*) lined up in threes in the square.
15. However foolish she may be, she is earning her own living.

B. Answer the following questions in Italian:
1. Perché il visitatore si sente imbarazzato quando torna al suo paesello?
2. Chi gli mostrava una cosí ardente simpatia?
3. Che cosa pensava il visitatore dei racconti del dottor Palumba?
4. Quand'era morta la moglie del dottor Palumba?
5. Perché il visitatore non aveva il coraggio di dire che non conosceva il dottore?

C. Translate into Italian:
1. Will you take my luggage up, please?
2. He told us to carry on as if nothing had happened.
3. The soldiers were cut off by the enemy while they were advancing (*avanzare*) towards the village.
4. We set up shop in the main street.
5. I would not have taken him at his word if I had known he was not honest.
6. We went away as soon as the play had finished.
7. He asked me if I was speaking seriously.
8. I think he was a man around sixty but I could not be sure of it.
9. We had to carry the chairs downstairs.
10. I ordered him to come down at once.

D. Put the correct preposition into the blank spaces:
1. Il signor Tosi è dottore — lettere.
2. Non avrei detto che fosse mediocre — Inglese.
3. Ci ha lasciati — due piedi.
4. Abbiamo costruito un muro — protezione del paese.
5. Le biciclette costano al giorno d'oggi — dieci — quindici sterline.

6. La casa era costruita — legno.
7. Non mi piace viaggiare — notte.
8. Mi dia quelle tazze — tè perché io le possa lavare.
9. L'ho chiamato — telefono.
10. Quattro — cinque fa venti.

E. Translate into Italian:

I decided one day to pay a visit to my village, although I had not been there for about twenty years. I rang up some old friends of the family and told them I should be arriving on the 26th September at ten o'clock in the morning. They were very happy and promised to meet me, together with one of my friends. Although I could not remember that any of my friends was still living in the village, I consented. When I arrived at the station, I was told that Dr. Palumba, my dearest friend, was sorry he could not meet me but his wife had died three days before and he was stricken with grief at his recent bereavement. I had never heard of Dr. Palumba and so I asked several other people who he was. They all looked at me as if I were mad and said: 'But he is your best friend.'

LESSON XL

A. CONJUNCTIONS IN ITALIAN

1. A number of conjunctions have already been dealt with since they require the subjunctive, but a more complete list, including those already examined, will now be given:

(a) *Simple conjunctions*

anche	*also, too*	mentre	*while*
ancora	*still, again*	né	*neither*
anzi	*rather, on the contrary*	o (od)	*or*
che	*that*	onde	*whence*
ché	*for*	però	*however*
come	*how*	pure	*also*
cosí	*thus*	quando	*when*
dove	*where*	quasi*	*as if*
dunque	*thus*	quindi	*thus*
e (ed)	*and*	se*	*if*
ma	*but*		

NOTE. (1) All conjunctions which require the subjunctive are marked with an asterisk.

(2) Some conjunctions can be used as masculine nouns:

Non ne so il perché.
I don't know the reason for it.

I ma e i se inceppano la volontà e ritardano l'azione.
Ifs and buts inhibit the will and delay action.

(3) **Come** may take the indicative or the subjunctive and is used in the following ways:

(i) Instead of **quanto** with the indicative:
Voi sapete come siamo felici.
You know how happy we are.

(ii) As a comparative with the indicative:
Facemmo cosí come avevamo deciso.
We acted just as we had decided.

(iii) In incidental clauses with the indicative:
Giovanni ed io, come sai, siamo andati in città ieri sera.
John and I, as you know, went to town last night.

(iv) In indirect questions with the subjunctive:
Non so come tu lo possa sopportare.
I don'i know how you can put up with him.

Io non vedo come si possa farlo.
I don't see how it can be done.

(v) With or without **se** with the subjunctive to mean *as if*:
Non mi parla piú, come (se) fossi stato io a fargli quel
brutto tiro.
*He doesn't speak to me any more, as if it were I who
played that dirty trick on him.*

(vi) In causal clauses one must replace **come** with
siccome:
Siccome non venne all'ora prefissa, me ne andai.
As he didn't come at the appointed time, I went away.

(4) **Che** can be used in a variety of ways in addition to
its normal function:

(i) With expressions of time:
Il giorno che l'incontrai, pioveva.
The day on which I met him it was raining.

(ii) To express purpose instead of **perché**:
Mi sbrigherò, che possa finire tutto il lavoro oggi.
I shall make haste, in order to finish all the work today.

(iii) To express result:
È pallido che fa pietà.
He is piteously pale.

Che hai che non mangi?
What's the matter that you are not eating?

Venga, che le dirò ciò che è successo.
Come, so that I can tell you what happened.

(5) **Se** may be used in exclamations as well as in conditional clauses:

Carlo sta male. — Se lo andassimo a vedere stasera!
Charles is ill. What if we went to see him this evening!

Conosci Giovanni? Se lo conosco! È il mio migliore
amico.
*Do you know John? Do I know him? He is my best
friend.*

(b) *Compound conjunctions*

acciocché*	*in order that*	non già che*	*not that*
a condizione	*on condition*	nonostante*	*notwithstanding*
che*	*that*	oppure	*or else*
affinché*	*in order to*	perché	*because*
a mano a	*proportionately*	perché*	*in order that*
mano che	*as*	perciò	*therefore*
a meno che		per quanto*	*however much*
. . . non*	*unless*	piuttosto che	*rather than*
ancorché*	*although*	poiché	*since*
anziché	*rather than*	(*causal*)	
a patto che*	*provided*	posto che*	*granted that*
benché*	*although*	prima che*	*before*
caso mai*	*in case*	purché*	*provided*
comunque*	*although*	qualora*	*if*
dacché (da	*since (tem-*	quand'anche*	*even if*
che)	*poral)*	quantunque*	*although*
dato che*	*granted that*	salvo che*	*except that,*
dopo che	*after*		*unless*
dovunque*	*wherever*	sebbene*	*although*
eccetto che	*except that*	senonché	*but*
eccetto che		senza che*	*without*
. . . non*	*unless*	sia . . . sia	*either . . . or*
eppure	*and yet*	sicché	
finché	*as long as*	(cosicché)	*so that*
finché* (*with*		supposto	
future		che*	*supposing*
meaning)	*until*	tanto che	*so much that*
fuorché	*except*	tanto piú che	*all the more so*
giacché	*since*		*because*
(*causal*)		tranne che	*except that*

malgrado		tranne che*	
che*	*despite that*	. . . non	*unless*
nel caso che*	*in case*	tuttavia	*yet, anyway*
nonché	*as well as*		

Examples of some of these conjunctions are as follows:

Dovunque si vada, l'uomo è sempre lo stesso.
Wherever one goes, man is always the same.

Giacché (poiché) sei andato in Italia, parlacene un po'.
Since you have been to Italy, tell us something about it.

Sia lui sia un altro, qualcuno mi ha rubato l'orologio.
Whether it be he or another, someone has stolen my watch.

Ci vado a condizione che egli non ci sia.
I shall go there on condition that he is not there.

Partimmo di buon'ora senonché scoppiò un temporale che ci costrinse a fermarci.
We left early but a storm broke out which forced us to stop.

NOTE. (1) **Caso mai** is capable of several meanings:

Caso mai tu trovassi un libro di novelle, ti spiacerebbe mandarmelo?
If by chance you find a book of short stories, would you mind sending it to me?

Caso mai è lui che l'ha rotto, non io!

or: È lui che l'ha rotto, caso mai!
It is he who broke it, if anything (not I)!

(2) **Sicché** also has several meanings:

Mi promise monti e mari, sicché alla fine mi lasciai persuadere.
He promised me the earth, so that I allowed myself to be persuaded in the end.

Sicché, non hai fatto il compito?
Well then, you haven't done your homework?

(3) Note the following constructions with **tranne che**:

Ci andrò, tranne che tu non voglia.
I shall go there, unless you don't want me to.

Tutti facciamo lo stesso lavoro, tranne che il mio è un po' piú difficile.
We all do the same work, except that mine is a little more difficult.

Tutto è lecito fra di noi, tranne che insultarci.
Everything but insulting one another is permissible between us.

The same constructions are possible with **eccetto che** and **salvo che**.

B. CERTAIN TRANSITIVE VERBS IN ITALIAN

1. Some verbs are transitive in Italian when intransitive in English:

ammettere	*to admit of*	domandare	*to ask for*
approvare	*to approve of*	guardare	*to look at*
ascoltare	*to listen to*	pagare	*to pay for*
aspettare	*to wait for*	presiedere	*to preside over*
cercare	*to look for*	soffrire†	*to suffer from*
chiedere	*to ask for*	sognare†	*to dream of*

Questa lingua non ammette un tale costrutto.
This language does not admit of such a construction.

Tutti hanno approvato la sua condotta.
Everyone approved of his conduct.

Ascoltiamo la radio!
Let's listen to the wireless.

Aspetto Giovanni.
I am waiting for John.

L'ho cercato dappertutto.
I have looked for him everywhere.

Glielo ho chiesto.
I asked him for it.

Non voglio guardarlo.
I don't want to look at it.

L'ho pagato duemila lire.
I paid two thousand lire for it.

Ho presieduto la conferenza.
I presided over the lecture.

Egli soffre il mal di fegato.
He suffers from liver trouble.

Ho sognato te.
I dreamt of you.

† These verbs may also take *di* with their complement.

IL VESUVIO

Simile a un osso antico, scarnito e levigato dalla pioggia e dal vento, stava il Vesuvio solitario e nudo nell'immenso cielo senza nubi, a poco a poco illuminandosi di un roseo lume segreto, come se l'intimo fuoco del suo grembo trasparisse fuori della sua dura crosta di lava, pallida e lucente come avorio: finché la luna ruppe l'orlo del cratere come un guscio d'uovo, e si levò chiara ed estatica, meravigliosamente remota, nell'azzurro abisso della sera. Salivano dall'estremo orizzonte, quasi portate dal vento, le prime ombre della notte. E fosse per la magica trasparenza lunare, o per la fredda crudeltà di quell'astratto, spettrale paesaggio, una delicata e labile tristezza era nell'ora, quasi il sospetto di una morte felice.

Ragazzi cenciosi, seduti sul parapetto di pietra a picco sul mare, cantavano volgendo gli occhi in alto, la testa lievemente inclinata sulla spalla. Avevano il viso pallido e scarno, gli occhi accecati dalla fame. Cantavano come cantano i ciechi, col viso riverso, gli occhi rivolti al cielo. La fame umana ha una voce meravigliosamente dolce e pura. Non v'è nulla di umano nella voce della fame. È una voce che nasce da una zona misteriosa della natura dell'uomo, dove ha radice quel senso profondo della vita che è la vita stessa, la nostra vita piú segreta e piú viva. L'aria era tersa, e dolce alle labbra. Una lieve brezza odorosa d'alga e di sale spirava dal mare, il grido dolente dei gabbiani faceva tremare il dorato riflesso della luna sulle onde, e laggiú, in fondo all'orizzonte, il pallido spettro del Vesuvio affondava a poco a poco nell'argentea caligine della notte. Il canto dei ragazzi faceva piú puro, piú astratto quel crudele, inumano paesaggio, cosí straniero alla fame e alla disperazione degli uomini.

— Non c'é bontà — disse Jack — non c'è misericordia, in questa meravigliosa natura.

— È una natura malvagia — dissi — ci odia, è nostra nemica. Odia gli uomini.

(CURZIO MALAPARTE: *La Pelle*)

EXERCISES

A. Translate into Italian:
1. He spoke as if he were afraid of what I should say to him.
2. Do you like this book? On the contrary, I think it is very bad.
3. Either you write to him now or you leave it for after dinner.
4. He is a policeman as I am myself.
5. He has gone to London today but I cannot tell you the reason why.
6. He asked me how I had succeeded in doing it.
7. He acted as if the whole factory belonged (*appartenere*) to him.
8. As he did not turn up (*farsi vedere*) at noon, I went home.
9. I met him the day I called on (*passare da*) you.
10. What is the matter with him that he looks so pale?
11. How can we let John know (it)? What if I write to him today!
12. I looked everywhere for Anthony; however, I could not find him.
13. What if we go to the cinema this evening!

B. Answer the following questions in Italian:
1. Dove si trova il Vesuvio?
2. A che cosa somiglia il Vesuvio nella descrizione di Malaparte?
3. Chi è seduto sul parapetto a picco sul mare?
4. Come cantano i ragazzi?
5. Chi, secondo lo scrittore, odia gli uomini?

C. Translate into Italian:
1. Although it was raining, Vesuvius appeared in the darkness, pale and shining like a huge pile of ivory.
2. Our duties are the same, but he has to work two hours more (*di più*) in the evening than me.
3. Rather than go with them to the theatre, I will stay at home.
4. As the sun set, the shadows became longer on the hills.
5. Who does it does not matter, but someone has to do it.
6. I shall do it myself, not that I hope to succeed, of course (*s'intende*), but because I do not wish to have to ask him for help.
7. He is the culprit, if anything, not John.
8. Well! You have not finished your work then!

306 MODERN ITALIAN GRAMMAR

9. I would like to see that film in spite of George.
10. He has passed his examination despite the fact that his teacher said he was lazy.

D. Translate into Italian:

Last year we went to visit Naples and saw Vesuvius in the distance with its hard crust of lava shining in the moonlight. The evening was very calm and we could hear ragged boys and girls singing as they sat on the parapet which overlooked the sea. Their voices seemed wonderfully sweet and pure and seemed to rise from a mysterious inner zone of life, like a rich music. Now and again, the sad cries of the seagulls interrupted (*interrompere*) their singing while the moon was reflected (*rispecchiarsi*) on the waves, over there, on the far horizon. Vesuvius disappeared little by little into the silvery mist of the night and Jack said to me that nature around Naples hated men since she frightened them by revealing to them her deepest secrets.

E. Translate into Italian:

1. I don't think he approves of what we have done.
2. I do not intend to wait for him any longer.
3. He said he dreamt of ghosts last night.
4. Since he did not send back my letter, I asked him for it.
5. John refused to preside over the meeting.
6. I paid two pounds for that pen and three pounds for a dozen exercise books.
7. We were listening to the radio when Charles knocked (*picchiare*) at the door.
8. I always used to suffer from seasickness when I crossed the Channel.
9. He asked us what we were looking at.
10. I am looking for a book which will help me do my homework.

A. PECULIARITIES OF CERTAIN VERBS

1. A number of verbs in Italian permit of several meanings, and others require a different construction from that generally used with their English equivalents. These verbs may be classified as follows:

(a) Verbs having various meanings and constructions:

aspirare (to aspire to, to breathe in):

Aspira a diventar medico. *He aspires to become a doctor.*

Aspiravo tutto quel fumo. *I was breathing in all that smoke.*

assistere (to help, to be present at, to attend):

Mi ha pregato di assisterlo. *He asked me to help him.*

Non potei assistere alla riunione. *I could not be present at the meeting.*

cedere (to give up, to yield):

Mi ha ceduto il posto. *He gave me his place.*

Ha ceduto solo alla forza. *He yielded only to force.*

credere (to believe, believe in):

Non credo ciò. *I don't believe that.*

Non credo al tuo amico. *I don't believe your friend.*

Non credo agli spettri. *I don't believe in ghosts.*

Credo in Dio. *I believe in God.*

NOTE. **Credere** requires the accusative of the thing, the dative of the person, and **a** or **in** with an article of faith.

chiedere, domandare (to ask for):

Domanda a tuo padre. *Ask your father.*

Ti voglio domandare una cosa. *I want to ask you something.*

Qualcuno chiede di Lei. *Someone is asking for you.*

NOTE. **Domandare** and **chiedere** require a dative of the

person when they mean *to ask*, a genitive when they mean
to enquire after.

intendere (to imply, to mean, hear, know about; of
course):

Non intende niente.	*He does not imply anything.*
Che cosa intendi?	*What do you mean?*
Ho inteso dire che è molto intelligente.	*I have heard he is very intelligent.*
Di lingue non se ne intende molto.	*He doesn't know much about languages.*
Si può essere stupidi, s'intende, ma non come lui.	*One can be stupid, of course, but not to that extent.*

mancare (to fail, break, lack, almost to do something,
to miss):

Non mancare di venire.	*Don't fail to come.*
Manca sempre di parola.	*He always breaks his word.*
Ci manca il tempo di andarci.	*We lack the time to go there.*
Gli manca tutto.	*He lacks everything.*
Mancò poco che non cascasse nel pozzo.	*He almost fell in the well.*
Tu mi manchi.	*I miss you.*
or: Sento la tua mancanza.	

provvedere (to provide):

Egli provvede a tutto.	*He provides for everything.*
Ha provvisto l'esercito di armi.	*He has provided the army with weapons.*

toccare (to touch, to touch on, to be the duty of, to
be the turn of, to fall to the lot of):

Non toccarlo.	*Don't touch it.*
Toccherò con lui questo affare.	*I will touch on this subject with him.*
Tocca a Lei migliorare le sue condizioni di vita.	*It is your duty to improve your way of living.*
Tocca a lui giocare.	*It is his turn to play.*

I tempi in cui gli era *The time in which it had*
toccato (di) vivere. *fallen to his lot to live.*
(Manzoni)

(b) Verbs which require **a** before a complement:

equivalere (to be equivalent to):

Una sterlina equivale a *A pound is equivalent to*
venti scellini. *twenty shillings.*

giovare (to be useful):

Questo non giova a niente. *This is quite useless.*

nuocere (to hurt):

Egli voleva nuocere a *He wanted to hurt every-*
tutti. *body.*

pensare (to think):

Pensate a me. *Think of me.*

NOTE. For the expression of opinion, however, **di** is required:

Che pensi di questo *What do you think of this*
libro? *book?*

resistere (to resist, to stand):

Non posso resistere al tuo *I can't resist your invitation.*
invito.

Non ci resisto. *I can't stand it.*

sopravvivere (to outlive, to survive):

Essa è sopravvissuta a suo *She has outlived her husband.*
marito.

ubbidire (to obey):

Ubbidisco ai miei genitori. *I obey my parents.*

In addition, the following are the most common
verbs requiring the dative of the person and the
accusative of the thing:

chiedere	*to ask*	imporre	*to impose*
comprare	*to sell*	insegnare	*to teach*
dare	*to give*	ispirare	*to inspire*
dire	*to say*	perdonare	*to pardon*
domandare	*to ask*	permettere	*to permit*
imparare	*to learn*	piacere	*to please*
impedire	*to prevent*	prendere	*to take*

scrivere	*to write*	vendere	*to sell*
suggerire	*to suggest*	vietare	*to forbid*
promettere	*to promise*		

Gli ho preso il fucile.   *I took his rifle from him.*

Gli ha perdonato tutto.   *He forgave him for everything.*

(c) Verbs that require **di** before a complement:

abbondare (to abound in):

Il paese abbonda di ogni ben di Dio.   *The country abounds in good things.*

abusare (to take advantage of):

Egli abusa della mia bontà.   *He takes advantage of my good nature.*

accorgersi (to notice):

Lei si accorge di tutto.   *You notice everything.*

affliggersi (to be affected by):

Si affligge di tutto.   *He is affected by everything.*

colmare (to load with):

L'hanno colmato di onori.   *They have loaded him with honours.*

contentarsi (to be contented):

Si contenta di poco.   *He is contented with little.*

decidere (to decide):

Abbiamo deciso della sua sorte.   *We have decided his fate.*

but occasionally:

Abbiamo deciso la sua sorte.

dubitare (to doubt):

Ne dubito io!   *I doubt it!*

Dubito della sua onestà.   *I doubt his honesty.*

fidarsi (to trust):

Non mi fido di lui.   *I don't trust him.*

impadronirsi (to take possession, to seize):

Egli si impadronisce di tutto.   *He seizes everything.*

incaricarsi (to undertake):

Non voglio incaricarmi di questa faccenda. / *I don't want to undertake this business.*

lagnarsi (to complain):

Essi si lagnano di tutto. / *They complain about everything.*

meravigliarsi (to be surprised at):

Mi meraviglio di ciò che dici. / *What you say surprises me.*

pentirsi (to repent of):

Si pente di ciò che ha detto. / *He repents saying what he did.*

profittare (to profit by, from):

Ha profittato della buona occasione. / *He has seized his opportunity.*

vivere (to live on):

Vive di pane ed acqua. / *He lives on bread and water.*

B. VERBAL ADJECTIVES

1. There are two kinds of verbal adjective in Italian, the one being formed by adding **-ante** to the stem of the infinitive of first conjugation verbs and **-ente** to the stem of the infinitives of the second and third conjugations, the other by removing the **-ato** ending of the past participle of certain first conjugation verbs.

2. The first type of verbal adjective is derived from the Latin present participle but it has lost its verbal force in most cases and is used simply as an adjective or noun:

il capitolo seguente	*the following chapter*
il merciaio ambulante	*the pedlar*
gli amanti	*the lovers*
il mittente	*the sender*

NOTE. **Mittente** from **mettere** is an irregular form, which is used only as a noun.

Other irregular forms are:

(a) **abbiente** (wealthy) in addition to **avente** (having) from **avere**.

(b) **senziente** (sensitive) in addition to **sentente** (feeling) from **sentire**.

(c) **nutriente** is the normal verbal adjective from **nutrire** (to feed).

(d) **ubbidiente** is the normal verbal adjective from **ubbidire** (to obey).

(e) **veniente** is the normal verbal adjective from **venire** and all its compounds have similar forms.

The irregular forms (a) and (b) are used in the following ways:

Tutti sapevano che era una persona abbiente.
Everybody knew he was a wealthy person.

L'orecchio è un organo molto senziente.
The ear is a very sensitive organ.

Note also: **gli abbienti e i non abbienti** (the Haves and the Have-nots).

3. Since most verbal adjectives have lost their verbal force, one should generally use a relative clause to translate an English present participle:

Una bambola che balla.	*A dancing doll.*
Un uccello che canta.	*A singing bird.*

The following verbal adjectives, however, still retain their verbal meaning:

attestante	*testifying*	concernente	*concerning*
comandante	*commanding*	contenente	*containing*
eccedente	*exceeding*	manifestante	*revealing*
formante	*forming*	proveniente	*deriving*
godente	*enjoying*	rappresentante	*representing*
indicante	*indicating*		

Queste sono delle pere provenienti dalla Spagna.
These are pears coming from Spain.

Il generale comandante la terza armata.
The general commanding the third army.

4. The verbal adjective is sometimes used in absolute phrases:

vivente il padre	*during his father's lifetime*
Enrico quarto regnante	*during Henry IV's reign*

5. A list of verbal adjectives formed from past participles is as follows:

adattato – adatto (*suitable*)   lessato – lesso (*boiled*)
avvezzato – avvezzo (*accustomed*) logorato – logoro (*worn out*)
caricato – carico (*loaded*)   pestato – pesto (*crushed*)
chinato – chino (*bowed, bent*)   privato – privo (*deprived*)
colmato – colmo (*full*)   scalzato – scalzo (*bare-footed*)
destato – desto (*awake*)   stancato – stanco (*weary*)
fermato – fermo (*still*)   svegliato – sveglio (*awake*)
gonfiato – gonfio (*swollen*)   troncato – tronco (*truncated*)
guastato – guasto (*spoilt*)

6. These adjectival forms are used when a state, not an action, is described:

Sono stanco.	*I am tired.*
but:	
Questo lavoro mi ha stancato.	*This work has tired me.*
La mia mano è gonfia.	*My hand is swollen.*
but:	
Dopo l'incidente, la mano mi si è gonfiata.	*After the accident my hand swelled up.*
Il mio orologio è guasto.	*My watch is broken.*
but:	
Mi hanno guastato l'orologio.	*They have broken my watch for me.*

LA BENEDIZIONE DEL TRATTORE SOVIETICO

Una sera don Camillo stava leggiucchiando in canonica quando apparve Peppone.

— Reverendo — disse Peppone, — qui la politica non c'entra. Qui c'entra la terra da arare, la terra da risanare, il pane per la gente che ha fame!

— E allora? — domandò, calmo, don Camillo.

— Allora io non so cos'abbia quel trattore nella pancia.

Non va! Appena finisco di accomodare a destra si guasta a sinistra. Appena ho finito di sistemarlo sotto, si svirgola sopra.

— Questa è una canonica, non un'officina meccanica — spiegò don Camillo.

— Ho fuori la moto, — continuò Peppone, — e si fa in un minuto. Venite a benedire quel canchero di trattore perché deve avere nella pancia tutte le maledizioni del creato.

Don Camillo scosse il capo:

— Per un trattore bolscevico io non mi muovo neanche se fosse in punto di morte.

Peppone strinse i pugni e scappò via, ma poco dopo don Camillo pedalava verso il *kolchoz*.

Alle Ghiaie tutto era buio. Un po' di luce soltanto nell'aia: seduto in mezzo a un mucchio di ferraglia, Peppone, con la chiave inglese in mano, stava guardando desolato il trattore attorno al quale aveva lavorato per otto ore consecutive.

— E allora? — domandò don Camillo.

— Non ci capisco più niente, — gemette Peppone premendosi la testa fra le mani. — Ho ripassato tutto, ho verificato tutto, ho messo a punto tutto, ho provato tutto. Non va. Non va!

La desolazione di Peppone era immensa, come la malinconia della terra nuda, come il silenzio della notte. E, sull'acqua del grande fiume, correva il vento della primavera.

Don Camillo si appressò alla macchina e levò l'aspersorio susurrando le parole del rito.

Quando ebbe finito, Peppone girò la manovella e la macchina si mise in moto tuonando e fumando come se stesse cacciando fuori il demonio dal tubo di scappamento.

Peppone salí, si mise al volante e innestò la marcia.

La macchina si avviò verso il solco incominciato.

E non si fermò.

(GIOVANNI GUARESCHI: *Mondo Piccolo*)

EXERCISES

A. Translate into Italian:
1. We were sorry we were unable to be present at the ceremony.
2. He said he didn't believe a word of what I had told him.
3. 'Somebody is at the door asking for you,' said Philip.
4. He doesn't know much about tractor motors.
5. We missed you in the meeting.
6. He told us that we would soon be provided with rifles.
7. We have heard that the Soviet tractor which Peppone received will not go.
8. Whose turn is it to play?
9. I was surprised to hear that that sickly (*malaticcio*) old man had outlived his wife.
10. We promised him a reward (*compenso*) if he succeeded in catching the thief (*ladro*).
11. He imposed a most difficult task upon us.
12. It is up to him to help his friends now he is in a position (*in grado di*) to do so.

B. Answer the following questions in Italian:
1. Perché Peppone è venuto alla canonica a vedere don Camillo?
2. Qual era la risposta di don Camillo?
3. Perché non voleva benedire il trattore?
4. Dove trovò Peppone alla fine?
5. Per quanto tempo aveva lavorato Peppone sul trattore?
6. Aveva verificato tutto il povero sindaco?
7. Che cosa fece don Camillo prima che Peppone girasse la manovella?
8. Che cosa sembrava facesse il trattore dopo la benedizione?
9. Cosa fece Peppone dopo esser salito in macchina?
10. Continuò a funzionare il trattore dopo la benedizione?

C. Translate into Italian:
1. Every time he sees me, Peppone always takes advantage of me, said don Camillo.
2. I did not notice what had happened at first.
3. The cart was loaded with hay (*fieno*).
4. I hope you are not doubting my word?
5. He is always complaining of the treatment (*trattamento*) he received when he was in hospital.
6. I told him he ought to profit from my mistakes.

7. I can't stand this noise (*chiasso*).
8. I certainly do not want to undertake the job of secretary to the society (*società*).
9. He refused to obey me when I ordered him to carry the goods into the warehouse.

D. Translate into Italian:
1. He was seen running barefoot down the road.
2. He came to see me this morning before I was awake.
3. It is the same story of the Haves and Have-nots again.
4. He gave me a bottle containing oil.
5. When John came in I noticed that his eye was swollen.
6. During the reign of Charles V, there was a plague (*peste (f.)*).
7. They deprived me of my books.
8. He entered the room with his head bent down.
9. My pen is broken, it seems.
10. We are not accustomed to eating that kind of thing.

E. Translate into Italian:
One evening when don Camillo was sitting by the fire reading a book, Peppone came to see him and told him that the Soviet tractor which he had just received would not go. 'What do you want me to do,' replied don Camillo, 'I am not an engineer.' Peppone explained that all the curses in creation seemed to be in that nuisance of a machine and he would like to have it blessed by the priest. Don Camillo laughed and said he would not bless a Soviet tractor even if it were at death's door, but he finally went to Peppone's home and blessed the tractor for him. The strange thing (*Il più strano . . .*) was that the tractor went afterwards and Peppone was able to plough his fields.

A. GENDERS OF NOUNS AND PLURALS OF COMPOUND NOUNS

1. The only declension which presents serious problems of gender in Italian is the third declension, since nouns ending in **-e** may be either masculine or feminine. However, one can often tell the gender of a noun in **-e** from its ending and a list of suffixes in **-e** are given below which are either predominantly masculine or feminine:

(a) Masculine endings:

-ame: ferrame (*scrap iron*); rottame (*wreckage*); *etc.* Exc.: la fame (*hunger*).

-ume: sudiciume (*filth*); biancume (*white stuff*); *etc.*

-iere or **-iero**: cavaliere (*horseman, cavalier*); passeggiero (*passenger*); *etc.*

-ile: campanile (*belfry*); fienile (*hay-loft*); *etc.* Exc.: la bile (*bile*).

-ele: miele (*honey*); fiele (*gall, bitterness*); *etc.*

-ese: Milanese (*a Milanese man*); arnese (*equipment*); *etc.*

-one: bastone (*stick*); librone (*large book*); *etc.* Exc.: la canzone (*song*).

-ore: splendore (*splendour*); spessore (*thickness*); *etc.* Exc.: folgore† (*thunder-bolt*).

-sore: difensore (*defender*); aggressore (*aggressor*); *etc.*

-tore: vincitore (*victor*); attore (*actor*); *etc.*

(b) Feminine endings:

-aggine: stupidaggine (*stupidity*); dabbenaggine (*ingenuousness*); *etc.*

-ie: specie (*kind*); superficie (*surface*); *etc.*

† The word is sometimes masculine in literary texts and also when it means *a great hero*: Un folgore di guerra (*A great hero in war*).

-rte: morte (*death*); sorte (*fate*); *etc.* Exc.: il pianoforte (*piano*); il consorte† (*consort*).

-sione: occasione (*occasion*); confusione (*confusion*);
etc.

-trice: attrice (*actress*); mitragliatrice (*machine-gun*);
etc.

-udine: altitudine (*altitude*); moltitudine (*multitude*);
etc.

-zione: lezione (*lesson*); intenzione (*intention*); *etc.*

Note. In addition to these suffixes, one can add the following,
although there are a number of exceptions in each case:

Masculine
-ale: canale (*canal*); but: la cambiale (*bill of exchange*).
-ente: agente (*agent*); but: la corrente‡ (*current*).

Feminine
-ice: radice (*root*); but: il pollice (*thumb, inch*).
-ione: ragione (*reason*); but: il bastione (*bastion*).

For most of these endings there are about a score of exceptions.

2. The formation of the feminine from the masculine noun
in Italian is done in many ways:

(a) With proper nouns by changing the final vowel or by
adding a diminutive:

Francesco – Francesca	Cesare – Cesarina
Giovanni – Giovanna	Clemente – Clementina
Giuseppe – Giuseppa	Giorgio – Giorgina
Paolo – Paola	Nicola – Nicoletta

(b) With some common nouns too the final vowel is
changed:

figlio – figlia (*son, daughter*) sarto – sarta (*tailor*)
infermiere – infermiera signore – signora (*Mr.,*
   (*nurse*)   *Mrs.*)

(c) Very often endings are added:

attore – attrice duca – duchessa
difensore – difenditrice poeta – poetessa

† Also *la consorte* when referring to a woman.
‡ Also *il corrente* (the joist).

(d) With animals the same processes are carried out:

asino – asina (*ass*)	elefante – elefantessa (*elephant*)
cavallo – cavalla (*horse*)	leone – leonessa (*lion*)
gatto – gatta (*cat*)	pavone – pavonessa (*peacock*)

(e) Some animals have different words for the masculine and feminine:

becco – capra (*goat*)	porco – scrofa (*pig*)
montone – pecora (*sheep*)	toro – vacca (*cow*).

(f) Some animals or birds have only the masculine or feminine forms and one has to use the adjectives **maschio** or **femmina** to indicate the other sex:

il falco – il falco femmina (*falcon*)
la lepre maschio – la lepre (*hare*)
la rondine maschio – la rondine (*swallow*)

Generally, however, the following words indicate an animal of both sexes:

aquila	*eagle*	lepre (*f.*)	*hare*
corvo	*crow*	pantera	*panther*
delfino	*dolphin*	rondine (*f.*)	*swallow*
falco	*falcon*	scorpione (*m.*)	*scorpion*
leopardo	*leopard*	etc., etc.	

3. The plurals of compound nouns are formed in the following ways:

(a) Most compound nouns form their plural in the usual way:

SINGULAR		PLURAL
l'arcobaleno	*rainbow*	gli arcobaleni
il capolavoro	*masterpiece*	i capolavori
il francobollo	*stamp*	i francobolli
il pianoforte	*piano*	i pianoforti

(b) Often when a noun is followed by an adjective, both words are made plural:

la cartastraccia	*wastepaper*	le cartestracce
la cassaforte	*strongbox*	le casseforti
la mezzaluna	*half-moon*	le mezzelune
la terracotta	*terracotta*	le terrecotte

(c) When there are two nouns of different genders, the
first noun alone is often made plural:

    il capostazione   *stationmaster*   i capistazione
    il pescespada   *swordfish*   i pescispada

(d) Masculine nouns formed from a verb or adverb and
a noun are usually invariable:

    il bucaneve   *snowdrop*   i bucaneve
    il retroterra   *hinterland*   i retroterra

(e) All nouns formed from verbs in conjunction with
adverbs, other verbs or plural nouns are invariable:

    il lustrascarpe   *the shoe-shine*   i lustrascarpe
    il portalettere   *postman*   i portalettere
    il saliscendi   *the see-saw*   i saliscendi

NOTE. Rules (b) and (c) and (d) have many exceptions,
especially with compounds of **capo**, but rule (e) admits of
no exceptions.

B. THE INFINITIVE WITH A CHANGE OF SUBJECT

1. Certain verbs are followed by an infinitive even when a
change of subject would normally require a subordinate
clause. These verbs may be classified as follows:

(a) Verbs of requesting and advising (**consigliare,
domandare, pregare, suggerire, supplicare,** *etc.*):

    L'ho pregato di partire.   *I begged him to leave.*
    L'ho consigliato di non   *I advised him not to do it.*
    farlo.

(b) Verbs of command (**comandare, imporre, ordinare,** *etc.*):

    Gli ordinò di non parlare in classe.
    He ordered him not to speak in class.

NOTE. It is not necessary for the verb to be regularly used
as a command provided it is so used in this type of

construction. For instance, one can use **dire** and **scrivere** in this way:

Gli ho detto di tornare a casa.   *I have told him to return home.*

Le ho scritto di non venire piú.   *I have written to her not to come again.*

(c) Verbs of prohibiting and preventing (**proibire, vietare, impedire,** *etc.*):

Gli ho vietato di seguirmi.   *I have forbidden him to follow me.*

Le ha impedito di scrivere alla sua amica.   *He has prevented her from writing to her friend.*

IL RITORNO DI DON ABBONDIO

Don Abbondio e Perpetua entrano in casa, senza aiuto di chiavi; ogni passo che fanno nell'*a*ndito, senton crescere un tanfo, un veleno, una peste, che li respinge indietro; con la mano al naso, vanno all'uscio di cucina; entrano in punta di piedi, studiando dove metterli, per iscansare piú che possono la porcher*i*a che copre il pavimento; e danno un'occhiata in giro. Non c'era nulla d'intero; ma avanzi e frammenti di quel che era stato, lí e altrove, se ne vedeva in ogni canto: piume e penne delle galline di Perpetua, pezzi di biancher*i*a, fogli dei calendari di don Abbondio, cocci di pentole e di piatti; tutto insieme o sparpagliato. Solo nel focolare si potevan vedere i segni d'un vasto saccheggio accozzati insieme, come molte idee sottintese, in un periodo steso da un uomo di garbo. C'era, dico, un rimasuglio di tizzi e tizzoni spenti, i quali mostravano d'essere stati un bracciolo di seggiola, un piede di tavola, uno sportello di armadio, una panca di letto, una doga della botticina, dove ci stava il vino che rimetteva lo stomaco di don Abbondio. Il resto era cenere e carboni . . .

'Ah porci!' esclamò Perpetua.

'Ah baroni!' esclamò don Abbondio; e, come scappando, andarono fuori per un altro uscio che metteva nell'orto.

(ALESSANDRO MANZONI: *I Promessi Sposi*)

EXERCISES

A. Put the definite article before the following nouns:

legname, canile, prestatore, dichiarazione, fanciullaggine, borghese, incisione, porcume, manovale, spedizione, bastone, portatore, difenditrice, bersagliere, burrone, cagione, ipotesi, mobile, motore, missione, cascaggine, odore, polmone, rottame, consuetudine, usciere, unzione, pallore, uccisore, presidente, ragioniere, rivendicatrice, onore.

B. Form the feminine of the following masculine nouns:

montone, asino, falco, poeta, Nicola, pavone, toro, scorpione, sarto, cavallo, leone, leopardo, marito, figlio, duca, porco, delfino, becco, corvo, Paolo, Giorgio.

C. Translate into Italian:

1. He ordered us to leave the town at once.
2. They asked him to write to them as soon as possible (*il più presto possibile*).
3. We implored her to do that.
4. I would have liked to tell him to go.
5. I suggested to him to go and see if you could help him.
6. Would you have liked to prevent him from returning home?
7. He begged me to sit down but I did not have time.
8. I forbade him to go out.
9. I requested my friend to accompany me to the station.
10. The police have prevented me from using those rifles.

D. Answer the following questions in Italian:

1. Chi accompagna don Abbondio a casa?
2. Che cosa li respinge quando entrano?
3. Perché entrano in punta di piedi?
4. Che cosa trovano sparpagliato dappertutto?
5. Cosa c'era nel focolare che attirava la loro attenzione?

E. Translate into Italian:

Don Abbondio had decided to leave home in a hurry (*in fretta*) because he had been threatened with death by don Rodrigo. On his return, some time later, he and his servant Perpetua found that their home had been ruined (*devastare*) by bandits. As they entered the house, a pestilential smell drove them back and they had to walk on the tips of their toes in order to avoid the filth that was on the floor. All they could find of what had once been the furniture (*mobilia*) was a burned table leg, the arm of a chair and a cupboard door.

Even the barrel which contained the wine that settled don Abbondio's stomach had been broken. 'What pigs these barons are,' said Perpetua as they went out into the garden to get a breath of fresh air.

REVISION EXERCISES (*Lessons XXXVI–XLII*)

1. Translate into Italian:
   1. Europe contains many large and small countries.
   2. The industrial strength of the United States is enormous.
   3. We intend to spend our holidays in Egypt.
   4. Writing letters seems to me to be a waste of time.
   5. On leaving, he shook me warmly by the hand.
   6. Having had dinner, we went out into the garden.
   7. They lived for two years in Mexico, but now they have returned to France.
   8. He has not yet ceased talking about that film, you know.
   9. I don't think his health has much improved.
   10. I was about to leave when he came up to me and asked me for help.
   11. The fact is that you have broken your word.
   12. Leave it alone, John will do it better than you.

2. Put the definite article before the following words:
   relazione, Brasile, canale, superficie, regione, serie, clima, auto, denaro, colore, avvenire, carbone, morte, fiume, salume, spessore, mitragliatrice, Giappone, crisi, sorte, moltitudine, folgore, cambiale.

3. Translate into Italian:
   1. Those hats must not be left here.
   2. He had John go and fetch the doctor.
   3. I was amazed when he came in.
   4. You could hear them singing in the street.
   5. In comparison with you (*a paragone suo*), he can hardly be called a student at all.
   6. I asked if John was in, but his mother said no.

7. What is that building opposite going to be used for?
8. We went right up to the top of the mountain.
9. When I was crossing the field I found myself suddenly confronted by a bull.
10. Since when has George been coming to visit us on Sundays

4. Put a preposition (if necessary) into the blank spaces:
   1. Non esiterò — dirglielo quando verrà.
   2. Questo non basta — pagare il suo conto.
   3. Mi riconobbe — l'accento.
   4. C'erano — cinquanta — sessanta ragazzi in quella classe.
   5. Vorrei un francobollo — cinquanta lire.
   6. Non c'è — sperare che egli sia generoso.
   7. Non c'è niente — altro da fare.
   8. I soldati si disposero — tre contro il muro.
   9. Egli è buono — tutto.
   10. Pesa — i quaranta chili.

5. Translate into Italian:
   1. I will come with you tomorrow unless you think it better for me to stay at home.
   2. He spoke to that poor girl as if she were nothing more than a servant in his home.
   3. He asked me how I had managed to get such an important job.
   4. As the sun went down, it began to grow cold.
   5. We get the same salary, except that he sometimes gets more money because he works longer in the evening.

6. Translate into Italian:
   1. Listen to those who love you.
   2. There is someone at the door asking for you.
   3. I dislike presiding over council meetings.
   4. The coat he was wearing was very worn.
   5. I would not have said that he was a wealthy person.

BUSINESS LETTERS IN ITALIAN

The following letters are typical of business inquiries, credit
arrangements and applications for posts as used in commercial
circles in Italy:

(a) *A business inquiry and order :*
Spett. Ditta Coxwell & Co. Ltd.,
12 Trafalgar Sq., London, W.C.1.   Milano, 20 febbraio 1959.
Spettabile Ditta,
  Abbiamo ricevuto il listino prezzi che avete allegato alla Vs.
lettera del 12 febbraio scorso. Le condizioni che ci fate sono
davvero interessanti e pensiamo che esse ci possano mettere in
grado di vincere la concorrenza la quale, come ben sapete, per
questo articolo e in questo particolare periodo è sensibilmente
acuta.

  Tuttavia il nostro compito sarebbe molto facilitato se almeno
per i primi ordinativi ci concedeste il pagamento a tre mesi data
della tratta. Nel caso accettaste questa nostra proposta, ci
preghiamo di ordinarvi 12 frigoriferi dei quali 7 del tipo piccolo
da 120 litri A/257 e 5 del tipo grande da 200 litri C/123 come
specificati nell'allegato modulo d'ordinazione. In attesa di una
Vs. conferma, vi inviamo i nostri piú cordiali saluti.

                              P. Algidafrig. Milano
                                Giuseppe Rossi
                                direttore ufficio acquisti

(b) *A business reply :*
Spett. Ditta Algidafrig. S.p.A.
Via Torino 14, Milano.   Londra, 2 marzo 1959.
Spett. Ditta,
  In risposta alla Vostra lettera del 20 febbraio scorso, e in
deroga ai nostri principii, per i quali non estendiamo il credito
oltre i 30 giorni, accettiamo con piacere le Vs. proposte. Speriamo
che ciò permetta l'inizio di una relazione d'affari vantaggiosa ai
reciproci interessi.

  La merce vi sarà spedita F.O.B. Londra entro il mese in corso.
                              Vostri,

                                p.pro Coxwell & Co.
                                John Maxwell
                                direttore ufficio vendite

(c) *An application for a post:*

Spett. Ditta Algidafrig. S.p.A.,
Via Torino 14, Milano.   Milano, 20 marzo 1959.

Spettabile Ditta,

Avendo letto l'inserzione pubblicata sul 'Corriere della Sera' del 18 marzo scorso, presento domanda per essere assunto quale corrispondente straniero. Oltre all'italiano, conosco alla perfezione il francese essendo figlio di madre francese. Conosco molto bene l'inglese poiché sono vissuto per due anni in quella nazione, e ho inoltre una discreta conoscenza del tedesco, sufficiente ad una corretta corrispondenza, poiché questa è la lingua che ho imparato a scuola.

Ho 35 anni, sono sposato con due figli, e fino a due mesi fa sono stato corrispondente straniero della fabbrica di frigoriferi Iceberg che, come ben sapete, è fallita in seguito a un dissesto finanziario. Quanto al trattamento le mie pretese non sono eccessive, ma vi faccio presente che ben pochi sono i corrispondenti che sappiano stenografare in tre lingue — italiano, francese, inglese — com'è il caso mio. Allego un benservito rilasciatomi dal Signor Barbieri, direttore della ditta presso la quale ero impiegato.

Con ossequio,
Marco Tommasei

(d) *A reference:*

Oggetto: benservito.   Milano, 19 dicembre 1958.

Il signor Marco Tommasei è stato al mio servizio per sei anni in qualità di corrispondente straniero. Conosce il francese e l'inglese alla perfezione, ed ha una buona padronanza del tedesco. Stenografa in tre lingue dimostrandosi cosí elemento di insostituibile rendimento. La sua pratica commerciale lo rende atto a mansioni piú vaste del semplice corrispondente e gli possono essere tranquillamente affidate mansioni direttive.

Fedele, leale, di comportamento irreprensibile, sa guadagnarsi la stima dei superiori e l'affetto degli inferiori. Lo si raccomanda caldamente come persona degna della migliore sistemazione.

L. Barbieri

NOTES

1. Abbreviations in order of appearance:

   Spett. (spettabile); *Esteemed*. This abbreviation is usually put on the envelope carrying a business letter.

   Vs. (Vostro): **Voi** is the usual form of address in business letters and the possessive adjective is often abbreviated.

P. (per): *On behalf of* (i.e., p.pro).
S.p.A. (Società per Azioni): Equivalent to English *Ltd.*
F.O.B.: *Free on Board.* Italians often use English abbreviations.
2. Business letters are largely made up of set phrases both in English and Italian, and the Italian equivalents of most English phrases can easily be found in any reputable commercial dictionary.

PREFIXES IN ITALIAN

1. Certain prefixes are added to adjectives to modify their meanings and among these **arci-**, **stra-** and **sopra** (or **sovra-**) are the most common. They may be added, though not indiscriminately, to a large number of adjectives:

> Dopo essere riuscito all'esame, era arcicontento.
> *After passing the examination, he was highly content.*
>
> La casa è stragrande.
> *The house is enormous.*
>
> Il carro era sovraccarico di fieno.
> *The cart was overloaded with hay.*

2. **Dis-** or **s-** usually indicates a negation of the positive quality of the adjective:

chiuso – schiuso	*shut – open*
garbato – sgarbato	*polite – impolite*
leale – sleale	*loyal – disloyal*
onesto – disonesto	*honest – dishonest*
uguale – disuguale	*equal – unequal.*

3. **Ri-** often reinforces the adjective without an appreciable change of meaning:

colmo – ricolmo	*full – brimful*
pieno – ripieno	*full – very full*
fornito – rifornito	*stocked – well-stocked.*

4. Verbs also take the prefix **dis-** or **s-** sometimes to negate the meaning and sometimes to reinforce it:

annodare – snodare	*to tie – to untie*
apparecchiare – sparecchiare	*to lay (table) – to clear (table)*
piacere – spiacere	*to please – to displease*

but:

battere – sbattere	*to beat – to batter*
cacciare – scacciare	*to send away – to drive away.*

A change of meaning is also brought about in some cases by these prefixes:

fondare – sfondare	*to found – to stave in*
piegare – spiegare	*to fold – to explain* (but also *to unfold*)
terminare – sterminare	*to finish – to exterminate.*

NOTE. Some verbs normally begin with **s impure** and should not be confused with verbs acquiring a prefix:

sbigottire	*to dismay, strike with fear*
scaldare	*to warm*
sprofondare	*to founder, sink.*

5. Other important prefixes used with verbs are:

intendere – fraintendere	*to hear, mean – to misunderstand*
porre – posporre	*to put – to reverse* (*order*)
tenere – trattenere	*to hold – to delay.*

In many cases, however, Italian verbs take the same prefixes as their English equivalents:

fare – sopraffare	*to do – to overcome, overwhelm*
leggere – rileggere	*to read – to reread*
scrivere – riscrivere	*to write – to rewrite*
stare – sottostare	*to stand – to submit, etc., etc.*

IRREGULAR VERBS

*Denotes verbs requiring **essere** in their compound tenses.

†Denotes verbs taking both **essere** and **avere** according to the construction.

* accadere, *to happen (impersonal)*; *see* cadere.
* accedere, *to accede*; *see* concedere.
accendere, *to light*; *p. def.*, accesi, accendesti, *etc.*; *p. part.*, acceso.
accludere, *to enclose*; *see* alludere.
accogliere, *to receive*; *see* cogliere.
* accorgersi, *to perceive*; *see* scorgere.
* accorrere, *to run up*; *see* correre.
accrescere, *to increase*; *see* crescere.
* addirsi, *to suit*; *(defective)*; *pres.*, si addice, si addicono; *impf.*, si addiceva, si addicevano; *pres. subj.*, si addica, si addicano; *impf. subj.*, si addicesse, si addicessero.
addurre, *to convey*; *pres. ind.*, adduco, adduci, *etc.*; *p. def.*, addussi, adducesti, *etc.*; *p. part.*, addotto; *fut.*, addurrò; *pres. subj.*, adduca, adduciamo, adduciate, adducano; *imper.*, adduci, adduciamo, adducete.
affiggere, *to stick, fasten*; *p. def.*, affissi, affiggesti, *etc.*; *p. part.*, affisso.
affliggere, *to afflict*; *p. def.*, afflissi, affliggesti, *etc.*; *p. part.*, afflitto.
aggiungere, *to add*; *see* giungere.
alludere, *to allude*; *p. def.*, allusi, alludesti, *etc.*; *p. part.*, alluso.
ammettere, *to admit*; *see* mettere.
* andare, *to go*; *pres. ind.*, vado *or* vo, vai, va, andiamo, andate, vanno; *fut.*, andrò; *pres. subj.*, vada, andiamo, andiate, vadano; *imper.*, va', andiamo, andate.
annettere, *to annex*; *p. def.*, annessi *or* annettei, annettesti, *etc.*; *p. part.*, annesso.
* apparire, *to appear*; *pres. ind.*, apparisco *or* appaio, apparisci *or* appari, apparisce *or* appare, appariamo, apparite, appariscono *or* appaiono; *p. def.*, apparvi, apparisti, *etc.*; *p. part.*, apparso; *pres. subj.*, apparisca *or* appaia, appariamo, appariate, appariscano *or* appaiano; *imper.*, apparisci, appariamo, apparite.
appartenere, *to belong*; *see* tenere.

appendere, *to hang*; *p. def.*, appesi, appendesti, *etc.*; *p. part.*, appeso.‡

apporre, *to affix*; *see* porre.

apprendere, *to learn*; *see* prendere.

aprire, *to open*; *p. def.*, apersi *or* aprii, apristi, *etc.*; *p. part.*, aperto.

ardere, *to burn*; *p. def.*, arsi, ardesti, *etc.*; *p. part.*, arso.

* arrendersi, *to surrender*; *see* rendere.

* ascendere, *to ascend*; *see* scendere.

aspergere, *to sprinkle*; *see* spargere.

assalire, *to assail, assault*; *pres. ind.*, assalisco *or* assalgo; *see* salire.

assolvere, *to absolve*; *p. def.*, assolsi *or* assolvei *or* assolvetti, assolvesti, *etc.*; *p. part.*, assoluto *or* assolto.

assumere, *to assume*; *p. def.*, assunsi, assumesti, *etc.*; *p. part.*, assunto.

* astenersi, *to abstain*; *see* tenere.

astrarre, *to abstract*; *see* trarre.

attendere, *to attend, wait*; *see* tendere.

attingere, *to draw up*; *see* tingere.

* avvedersi, *to perceive*; *see* vedere.

* avvenire, *to happen* (*impersonal*); *see* venire.

benedire, *to bless*; *see* dire.

bere, *to drink*; *pres. ind.*, bevo; *p. def.*, bevvi *or* bevei *or* bevetti, bevesti, *etc.*; *p. part.*, bevuto; *fut.*, berrò; *pres. subj.*, beva; *imper.*, bevi, beviamo, bevete.

* cadere, *to fall*; *p. def.*, caddi, cadesti, *etc.*; *fut.*, cadrò.

chiedere, *to ask*; *pres. ind.*, chiedo, chiedi, chiede, chiediamo, chiedete, chiedono; *p. def.*, chiesi, chiedesti, *etc.*; *p. part.*, chiesto; *pres. subj.*, chieda; *imper.*, chiedi, chiediamo, chiedete.

chiudere, *to close*; *p. def.*, chiusi, chiudesti, *etc.*; *p. part.*, chiuso.

cingere, *to gird, embrace*; *p. def.*, cinsi, cingesti, *etc.*; *p. part.*, cinto.

cogliere, *to gather*; *pres. ind.*, colgo, cogli, coglie, cogliamo, cogliete, colgono; *p. def.*, colsi, cogliesti, *etc.*; *p. part.*, colto; *pres. subj.*, colga; *imper.*, cogli, cogliamo, cogliete.

commettere, *to commit*; *see* mettere.

commuovere, *to move, affect*; *see* muovere.

* comparire, *to appear*; *see* apparire.

* compiacere, *to please*; *see* piacere.

compiangere, *to pity*; *see* piangere.

comporre, *to compose*; *see* porre.

‡ pendere, *to hang*, is regular.

comprendere, *to comprehend*; *see* prendere.

comprimere, *to compress*; *p. def.*, compressi, comprimesti, *etc.*; *p. part.*, compresso.‡

concedere, *to concede, grant*; *p. def.*, concessi *or* concedei *or* concedetti, concedesti, *etc.*; *p. part.*, concesso *or* conceduto.§

concludere, *to conclude*; *see* alludere.

concorrere, *to concur*; *see* correre.

* condolersi, *to complain, condole with*; *see* dolere.

condurre, *to lead*; *see* addurre.

configgere, *to drive in*; *see* figgere.

confondere, *to confound*; *see* fondere.

† congiungere, *to join, match*; *see* giungere.

connettere, *to connect*; *see* annettere.

conoscere, *to know*; *p. def.*, conobbi, conoscesti, *etc.*

consumere (*defective*), *to consume*; *p. def.*, consunsi, consumesti, *etc.*; *p. part.*, consunto.

contendere, *to contend*; *see* tendere.

contenere, *to contain*; *see* tenere.

contorcere, *to twist*; *see* torcere.

contraddire, *to contradict*; *see* dire.

contraffare, *to counterfeit*; *see* fare.

contrarre, *to contract*; *see* trarre.

† convenire, *to agree*; *to gather together*; *see* venire.

convincere, *to convince*; *see* vincere.

coprire, *to cover*; *see* aprire.

correggere, *to correct*; *see* reggere.

† correre, *to run*; *p. def.*, corsi, corresti, *etc.*; *p. part.*, corso.

corrispondere, *to correspond*; *see* rispondere.

corrompere, *to corrupt*; *see* rompere.

costringere, *to force*; *see* stringere.

costruire, *to construct, build*; *p. def.*, costrussi *or* costruii, costruisti, *etc.*; *p. part.*, costrutto *or* costruito.

† crescere, *to grow, raise*; *p. def.*, crebbi, crescesti, *etc.*

cuocere, *to cook*; *pres. ind.*, cuocio, cuoci, cuoce, cociamo *or* cuociamo, cocete *or* cuocete, cuociono; *p. def.*, cossi, cocesti, *etc.*; *p. part.*, cotto; *pres. subj.*, cuocia; *imper.*, cuoci, cociamo, cocete.

dare, *to give*; *pres. ind.*, do, dai, dà, diamo, date, danno; *p. def.*, diedi *or* detti, desti, *etc.*; *p. part.*, dato; *fut.*, darò; *pres. subj.*, dia, diamo, diate, diano; *imper.*, da', diamo, date.

‡ premere, *to press*, is regular.

§ All compounds of *cedere*, except *concedere*, *succedere*, *retrocedere*, are regular. The p. part. of *succedere* is *succeduto* when it means 'to follow on'.

dec*i*dere, *to decide*; *p. def.*, decisi, decidesti, *etc.*; *p. part.*, deciso.

* decrescere, *to decrease*; *see* crescere.

dedurre, *to deduce, deduct*; *see* addurre.

del*u*dere, *to delude*; *see* all*u*dere.

deporre, *to depose, bear witness*; *see* porre.

depr*i*mere, *to depress*; *see* compr*i*mere.

der*i*dere, *to deride*; *see* r*i*dere.

descrivere, *to describe*; *see* scrivere.

difendere, *to defend*; *p. def.*, difesi, difendesti, *etc.*; *p. part.* difeso.

diffondere, *to diffuse*; *see* fondere.

* dipendere, *to depend*; *see* appendere.

dip*i*ngere, *to paint*; *see* p*i*ngere.

dire, *to say, tell*; *pres. ind.*, dico, dici, dice, diciamo, dite d*i*cono; *p. def.*, dissi, dic*e*sti, *etc.*; *p. part.*, detto; *fut.* dirò; *pres. subj.*, dica, diciamo, diciate, d*i*cano; *imper.*, di', diciamo, dite.

dir*i*gere, *to direct*; *p. def.*, diressi, dirigesti, *etc.*; *p. part.*, diretto.

* discendere, *to descend*; *see* scendere.

dischi*u*dere, *to disclose, open*; *see* chi*u*dere.

disci*o*gliere, *to untie*; *see* sci*o*gliere.

discorrere, *to talk*; *see* correre.

disc*u*tere, *to discuss*; *p. def.*, discussi, discutesti, *etc.*; *p. part.*, discusso.

disfare, *to undo*; *see* fare.

disgi*u*ngere, *to disjoin, separate*; *see* gi*u*ngere.

disill*u*dere, *to disappoint*; *see* all*u*dere.

disperdere, *to disperse*; *see* perdere.

* dispiacere, *to displease*; *see* piacere.

disporre, *to dispose*; *see* porre.

dissuadere, *to dissuade*; *see* persuadere.

distendere, *to stretch*; *see* tendere.

distinguere, *to distinguish*; *p. def.*, distinsi, distinguesti, *etc.*; *p. part.*, distinto.

distogliere, *to dissuade*; *see* togliere.

distrarre, *to distract*; *see* trarre.

distr*u*ggere, *to destroy*; *see* str*u*ggere.

* divenire, *to become*; *see* venire.

div*i*dere, *to divide*; *p. def.*, divisi, dividesti, *etc.*; *p. part.*, diviso.

* dolere, *to ache, pain*; *pres. ind.*, dolgo, duoli, duole, doliamo, dolete, dolgono; *p. def.*, dolsi, dolesti, *etc.*; *fut.*, dorrò; *pres. subj.*, dolga, doliamo, doliate, dolgano.

† dovere, *to have to, be obliged, must*; *pres. ind.*, devo *or* debbo, devi, deve, dobbiamo, dovete, devono *or* debbono; *fut.*, dovrò; *pres. subj.*, debba, dobbiamo, dobbiate, debbano.

effondere, *to pour out*; *see* fondere.

eleggere, *to elect*; *see* leggere.

elidere, *to elide*; *p. def.*, elisi, elidesti, *etc.*; *p. part.*, eliso.

eludere, *to elude*; *see* alludere.

* emergere, *to emerge*; *p. def.*, emersi, emergesti, *etc.*; *p. part.*, emerso.

emettere, *to emit*; *see* mettere.

ergere, *to erect, raise*; *p. def.*, ersi, ergesti, *etc.*; *p. part.*, erto.

erigere, *to erect*; *see* dirigere.

escludere, *to exclude*; *see* alludere.

esigere, *to exact*; *p. part.*, esatto.

* esistere, *to exist*; *p. part.*, esistito.

espellere, *to expel*; *p. def.*, espulsi, espellesti, *etc.*; *p. part.*, espulso.

* esplodere, *to explode*; *p. def.*, esplosi, esplodesti, *etc.*; *p. part.*, esploso.

esporre, *to expose*; *see* porre.

esprimere, *to express*; *see* comprimere.

estendere, *to extend*; *see* tendere.

estinguere, *to extinguish*; *see* distinguere.

estrarre, *to extract*; *see* trarre.

* evadere, *to evade*; *p. def.*, evasi, evadesti, *etc.*; *p. part.*, evaso.

fare,‡ *to do, make*; *pres. ind.*, faccio *or* fo, fai, fa, facciamo, fate, fanno; *p. def.*, feci, facesti, *etc.*; *p. part.*, fatto; *fut.*, farò; *pres. subj.*, faccia, facciamo, facciate, facciano; *imper.*, fa', facciamo, fate.

fendere, *to split*; *p. part.*, fesso.

figgere, *to fix*; *p. def.*, fissi, figgesti, *etc.*; *p. part.*, fitto.

fingere, *to feign, pretend*; *see* cingere.

fondere, *to cast, to melt*; *p. def.*, fusi, fondesti, *etc.*; *p. part.*, fuso.

frammettere, *to interpose, insert*; *see* mettere.

frangere, *to break*; *p. def.*, fransi frangesti, *etc.*; *p. part.*, franto.

frapporre, *to interpose, insert*; *see* porre.

friggere, *to fry*; *p. def.*, frissi, friggesti, *etc.*; *p. part.*, fritto.

giacere, *to lie*; *pres. ind.*, giaccio, giaci, giace, giaciamo *or* giacciamo, giacete, giacciono; *p. def.*, giacqui, giacesti, *etc.*; *pres. subj.*, giaccia; *imper.*, giaci, giaciamo, giacete.

* giungere, *to arrive, reach*; *p. def.*, giunsi, giungesti, *etc.*; *p. part.*, giunto.

illudere, *to delude, beguile*; *see* alludere.

immergere, *to immerse*; *see* emergere.

imporre, *to impose*; *see* porre.

‡ All compounds follow *fare* except *soddisfare* which conforms to regular first conjugation forms.

imprimere, *to imprint, impress*; *see* comprimere.

incidere, *to cut*; *see* decidere.

includere, *to include*; *see* alludere.

* incorrere, *to incur*; *see* correre.

* increscere, *to cause sorrow*; *see* crescere.

incutere, *to strike*; *see* discutere.

indurre, *to induce*; *see* addurre.

inferire,‡ *to strike, inflict (a blow, etc.)*; *p. def.*, infersi, inferisti, *etc.*; *p. part.*, inferto.

infliggere, *to inflict*; *see* affliggere.

infondere, *to infuse*; *see* fondere.

intendere, *to intend, understand*; *see* tendere.

intercedere, *to intercede*; *see* concedere (*or regular*).

interdire, *to prohibit*; *see* dire.

interporre, *to interpose*; *see* porre.

interrompere, *to interrupt*; *see* rompere.

* intervenire, *to intervene*; *see* venire.

intraprendere, *to undertake*; *see* prendere.

introdurre, *to introduce*; *see* addurre.

* intrudersi, *to intrude*; *p. def.*, intrusi, intrudesti, *etc.*; *p. part.*, intruso.

invadere, *to invade*; *see* evadere.

involgere, *to wrap*; *see* volgere.

irrompere, *to rush in upon*; *no p. part.*; *see* rompere.

iscrivere, *to inscribe*; *see* scrivere.

istruire, *to instruct*; *see* costruire.

leggere, *to read*; *p. def.*, lessi, leggesti, *etc.*; *p. part.*, letto.

maledire, *to curse*; *see* dire.

mantenere, *to maintain*; *see* tenere.

mettere, *to put*; *p. def.*, misi, mettesti, *etc.*; *p. part.*, messo.

mordere, *to bite*; *p. def.*, morsi, mordesti, *etc.*; *p. part.*, morso.

* morire, *to die*; *pres. ind.*, muoio, muori, muore, moriamo, morite, muoiono; *p. part.*, morto; *fut.*, morirò or morrò; *pres. subj.*, muoia, moriamo, moriate, muoiano; *imper.*, muori, moriamo, morite.

mungere, *to milk*; *p. def.*, munsi, mungesti, *etc.*; *p. part.*, munto.

muovere *or* movere, *to move*; *pres. ind.*, muovo *or* movo, muovi *or* movi, muove *or* move, moviamo *or* muoviamo, movete *or* muovete, muovono *or* movono; *p. def.*, mossi, movesti, *etc.*; *p. part.*, mosso; *pres. subj.*, muova *or* mova, moviamo *or* muoviamo, moviate *or* muoviate, muovano *or* movano; *imper.*, muovi *or* movi, moviamo, movete.

‡ Regular when it means *to infer*.

*nascere, *to be born*; *p. def.*, nacqui, nascesti, *etc.*; *p. part.*, nato.

nascondere, *to hide, conceal*; *p. def.*, nascosi, nascondesti, *etc.*; *p. part.*, nascosto.

negligere, *to neglect*; *p. def.*, neglessi, negligesti, *etc.*; *p. part.*, negletto.

nuocere *or* nocere, *to hurt, prejudice*; *pres. ind.*, noccio, nuoci, nuoce, nociamo, nocete, nocciono; *p. def.*, nocqui, nocesti, *etc.*; *pres. subj.*, noccia, nociamo, nociate, nocciano; *imper.*, nuoci *or* noci, nociamo, nocete.

* occorrere, *to be necessary*; (*impersonal*); *see* correre.

offendere, *to offend*; *see* difendere.

offrire, *to offer*; *p. def.*, offersi *or* offrii, offristi, *etc.*; *p. part.*, offerto.

omettere, *to omit*; *see* mettere.

opporre, *to oppose*; *see* porre.

opprimere, *to oppress*; *see* comprimere.

ottenere, *to obtain*; *see* tenere.

* parere, *to seem, appear*; *pres. ind.*, paio, pari, pare, paiamo, parete, paiono; *p. def.*, parvi, paresti, *etc.*; *p. part.*, parso; *fut.*, parrò; *pres. subj.*, paia, paiamo, pariate, paiano.

percorrere, *to run over*; *see* correre.

percuotere, *to strike*; *see* scuotere.

perdere, *to lose*; *p. def.*, persi *or* perdei *or* perdetti, perdesti, *etc.*; *p. part.*, perso *or* perduto.

permettere, *to permit*; *see* mettere.

persuadere, *to persuade*; *p. def.*, persuasi, persuadesti, *etc.*; *p. part.*, persuaso.

* pervenire, *to arrive at*; *see* venire.

* piacere, *to please*; *pres. ind.*, piaccio, piaci, piace, piacciamo *or* piaciamo, piacete, piacciono; *p. def.*, piacqui, piacesti, *etc.*; *pres. subj.*, piaccia, piacciamo, piacciate, piacciano; *imper.*, piaci, piacciamo, piacete.

piangere, *to weep*; *p. def.*, piansi, piangesti, *etc.*; *p. part.*, pianto.

pingere, *to paint*; *p. def.*, pinsi, pingesti, *etc.*; *p. part.*, pinto.

† piovere, *to rain* (*impersonal*); *p. def.*, piovve.

porgere, *to offer*; *p. def.*, porsi, porgesti, *etc.*; *p. part.*, porto.

porre, *to place, to put*; *pres. ind.*, pongo, poni, pone, poniamo, ponete, pongono; *p. def.*, posi, ponesti, *etc.*; *p. part.*, posto; *fut.*, porrò; *pres. subj.*, ponga, poniamo, poniate, pongano; *imper.*, poni, poniamo, ponete.

posporre, *to postpone*; *see* porre.

possedere, *to possess*; *see* sedere.

†potere, *to be able*; *pres. ind.*, posso, puoi, può, possiamo, potete, possono; *fut.*, potrò; *pres. subj.*, possa, possiamo, possiate, possano.

prediligere, *to prefer*; *p. def.*, predilessi, prediligesti, *etc.*; *p. part.*, prediletto.

predire, *to predict*; *see* dire.

prendere, *to take*; *p. def.*, presi, prendesti, *etc.*; *p. part.*, preso.

preporre, *to prefer*; *see* porre.

prescegliere, *to choose from*; *see* scegliere.

prescrivere, *to prescribe*; *see* scrivere.

presumere, *to presume*; *see* assumere.

pretendere, *to pretend, to claim*; *see* tendere.

prevedere, *to foresee*; *fut.*, prevederò; *see* vedere.

prevenire, *to arrive before, forewarn*; *see* venire.

produrre, *to produce*; *see* addurre.

proferire, *to utter*; *see* inferire.

promettere, *to promise*; *see* mettere.

promuovere, *to promote*; *see* muovere.

proporre, *to propose*; *see* porre.

prorompere, *to burst out*; *no p. part.*; *see* rompere.

proscrivere, *to proscribe*; *see* scrivere.

proteggere, *to protect*; *p. def.*, protessi, proteggesti, *etc.*; *p. part.*, protetto.

* provenire, *to proceed from*; *see* venire.

provvedere, *to provide*; *fut.*, provvederò, *etc.*; *see* vedere.

pungere, *to sting*; *p. def.*, punsi, pungesti, *etc.*; *p. part.*, punto.

raccogliere, *to gather*; *see* cogliere.

radere, *to shave*; *p. def.*, rasi, radesti, *etc.*; *p. part.*, raso.

raggiungere, *to overtake*; *see* giungere.

* rapprendere, *to congeal*; *see* prendere.

rattenere, *to restrain*; *see* tenere.

rattorcere, *to wring*; *see* torcere.

* rattrarsi, *to shrink*; *see* trarre.

* ravvedersi, *to repent*; *fut.*, ravvederò; *see* vedere.

ravvolgere, *to wrap up*; *see* volgere.

recidere, *to cut off*; *see* decidere.

redigere, *to draw up*; *p. def.*, redassi *or* redigei, redigesti, *etc.*; *p. part.*, redatto.

redimere, *to redeem*; *p. def.*, redensi, redimesti, *etc.*; *p. part.*, redento.

reggere, *to rule, to support, to govern*; *p. def.*, ressi, reggesti, *etc.*; *p. part.*, retto.

rendere, *to render*; *p. def.*, resi, rendesti, *etc.*; *p. part.*, reso.

reprimere, *to repress*; *see* comprimere.

respingere, *to push back*; *see* spingere.

restringere *or* ristringere, *to restrain*; *see* stringere.

* ricadere, *to fall again*; *see* cadere.

richiedere, *to request*; *see* chiedere.

riconoscere, *to recognize*; *see* conoscere.

ricoprire, *to cover again*; *see* coprire.

† ricorrere, *to run again, have recourse*; *see* correre.

ridere, *to laugh*; *p. def.*, risi, ridesti, *etc.*; *p. def.*, riso.

ridire, *to say again*; *see* dire.

ridurre, *to reduce*; *see* addurre.

rifare, *to do again, make again*; *see* fare.

rifrangere, *to refract*; *p. part.*, rifratto; *see* frangere.

* rimanere, *to remain*; *pres. ind.*, rimango, rimani, rimane, rimaniamo, rimanete, rimangono; *p. def.*, rimasi, rimanesti, *etc.*; *p. part.*, rimasto; *fut.*, rimarrò; *pres. subj.*, rimanga, rimaniamo, rimaniate, rimangano; *imper.*, rimani, rimaniamo, rimanete.

rimettere, *to replace, set again*; *see* mettere.

* rimordere, *to bite again, feel remorse*; *see* mordere.

rimpiangere, *to regret*; *see* piangere.

* rinascere, *to be born again*; *see* nascere.

* rincrescere, *to regret (impersonal)*; *see* crescere.

* rinvenire, *to find again*; *fut.*, rinverrò *or* rinvenirò, *etc.*; *see* venire.

ripercuotere, *to repercuss, strike back*; *see* percuotere.

riporre, *to put again*; *see* porre.

riprendere, *to retake, recover*; *see* prendere.

riprodurre, *to reproduce*; *see* addurre.

riscuotere, *to cash*; *see* scuotere.

risolvere, *to resolve*; *see* assolvere.

* risorgere, *to rise up again*; *see* sorgere.

rispondere, *to answer, reply*; *p. def.*, risposi, rispondesti, *etc.*; *p. part.*, risposto.

* ristare, *to desist*; *see* stare.

ritenere, *to retain*; *see* tenere.

ritrarre, *to draw*; *see* trarre.

* riuscire, *to succeed*; *see* uscire.

rivedere, *to see again*; *see* vedere.

* rivivere, *to live again*; *see* vivere.

rivolgere, *to turn*; *see* volgere.

rodere, *to gnaw*; *p. def.*, rosi, rodesti, *etc.*; *p. part.*, roso.

rompere, *to break*; *p. def.*, ruppi, rompesti, *etc.*; *p. part.*, rotto.

† salire, *to ascend, climb*; *pres. ind.*, salgo, sali, sale, saliamo, salite, salgono; *pres. subj.*, salga, saliamo, saliate, salgano; *imper.*, sali, saliamo, salite.

sapere, *to know*; *pres. ind.*, so, sai, sa, sappiamo, sapete, sanno; *p. def.*, seppi, sapesti, *etc.*; *fut.*, saprò; *pres. subj.*, sappia, sappiamo, sappiate, sappiano; *imper.*, sappi, sappiamo, sappiate.

* scadere, *to fall due*; *see* cadere.

scegliere, *to select*; *pres. ind.*, scelgo, scegli, sceglie, scegliamo, scegliete, scelgono; *p. def.*, scelsi, scegliesti, *etc.*; *p. part.*, scelto; *pres. subj.*, scelga, scegliamo, scegliate, scelgano; *imper.*, scegli, scegliamo, scegliete.

† scendere, *to descend*; *p. def.*, scesi, scendesti, *etc.*; *p. part.*, sceso.

schiudere, *to open, to disclose*; *see* chiudere.

scindere, *to separate*; *p. def.*, scissi, scindesti, *etc.*; *p. part.*, scisso.

sciogliere, *to untie, loosen*; *pres. ind.*, sciolgo, sciogli, scioglie, sciogliamo, sciogliete, sciolgono; *p. def.*, sciolsi, sciogliesti, *etc.*; *p. part.*, sciolto; *pres. subj.*, sciolga, sciogliamo, sciogliate, sciolgano; *imper.*, sciogli, sciogliamo, sciogliete.

scommettere, *to bet*; *see* mettere.

scomparire, *to disappear*; *see* apparire.

scomporre, *to disarrange*; *see* porre.

sconfiggere, *to defeat*; *see* figgere.

sconnettere, *to disconnect*; *see* annettere.

sconoscere, *to pay with ingratitude*; *see* conoscere.

scontorcere, *to contort, twist*; *see* torcere.

sconvolgere, *to overturn*; *see* volgere.

scoprire, *to discover*; *see* aprire.

scorgere, *to perceive*; *p. def.*, scorsi, scorgesti, *etc.*; *p. part*, scorto.

* scorrere, *to flow*; *see* correre.

scrivere, *to write*; *p. def.*, scrissi, scrivesti, *etc.*; *p. part.*, scritto.

scuotere, *to shake*; *pres. ind.*, scuoto, scuoti, scuote, scuotiamo, scuotete, scuotono; *p. def.*, scossi, scotesti, *etc.*; *p. part.*, scosso; *fut.*, scuoterò; *pres. subj.*, scuota, scuotiamo, scuotiate, scuotano; *imper.*, scuoti, scuotiamo, scuotete.

* sedersi, *to sit*; *pres. ind.*, mi siedo, ti siedi, si siede, ci sediamo, vi sedete, si siedono; *pres. subj.*, si sieda, ci sediamo, vi sediate, si siedano; *imper.*, siediti, sediamoci, sedetevi.

seppellire, *to bury*; *p. part.*, seppellito *or* sepolto.

smettere, *to cease*; *see* mettere.

smuovere, *to move*; *see* muovere.

socchiudere, *to half shut*; *see* chiudere.

† soccorrere, *to assist*; *see* correre.
soffrire, *to suffer*; *p. def.*, soffersi *or* soffrii, soffristi, *etc.*; *p. part.*, sofferto.
soggiungere, *to add*; *see* giungere.
* solere, *to be accustomed (defective)*; *pres. ind.*, soglio, suoli, suole, sogliamo, solete, sogliono; *impf. ind.*, solevo, *etc.*; *pres. subj.*, soglia, sogliamo, sogliate, sogliano; *p. part.*, solito.
solvere, *to solve*; *see* assolvere.
sommergere, *to submerge*; *see* emergere.
sopprimere, *to suppress*; *see* comprimere.
* sorgere, *to arise*; *p. def.*, sorsi, sorgesti, *etc.*; *p. part.*, sorto.
sorprendere, *to surprise*; *see* prendere.
sorreggere, *to support*; *see* reggere.
sorridere, *to smile*; *see* ridere.
sospendere, *to suspend*; *see* appendere.
sospingere, *to push*; *see* spingere.
sostenere, *to support*; *see* tenere.
sottintendere, *to hint at*; *see* tendere.
* sovvenire, *to aid*; *see* venire.
spandere, *to spread*; *p. part.*, spanto.
spargere, *to scatter*; *p. def.*, sparsi, spargesti, *etc.*; *p. part.*, sparso.
* sparire, *to disappear*; *see* apparire.
spegnere, *to extinguish*; *pres. ind.*, spengo, spegni, spegne, spegniamo, spegnete, spengono; *p. def.*, spensi, spegnesti, *etc.*; *p. part.*, spento.
spendere, *to spend*; *p. def.*, spesi, spendesti, *etc.*; *p. part.*, speso.
* sperdersi, *to disappear*; *see* perdere.
spiacere, *to displease*; *see* piacere.
spingere, *to push*; *p. def.*, spinsi, spingesti, *etc.*; *p. part.*, spinto.
sporgere, *to hold out*; *see* porgere.
* stare,‡ *to stay, stand, be*; *pres. ind.*, sto, stai, sta, stiamo, state, stanno; *p. def.*, stetti, stesti, *etc.*; *pres. subj.*, stia, stiamo, stiate, stiano; *fut.*, starò; *imper.*, sta', stiamo, state.
stendere, *to stretch out*; *see* tendere.
storcere, *to twist*; *see* torcere.
stringere, *to squeeze, tighten*; *p. def.*, strinsi, stringesti, *etc.*; *p. part.*, stretto.
struggere, *to melt, to consume*; *p. def.*, strussi, struggesti, *etc.*; *p. part.*, strutto.
* succedere, *to succeed, happen*; *see* concedere.
supporre, *to suppose*; *see* porre.

‡ All compounds follow the conjugation of *stare*, except *prestare*, *costare*, *constare*, *sostare*, which are regular.

svellere, *to root out*; *pres. ind.*, svello *or* svelgo, svelli, svelle, svelliamo, svellete, svellono *or* svelgono; *p. def.*, svelsi, svelgesti, *etc.*; *p. part.*, svelto; *pres. subj.*, svella *or* svelga, svelliamo, svelliate, svellano *or* svelgano; *imper.*, svelli, svelliamo, svellete.

* svenire, *to faint away*; *fut.*, svenirò, *etc.*; *see* venire.

svolgere, *to unfold*; *see* volgere.

tacere, *to be silent*; *pres. ind.*, taccio, taci, tace, taciamo, tacete, tacciono; *p. def.*, tacqui, tacesti, *etc.*; *pres. subj.*, taccia, taciamo, taciate, tacciano; *imper.*, taci, taciamo, tacete.

tendere, *to tend*; *p. def.*, tesi, tendesti, *etc.*; *p. part.*, teso.

tenere, *to hold, have*; *pres. ind.*, tengo, tieni, tiene, teniamo, tenete, tengono; *p. def.*, tenni, tenesti, *etc.*; *fut.*, terrò; *pres. subj.*, tenga, teniamo, teniate, tengano; *imper.*, tieni, teniamo, tenete.

tergere, *to dry*; *p. def.*, tersi, tergesti, *etc.*; *p. part.*, terso.

tingere, *to dye*; *p. def.*, tinsi, tingesti, *etc.*; *p. part.*, tinto.

togliere, *to take from*; *pres. ind.*, tolgo, togli, toglie, togliamo, togliete, tolgono; *p. def.*, tolsi, togliesti, *etc.*; *p. part.*, tolto; *pres. subj.*, tolga, togliamo, togliate, tolgano; *imper.*, togli, togliamo, togliete.

torcere, *to twist*; *p. def.*, torsi, torcesti, *etc.*; *p. part.*, torto.

tradurre, *to translate*; *see* addurre.

trafiggere, *to run through*; *see* figgere.

trarre, *to draw, pull*; *pres. ind.*, traggo, trai, trae, traiamo, traete, traggono; *p. def.*, trassi, traesti, *etc.*; *p. part.*, tratto; *fut.*, trarrò; *pres. subj.*, tragga, traiamo, traiate, traggano; *imper.*, trai, traiamo, traete.

* trascorrere, *to pass over*; *see* correre.

trascrivere, *to transcribe*; *see* scrivere.

trasmettere, *to transmit, send*; *see* mettere.

* trasparire, *to shine forth*; *see* apparire.

trattenere, *to detain*; *see* tenere.

travedere, *to see dimly*; *see* vedere.

uccidere, *to kill*; *p. def.*, uccisi, uccidesti, *etc.*; *p. part.*, ucciso.

udire, *to hear*; *pres. ind.*, odo, odi, ode, udiamo, udite, odono; *pres. subj.*, oda, udiamo, udiate, odano; *imper.*, odi, udiamo, udite.

ungere, *to grease*; *p. def.*, unsi, ungesti, *etc.*; *p. part.*, unto.

* uscire, *to go out*; *pres. ind.*, esco, esci, esce, usciamo, uscite, escono; *pres. subj.*, esca, usciamo, usciate, escano; *imper.*, esci, usciamo, uscite.

* valere, *to be worth*; *pres. ind.*, valgo, vali, vale, valiamo, valete, valgono; *p. def.*, valsi, valesti, *etc.*; *p. part.*, valso; *fut.*, varrò; *pres. subj.*, valga, valiamo, valiate, valgano.

vedere, *to see*; *p. def.*, vidi, vedesti, *etc.*; *p. part.*, visto *or* veduto; *fut.*, vedrò.

* venire, *to come*; *pres. ind.*, vengo, vieni, viene, veniamo, venite, vengono; *p. def.*, venni, venisti, *etc.*; *p. part.*, venuto; *fut.*, verrò; *pres. subj.*, venga, veniamo, veniate, vengano; *imper.*, vieni, veniamo, venite.

vincere, *to win*; *p. def.*, vinsi, vincesti, *etc.*; *p. part.*, vinto.

† vivere, *to live*; *p. def.*, vissi, vivesti, *etc.*; *p. part.*, vissuto.

† volere, *to will, wish, want*; *pres. ind.*, voglio, vuoi, vuole, vogliamo, volete, vogliono; *p. def.*, volli, volesti, *etc.*; *fut.*, vorrò; *pres. subj.*, voglia, vogliamo, vogliate, vogliano; *imper.*, vogli, vogliamo, vogliate.

volgere, *to turn, revolve*; *p. def.*, volsi, volgesti, *etc.*; *p. part.*, volto.

APPENDIX IV

A SELECTIVE LIST OF INTRANSITIVE VERBS REQUIRING *ESSERE* AS THEIR AUXILIARY

Verbs preceded by an asterisk require **avere** as their auxiliary when used transitively.

abbisognare	*to require*	* avanzare	*to advance*
accadere	*to happen*	avvampare	*to blaze up*
accorrere	*to run up*	avvenire	*to happen*
affluire	*to flow in*	balenare†	*to flash, lighten*
* affogare	*to drown, stifle*		
* alzare	*to rise*	bastare	*to suffice*
* ammontare	*to amount*	bisognare	*to need*
* ammutolire	*to be silent*	cadere	*to fall*
andare	*to go*	* campare	*to earn (living)*
* annerire	*to blacken*	capitare	*to arrive, happen*
annottare	*to grow dark*		
apparire	*to appear*	capitombolare	*to fall head first*
appassire	*to wither*		
* arricchire	*to grow rich*	cascare	*to fall*
arrivare	*to arrive*	comparire	*to appear*
arrossire	*to blush*	consistere	*to consist*
* ascendere	*to go up*	* convenire	*to gather to-gether*
assiderare	*to become numb*		
* aumentare	*to increase*	costare	*to cost*
		crepare	*to break*

crescere	to grow	* migliorare	to improve
decadere	to decay	* montare	to mount
decorrere	to elapse	morire	to die
decrescere	to decrease	nascere	to be born
deperire	to waste away	nevicare†	to snow
derivare	to derive	occorrere	to be necessary
dipendere	to depend	parere	to seem
discendere	to go down	partire	to set out
dispiacere	to displease	passare	to pass
divenire	to become	* peggiorare	to worsen
diventare	to become	perire	to perish
dolere	to ache	pervenire	to reach
entrare	to enter	piacere	to please
equivalere	to be equiva- lent	piovere†	to rain
		provenire	to issue from
esistere	to exist	restare	to stay
esplodere	to explode	ricorrere	to have re- course to
essere	to be		
evadere	to evade	rimanere	to remain
fallire	to fail	rincrescere	to be sorry
* fuggire	to flee	risultare	to result
fulminare†	to flash, lighten	ritornare	to return
		riuscire	to succeed
gelare†	to freeze	* rovinare	to fall to ruin
ghiacciare	to freeze	* salire	to go up
giungere	to reach	sbiadire	to wither
* gonfiare	to swell	sbucare	to come out
grandinare†	to hail	scadere	to fall due
* guarire	to be cured	scappare	to escape
* imbiancare	to turn white	* scendere	to go down
imbrunare, -ire	to grow dark	scivolare	to slip
impazzire	to grow mad	* scoccare	to shoot out
importare	to matter	scomparire	to disappear
inciampare	to stumble against	scoppiare	to burst out
		scorrere	to flow
incominciare	to begin	sdrucciolare	to slip
* incontrare	to meet	sembrare	to seem
incorrere	to incur	* smontare	to dismount
* indebolire	to weaken	sopraggiungere	to arrive
insorgere	to rebel, rise	sopravvivere	to survive
intervenire	to intervene	sorgere	to rise
invecchiare	to age	sottostare	to submit
mancare	to lack	sovrastare	to surpass
maturare	to ripen	sparire	to disappear

stare	to stand	trascorrere	to pass
* stordire	to be amazed	uscire	to go out
svanire	to vanish	valere	to be worth
* terminare	to end	venire	to come
tornare	to return	* vivere	to live
tramontare	to set (sun)		

† Verbs dealing with the weather take **avere** or **essere** as auxiliaries.

VOCABULARIES
A. ITALIAN — ENGLISH

Many of the words included in the previous vocabularies have been omitted here for reasons of space.

abbassare, *to lower*
abbondante, *abundant*
abbrustolito, *roasted*
abisso, *abyss*
abito, *clothes, suit*
abituarsi, *to become accustomed to*
abitudine (*f.*), *habit, custom*
accadere, *to happen*
accecare, *to blind*
accendere, *to light*
accennare, *to point to, hint at*
acceso, *lit up, illuminated*
acchiappare, *to catch*
acciaio, *steel*
accidente! *goodness! what on earth!*
acciò che, *in order that*
accogliere, *to welcome, receive*
accomodare, *to adjust, arrange, mend*
acconciarsi, *to settle*
acconciatura, *style of hairdressing*
accordo, *agreement, harmony*
accostarsi, *to approach*
accozzare, *to jumble together*
acido fenico, *carbolic acid*
acquisto, *purchase, acquisition*
addirittura, *even, really*
additare, *to point out*
addormentarsi, *to go to sleep*
addormentato, *sleeper*
affacciarsi, *to appear, to show oneself*
affare (*m.*), *business*

affarista, *business seeking*
affatturare, *to bewitch*
affetto, *affection*
affettuoso, *affectionate*
affinché, *in order that, so that*
affitto, *rent*
affollare, *to crowd*
affollato, *crowded*
affondare, *to sink, to bury*
agente (*m.*), *agent*
aggiudicare, *to grant, adjudge*
aggiungere, *to add, join*
aggiustare, *to adjust, settle*
aggiustare i conti, *to settle accounts, matters*
agricolo, *agricultural*
aia, *threshing floor, yard*
alba, *dawn*
alga, *seaweed*
alito, *breath, breeze*
allegare, *to attach*
allinearsi, *to line up*
alloggiare, *to lodge, put up*
allontanarsi, *to go away*
allora, *then, at that time*
alludere, *to allude to, hint at*
almanacco, *almanac, calendar*
alquanto, *somewhat*
alto, *high, tall, loud*
  ad alta voce, *aloud*
altrimenti, *otherwise*
altro, *other*
  tra l'altro, *among other things*
  altroché! *rather!*
  senz'altro, *certainly*
  tutt'altro, *on the contrary*

altrove, *elsewhere*
alzare, *to lift*
alzarsi, *to get up, rise*
amante (*m. & f.*), *lover*
amare, *to love*
amaro, *bitter*
ambedue, *both*
ammalato, *sick, ill*
ammazzare, *to kill, murder*
ammettere, *to admit (of)*
ammucchiare, *to heap up, pile up*
ampiezza, *size, amplitude, extension*
anarchico, *anarchist,* (*adj.*) *anarchic*
andare, *to go, suit*
  andarsene, andare via, *to go away*
  andare su, giú, *to go up, down*
andito, *passage*
annuale, *yearly, annual*
annunziare (annunciare), *to announce*
ansioso, *anxious*
anticipo, *advance*
  in anticipo, *in advance*
antico, *old, ancient*
anzi, *rather, on the contrary*
anziché, *rather than*
aperto, *open*
  bell'e aperto, *well and truly open*
apparecchio, *apparatus, aeroplane, radio set*
appartamento, *flat*
appena, *hardly*
applauso, *applause*
appoggiare, *to lean, prop, support*
apprendere, *to learn*
appressarsi, *to approach*

appuntamento, *appointment*
appunto, *note,* (*adv.*) *precisely*
  prendere appunti, *to take notes*
arare, *to plough*
arbitrare, *to arbitrate*
archivio, *archive*
argenteo, *silvery*
aria, *air, song, appearance*
armadio, *cupboard*
armi (*f.pl.*), *weapons, arms*
arrampicarsi, *to climb, cling to*
arrivederla, *goodbye*
arte (*f.*), *art*
asciutto, *dry*
ascoltare, *to listen (to)*
asino, *ass, donkey*
aspersorio, *holy-water sprinkler*
aspettare, *to wait for, await, expect*
aspettativa, *expectation*
aspetto
  sala d'aspetto, *waiting-room*
assai, *very much*
assassinio, *murder*
assenza, *absence*
asserire, *to assert, affirm*
assistere, *to assist, help, be present at*
asso, *ace (in cards)*
  piantare in asso, *to leave in the lurch*
associarsi con, *to become associated with, join*
assoluto, *absolute*
assumere *to appoint*
asta, *lance, pole*
  vendere all'asta, *to sell by auction*
astratto, *abstract*
attendere, *to await, expect, attend to*
attento, *careful*

atterrare, *to lay low, overthrow, land*

attesa, *expectation*
  in attesa di, *while waiting for*

atto, *act,* (*adj.*) *suitable*

attorto, *twisted*

attraversare, *to cross*

attraverso, *across*

augurale, *promising*

aumento, *increase*

autonomia, *autonomy*

avanti (di), *before*
  avanti che (*conj.*)(+ *subj.*), *before*

avanzo, *remnant, scrap*

avere, *to have*
  che hai? *What is the matter?*

avido, *greedy*

avorio, *ivory*

avvenimento, *event*

avvenire, *to happen,* (*subs., adj.*) *future*

avventato, *rash*

avventura, *adventure*

avvertire, *to inform, warn, let know*

avvezzo, *accustomed*

avvicinarsi, *to approach*

avvilimento, *humiliation*

azione (*f.*), *action, share*

azzurro, *blue*

bacillo, *microbe*
  porta-bacilli, *germ-carrier*

badare, *to mind, take care to, pay attention to*

bagnare, *to bathe, wet*

bagnato, *soaked*

baiocco, *brass farthing*

balcone (*m.*), *balcony*

balconata, *public gallery*

bara, *coffin*

baraonda, *confusion*

barca, *boat*

barone (*m.*), *baron, rascal*

bastare, *to be enough, suffice*

bastone (*m.*), *stick*

battere, *to beat*
  batter d'occhio, *in a flash*

beato, *blessed*

beffa, *trick*

ben di Dio, *God's abundance*

benedire, *to bless*

benedizione (*f.*), *benediction, blessing*

benservito, *reference*

benvenuto, *welcome*

bestiame (*m.*), *cattle*

biancheria, *linen*

bianco, *white*

biasimare, *to blame*

biondo, *blond*

biondiccio, *yellowish, blond*

birichinata, *prank*

bisogno, *need*
  aver bisogno, *to be in need*

bocca, *mouth*

boccata, *mouthful*
  boccata d'aria, *breath of fresh air*

bollire, *to boil*

bollito, *boiled food*

bolscevico, *bolshevik*

bontà, *kindness*

botte (*f.*), *barrel*

botticina, *little barrel*

bracciolo, *arm (of chair)*

brezza, *breeze*

brigadiere, *police-sergeant*

brillare, *to shine*

bruciare, *to burn (out)*

brughiera, *heath*

buco, *hole*

buffo, *comic*

buio, *darkness,* (*adj.*) *dark*

buono, *good*
  a buon mercato, *cheap*
  alla buona, *simply*
  di buon'ora, *early*
burla, *joke, trick*
buttare, *to throw*

cabala, *plot, intrigue*
cacciare, *to chase, hunt*
  cacciare fuori, *to bring out*
  cacciarsi, *to thrust one's way
    into*
cadere, *to fall*
calamaio, *inkstand*
calcarsi, *to ram down*
caldo, *hot*
  far caldo, *to be warm (of
    weather)*
calesse (*m.*), *trap, carriage*
calice (*m.*), *goblet*
caligine (*f.*), *mist*
calunnia, *calumny*
calza, *stocking*
cambiare, *to change*
camera, *room, bedroom*
cameriera, *maidservant*
camerista, *chambermaid*
camminare, *to walk, march*
campana, *bell*
campanile (*m.*), *belfry*
campione (*m.*), *champion, sample*
campo, *field, camp*
  campo d'aviazione, *airfield*
canchero, *nuisance*
candela, *candle*
cane (*m.*), *dog*
canonica, *presbytery*
canonico, *canon*
cantare, *to sing*
canterellare, *to hum*
cantina, *cellar*
canto, *song, corner*
capace, *capable*

capanna, *hut*
capello, *hair*
capitare, *to happen, arrive*
capo, *head*
  in capo a, *at the end of (time)*
  capo di vestiario, *item of
    clothing*
capoluogo, *chief town*
capomastro, *head foreman*
caporeparto, *shop manager, de-
    partmental manager*
cappello, *hat*
capro, *goat*
  capro espiatorio, *scapegoat*
carbone (*m.*), *coal, charcoal*
carico, *loaded*
carne (*f.*), *meat*
  in carne ed ossa, *in flesh and
    blood*
carrozza, *carriage, coach*
cascare, *to fall*
caso, *chance, fate*
  caso mai, *if by chance*
  fare al caso mio, *to suit my
    purpose*
  nel caso che, *in case*
  in caso di, *in a position to*
casupola, *hovel*
catena, *chain*
causa, *cause*
  a causa di, *because of*
cauzione (*f.*), *security*
cava, *quarry*
cavaliere, *knight*
cavarsela, *to get out of*
cedere, *to give up, yield*
celare, *to hide*
cenare, *to sup*
cencioso, *ragged*
ceneri (*f.pl.*), *ashes*
cenno, *nod*
cerca, *search, quest*
  in cerca di, *in search of*

certo, *certain*
cervello, *brain*
cervo, *stag*
cessare, *to cease*
chiacchierare, *to gossip*
chiacchierino, *gossiping*
chiamarsi, *to be called*
chiarire, *to clarify, clear up*
chiaro, *clear*
chiave (*f.*), *key*
   chiave inglese, *spanner*
chiazza, *splash, pool, spot*
chiedere, *to ask, enquire*
   chieder scusa, *to ask for pardon*
china, *slope*
chinare, *to bend, bow, lean*
chino, *bent, bowed*
chioma, *foliage, locks (of hair)*
chiudere, *to close, shut*
ciambella, *doughnut*
cifra, *figure, number*
ciglio, *eyelid, edge*
cima, *summit*
cinta, *surrounding wall*
circa, *about, nearby*
cittadina, *small town*
clima (*m.*), *climate*
coccio, *piece, shard*
cogliere, *to gather*
collana, *necklace*
collina, *hill*
colpevole, *guilty*, (*subs.*) *culprit*
colpo, *blow*
   ad un colpo, di colpo, *suddenly, at once*
combattere, *to fight*
comitiva, *company, party*
commovente, *touching*
comparire, *to appear*
compera, *purchase*
   fare delle compere, *to go shopping*

compire (compiere), *to accomplish*
completo, *complete*
complimentare, *to compliment*
comporre, *to compose, make up*
comportamento, *behaviour*
comprendere, *to comprise, include, understand*
compreso, *including*
comune (*m.*), *commune, municipality,* (*adj.*) *common, ordinary*
conca, *hollow*
concedere, *to concede*
concorrenza, *competition*
condizione (*f.*), *condition, position, situation*
condoglianza, *condolence*
conducente (*m.*), *driver*
condurre, *to conduct, lead*
   condurre a termine, *to bring to an end*
conferma, *confirmation*
confusione (*f.*), *confusion*
congegno, *assemblage*
   congegno dell' universo, *creation of the universe*
congratularsi con, *to congratulate*
conoscente (*m. & f.*), *acquaintance*
conoscere, *to know, be acquainted with*
consacrare, *to consecrate, dedicate*
conseguenza, *consequence*
consigliare, *to advise*
   consigliarsi, *to consult, seek advice*
consultarsi, *to deliberate, confer*
contanti (*m.pl.*), *ready money*
   a contanti, *in cash*
contare, *to count*

contemporaneo, *contemporary*
conto, *account*
contro, *against*
convenienza, *propriety*
convincere, *to convince*
convocare, *to convoke, summon*
coperto, *covered, overcast*
coppia, *couple*
coprire, *to cover*
coraggio, *courage*
cordoglio, *grief*
corno, *horn*
    rompere le corna, *to break one's neck, defeat*
corpo, *body*
corporale, *bodily*
correre, *to run*
corsa, *race*
in corso, *present*
corteo, *procession*
cortese, *polite*
cortile (*m.*), *courtyard*
corto, *short*
cospiratore, *plotter*
costeggiare, *to coast, run along*
costituzione (*f.*), *constitution*
costringere, *to compel*
    costretto a, *forced to*
costruire, *to build*
costume (*m.*), *custom, habit*
cotto, *cooked*
cratere (*m.*), *crater*
creato, *creation*
credito, *credit*
credulone (*m.*), *credulous person*
crepuscolo, *twilight*
crescere, *to grow*
crollare, *to collapse*
crosta, *crust*
crudele, *cruel*
crudeltà, *cruelty*
crudo, *raw, crude*
cucina, *kitchen*

culturale, *cultural*
cumulo, *heap, pile*
cuocere, *to cook*
cuore (*m.*), *heart*
    stare a cuore, *to be dear to*
cupo, *dark, deep*

dabbene, *good*
dacché (da che), *since (time)*
dama, *draughts, lady*
danaro (denaro), *money*
dappertutto, *everywhere*
dapprima, *at first*
dare, *to give*
    dare da mangiare, *to feed (animals)*
    dare risposta, *to further, carry out (reply)*
    può darsi (+*subj.*), *it is possible that*
data, *date*
dato che (+*subj.*), *granted that*
davvero, per davvero, *really in earnest*
degno, *worthy*
deliberare, *to deliberate, decide*
delitto, *crime*
demonio, *devil*
dente (*m.*), *tooth, jag*
dentellato, *jagged*
dentro, *inside, in*
derisione (*f.*), *derision*
deroga, *cancellation*
    in deroga a, *as an exception to*
desiderare, *to want, wish, desire*
desolato, *desolate*
desolazione (*f.*), *desolation*
desto, *awake, lively*
destra, *right*
    a destra, *to the right*
detta, *saying*
    a detta di, *according to*

detto, *opinion*
   lasciare detto, *to leave word*
difetto, *defect, fault*
diffidenza, *distrust*
diga, *dyke*
dignità, *dignity*
dimenticare (-arsi), *to forget*
dimostrazione (*f.*), *demonstrate*
Dio, *God*
   come è vero Dio, *as God is my judge*
   Dio mio! *Good gracious!*
dipendere, *to depend*
dire
   un bel dire, *to say in vain*
   dirne di tutti i colori, *to tell off*
diretto, *heading for, on the way to, direct*
diritto, *right*, (*adj.*) *straight, erect*
discernere, *to discern*
discorso, *talk, speech*
discreto, *reasonable, discreet*
disgrazia, *ill-luck, misfortune, disgrace*
disperazione (*f.*), *despair*
dispiacere, *to displease*, (*subs.*) *dislike, grief, misfortune*
disporre (disposto), *to arrange, dispose*
dissesto, *financial troubles*
distratto, *absent-minded*
dito, *finger*
   dito indice, *index finger*
divertirsi, *to enjoy oneself, amuse oneself*
dividere, *to divide, share, separate*
doga, *stave*
dolente, *mournful*
dolore (*m.*), *pain, grief*
domani, *tomorrow*

dono, *gift*
dopodomani, *the day after tomorrow*
doppio, *double*
dorato, *golden, gilded*
dovere, *to owe, have to*
dovunque, *wherever*
dozzina, *dozen*
dubbio, *doubt*
dubitare, *to doubt*
duca, *duke*
duna, *dune*
dunque, *thus, then*
duomo, *cathedral*
durare, *to last*

eccellente, *excellent*
   per eccellenza, *par excellence*
eccessivo, *excessive*
edificio, *building*
effetto, *effect*
elevare, *to elevate*
ente (*m.*), *being, entity*
entro, *within* (*time*)
eppure, *and yet*
era, *era*
esame (*m.*), *examination*
esclamare, *to exclaim*
esercizio, *exercise*
esile, *slender*
esistenza, *existence*
esitare, *to hesitate*
essere, *to be*
   essere per, *to be about to*
   esserne di, *to become of*
estate (*f.*), *summer*
estatico, *ecstatic*
estendere (-ersi), *to extend*
estero (all'estero), *abroad*
estremità, *end*
età, *age*
evitare, *to avoid*

fabbrica, *factory*
faccia, *face*
  in faccia a, *in the face of*
facilitare, *to facilitate*
falda, *foot (of hill)*
fallire, *to go bankrupt, fail*
fame (*f.*), *hunger*
  aver fame, *to be hungry*
fango, *mud*
farabutto, *rascal*
fare, *to do, make*
  farsi, *to become*
  far cadere, *to emphasize*
  fare né caldo né freddo, *to be indifferent*
  fare in tempo, *to be in time*
  far finta di, *to pretend*
farmacia, *chemist's shop*
farmaco, *medicine*
fatato, *magic, bewitched*
fatatura, *enchantment, spell*
fatica, *fatigue, tiredness*
faticoso, *tiring*
fatto, *fact, (plu.) business*
  saper il fatto suo, *to know one's job*
fattoria, *farm*
fattucchiera, *witch*
fava, *bean*
favore (*m.*), *favour*
  per favore, *please*
fegato, *liver*
felicità, *happiness*
ferita, *wound, injury*
fermare (-arsi), *to stop*
fermo, *firm, standing*
feroce, *ferocious*
ferraglia, *scrap-iron*
ferrovia, *railway*
ferroviario, *of the railway*
festa, *merrymaking, holiday*
fetore (*m.*), *bad smell, stench*
fetta, *slice*

feudo, *estate*
fico, *fig, figtree*
fidarsi di, *to trust*
figliastra, *step-daughter*
figlio, -a, *son, daughter*
figurarsi, *to imagine, fancy*
filare (*m.*), *row (of trees)*
filtro, *potion*
finché, *as long as, until (+ subj.)*
fine (*m.*), *aim, goal*
fine (*f.*), *end*
finestra, *window*
fino a, *as far as*
finto, *false*
  fare finto, *to pretend*
Firenze, *Florence*
fiotto, *wave, surge*
firmare, *to sign*
fischiare, *to whistle*
fisico, *constitution*
fisso, *fixed*
fiume (*m.*), *river*
fiutata, *sniff*
fluente, *flowing*
focolare (*m.*), *fireplace*
focoso, *fiery*
foglia, *leaf*
foglio, *sheet (of paper)*
folto, *dense*
fondo, *bottom*
  in fondo a, *at the end of, at the bottom of*
forse, *perhaps*
  rimanere in forse, *to remain in doubt*
fortunato, *lucky, fortunate*
forza, *force, strength*
fracasso, *crash*
frammento, *fragment*
frangersi, *to break*
frangia, *fringe*
frastuono, *din*
fratello, *brother*

fresco, *fresh*
frigorifero, *refrigerator*
fritto, *fried*
frizzante, *sparkling*, *tingling*
fronte, *forehead*
   di fronte a, *face to face with*, *in front of*
fu, *late*
fucile (*m.*), *rifle*
fuga, *flight*
fuggire, *to flee*
fumare, *to smoke*
fumigare, *to smoke*
fumo, *smoke*
fuoco, *fire*
fuorché, *except*
furibondo, *furious*

gabbiano, *seagull*
galantuomo, *gentleman*
galleria, *tunnel*
   galleria d'arte, *art gallery*
gallina, *hen*, *chicken*
gara, *rivalry*
   fara a gara, *to vie with*
garbo, *charm*, *culture*
garzone (*m.*), *labourer*
gatto, *cat*
gattino, *kitten*
gelare, *to freeze*
geloso, *jealous*
gemere, *to moan*
genere (*m.*), *kind*, *gender*
genitore, -trice, *parent*
gente (*f.*), *people*
Germania, *Germany*
gesto, *gesture*
ghiaia, *gravel*
ghiotto, *greedy*
già, *yes*, *already*
giacca, *jacket*
giacché, *since* (*cause*)

giacente, *prostrate*
giacere, *to lie*
giallo, *yellow*
giardiniera, *mixed pickles*
ginocchio, *knee*
giocare, *to play*
gioco (giuoco), *game*
gioia, *joy*
giovane, *young*
giovanile, *of youth*
giovare, *to be useful*
girare, *to turn*, *go around*
   gira e rigira, *whichever way you look at it*
giravolta, *turn about*
giro, *turn*, *ride*
   in giro, *around*
giú, *down*
   giú di morale, *downcast*
giungere, *to reach*
giunta, *council*
giustizia, *justice*
giusto, *right*, *just*, *clearly*
godere (-ersi), *to enjoy*
gomito, *elbow*
gonfio, *swollen*
gorgoglio, *gurgling*
gradino, *step*
grado, *degree*
   essere in grado di, *to be in a position to*
grasso, *fat*, *stout*
grattacielo, *skyscraper*
greco, *Greek*
grembo, *bosom*
gridare, *to shout*
grido, *shout*
grigio, *grey*
grondante, *dripping*
grosso, *big*
guadagnare, *to earn*, *win*
guanciale, *pillow*
guanto, *glove*

guardare, *to look at*
guarigione (*f.*), *cure*
guastare, *to spoil*
guastarsi, *to go bad*
guasto, *accident, damage, (adj.) spoilt*
guerra, *war*
guizzante, *quivering*
guscio, *shell (of egg)*

illuminare (-arsi), *to light up*
imbarazzo, *embarrassment*
imbrogliare, *to cheat, swindle*
immaginare (-arsi), *to imagine*
immobile, *motionless*
immune, *immune to*
impari, *uneven*
impedire, *to prevent*
impegno, *obligation, duty, work*
impervio, *impossible, impervious*
impiegare, *to employ*
impiego, *employment, use*
imporre, *to impose*
importare, *to matter*
impostare, *to post*
impressionato, *alarmed*
improvviso, *unexpected*
  all'improvviso, *suddenly*
inanellato, *ringed*
inaspettato, *unexpected*
incamminarsi, *to set out, walk along*
incantare, *to enchant, bewitch, delight*
incantevole, *enchanting*
incaricare, *to undertake*
incarnato, *complexion*
inchinarsi, *to bow*
inchino, *bow*
incominciare, *to begin*
incoraggiare, *to encourage*
incredulità, *incredulity*

increspato, *churned up*
incriminare, *to incriminate*
indice, *index*
indirizzo, *address*
  all'indirizzo di, *at*
indole (*f.*), *disposition*
indovinare, *to guess, divine*
industrializzare, *to industrialize*
industrioso, *industrious*
inesauribile, *inexhaustible*
infanzia, *infancy, childhood*
infatti, *in fact*
infezione (*f.*), *infection*
infine, *finally, in the end*
influenza, *influence, influenza*
infrangibilità, *unbreakableness*
ingegnere (*m.*), *engineer*
ingenuo, *simple, ingenuous*
Inghilterra, *England*
inglese, *English*
iniziare, *to begin*
innamorato, *in love*
innanzi, *before, in front of*
  d'ora innanzi, *from now on*
innestare, *to engage (gear)*
inoltre, *moreover, besides*
inserzione (*f.*), *advertisement*
insieme (con), *together (with)*
insistere, *to insist*
insomma, *in conclusion, in short*
insopportabile, *unbearable*
insorgere, *to rebel*
insostituibile, *irreplaceable*
insulare, *insular (of islands)*
intanto, *meanwhile*
intendere, *to mean, understand, intend*
  s'intende, *of course*
  intendersene, *to know about*
intenzione (*f.*), *intention*
  aver intenzione, *to intend*
interesse (*m.*), *interest*
interno, *interior, inside*

intero, *whole*
intervallo, *interval*
inteso, *agreed*
intimo, *inner, intimate*
inumano, *inhuman*
inutile, *useless*
invariabile, *invariable*
inverno, *winter*
investire, *to run over*
invidioso, *envious*
inviperito, *vindictive*
irregolarità, *irregularity*
irreparabile, *irreparable*
irreprensibile, *faultless*
isola, *island*

là, *there*
labile, *slight*
laborioso, *industrious*
laggiú, *down there, over there,
    on earth*
lagnarsi, *to complain*
lago, *lake*
lampeggiare, *to lighten*
lana, *wool*
landa, *heath*
lanciare, *to throw, fling, launch*
lapis (*m.*), *pencil*
larghezza, *width*
largo, *wide*
lasciare, *to leave*
    lasciare in asso, *to leave in the
        lurch*
lato, *side*
    allato, *beside*
latte (*m.*), *milk*
lava, *lava*
lavagna, *blackboard*
lavata (di capo), *telling off, row*
Lazio, *Latium*
leccare, *to lick*
lecito, *allowed*

legare, *to bind, tie up*
leggere, *to read*
leggiero, *light, slight*
leggiucchiare, *to read*
legno, *wood, timber*
lenzuolo, *sheet (of bed)*
lepre (*f.*), *hare*
    leprotto, *young hare*
lettera, *letter*
    lettera raccomandata, *regis-
        tered letter*
letto, *bed*
levarsi, *to rise, lift*
levigato, *polished*
libertario, *libertarian*
lido, *shore*
lieto, *happy*
lieve, *slight*
lingua, *language, tongue*
liscio, *smooth*
lista, *list, menu*
listino, *price-list*
lite (*f.*), *quarrel*
litorale (*m.*), *coast*
lodare, *to praise*
Londra, *London*
lontano, *far, distant*
    in lontananza, *in the distance*
luce (*f.*), *light*
lucente, *sparkling, shining*
lume (*m.*), *light*
    lume a petrolio, *paraffin
        lamp*
luna, *moon*
lunario, *almanac*
lunare, *of the moon*
lunghezza, *length*
lungi da, *far from*
lungo, *long*
    di gran lunga, *by far*
luogo, *place*
    avere luogo, *to take place*
lupino, *lupin seed*

maestro, *teacher, master*

mai, *ever, never*
  come mai, *how on earth*
  se mai, *in case*

malattia, *illness, disease*

malavoglia, *sloth*
  di malavoglia, *unwillingly*

male, *bad,* (subs.) *illness*
  mal di mare, *sea-sickness*

malgrado, *in spite of*

malinconia, *melancholy*

malvagio, *wicked*

manata, *hanàful*

mancare, *to fail, lack, miss*
  mancare poco che, *almost (to do something)*

mandare, *to send*

manica, *sleeve*
  la Manica, *the English Channel*

maniera, *manner*

mano (*f.*), *hand*
  man mano, *as*

manovella, *handle*

mansione (*f.*), *duty, function*

mantice (*m.*), *bellows*

manzo, *beef*

marcia, *march, gear (of car)*

marchese, *marquis*

marciapiede (*m.*), *pavement, platform*

mare (*m.*), *sea*

margine, *edge*

marinaio (-aro), *sailor,* (adj.) *maritime*

marito, *husband*

massaia, *housewife*

mastro, *master*

matita, *pencil*

matrigna, *step-mother*

mattina (-ino), *morning*

matto, *mad, madman*

mattone (*m.*), *brick*

meccanico, *mechanical engineering*

mediante, *by means of*

medicamento, *medicine*

medico, *doctor*

medio (subs.), *middle finger*

meglio, *better*

membro, *limb, member*

memoria, *memory*

meno, *less*
  in meno di, *in less than*
  a meno che . . . non, *unless*

mensa, *table*

meraviglia, *wonder, surprise astonishment*

meravigliarsi, *to be amazed, be surprised, wonder*

meraviglioso, *amazing, wonderful*

mercante (*m.*), *trader*

mercato, *market*
  a buon mercato, *cheap*

merce (*f.*), *merchandise, goods*

meridionale, *southern*

mestiere (*m.*), *trade, profession*

metà, *half*

mettere, *to put, lead on to*
  mettersi a, *to begin to, set about*
  mettere a soqquadro, *to turn upside down*
  mettere in moto, *to start (of machine)*
  mettere a punto, *to put right*

mezzo, *half, middle*
  da mezzo, *in the middle*
  nel mezzo di, *in the middle of*
  in mezzo a, *in the middle of*
  per mezzo di, *by means of*

mica
  non . . . mica, *not at all, not in the least*
  mica tanto, *not so much*

miglio, *mile*
migliore, *better*
minacciare, *to threaten*
minestra, *stew*
minestrone, *vegetable stew*
minuto, *minute*
  al minuto, *retail*
misericordia, *mercy, pity*
misurare, *to measure*
modo, *way, manner*
modulo, *form*
mogio, *crestfallen*
molticolore, *many-coloured*
mondo, *world, a lot*
montagna, *mountain*
monte (*m.*), *mountain*
  mandare a monte, *to forget about, annul*
morale (*f.*), *morality*
  giú di morale, *dispirited*
mordere, *to bite*
morire, *to die*
mormorio, *murmur*
morte (*f.*), *death*
mortificare, *to mortify*
mosca, *fly*
  a mosca cieca, *blind man's buff*
moscatello, *muscatel wine*
moto (*f.*), *motor-bike*
mucchio, *pile, heap*
mugnaio, *miller*
mulino, *mill*
munito, *provided*
muovere, *to move*
muraglia, *large wall*
muro, *wall*
muscolo, *mussel*
musica, *music*
muto, *silent, dumb*

napoletano, *Neapolitan*
nascere, *to be born*

nascondere, *to hide*
nascosto, *hidden*
  di nascosto, *secretly, stealthily*
naso, *nose*
  naso a naso con, *face to face*
naturalmente, *of course*
né . . . né, *neither . . . nor*
nebbia, *mist, fog*
necessario, *necessary*
negare, *to deny*
negozio, *shop*
  negozio di generi alimentari, *grocer's shop*
nemico, *enemy*
nemmeno, *not even, neither*
neppure, *not even, neither*
nervoso, *nervous*
nessuno, *no one,* (*adj.*) *no, any*
neve (*f.*), *snow*
nevicare, *to snow*
nevvero? *is it not?*
niente, *nothing*
  niente affatto, *not at all,* (*adj.*) *no*
  per niente, *by no means*
nipote (*m & f.*), *nephew, niece*
nipotino, -a, *grandchild*
nocciola, *nut*
nocivo, *harmful*
noia, *trouble*
  dar noia, *to trouble*
noleggiare, *to hire*
nome (*m.*), *name*
nominare, *to name, appoint*
non, *not*
  non già che, *not that*
  non che, *as well as*
nonno, -a, *grandfather, grandmother*
nonostante (*+subj.*), *notwithstanding*
nostalgia, *homesickness*
nota, *note*

notaio, *lawyer*
notare, *to note, notice*
notarile, *of lawyers*
notevole, *notable*
noto, *well-known*
novella, *short story*
novità, *news, novelty*
nube (*f.*), *cloud*
nudo, *bare, nude*
numero, *number*
nuocere, *to hurt*

obbligare (- irsi), *to oblige, undertake*
occhiali (*m.pl.*), *glasses, spectacles*
occhiata, *glance*
    occhiata di solluchero, *a sugary glance*
occhio, *eye*
occorrere, *to be necessary*
odiare, *to hate*
odio, *hate*
odore (*m.*), *smell, odour*
offerta, *offer, tender*
officina, *workshop*
offrire, *to offer*
oggetto, *object, article*
olio, *oil*
    sott'olio, *in oil*
oltre, *besides, beyond*
ombra, *shadow, shade*
onda, *wave*
ondeggiare, *to sway, wave*
onorare, *to honour*
operaio, *workman,* (*adj.*) *of workmen*
operoso, *industrious*
opinione (*f.*), *opinion*
opposizione (*f.*), *opposition*
ora, *now*
    non veder l'ora di, *to be longing to*

d'ora innanzi, *from now on*
orcio, *pitcher*
ordinare, *to order*
ordinativo, *order*
ordinazione (*f.*), *order*
ordine, *order, row*
orgoglioso, *proud*
orizzonte (*m.*), *horizon*
orlo, *brink, edge, brim*
orologio, *clock, watch*
osare, *to dare*
ossequio, *respect*
osservare, *to observe*
osservazione (*f.*), *observation*
ostinarsi a, *to persist in*
ottenere, *to obtain*
ottimo, *very good*
ovunque, *wherever, everywhere*

pacifico, *peaceful*
padronanza, *command*
padrone, -a, *head, chief, boss, landlady, mistress, proprietor*
paesaggio, *landscape*
paese (*m.*), *country, village*
pagamento, *payment*
palazzo, *building, palace*
palazzotto, *fortress*
palcoscenico, *stage*
palla, *ball*
pallido, *pale*
pallone (*m.*), *football*
paludoso, *marshy*
panca, *board* (*of bed*)
pancia, *stomach, inside*
paralume (*m.*), *lampshade*
parapetto, *parapet*
parecchio, *very much*
parente (*m. & f.*), *relation*
parere, *to seem, appear*
pari, *equal*

parità, *equality*
parola, *word*
parte (*f.*), *part, share*
  da parte sua, *on his part*
  da parte, *aside*
partenza, *departure*
particolare, *particular*
partire, *to set out, leave*
partita, *game*
pascere, *to pasture*
passaggio, *crossing*
passante (*m. & f.*), *passer-by*
passare, *to pass*
  passare da, *to call on*
passato, *the past*
passeggero, *passenger*
passeggiata, *walk*
passo, *step*
pastasciutta, *pastasciutta*
pasticceria, *confectioner's*
pasto, *meal*
paterno, *paternal*
patria, *native land*
patto, *condition*
  a patto che, *on condition that*
paura, *fear*
  aver paura, *to be afraid*
pausa, *pause*
  far pausa, *to pause*
pavimento, *floor*
pazzo, *bread*
peccato, *pity, sin*
pedalare, *to pedal*
peggio, *worse*
  di male in peggio, *from bad to worse*
pelato, *bald*
pelle (*f.*), *skin, hide*
pendere, *to hang*
penna, *pen, plume, feather*
pensare, *to think*
pensiero, *thought*
  sopra pensiero, *in thought*

pensione(*f.*), *boarding-house*
pentimento, *regret, repentence*
pentirsi, *to repent*
pentola, *saucepan*
pera, *pear*
perché, *because, in order that* (+*subj.*)
perdere, *to lose*
perdonare, *to forgive*
pericoloso, *dangerous*
periodo, *period, sentence*
perla, *pearl*
permesso! *excuse me!* (*subs.*) *permission*
permettere, *to permit, allow*
perplesso, *perplexed*
persino, *even*
personalità, *personality*
personale di bordo, *crew*
persuadere, *to persuade*
pesca, *peach*
pesce (*m.*), *fish*
pessimo, *very bad*
peste (*f.*), *plague, bad smell*
petrolio, *paraffin*
pettinare, *to comb*
pettine (*m.*), *comb*
petto, *chest*
pezzo, *piece*
piacere, *to like, please*
piacevole, *agreeable, pleasing, nice*
piangere, *to weep*
piano, *floor*
  pian piano, *softly, slowly*
piantare, *to abandon*
  piantare in asso, *to leave in the lurch*
pianura, *plain*
  pianura padana, *Po Valley*
piatto, *plate, flat dish*
picco, *peak*
  a picco, *perpendicularly over*

piede (m.), foot
  su due piedi, instantly
Piemonte, Piedmont
pietà, pity
  far pietà, to cause pity
pietra, stone
pigliare, to take, catch
pila, pile
pioggia, rain
piovigginoso, drizzling
pista, track
  pista di decollo, runway
piú, more
  per lo piú, mostly
  piú in là, further on
  non . . . piú, no longer
piuma, quill, feather
poetico, poetic
poiché, since (causal)
politica, politics
pollice (m.), inch, thumb
polpastrelli, balls of fingers
poltrona, armchair
polvere (f.), dust
ponte, deck, bridge
popoloso, populous
poppa, stern
porcaro, pig-keeping
porcheria, dirt, filth
porcile (m.), pig-sty
porcino, of pigs
porgere, to offer
porta, door
porta-bacilli, germ-carrier
portabile, portable
portare, to carry, to wear, bear
  portare su, giú, via, to carry
    up, down, away
portinaia, door-keeper's wife
porto, port
possedere, to possess
posto, place
  posto di ritrovo, rendez-vous

posto di sicurezza, police-
    station
posto che (+ subj.), supposing
potere, to be able, (subs.) power
  non ne posso piú, I am ex-
    hausted
pozzanghera, puddle
pozzo, well
pranzare, to dine
pranzo, dinner
precorrere, to anticipate, go
    around
predica, sermon
preferenza, preference
  di preferenza, preferably
prefisso, appointed
premere, to press
prendere, to take, catch
  prendersela con, to get angry
    with
preoccupato, worried
prepararsi, to prepare
prescindendo da, apart from
presentazione (f.), presentation
presiedere, to preside over
presso, at, near, beside, nearby
prestare, to lend
prestare aiuto, to lend a hand
presto, quick, soon
  far presto, to be quick
prete (m.), priest
pretendere, to claim
pretesa, claim, pretention
pretesto, pretext
prevedere, to foresee
prevosto, provost
prezzo, price
prima di, before
  in prima, at first
primavera, Spring
principessa, princess
proclamare, to proclaim
produzione (f.), production

proferire, *to utter*
profittare, *to profit*
progetto, *project, plan*
promettere, *to promise*
promontorio, *headland*
promosso
  essere promosso in, *to pass (exams.)*
pronto, *ready, hello!*
pronunciare, *to pronounce*
proposta, *proposal, proposition*
proprio, *own, (adv.) really*
prosciutto, *ham*
protendersi, *to stretch*
provare, *to prove, try, test*
provenire, *to come from, issue forth*
provincia, *province*
provvedere, *to provide*
pubblico, *public, audience*
pugno, *fist, blow*
puntiglio, *spite*
punto (-a), *point*
  in punta di piedi, *on tiptoe*
  in punto di morte, *at death's door*
  punto di vista, *point of view*
purché (+ *subj.*), *provided*
pure, *also, too*
  pur di, *provided*
purtroppo, *unfortunately*

quaderno, *exercise-book*
quadro, *picture*
qualità, *quality*
  in qualità di, *in the position of*
qualunque, *whatever, whichever*
quando, *when, if* (+ *subj.*)
  di quando in quando, *from time to time*
quanto, *how much?*
  in quanto, *inasmuch*
  quanto a, *as for*

quantunque, *although*
quasi, *nearly, as if* (+ *subj.*)
quello, *that*
questione (*f.*), *dispute, problem*
questura, *prefecture (of police)*
qui (qua), *here*
quindi, *thus*
quindici (giorni), *a fortnight*
quintale (*m.*), *100 kilos*
quota, *quota, height*
  prendere quota, *to gain height*

rabbrividire, *to shudder*
raccolta, *harvest*
raccomandabile, *recommendable*
raccomandato
  lettera raccomandata, *registered letter*
radice (*f.*), *root*
raggiungere, *to join, overtake*
ragia, *resin, scolding*
rallentare, *to slow down*
rammentare, *to recall*
rappresentare, *to present, represent, perform*
raso, *satin*
re, *king*
recinto, *enclosure*
regalare, *to present*
regale, *regal*
regina, *queen*
regno, *reign, kingdom*
relazione, *connection, relation*
remo, *oar*
remoto, *remote*
rendere, *to render*
rendersi conto di, *to realize*
resistere, *to stand, resist, put up with*
resoconto, *report, account*
respingere, *to drive back*
restare, *to stay*
resto, *rest*

retto, *straight*

ribalta, *footlights*

ribelle, *rebellious*

ricco, *rich*

ricercare, *to inquire into, research*

ricevitore, *receiver (telephone)*

richiamare, *to recall*

richiesta, *request, enquiry*

richiedere, *to require*

riconoscere, *to recognize*

ricordare (-arsi), *to remember*

ridere, *to laugh*

riempire, *to fill in*

rifare, *to do again, repeat*

riferire, *to tell, relate*

rifiutare, *to refuse*

riflesso, *reflection*

rigido, *severe, rigid*

riguardo, *respect*

   per riguardo a, *out of respect for*

rilasciare, *to grant, release*

rimanente (*m.*), *remainder*

rimanere, *to remain*

rimasuglio, *remains*

rimescolare, *to stir, mingle*

rimettere, *to settle*

rincorrersi, *to chase after, run after*

rincrescere, *to be sorry*

ripassare, *to check*

riprendere, *to take up again*

risanare, *to restore*

rischiarare, *to light up*

riso, *laughter*

risparmiare, *to save, spare*

rispetto a, *with regard to*

rispettivo, *respective*

risposta, *reply*

ristorante (*m.*), *restaurant*

ritardo; in ritardo, *late*

ritegno, *reserve*

ritirare, *to draw back, withdraw, take back*

rito, *ritual*

   essere di ritorno, *to be back*

ritto, *erect*

rituffarsi, *to plunge again*

riunione (*f.*), *meeting*

riunirsi, *to meet*

riva, *shore, bank*

   in riva a, *on the shore of*

riverso, *upturned*

ritorno, *return*

riviera, *coast*

   Riviera di Levante, *Eastern Riviera*

rivivere, *to live again, revive*

rivolgersi, *to apply to*

rivolto, *turned*

roba, *goods, material*

roccia, *rock, cliff*

rompere, *to break*

   rompersi le corna, *to break one's neck*

roseo, *rosy-cheeked, reddish*

rosso, *red*

rotaia, *rail*

rotondo, *round*

rotta, *breach*

   a rotta di collo, *at breakneck speed*

rubare, *to steal*

rumore (*m.*), *noise*

sabbia, *sand*

saccheggio, *plundering*

sacco, *sack*

saccocciata, *sackful*

sacerdote (*m.*), *priest*

sala, *room*

   sala d'aspetto, *waiting-room*

   sala da pranzo, *dining-room*

sale (*m.*), *salt*

salire, *to go up, climb*
salone (*m.*), *reception-room*
salotto, *drawing-room, parlour*
saltare, *to jump*
salutare, *to greet*
salute (*f.*), *health, safety*
salvarsi, *to save oneself*
sapere, *to know, taste of*
  saperne di, *to hear of*
Sardegna, *Sardinia*
sardo, *Sardinian*
sbalordire, *to dumbfound*
sbirro, *policeman*
sbucciare, *to peel*
scacco, *check, repulse*
  a scacco, *checked*
scaffale (*m.*), *shelf*
scala, *scale, ladder*
  le scale, *staircase*
scalzo, *barefooted*
scambiare, *to exchange*
scansare, *to avoid*
scappare, *to escape*
scarnito, *thin, emaciated*
scarno, *thin, emaciated*
scarpa, *shoe*
scatola, *box*
scena, *scene*
scenata, *angry scene*
scenario, *scenery*
scherzo, *joke, jest, prank*
schifo, *disgust*
  che schifo! *how disgusting!*
sciagura, *disaster, bereavement*
scialle (*m.*), *shawl*
sciocco, *foolish, silly*
scivolare, *to slide, slip*
scoglio, *rock*
scolaro, *schoolboy*
scommettere, *to bet*
scomparire, *to disappear, vanish*
scongiurare, *to implore*
scontrare, *to meet*

scoperta, *discovery*
scoppiare, *to burst*
scorso, *last*
scrofa, *sow*
scuola, *school*
scuotere, *to shake*
scuro, *dark*
scusa, *excuse*
  chieder scusa, *to ask for pardon*
scusare, *to excuse*
scusarsi, *to apologize*
sdegno, *indignation*
se, *if, whether*
sebbene (+ *subj.*), *although*
seccato, *vexed*
secchia, -io, *bucket*
secolo, *century*
seconda, *second (mus.)*
  a seconda di, *according to*
secondo, *according to*
sedersi, *to sit down*
sedia, *chair*
segato, *cleft*
seggiola, *chair*
segnare, *to mark*
segno, *mark, sign*
segreto, *secret*
seguire, *to follow*
seguito, *retinue, sequel*
  in seguito, *later on*
selvaggio, *wild*
semplice, *simple*
sempre, *always*
  per sempre, *for ever*
  sempre piú, *more and more*
senseria, *fee*
sensibile, *notable, extreme*
sentire, *to feel, hear, smell*
  sentirsi, *to feel (ill, etc.)*
  sentite qua! *look here!*
senza, *without*
sera, *evening*

serio, *serious*
  sul serio, *in earnest*
serva, *maid, servant*
servire, *to serve*
  servirsi di, *to use*
servizievole, *humble*
sete (*f.*), *thirst*
  aver sete, *to be thirsty*
setola, *bristle*
settentrionale, *northern*
sfiorare, *to graze, touch lightly*
sfortunatamente, *unfortunately*
sforzarsi, *to strive, struggle*
sforzo, *effort*
sguardo, *look, glance*
sicché, *so that, well then!*
siccome, *just as, as*
sigaretta, *cigarette*
silenzio, *silence*
silenzioso, *silent*
simile, *like*
simpatia, *liking, sympathy*
sindaco, *mayor*
sinistra
  a sinistra, *to the left*
sino a, *as far as*
  sin d'ora, *even now, from now on*
sistemare, *to arrange, put in order*
sistemazione (*f.*), *placing*
smarrirsi, *to get lost*
smettere, *to stop, cease*
smorfioso
  fare la smorfiosa, *to be affectedly polite*
soddisfatto, *satisfied*
soddisfazione (*f.*), *satisfaction*
soffermarsi, *to linger*
soffiata, *gasp*
soffio, *breath, lick*
soffrire, *to suffer*
soglia, *threshold*

sognare, *to dream*
solco, *furrow*
sole (*m.*), *sun*
solido, *solid*
solitario, *solitary*
solito, *usual*
  di solito, *usually*
sollevare, *to relieve*
solluchero
  di solluchero, *sugary*
solo, *alone, only*
soltanto, *only*
somigliare, *to resemble*
somma, *sum*
sonno, *sleep*
  aver sonno, *to be sleepy*
sopportare, *to put up with*
sopra, *on, upon*
soprattutto, *above all*
sopravanzare, *to overhang*
sopravvenire, *to happen, supervene*
sopravvivere, *to outlive, survive*
soqquadro (*see* mettere)
sor (signore)
sorgere, *to rise*
sorpresa, *surprise*
sorridere, *to smile*
sorriso, *smile*
sorte, *destiny, fate*
sospettare, *to suspect*
sospetto, *suspicion*
sosta, *pause*
sostenere, *to maintain*
sottaceti, *pickles*
sottinteso, *hint*
sotterfugio, *subterfuge*
sottolineare, *to emphasize, underline*
sottovoce, *in a low voice, in an undertone*
sovietico, *Soviet*
Spagna, *Spain*

spalla, *shoulder*
    dare una spallata, *to give a shrug*
    alle spalle di, *at the expense of*
    sulle spalle, *on one's hands*
spargere, *to scatter*
sparpagliato, *scattered*
spaventare, *to frighten*
specchiarsi, *to mirror*
specchio, *mirror*
specie (*f.*), *kind, sort*
spendere, *to spend*
spesa, *expense*
spessore (*m.*), *thickness*
spettabile, *esteemed*
spettro, *ghost*
spettrale, *ghostly*
spiaggia, *beach*
spiegare, *to explain*
spiegazione (*f.*), *explanation*
spingere, *to push*
spirare, *to blow*
sponda, *edge, bank*
sporgersi, *to lean out*
sportello, *door (of car, etc.), window (of booking office)*
    sportello della biglietteria, *booking-office window*
sposo, *bridegroom*
sprecare, *to waste*
sprofondare, *to plunge*
squadra, *team*
squarciagola
    a squarciagola, *at the top of one's voice*
squillare, *to ring*
squillo, *ringing*
staccarsi, *to draw away*
stagione (*f.*), *season*
stamani, *this morning*
stare, *to be, stand*
    come sta? *how are you?*
    starsene, *to remain*

stato, *state*
    Stati Uniti, *United States*
statura, *size, stature*
statuto, *constitution*
stazza, *displacement*
stemmato, *crested*
stendere, *to stretch, write up, draw up*
stento, *hardship*
    a stento, *with difficulty*
sterlina, *pound*
stima, *esteem*
stimare, *to esteem, value*
stimolare, *to stimulate*
stomaco, *stomach*
stordito, *stunned*
storia, *story*
storico, *historian*
storto, *twisted, crooked*
strada, *street*
    strada facendo, *on the way*
stradale, *of the street*
strage (*f.*), *slaughter*
stralunare, *to open wide*
straniero, *foreign*
strano, *strange*
strappare, *to tear out*
stravolto, *cast up*
strega, *witch*
stridore (*m.*), *squeal*
stringere, *to tighten, grasp*
    stringersi la mano, *to shake hands*
striscia, *strip*
studio, *study, studio*
    essere allo studio, *to be under study*
stufato, *boiled*
stupidaggine (*f.*), *stupidity*
stupido, *stupid*
stupore (*m.*), *amazement*
su, *on*
    su su per, *up along*

successo, *success*

suggerire, *to suggest*

superficie (*f.*), *surface*

susurrare, *to murmur*

sveglio, *awake*

sviluppo, *development*

svirgolarsi, *to go wrong, awry*

tacere, *to be silent*

tagliare, *to cut*

  tagliare fuori, *to cut off*

taluno, *someone*

talvolta, *sometimes*

tanfo, *stench*

tanto, *so much*

  ogni tanto, *every now and again*

  di tanto in tanto, *from time to time*

tardare, *to delay*

tardi, *late*

telegramma (*m.*), *telegram*

temere, *to fear*

tempo, *time* ~

temporale, *storm*

tenebre (*f. pl.*), *darkness*

tenere, *to hold, keep*

tentare, *to attempt*

tenuta, *estate*

terreno, *ground, field*

terso, *clear (of sky)*

testa, *head*

tirare, *to draw, pull, fire*

  tirare vento, *to blow (of wind)*

  tirare via, *to carry on*

  tirare su, *to pull up*

  tirare per le lunghe, *to drag out*

tiro, *trick*

tizzo, *brand*

tizzone, *burnt wood*

toccare, *to touch, fall to one's lot*

  tocca a te, *it's your turn*

togliere, *to take off, take away*

tonfo, *splash*

tonnellata, *ton*

tornare a, *to do again*

toro, *bull*

torre (*f.*), *tower*

  torre di controllo, *control tower*

torretta, *bridge (of ship)*

torta, *tart*

torto, *fault*

  aver torto, *to be wrong*

tosse (*f.*), *cough*

tradimento, *treachery*

tradire, *to betray*

tramonto, *sunset*

tranne, *except*

  tranne che . . . non, *unless*

trascurare, *to neglect*

trasecolare, *to be amazed*

trasmettere, *to transmit*

trasparenza, *fluidity*

trasparire, *to appear*

tratta, *transaction*

trattamento, *treatment, salary*

trattenere, *to restrain, stay*

tratto

  ad un tratto, *suddenly*

trattore (*m.*), *tractor*

tremolare, *to quiver*

triangolo, *triangle*

trionfante, *exultant*

triste, *sad*

tristezza, *sadness*

trovare, *to find*

tubo di scappamento, *exhaust pipe*

tumulto, *riot, uproar*

tuonare, *to thunder*

turistico, *tourist*

tuttavia, *yet, still, anyhow*

uccidere, *to kill*

udire, *to hear*
umido, *moist*
urlo, *cry, shriek*
urtare, *to hit*
usciere (*m.*), *usher*
uscio, *door*
uscire, *to go out*
uscirsene, *to go out*
uso, *use, usage, custom*
usufruente, *enjoying*
utile, *useful*

vacanza, *holiday*
vago, *pretty, vague, beautiful*
valere, *to be worth*
    valere la pena di, *to be worth
      while to*
valore (*m.*), *value*
valvola, *valve*
vantaggio, *advantage*
vantarsi, *to boast*
vecchio, *old*
vedere, *to see*
    non veder l'ora di, *to long to*
vedovo, -a, *widower, widow*
vegliare, *to be on the watch*
veleno, *poison, poisonous smell*
vendere, *to sell*
vendita, *sale*
venire, *to come*
    venire incontro, *to come up*
vento, *wind*
venturo, *next*
verificare, *to verify*
vero, *true*
    non è vero? *isn't it?*
versare, *to pour*
vertice (*m.*), *vertex, top*
vestibolo, *hall, vestibule*
vestire, *to dress*
vestito, *dress, clothing*
vetrina, *shop-window*

vetta, *peak, summit*
via, *way, road,* (*adv.*) *away*
    per via di, *because of*
viavai (*m.*), *coming and going,
    bustle*
viaggio, *journey*
vibrare, *to vibrate*
video, *screen*
vietare, *to forbid*
vincere, *to win, conquer*
vincitore, *winner*
visibile, *obvious*
vista, *view*
    a vista d'occhio, *under one's
    nose*
vita, *life*
vitello, *calf*
vivere, *to live*
voce (*f.*), *voice*
    a viva voce, *by word of
    mouth*
voglia, *wish*
    aver voglia, *to want*
volante (*m.*), *steering-wheel*
volare, *to fly*
volenteroso, *willing*
volentieri, *willingly*
volere, *to want, wish*
    volere bene, *to love*
    volerci, *to lack, need*
volgersi, *to turn*
volontà, *will*
volta, *time, turn*
    a volte, *at times*
    alla volta, *at a time*
voltarsi, *to turn round*
vuoto, *empty*

zampino, *leg of veal*
zitto, *silent, quiet*
    star zitto, *to be quiet*

B. ENGLISH — ITALIAN

to abandon, *abbandonare*
to be able, *potere*
about, *circa, intorno a*
abroad, *all'estero*
to accept, *accettare*
accident, *incidente* (*m.*)
to accompany, *accompagnare*
according to, *secondo*
to be accustomed, *abituarsi*
accustomed to, *avvezzo a*
act, *atto*
to act, *agire*
administration, *amministrazione* (*f.*)
to advance, *avanzare*
in advance, *in anticipo*
advantage
   to take advantage, *abusare di*
adventure, *avventura*
to advise, *consigliare*
aerial, *antenna*
aeroplane, *aereo*
to be afraid, *aver paura di*
after, *dopo, dopo che*
afternoon, *pomeriggio*
age, *età,* era
ago, *fa*
airfield, *campo d'aviazione*
all, *tutto*
   all that, *tutto ciò che*
almost, *quasi, per poco ... non ...*
alone, *solo*
along, *lungo*
alps, *Alpi* (*f.*)
already, *già*
although, *benché, sebbene, quantunque*
always, *sempre*
amazed, *stupito*

America, *America*
to amuse, *divertirsi*
anarchist, *anarchico*
and, *e* (*ed*)
angry, *arrabbiato*
   to get angry, *arrabbiarsi*
animal, *animale* (*m.*)
to annul, *mandare a monte*
anxiously, *ansiosamente*
anyone, *qualcuno*
   anyone who, *chi*
apology, *scusa*
appartment, *appartamento*
to appear, *parere, apparire* (of persons), *comparire* (of persons)
apple, *mela*
to appoint, *nominare*
appointment, *appuntamento*
to approach, *avvicinarsi*
to approve, *approvare*
arm, *braccio, bracciolo* (of chair)
around, *intorno* (*attorno*) *a*
arrival, *arrivo*
to arrive, *arrivare*
art, *arte* (*f.*)
artistic, *artistico*
as, *come, siccome* (causal), *mentre*
to ask, *domandare, chiedere*
to astonish, *stupire*
at, *a, da, all'indirizzo di*
to attract (attention): *dare nell'occhio*
to auction, *vendere all'asta*
aunt, *zia*
autumn, *autunno*
to average, *aggirarsi*
average, *media*
to await, *aspettare*
awake, *sveglio*

away, *lontano*, *distante*, *via*

baby, *bambino*
back, *dorso*, *schiena*
bad, *cattivo*
bag, *sacco*
ball, *palla*
    balls of fingers, *polpastrelli*
bandit, *bandito*
bar, *bar* (*m.*)
barefoot (-ed), *scalzo*
baron, *barone* (*m.*)
barrel, *botte* (*f.*), *botticina*
to be, *essere*
    to be about, *trattarsi di*
    to be about to, *stare per*
    to be up to, *stare facendo*,
        toccare (duty)
    to be back, *essere di ritorno*
beach, *spiaggia*
bean, *fava*
to bear, *portare*
to beat, *battere*
beautiful, *bello*
because, *perché*
to become, *diventare*
bed, *letto*
bedroom, *camera* (*da letto*)
before, *prima di*, *prima che*,
    davanti a (position)
to beg, *pregare*
to begin, *cominciare*
behind, *dietro*
belfry, *campanile* (*m.*)
belonging (to village), *conter-
    raneo*
belongings, *roba*
bent (down), *chino*
bereavement, *sciagura*
beside, *accanto a*
to betray, *tradire*
between, *fra*, *tra*

to bewitch, *affatturare*
big, *grande*, *grosso*
birdseed, *becchime* (*m.*)
bit, *un po' di*
black, *nero*
blackboard, *lavagna*
to blame, *biasimare*
bloodcurdling, *sanguinoso*
blue, *azzurro*, *blu*
on board, *a bordo*
to boast, *vantarsi di*
boat, *barca*, *battello*, *nave* (*f.*)
bone, *osso*
book, *libro*
to bore, *stancare*, *seccare*
to be born, *nascere*
both, *tutti e due*
bottle, *bottiglia*
box, *scatola*
box-office, *sportello della bigliet-
    teria*
Brazil, *Brasile* (*m.*)
to break, *rompere*, *frangersi* (of
    waves)
    to break out, *scoppiare*
    to break one's word, *mancare
        di parola*
breath (of fresh air), *una
    boccata d'aria fresca*
breeze, *brezza*, *venticello*
bridge, *ponte* (*m.*)
to bring, *portare*
brother, *fratello*
brother-in-law, *cognato*
to build, *costruire*
building, *edificio*, *palazzo*
bull, *toro*
to burn, *bruciare*
to bury, *seppellire*, *affondare*
bus, *autobus* (*m.*)
business, *affari* (*m.*), *impresa*
    (undertaking)
busy, *occupato*

but, *ma*
to buy, *comprare*
by, *da*

cabbage, *cavolo*
cabin, *cabina*
cage, *gabbia*
calendar, *calendario, almanacco*
to call, *chiamare*
   to call in, *passare da*
   to call (on telephone), *telefonare*
   a telephone call, *telefonata*
calm, *calmo, tranquillo*
Canada, *Canadà* (*m.*)
canon, *canonico*
capital, *capitale* (*f.*)
car, *macchina, auto* (*f.*)
card, *carta*
care
   to take care, *badare di*
   to care for, *piacere*
careful
   to be careful, *stare attento*
carpet, *tappeto*
carriage, *carrozza, vettura*
   carriage door, *sportello*
to carry, *portare*
   to carry on, *tirare via*
cart, *carro*
case, *caso, valigia* (suitcase)
   in case, *caso mai*
to cast up, *stravolgere*
castle, *castello*
cat, *gatto*
to catch, *prendere, pigliare*
cattle, *bestiame* (*m.*)
celebration, *festa*
central, *centrale*
centre, *centro*
chain, *catena*
chair, *sedia*

chalk, *gesso*
to change, *cambiare*
Channel, *Manica*
chapter, *capitolo*
charge
   those in charge, *i responsabili* (*m.*)
to chase one another, *rincorrersi*
to chatter, *parlottare*
cheese, *formaggio*
chemist, *farmacista*
cherry, *ciliegia*
chicken, *pollo*
child, *bambino, figlio*
to choose, *scegliere*
church, *chiesa*
cigarette, *sigaretta*
cinema, *cinema, cine* (*m.*)
circle, *giro, cerchio*
to claim, *pretendere*
class, *classe* (*f.*)
to clean, *pulire*
clerk, *impiegato*
client, *cliente* (*m. & f.*)
climate, *clima* (*m.*)
to climb, *arrampicarsi, salire*
cloth, *stoffa*
to clothe, *vestire*
clothes, *vestiti, abiti*
coal, *carbone* (*m.*)
coast, *costa, litorale* (*m.*)
cobbler, *calzolaio*
coffee, *caffè* (*m.*)
cold, *freddo*
   to be cold, *aver freddo, far freddo* (weather)
to collapse, *crollare*
to collect, *raccogliere*
colour, *colore* (*m.*)
to come, *venire*
   to come back, *tornare*
   to come near, *accostare*

commission, *commissione* (*f.*)
to complain, *lagnarsi*
to complete, *completare*
completely, *del tutto*
condition, *condizione* (*f.*)
to confine, *limitarsi a*
to congratulate, *congratularsi con*
to consent, *consentire*
consequence, *conseguenza*
to consider, *considerare*
to consult, *consigliarsi*
to contain, *comprendere, contenere*
to continue, *continuare*
to convey, *presentare* (excuses)
to count on, *contare su*
countess, *contessa*
country, *paese, campagna*
course
  of course, *naturalmente*
courtyard, *cortile* (*m.*)
to cover, *coprire*
covered with, *coperto di*
crash, *fracasso*
creation, *creato*
to cross, *attraversare*
crowd, *folla*
crowded, *affollato*
  crowded together, *ammucchiato*
crust, *crosta*
cry, *grido, pianto*
culprit, *colpevole*
cup, *tazza*
cupboard, *armadio*
curse, *maledizione* (*f.*)
customer, *cliente* (*m. & f.*)
to cut, *tagliare*
  to cut off, *tagliare fuori*

daddy, *babbo*
danger, *pericolo*

to dare, *osare*
darkness, *buio, tenebre, oscurità*
daughter, *figlia*
  daughter-in-law, *nuora*
day, *giorno, -ata*
dead, *morto*
deal
  a great deal, *molto*
to deal, *trattare*
dear, *caro*
death, *morte* (*f.*)
to decide, *decidere*
deck, *ponte* (*m.*)
declaration, *dichiarazione* (*f.*)
to declare, *dichiarare*
deep, *profondo*
to delight, *dilettare, divertire*
to demonstrate, *dimostrare*
dentist, *dentista* (*m.*)
to deny, *negare*
to depart, *partire*
to deprive, *privare*
to descend, *scendere*
desk, *scrivania*
despite (the fact that), *malgrado che*
to die, *morire*
different, *diverso, differente*
difficult, *difficile*
difficulty, *difficoltà*
dilemma, *dilemma* (*m.*)
dining-room, *sala da pranzo*
dinner, *pranzo*
directly, *subito*
director, *principale* (*m.*), *direttore* (*m.*)
disagreeable, *spiacevole, sgradevole*
to discover, *scoprire*
to discuss, *discutere*
disease, *malattia*
disgrace, *disgrazia*
dish, *piatto*

to dislike, *spiacere, non piacere*
displeased, *scontento*
distance
  in the distance, *in lontananza*
distant, *distante*
to distinguish, *distinguere*
to disturb, *disturbare*
to do, *fare*
  to do good, *fare bene*
doctor, *medico*
document, *documento*
dog, *cane* (*m.*)
door, *porta, sportello*
  at death's door, *in punto di morte*
  door-keeper's wife, *portinaia*
to doubt, *dubitare*
  without doubt, *senza dubbio*
down, *giú*
  down-stairs, *giú*
drawing-room, *salotto*
dream, *sogno*
dress, *vestito*
to drink, *bere*
to drive back, *respingere*
to dry, *asciugare*
dune, *duna*
during, *durante*
duty, *dovere* (*m.*)

each, *ciascuno*
earlier, *piú presto*
early, *presto, di buon'ora, primo* (*adj.*)
to earn, *guadagnare*
easy, *facile*
to eat, *mangiare*
effect, *effetto*
Egypt, *Egitto*
elbow, *gomito*
to elect, *eleggere*
else, *altrimenti*
  or else, *oppure*

employee, *impiegato*
end, *fine* (*f.*)
  to end up, *finire con*
enemy, *nemico*
engineer, *ingegnere* (*m.*)
England, *Inghilterra*
English, *inglese*
to enjoy, *godere di*
enough, *abbastanza*
  to be enough, *bastare*
to enter, *entrare*
estate, *tenuta, feudo*
estimated, *previsto*
Europe, *Europa*
even, *anche*
  not even, *neanche*
evening, *sera*
ever, *mai*
every, *ogni*
everywhere, *dappertutto*
examination, *esame* (*m.*)
to examine, *visitare* (of doctor)
to exchange, *scambiare*
excitement, *eccitazione* (*f.*)
to excuse oneself, *scusarsi*
exercise-book, *quaderno*
exhausted
  to be completely exhausted, *non poterne piú*
exit, *uscita*
expansion, *espansione* (*f.*), *sviluppo*
expectancy, *aspettativa*
expense
  at someone's expense, *alle spese* (*spalle*) *di*
to explain, *spiegare*
extreme, *estremo,* u*ltimo*
eye, *occhio*

face, *faccia, volto*
fact, *fatto*
factory, *fabbrica*

to fail, *mancare*
to fall, *cadere*
family, *famiglia*
famous, *famoso*, *celebre*
to fancy, *figurarsi*
far, *lontano*
  far from, *tutt'altro*
farm, *fattoria*
fast, *veloce*, *rapido*
fat, *grasso*
father, *padre* (*m.*)
fault
  to be one's fault, e*sser colpa sua*
favour, *favore* (*m.*), *servizio*
to feed, *nutrire*, *dare da mangiare* (animals)
to feel, *sentire*
  to feel ill, etc., *sentirsi male*, etc.
fellow, *tipo*, *costui* (*derog.*)
few, *alcuni*, *qualche*, *pochi*
field, *campo*
to fight, *combattere*
filth, *porcheria*
finally, *alfine*, *finalmente*
financial, *finanziario*
to find, *trovare*
finger, *dito*
to finish, *finire*
fire, *fuoco*
fish, *pesce* (*m.*)
to flash, *balenare*
flat (on one's face), *bocconi*
to flee, *scappare*, *fuggire*
floor, *pavimento*, *piano* (*i.e.* storey)
Florence, *Firenze*
flower, *fiore* (*m.*)
to follow, *seguire*
following, *seguente*
fond
  to be fond of, *amare*, *piacere*

foolish, *sciocco*
foot, *piede*
  on foot, *a piedi*
for, *per*
to forbid, *vietare*
to foresee, *prevedere*
to forget, *dimenticare* (*-arsi*)
former, *quegli*, *primo*
fortnight, *quindici giorni*
fortress, *palazzotto*, *fortezza*
four-engined, *quadrimotore* (*m.*)
France, *Francia*
free, *libero*
French, *francese*
to frighten, *spaventare*
front
  in front of, *davanti a*
frontier, *frontiera*
  frontier-post, *posto di confine*
fruit, *frutta*
fruitseller, *fruttivendolo*
fruit-tree, a*lbero da frutta*
full, *pieno*
funny, *comico*, *buffo*
furious, *furibondo*
further on, *più in là*
future, *futuro*, *avvenire* (*m.*)

to gain, *guadagnare*
  to gain height, *prender quota*
gallery, *galleria* (*d'arte*)
game, *gioco*
gang, *banda*
garden, *giardino*
  kitchen-garden, *orto*
garnishing, *contorno*
to gather, *cogliere*, *raccogliere*
generally, *di solito*
genius
  of genius, *geniale*
gentleman, *signore* (*m.*)
German, *tedesco*

to get, *ottenere*
  to get off, *cavarsela*
  to get up, *alzarsi*
  to get short, *mancare*
ghost, *spettro*
ghost of a voice, *filo di voce*
girl, *ragazza*
to give, *dare*
  give back, *rendere, consegnare*
  to give rise to, *dare origine a*
glance, *occhiata*
  sugary glance, *occhiata di solluchero*
glass, *bicchiere* (m.)
to go, *andare*
  to go away, *andar via*
  to go in, *entrare*
  to go out, *uscire, spegnere* (fire, lights, *etc.*)
  to go up, *salire*
  to go up to, *andare incontro a*
golf
  to play golf, *giocare a golf*
good, *buono*
goods, *merce* (f.)
grandchild, *nipotino -a*
grape, *uva*
great, *grande*
green, *verde*
to greet, *salutare*
grief, *dolore* (m.)
grocer's, *negozio di generi alimentari*
ground, *terra*
to grow, *crescere*

to hail, *grandinare*
half, *mezzo*
half-brother, *fratellastro*
ham, *prosciutto*
hand, *mano* (f.)
handling, *manovra*
to hang, *pendere*

to happen, *succedere, accadere*
happy, *felice, lieto*
hardly, *appena*
harmlessness, *innocuità*
harvest, *raccolto*
hat, *cappello*
hate, *odio*
to hate, *odiare*
to have, *avere*
  to have to, *dovere*
  haves and have nots, *gli abbienti e i non abbienti*
hay, *fieno*
head, *capo, testa*
  to head for, *puntare*
  head of department, *caporeparto*
health, *salute* (f.)
to hear, *sentire, udire*
heart, *cuore* (m.)
heath, *brughiera*
heavy, *pesante, forte*
height
  to gain height, *prender quota*
to help, *aiutare*
here, *qui, qua*
to hesitate, *esitare*
high, *alto, principale* (street)
hill, *collina*
historian, *storico*
hobby, *passatempo*
to hold, *tenere*
hole, *buco, buca*
holiday, *vacanza*
  bank-holiday, *ferie* (f.pl.)
home, *casa*
homework, *compito*
honest, *onesto*
to hope, *sperare*
horizon, *orizzonte* (m.)
horn, *corno*
hors-d'œuvre, *antipasto*
hospital, *ospedale* (m.)

hot, *caldo*
how, *come*
hundred and fifty, *centocinquanta*
to hurl, *lanciare, buttare*
to hurry, *far presto, affrettarsi*
   to hurry off, *partire in fretta*
to hurt, *nuocere*
husband, *marito*

I, *io*
idea, *idea*
ideal, *ideale (m.)*
if, *se*
ill, *(am)malato*
to imagine, *immaginare*
immediate, *subito, immediato*
to implore, *supplicare*
important, *importante*
to impose, *imporre*
impossible, *impossibile*
to improve, *migliorare*
in, *in, a*
indeed, *davvero, infatti*
indigestion, *indigestione (f.)*
industrial, *industriale*
information, *informazione (f.)*
inkwell, *calamaio*
inner, *interno, intimo*
inquiry, *richiesta*
ins and outs of, *per filo e per segno*
to insist, *insistere*
instead of, *invece di*
insular, *insulare*
intelligent, *intelligente*
to intend, *intendere, aver intenzione di*
intention, *intenzione (f.)*
interest, *interesse (m.)*
international, *internazionale*
to introduce, *presentare*
invective, *invettiva*

invitation, *invito*
to invite, *invitare*
iron, *ferro*
Italy, *Italia*
Italian, *italiano*
ivory, *avorio*

to jabber, *parlottare*
jagged, *dentellato*
Japanese, *giapponese*
jealous, *geloso*
jet-engine, *motore a reazione*
job, *posto, lavoro*
joke, *scherzo, beffa*
journalist, *giornalista (m.)*
journey, *viaggio*
joy, *gioia*
July, *luglio*
just, *appena, proprio adesso, giusto*

to keep, *tenere, trattenere*
   to keep on, *continuare*
to kill, *uccidere*
kind, *specie (f.), gentile (adj.)*
kindly, *gentile, benevolo*
king, *re (m.)*
kitchen, *cucina*
kitten, *gattino*
to know, *sapere, conoscere*

labour, *lavoro*
laconic, *laconico*
lake, *lago*
lamp, *lampada*
lampshade, *paralume (m.)*
land, *paese, terra*
   to land, *atterrare*
last, *ultimo, scorso*
   last night, *ieri sera*
late, *tardi, in ritardo, fu (defunct)*
   late at night, *a tarda notte*

latter, u*ltimo, questi*
laugh(ter), *riso*
to laugh, *ridere*
    to be laughable, *far ridere*
lawyer, *avvocato*
lazy, *pigro*
to lead, *condurre*
    to lead the way, *far strada a*
to learn, *imparare*
least
    at least, *almeno*
to leave, *lasciare, partire*
    to leave off, *lasciare*
    to leave word, *lasciare detto*
lecture, *conferenza*
left
    to the left, *a sinistra*
lesson, *lezione (f.)*
lest, *per paura che, nel caso che*
to let, *lasciare*
    to let know, *far sapere*
letter, *lettera*
licence, *abbonamento* (radio, etc.)
to lick, *leccare*
life, *vita*
to lift, *sollevare*
to light (up), *illuminare*
like, *come, da*
    to like, *piacere*
to line up, *allinearsi*
to link, *legare*
lion, *leone (m.)*
lip, *labbro*
to listen, *ascoltare*
little, *piccolo*
    a little, *un po'*
to live, *vivere*
living, *vita*
to look at, *guardare*
    to look for, *cercare*
    to look like, *somigliare a*

look, *sguardo*
to lose, *perdere*
    to lose sight of, *perdere di vista*
lot, *molto*
loud, *forte, alto, grande*
love, *amore (m.)*
lovely, *bello*
low, *basso*
luggage, *bagaglio, valigie (f.pl.)*
lump (of sugar), *zolletta*
lunch, *pranzo*
lupin-seed, *lupino*

machine, *macchina*
mad, *pazzo, verticoso* (of machines)
to make, *fare*
    to make one's way, *farsi strada*
    to make one's way (to go along), *incamminarsi*
    to make for oneself, *farsi*
    to make up, *confezionare*
    to make mistakes, *sbagliare*
man, *uomo*
to manage, *riuscire*
many, *molti*
marchioness, *marchesa*
to mark down, *segnare*
market, *mercato*
marquis, *marchese*
match, *partita, fiammifero* (safety match)
material, *stoffa*
matter, *faccenda, cosa*
    what's the matter? *cosa c'è?*
    what's the matter with? *cosa ha?*
    to matter, *importare*
mayor, *sindaco*
meal, *pasto*
meantime (-while), *intanto*

to measure, *misurare*
medicine, *medicamento*
to meet, *incontrare*
meeting, *riunione* (*f.*)
member, *membro*
mention
    don't mention it, *non c'è di che! Di niente*
merchant, *mercante* (*m.*)
message, *messaggio*
metre, *metro*
microphone, *microfono*
middle, *mezzo*
    in the middle of, *nel mezzo di, in mezzo a*
mile, *miglio*
to mind, *badare a*
minister, *ministro*
minute, *minuto*
mirror, *specchio*
    to mirror, *rispecchiarsi*
to miss, *mancare, sentire la mancanza di* (of person)
mist, *nebbia*
mistake, *sbaglio*
to mistake, *sbagliare*
mistress, *padrona*
modernization, *rimodernamento*
moment, *momento*
money, *danaro*
monkey, *scimmia*
month, *mese* (*m.*)
monument, *monumento*
moonlight, *chiaro di luna*
more, *più*
    any more, *non . . . più*
    more and more, *sempre più*
morning, *mattina*
mother, *madre* (*f.*)
motionless, *immobile*
motor, *motore* (*m.*)
mountain, *montagna*
to move, *muovere*

to move off, *staccarsi*
much, *molto*
multicoloured, *multicolore*
museum, *museo*
music, *musica*
must, *mosto*
mysterious, *misterioso*

Naples, *Napoli*
nasty, *cattivo*
nature, *natura*
naughty, *cattivo*
near, *vicino a*
necessary
    to be necessary, *occorrere*
to need, *aver bisogno di*
nephew, *nipote* (*m.*)
network, *rete* (*f.*)
new, *nuovo*
news, *notizia*
newspaper, *giornale* (*m.*)
next, *prossimo, seguente*
nice, *gentile*
niece, *nipote* (*f.*)
no, *no, nessuno* (*adj.*)
    no one, *nessuno* (*pro.*)
noon, *mezzogiorno*
northern, *settentrionale*
nose, *naso*
    under one's nose, *a vista d'occhio*
not, *non*
note, *appunto*
    to take note, *prendere nota*
nothing, *niente, nulla*
to notice, *notare, accorgersi di*
now, *adesso, ora*
    now and again, *di tanto in tanto, di quando in quando*
nuisance, *canchero*
number, *numero*
nut, *nocciuola*

oar, *remo*
oath, *ingiuria*
to obey, *ubbidire a*
observation, *osservazione* (*f.*)
of, *di*
offer, *offerta*
to offer, *offrire*
office, *ufficio, azienda*
   branch office, *filiale* (*f.*)
often, *spesso*
oil, *olio*
   oil-lamp, *lampada a olio*
old, *vecchio*
onlooker, *presente* (*m.*), *astante*
   (*m.*)
once, *una volta*
   at once, *subito*
one-armed, *monco*
only, *solo*
to open, *aprire*
   open, *aperto*
   wide-open, *stralunato* (of
   eyes)
opinion, *parere* (*m.*), *opinione*
   (*f.*)
opposite, *dirimpetto a*
orange, *arancia*
order, *ordine* (*m.*)
   in order to, *per, affinché*
other, *altro*
otherwise, *altrimenti*
out, *fuori*
outside, *fuori di*
to outlive, *sopravvivere a*
to overlook, *dare su*
own, *proprio*

pain, *dolore* (*m.*)
pale, *pallido*
paper
   newspaper, *giornale* (*m.*)
parapet, *parapetto*
pardon, *perdono*

to ask for pardon, *chieder
   scusa*
parent, *genitore* (*m.*), *genitrice*
   (*f.*)
Paris, *Parigi*
part, *parte* (*f.*)
particular, *particolare* (subs. &
   adj.)
to pass, *passare*
   to pass an examination, *essere
     promosso in*
   to pass through, *passare per*
passenger, *passeggiero* (*m.*)
past, *passato*
to pasture, *pascere*
path, *sentiero*
to pay (for), *pagare*
   to pay a visit, *fare una visita*
peach, *pesca*
peak, *vetta*
pear, *pera*
peasant, *contadino*
pen, *penna*
   fountain pen, *penna stilo-
     grafica*
pencil, *matita*
people, *gente* (*f.*), *popolo* (*m.*)
perfect, *perfetto*
performance, *rappresentazione*
   (*f.*)
to permit, *permettere*
perplexed, *perplesso*
to persist in, *ostinarsi a*
pestilential smell, *tanfo*
pianist, *pianista* (*m.*)
to pick, *cogliere, raccogliere*
picture, *quadro*
piece, *pezzo*
pig, *porco*
pile, *mucchio, pila*
pitching and tossing, *beccheggio
   e rullio*
pity, *peccato*

what a pity, *che peccato!*
place, *posto, luogo*
public place, *locale* (*m.*)
plane, *aereo, apparecchio*
plate, *piatto*
platform, *marciapiede* (*m.*)
to play, *giocare*
   to play cards, draughts, *giocare a carte, a dama*
play, *dramma* (*m.*)
player, *giocatore* (*m.*)
pleasant, *piacevole*
to please, *piacere*
pleasure, *piacere* (*m.*)
to plough, *arare*
plunging, *tonfo*
pneumonia, *polmonite* (*f.*)
poet, *poeta* (*m.*)
point, *punto*
to point, *additare*
police, *polizia*
policeman, *poliziotto*
police-station, *posto di sicurezza*
pool, *chiazza*
poor, *povero*
popular, *popolare*
port, *porto*
porter, *facchino*
position, *posizione* (*f.*), *situazione* (*f.*)
possible, *possibile*
post, *posto, posta* (post-office)
potato, *patata*
potion, *filtro*
precisely, *appunto, proprio*
to prefer, *preferire*
prefecture, *questura*
to prescribe, *prescrivere*
present
   to be present, *assistere a*
to preside, *presiedere*
president, *presidente* (*m.*)
pressing, *pigiatura*

pretext, *pretesto*
to prevent, *impedire*
price, *prezzo*
priest, *prete* (*m.*)
probable, *probabile*
problem, *problema* (*m.*)
product, *prodotto*
production, *produzione* (*f.*)
to profit, *profittare di*
programme, *programma* (*m.*)
to prohibit, *proibire*
to promise, *promettere*
promontory, *promontorio*
to pronounce, *pronunciare*
propeller, *elica*
propriety, *convenienza*
proud, *orgoglioso*
to provide, *provvedere*
provided, *purché*
provost, *prevosto*
public, *pubblico*
punctual, *puntuale*
purchase, *acquisto*
to purr, *fare le fusa*
to put, *mettere*

quay, *banchina*
queen, *regina*
quick, *presto*

to race, *correre*
radar, *radar*
radio, *radio* (*f.*)
ragged, *cencioso*
rail, *rotaia, binario* (pair of rails)
rain, *pioggia*
to rain, *piovere*
rare, *raro*
rather than, *anziché*
to reach, *giungere*
to read, *leggere*
to realize, *rendersi conto di*

to receive, *ricevere*
received, *avuto, ricevuto*
recent, *recente*
red, *rosso*
referee, a*rbitro*
reflection, *riflesso*
to refuse, *rifiutare*
region, *regione (f.)*
to relate, *raccontare*
relation, *parente (m. & f.)*
to remind, *ricordare a*
repeating, *ripetitore, -trice*
to repent, *pentirsi*
to reply, *rispondere*
to reply to, *rispondere, dare risposta a*
report, *resoconto*
republican, *repubblicano*
to request, *pregare*
resignation, *rassegnazione (f.)*
to resolve, *risolvere*
to respect, *rispettare, stimare*
respect, *rispetto*
restaurant, *ristorante (m.)*
return, *ritorno*
to return, *tornare*
to reveal, *rivelare*
revolution, *rivoluzione (f.)*
rich, *ricco*
to be rife, *far strage*
rifle, *fucile (m.)*
right now, *proprio adesso*
    to be right, *aver ragione*
    right to, *fino a*
    to the right, *a destra*
    to go right, *andar bene*
ripe, *maturo*
rippling, *increspato*
to rise, *sorgere*
to rival, *rivaleggiare con*
river, *fiume (m.)*
road, *strada, via*
roar, *ruggito*

roast, *arrosto*
rock, *roccia*
rogue, *farabutto, mascalzone (m.)*
Rome, *Roma*
room, *sala, camera, stanza*
row, *filare (m.)*
rubbish, *robaccia*
to run over, *investire*
runway, *pista di decollo*

sad, *triste*
salad, *insalata*
salame, *salame (m.)*
salary, *trattamento*
sale, *vendita*
same, *stesso*
sample, *campione (m.)*
to say, *dire*
scale
    on a large scale, *su larga scala*
schoolboy, *alunno, scolaro*
scoundrel, *mascalzone (m.)*
screen, *schermo*
sea, *mare (m.)*
seagull, *gabbiano*
seasickness, *mal di mare*
to search, *ricercare*
seat, *posto*
second, *secondo*
secret, *segreto*
secretary, *segretario*
to seem, *sembrare, parere*
to sell, *vendere*
seller, *venditore (m.)*
to send, *mandare*
seriously, *sul serio*
sermon, *predica*
servant, *servo, -a*
to serve, *servire*
    it serves me right! *ben mi sta!*
to set out, *partire*

to set up, *mettere su*

set, *apparecchio*

to shake (hands), *stringere la mano a*

to share, *dividere*

sheet, *lenzuolo*

shelf, *scaffale (m.)*

ship, *piroscafo*, *nave (f.)*

shoe, *scarpa*

shop, *bottega*, *negozio*

shore, *riva*, *costa*

short, *breve*, *corto*

shoulder, *spalla*

to shout, *gridare*

to show, *mostrare*, *far vedere*

shrill, *acuto*

shrug (of shoulders), *dare una spallata*

to sigh, *singhiozzare*

sight, *vista*, *spettacolo*

to sight, *inquadrare*

to sign, *firmare*

signature, *firma*

silence, *silenzio*

silent, *silenzioso*

to be silent, *tacere*

silk, *seta*

silvery, *argenteo*

since, *da che*, *poiché (causal)*

sister, *sorella*

to sit, *sedersi*

sky, *cielo*

skyscraper, *grattacielo*

to sleep, *dormire*

slice, *fetta*

to slip off, *scapparsene*

slow, *lento*, *piano*

small, *piccolo*

smile, *sorriso*

smoke, *fumare*

smooth, *liscio*, *calmo*

snappily, *giulivo*

to snivel, *piagnucolare*

to snow, *nevicare*

so, *così*

so so! *così così!*

soak

soaking wet, *tutto bagnato*

soft, *morbido*, *dolce*

to solve, *risolvere*

some, *alcuni*, *qualche*

something, *qualcosa*

song, *canto*, *canzone (f.)*

soon, *presto*

as soon as, *appena*

sorry

to be sorry, *dispiacere*

south, *sud*, *meridionale (adj.)*

soviet, *sovietico*

sow, *scrofa*

to speak, *parlare*

spectacles, *occhiali (m.p.)*

speech, *discorso*

to spend, *passare (time)*

to spin, *girare*

spoon, *cucchiaio*

spot

on the spot, *subito*, *su due piedi*

square, *piazza*

squash, *zucchino*

stairs, *scale (pl.)*

stall, *platea*

to stand, *stare*, *resistere a*

to start, *cominciare*, *iniziare*

to steal, *rubare*

steam, *vapore (m.)*

steamer, *piroscafo*

steel, *acciaio*

step-brother, *fratellastro*

step-mother, *matrigna*

step-sister, *sorellastra*

still, *ancora*

stone, *pietra*

stone-quarry, *cava*

to stop, *fermarsi*, *smettere*

storm, *temporale (m.)*, *tempesta (f.)*
straight, *direttamente*
to stretch, *stendersi*
stricken, *sprofondato*
strip, *striscia*
to stroll, *passeggiare*
strong, *forte*
struggle, *lotta*
study, *studio*
stupid, *stupido*
to succeed, *riuscire*
such, *tale*
suddenly, *subito*
to suffer, *soffrire*
sugar, *zucchero*
to suggest, *suggerire*
suit, *abito, completo*
    to suit, *convenire, stare, andare* (of clothes)
suitcase, *valigia*
summer, *estate (f.)*
summit, *vetta, cima*
sun, *sole (m.)*
supper, *cena*
sure, *sicuro*
surface, *superficie (f.)*
surprised, *sorpreso*
to suspect, *sospettare*
swaying, *ondeggiante*
to swear, *giurare*
sweet, *(subs.) caramella*, (of meals) *dolce (m.)*, *(adj.) dolce*
to swim, *nuotare*
Switzerland, *Svizzera*
swollen, *gonfio*

table, *tavola*
tail between legs, *mogio mogio*
tailor, *sarto*
tailor-made costume, *tailleur (m.)*

to take, *prendere*
    to take off (of planes), *decollare*, (of clothes) *togliere*
    to take back, *riportare*
to talk, *parlare*
task, *compito*
taxi, *taxi (m.)*
tea, *tè (m.)*
teacher, *professore (m.)*
team, *squadra*
telephone, *telefono*
television, *televisione (f.)*
to tell, *dire*
    to tell off, *dirne di tutti i colori*
terrible, *terribile*
territory, *territorio*
thank (you), *grazie*
that, *quello*
theatre, *teatro*
them, *loro*
then, *poi, allora*
there, *là, ci, vi*
thing, *cosa*
to think, *pensare*
this, *questo*
to threaten, *minacciare*
throughout, *in*
to throw, *gettare*
ticket, *biglietto*
tiger, *tigre (f.)*
timber, *legno*
time, *tempo*
    every time, *ogni volta*
    in time, *in tempo*
tip, on tiptoes, *in punta di piedi*
tired, *stanco*
today, *oggi*
together, *insieme*
tomorrow, *domani*
tonight, *stasera, stanotte*
too, *troppo, anche*

top, *cima*
  top of one's voice, *a squar-ciagola*
to touch, *toccare*
  a touch of, *un po' di*
tourist, *turista* (*m.*)
towards, *verso*
tower, *torre* (*f.*)
tractor, *trattore* (*m.*)
tradition, *tradizione* (*f.*)
train, *treno*
transformer, *trasformatore* (*m.*)
to transmit, *trasmettere*
trap, *calesse* (*m.*)
to travel, *viaggiare*; -er, *viag-giatore* (*m.*)
to treat, *trattare*
tree, *albero*
trick, *tiro*
to triple, *triplicare*
to trot, *trotterellare*
troublesome, *noioso*
truth, *verità*
to try, *tentare*
tumult, *baraonda*
turn, *volta*
  in turn, *a vicenda*
  to turn round, *voltarsi*
  to turn on, *metter in moto*
  to turn upside down, *metter a soqquadro*
  whose turn? *a chi tocca?*
two, *due*
type, *tipo*
  to type, *scrivere a macchina*

unbreakableness, *infrangibilità*
uncle, *zio*
to underline, *sottolineare*
to understand, *capire*
to undertake, *incaricarsi*
to undulate, *ondeggiare*
unequal, *impari, inuguale*

unfortunate, *sfortunato*
unless, *a meno che* . . . *non*
us, *noi, ci*
useful, *utile*
useless, *inutile*
usher, *usciere* (*m.*)
usual, *solito*

vain, *vanitoso*
  to speak in vain, *aver un bel dire*
valve, *valvola*
various, *vario*
veal, *vitello*
vegetables, *verdura*
very, *molto*
view, *vista*
vineyard, *vigna*
violinist, *violinista* (*m.*)
visit, *visita*
  to visit, *visitare*
voice, *voce* (*f.*)
voyage, *viaggio*

to wait, *aspettare*
  waiting-room, *sala d'aspetto*
wall, *muro*, (city walls) *mura* (*f. pl.*)
to want, *volere*
war, *guerra*
warehouse, *magazzino*
warm, *caldo, caloroso*
to wash, *lavarsi*
to waste, *sprecare*
to watch, *guardare*
water, *acqua*
wave, *flutto, onda*
way, *via*
  on the way to, *diretto a*
weather, *tempo*
week, *settimana*
week-end, *fine settimana*
to weep, *piangere*

well, *bene*
  as well, *anche*
  well-known, *noto*
what, *che, ciò che*
  what a lot of, *quanto*
  what on earth, *che mai*
wheat, *frumento*
whether, *se*
while, *mentre*
to whistle, *sibilare*
white, *bianco*
  white stuff, *biancume* (*m.*)
whoever, *chiunque*
whole, *tutto*
  on the whole, *insomma*
why, *perché*
wide, *largo*
wife, *moglie* (*f.*)
wild, *selvaggio*
to win, *vincere*
wind, *vento*
window, *finestra*
wine, *vino*
  wine-harvest, *vendemmia*
winter, *inverno*
wireless, *radio* (*f.*)
  wireless-operator, *radiotelegrafista* (*m.*)

witch, *fattucchiera, strega*
with, *con*
without, *senza*
witness, *testimonio*
woman, *donna*
wonderful, *meraviglioso*
worker, *lavoratore* (*m.*)
to worry, *preoccuparsi*
worse, *peggiore, peggio* (*adv.*)
to be worth, *valere*
  to be worth while, *valere la pena di*
worthy, *degno*
to write, *scrivere*
to be wrong, *aver torto*

year, *anno*
yellow, *giallo*
yes, *sì*
yesterday, *ieri*
yet, *ancora*
you, *Lei*
youth, *giovane* (*m.*)

zero, *zero*
zone, *zona*
zoo, *giardino zoologico*

INDEX